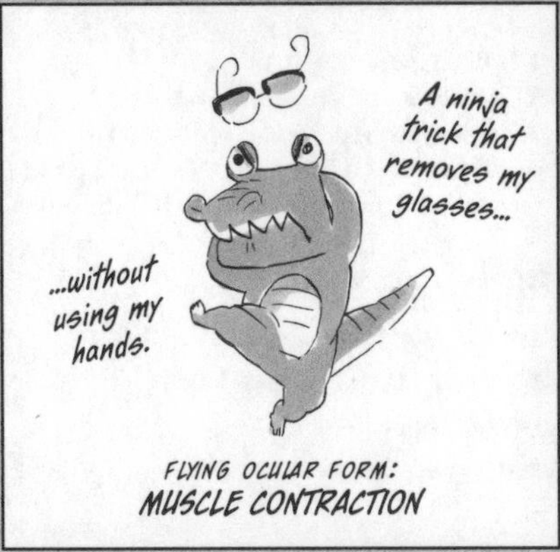
A ninja trick that removes my glasses...
...without using my hands.
FLYING OCULAR FORM:
MUSCLE CONTRACTION

KOYOHARU GOTOUGE

Hi, I'm Gotouge. Lately, I've been eating a lot of Chinese onions. What have you been eating? Thank you, from the bottom of my heart, for the continuous support through letters and gifts. I apologize for not responding to any of them yet. Please wait a little longer for my response to each and every one of you. (*Tears*) I want to say "Baby potter anzun," almond. Keep moving forward, baby potter anzun. I'll work hard!

DEMON SLAYER:
KIMETSU NO YAIBA
VOLUME 20
Shonen Jump Edition

Story and Art by
KOYOHARU GOTOUGE

KIMETSU NO YAIBA
© 2016 by Koyoharu Gotouge
All rights reserved. First published in Japan
in 2016 by SHUEISHA Inc., Tokyo. English
translation rights arranged by SHUEISHA Inc.

TRANSLATION John Werry
ENGLISH ADAPTATION Stan!
TOUCH-UP ART & LETTERING John Hunt
DESIGN Jimmy Presler
EDITOR Mike Montesa

Printed in the U.S.A

Published by VIZ Media, LLC
P.O. Box 77010
San Francisco, CA 94107

10 9 8 7 6 5 4 3 2 1
First printing, February 2021

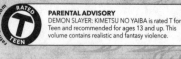

viz.com

DEMON SLAYER

KIMETSU NO YAIBA

THE PATH OF OPENING A STEADFAST HEART

KOYOHARU GOTOUGE

CHARACTERS

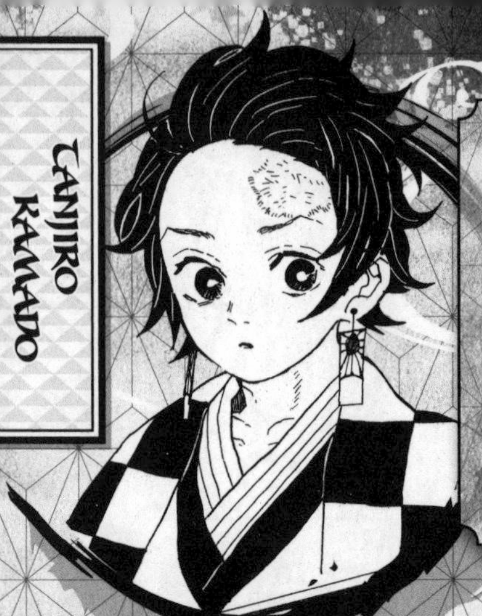

TANJIRO KAMADO

A kind boy who saved his sister and now aims to avenge his family. He can smell the scent of demons and an opponent's weakness.

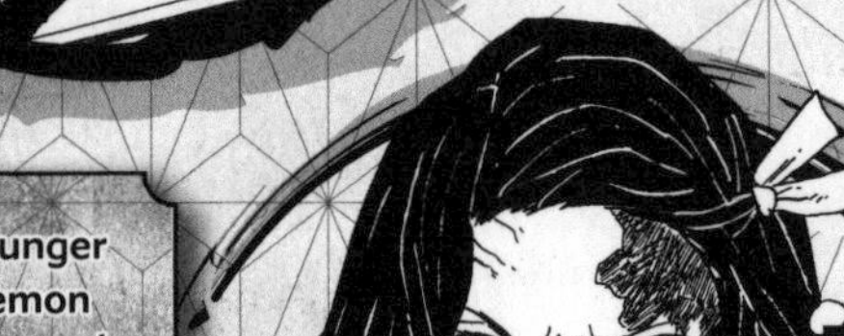

NEZUKO KAMADO

Tanjiro's younger sister. A demon attacked her and turned her into a demon. But unlike other demons, she fights her urges and tries to protect Tanjiro.

STORY

In Taisho-era Japan, young Tanjiro makes a living selling charcoal. One day, demons kill his family and turn his younger sister Nezuko into a demon. Tanjiro and Nezuko set out to find a way to return Nezuko to human form and defeat Kibutsuji, the demon who killed their family!

After joining the Demon Slayer Corps, Tanjiro meets Tamayo and Yushiro—demons who oppose Kibutsuji—who provide a clue to how Nezuko may be turned back into a human.

Nezuko finally manifests the ability to withstand sunlight, so Kibutsuji comes for her and attacks Ubuyashiki Mansion. The Demon Slayers plunge into Infinity Castle and defeat the Upper Rank 2 and 3 demons—but not without losses of their own. Then Himejima and Shinazugawa, the Wind and Stone Hashiras, clash with the Upper Rank 1 demon, and his strength overwhelms them!!

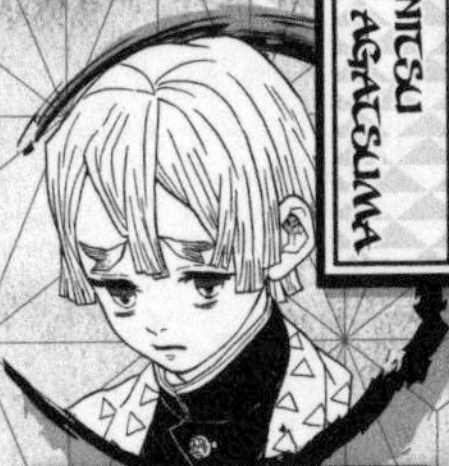

ZENITSU AGATSUMA

He went through Final Selection at the same time as Tanjiro. He's usually cowardly, but when he falls asleep, his true power comes out.

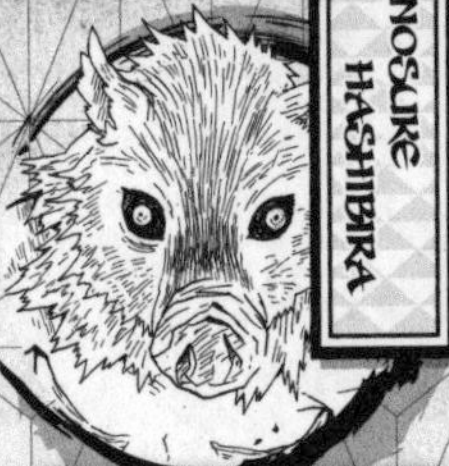

INOSUKE HASHIBIRA

He also went through Final Selection at the same time as Tanjiro. He wears the pelt of a wild boar and is very belligerent.

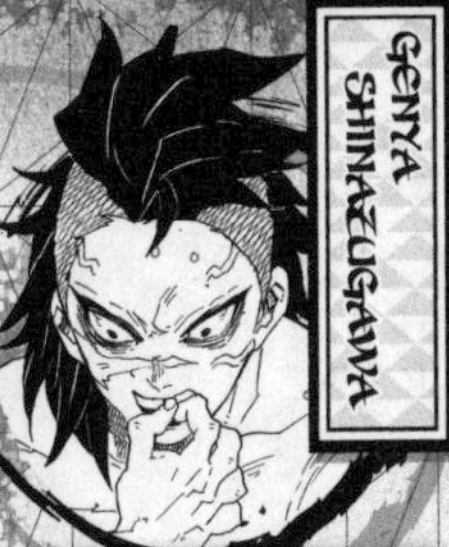

GENYA SHINAZUGAWA

He went through Final Selection at the same time as Tanjiro. His elder brother is Sanemi, the Wind Hashira. He gains demonic strength by eating demon flesh.

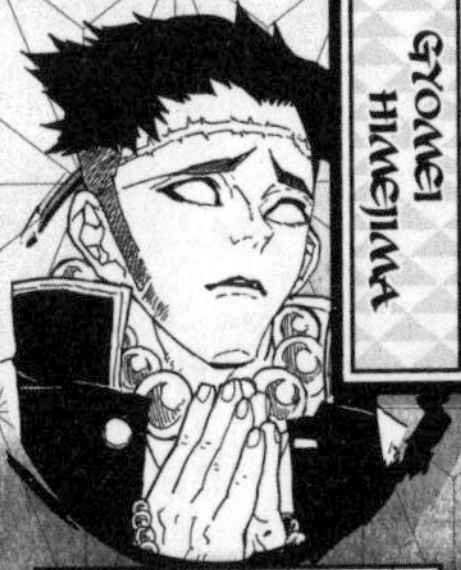

GYOMEI HIMEJIMA

Stone Hashira in the Demon Slayer Corps. He is always holding a rosary and reciting Buddhist prayers.

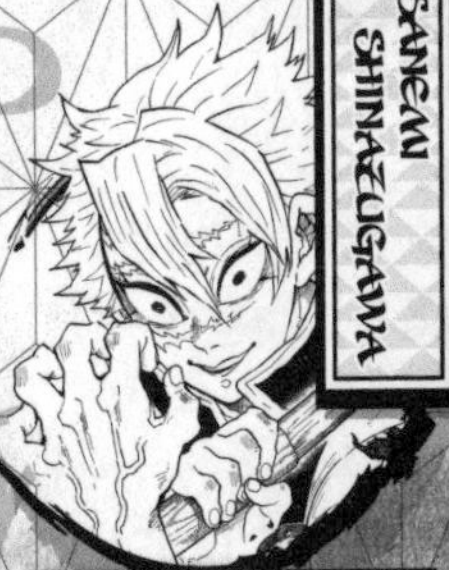

SANEMI SHINAZUGAWA

Wind Hashira in the Demon Slayer Corps. He has a harsh attitude toward his younger brother Genya.

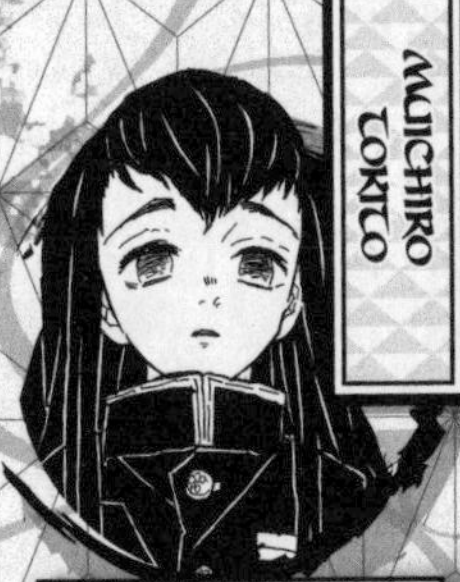

MUICHIRO TOKITO

Mist Hashira in the Demon Slayer Corps. The descendant of users of Sun Breathing, the first breathing technique.

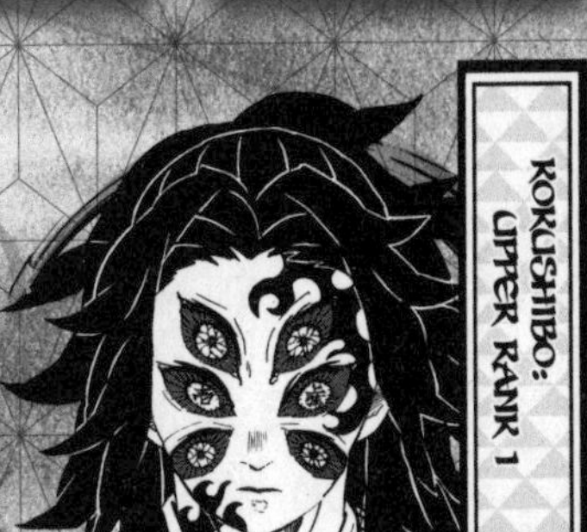

KOKUSHIBO: UPPER RANK 1

He carries a katana and is a demon, but uses the Moon Breathing sword technique.

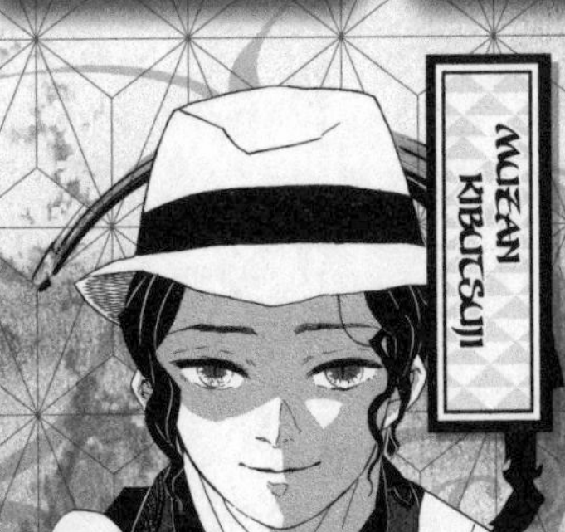

MUZAN KIBUTSUJI

Kibutsuji turned Nezuko into a demon. He is Tanjiro's enemy and hides his nature in order to live among human beings.

CONTENTS

DEMON SLAYER
KIMETSU NO YAIBA

20

THE PATH OF OPENING A STEADFAST HEART

CHAPTER 170: THE IMMOVABLE HASHIRA

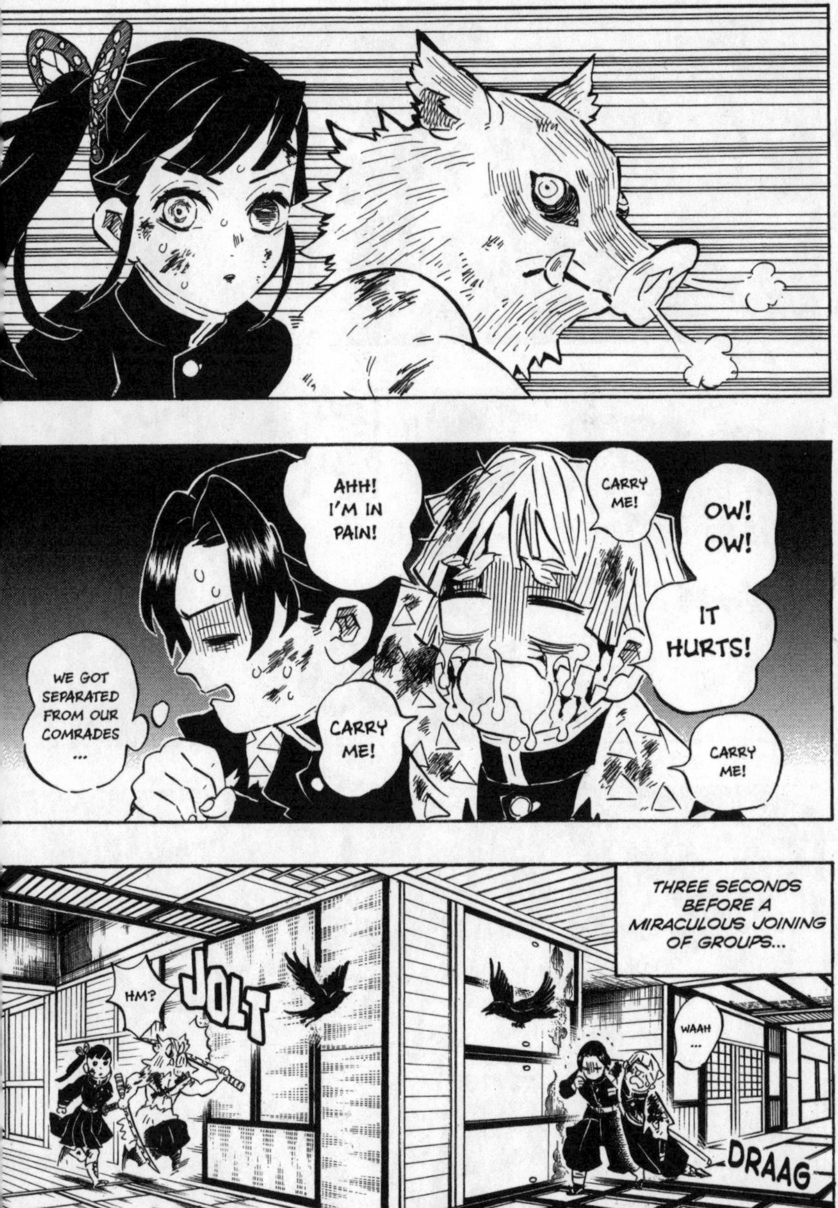
OW! OW!
CARRY ME!
AHH! I'M IN PAIN!
IT HURTS!
CARRY ME!
CARRY ME!
WE GOT SEPARATED FROM OUR COMRADES ...
THREE SECONDS BEFORE A MIRACULOUS JOINING OF GROUPS...
WAAH ...
DRAAG
JOLT
HM?

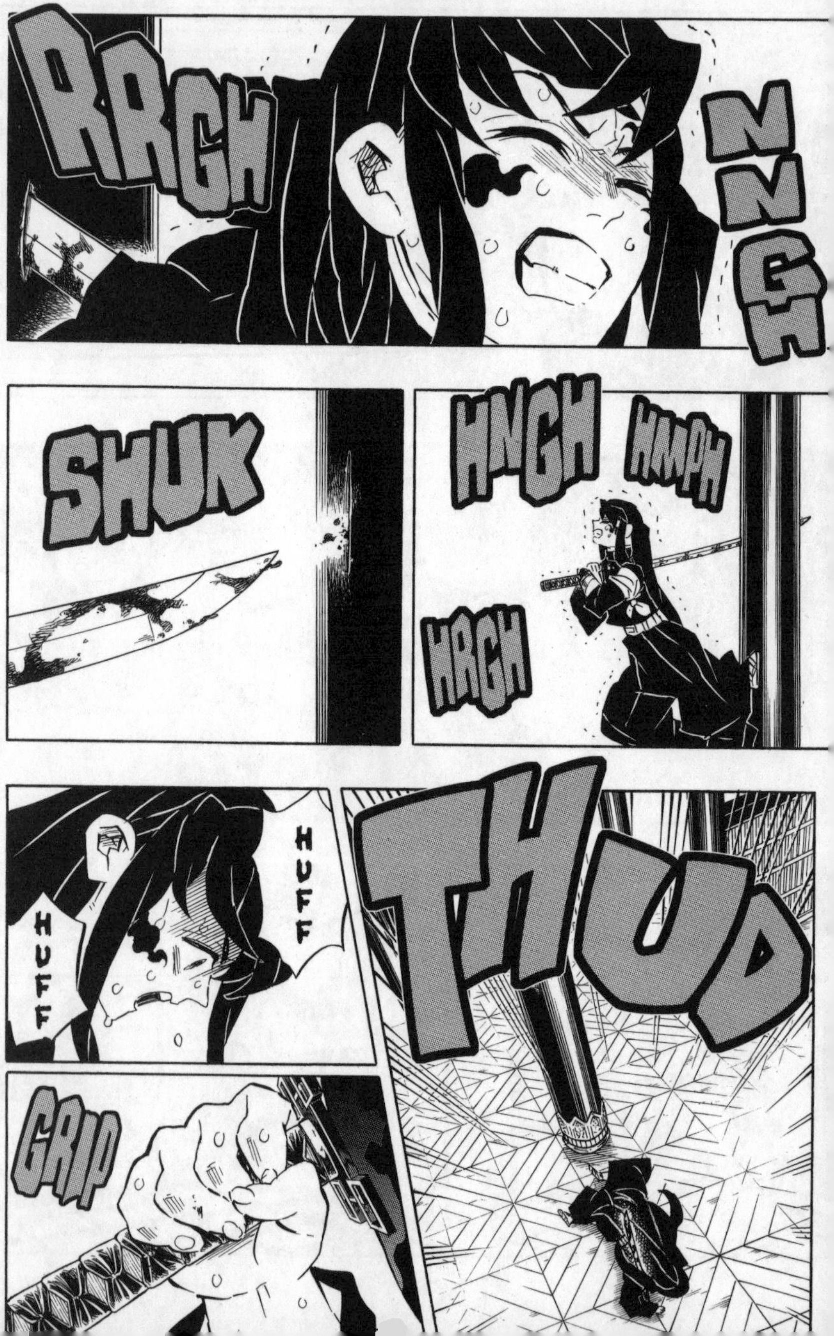
NNGH
ARRGH
HMPH
HNGH
HRGH
SHUK
THUD
HUFF
HUFF
GRIP

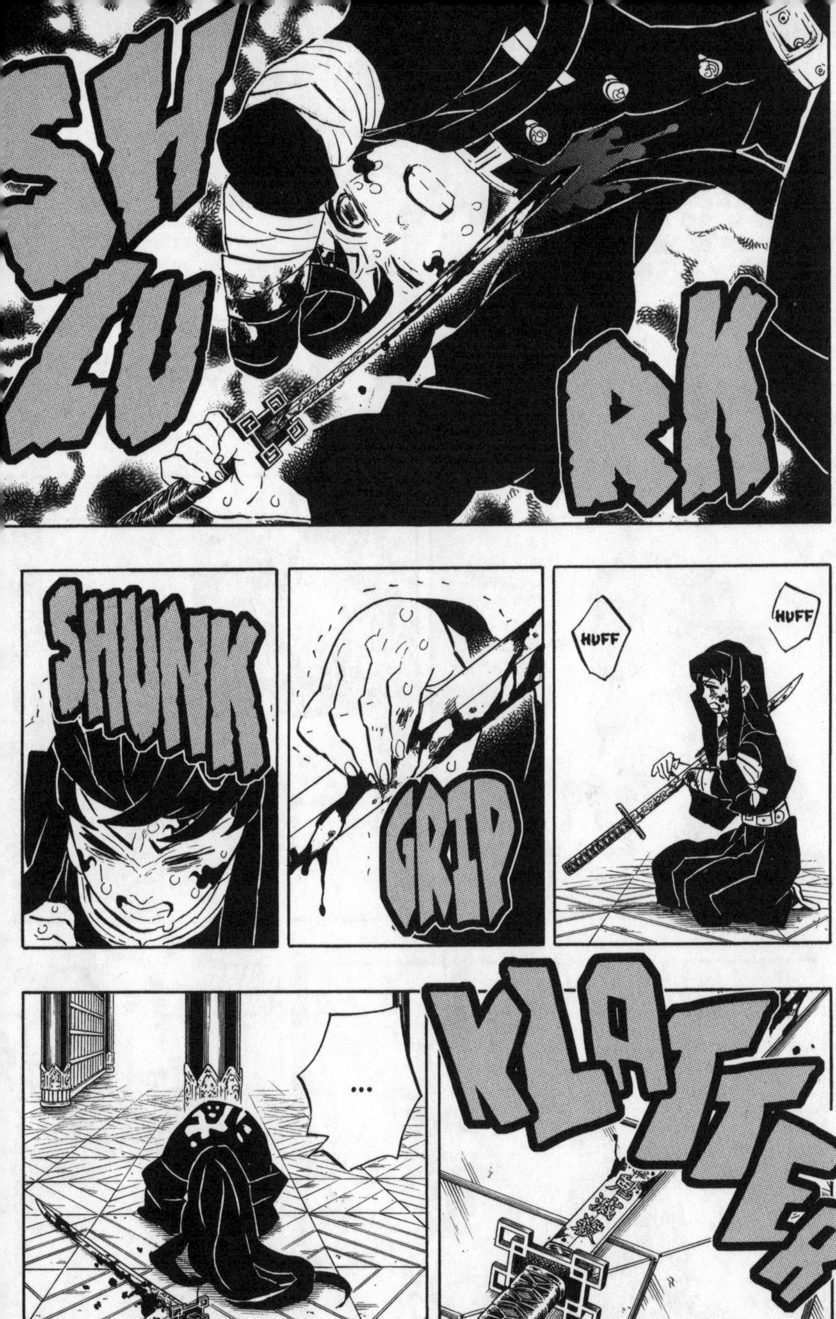
SHLURK
HUFF
HUFF
GRIP
SHUNK
KLATTER
...

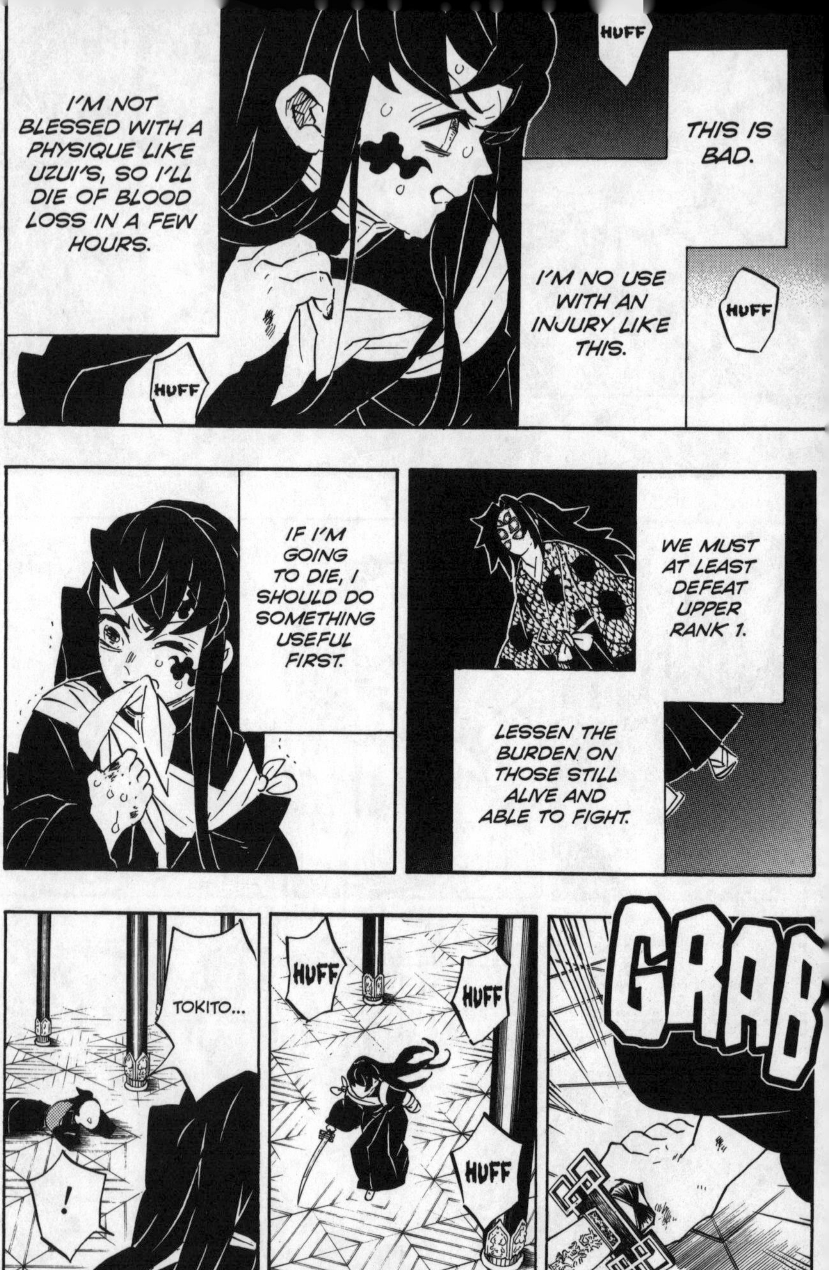
HUFF
THIS IS BAD.
HUFF
I'M NO USE WITH AN INJURY LIKE THIS.
I'M NOT BLESSED WITH A PHYSIQUE LIKE UZUI'S, SO I'LL DIE OF BLOOD LOSS IN A FEW HOURS.
HUFF
WE MUST AT LEAST DEFEAT UPPER RANK 1.
LESSEN THE BURDEN ON THOSE STILL ALIVE AND ABLE TO FIGHT.
IF I'M GOING TO DIE, I SHOULD DO SOMETHING USEFUL FIRST.
GRAB
HUFF
HUFF
HUFF
TOKITO...
!

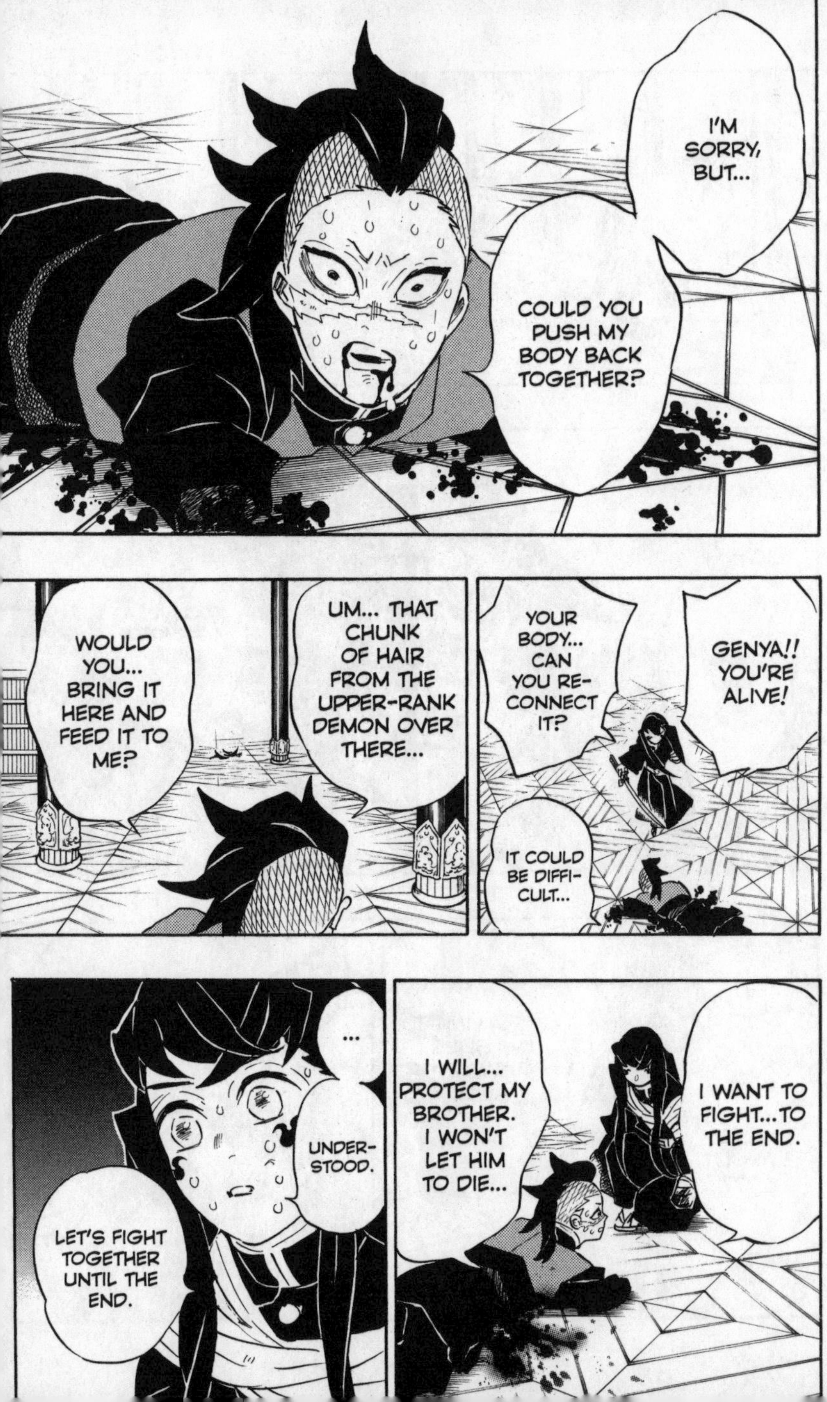
I'M SORRY, BUT...
COULD YOU PUSH MY BODY BACK TOGETHER?
GENYA!! YOU'RE ALIVE!
YOUR BODY... CAN YOU RE-CONNECT IT?
IT COULD BE DIFFI-CULT...
UM... THAT CHUNK OF HAIR FROM THE UPPER-RANK DEMON OVER THERE...
WOULD YOU... BRING IT HERE AND FEED IT TO ME?
I WANT TO FIGHT...TO THE END.
I WILL... PROTECT MY BROTHER. I WON'T LET HIM TO DIE...
...
UNDER-STOOD.
LET'S FIGHT TOGETHER UNTIL THE END.

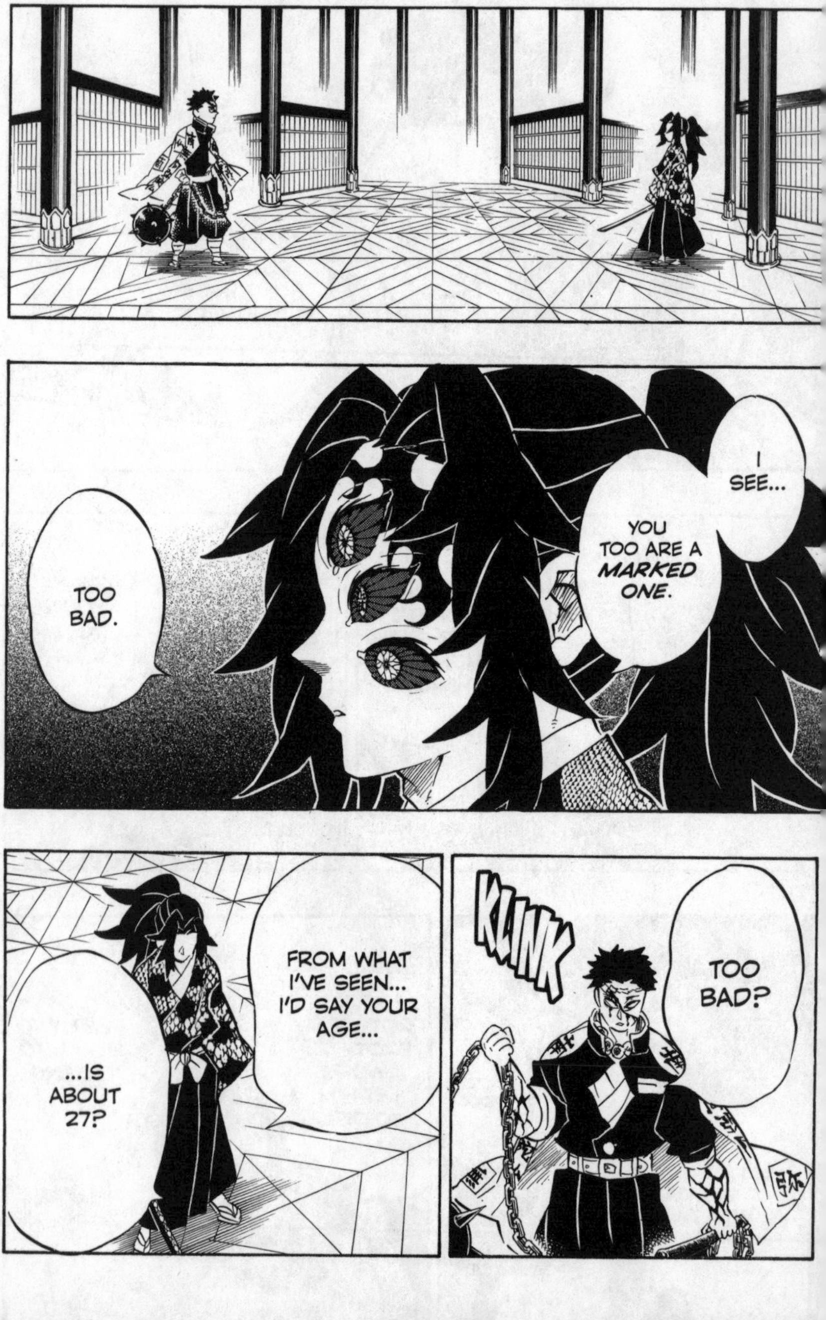
I SEE...
YOU TOO ARE A *MARKED* ONE.
TOO BAD.
KLINK
TOO BAD?
FROM WHAT I'VE SEEN... I'D SAY YOUR AGE...
...IS ABOUT 27?

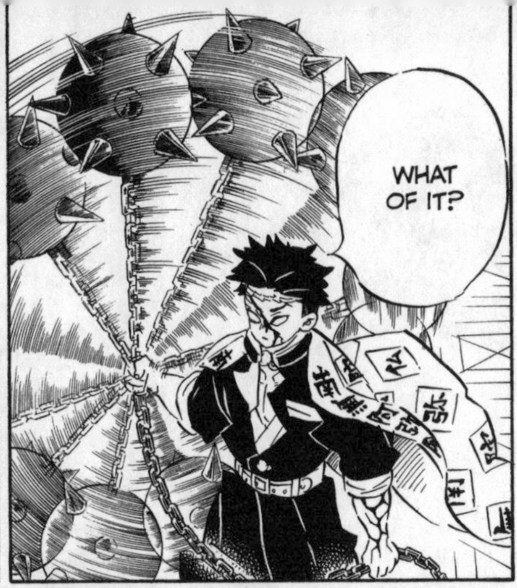
WHAT OF IT?
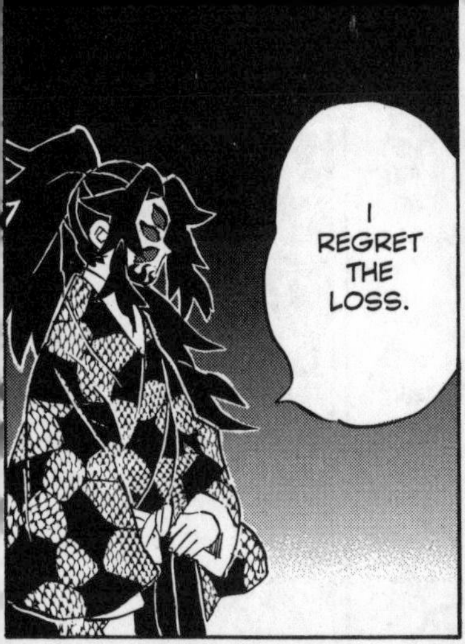
I REGRET THE LOSS.

*EYES: UPPER 1

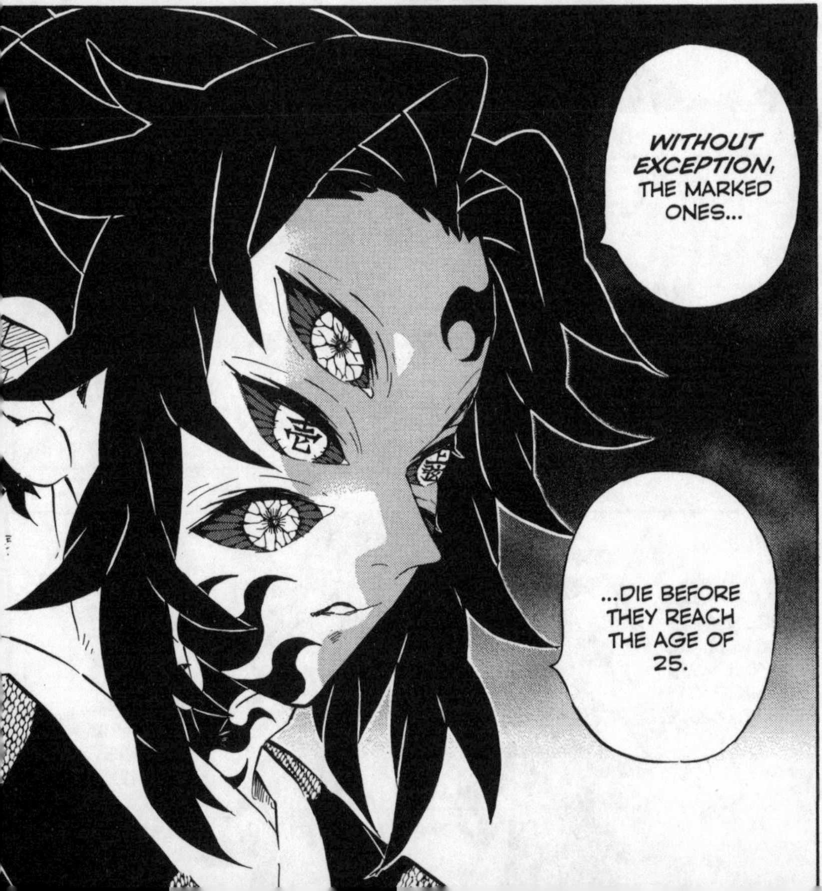
WITHOUT EXCEPTION, THE MARKED ONES...
...DIE BEFORE THEY REACH THE AGE OF 25.

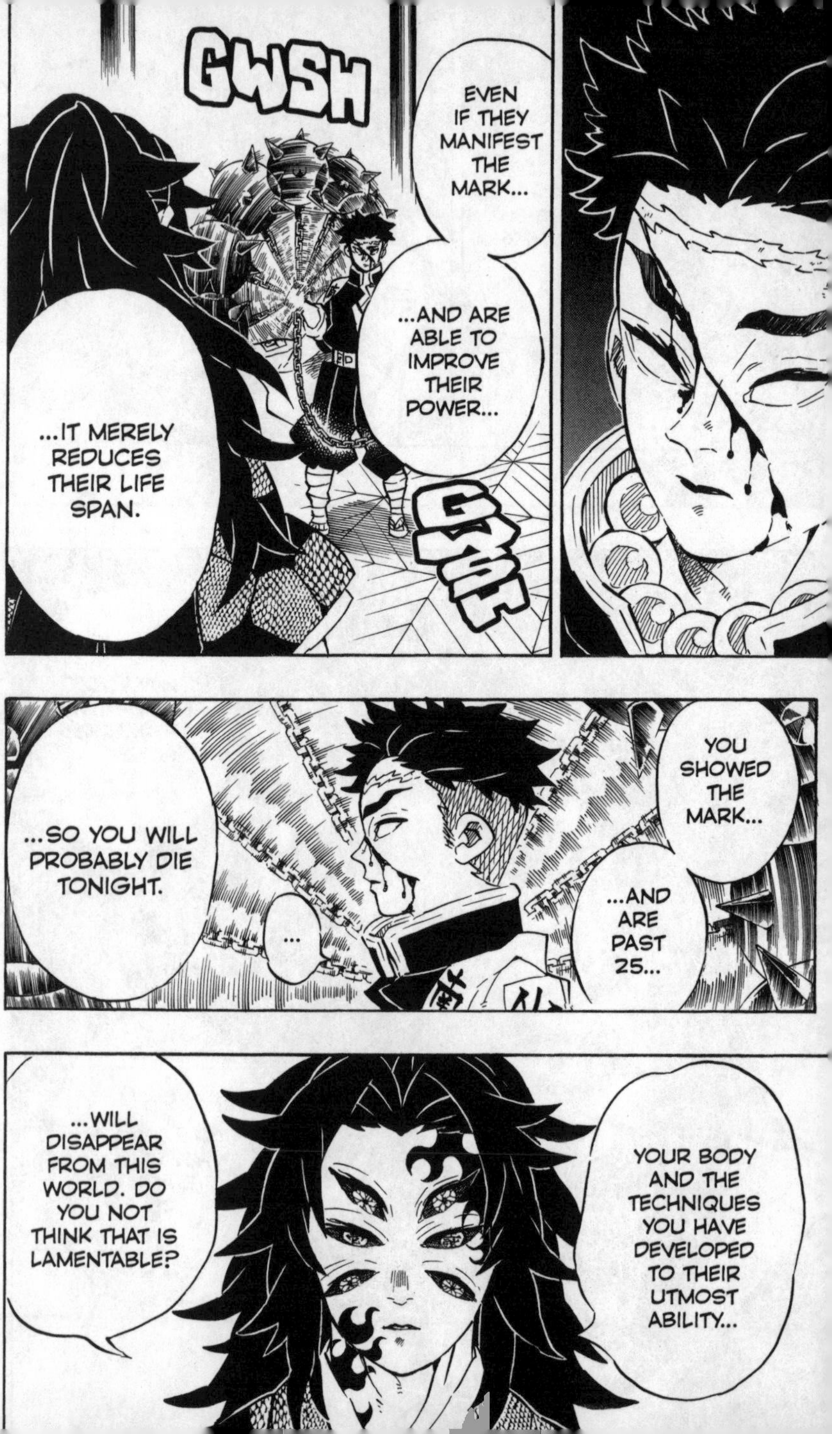
GWSH
EVEN IF THEY MANIFEST THE MARK...
...AND ARE ABLE TO IMPROVE THEIR POWER...
...IT MERELY REDUCES THEIR LIFE SPAN.
YOU SHOWED THE MARK...
...AND ARE PAST 25...
...
...SO YOU WILL PROBABLY DIE TONIGHT.
YOUR BODY AND THE TECHNIQUES YOU HAVE DEVELOPED TO THEIR UTMOST ABILITY...
...WILL DISAPPEAR FROM THIS WORLD. DO YOU NOT THINK THAT IS LAMENTABLE?

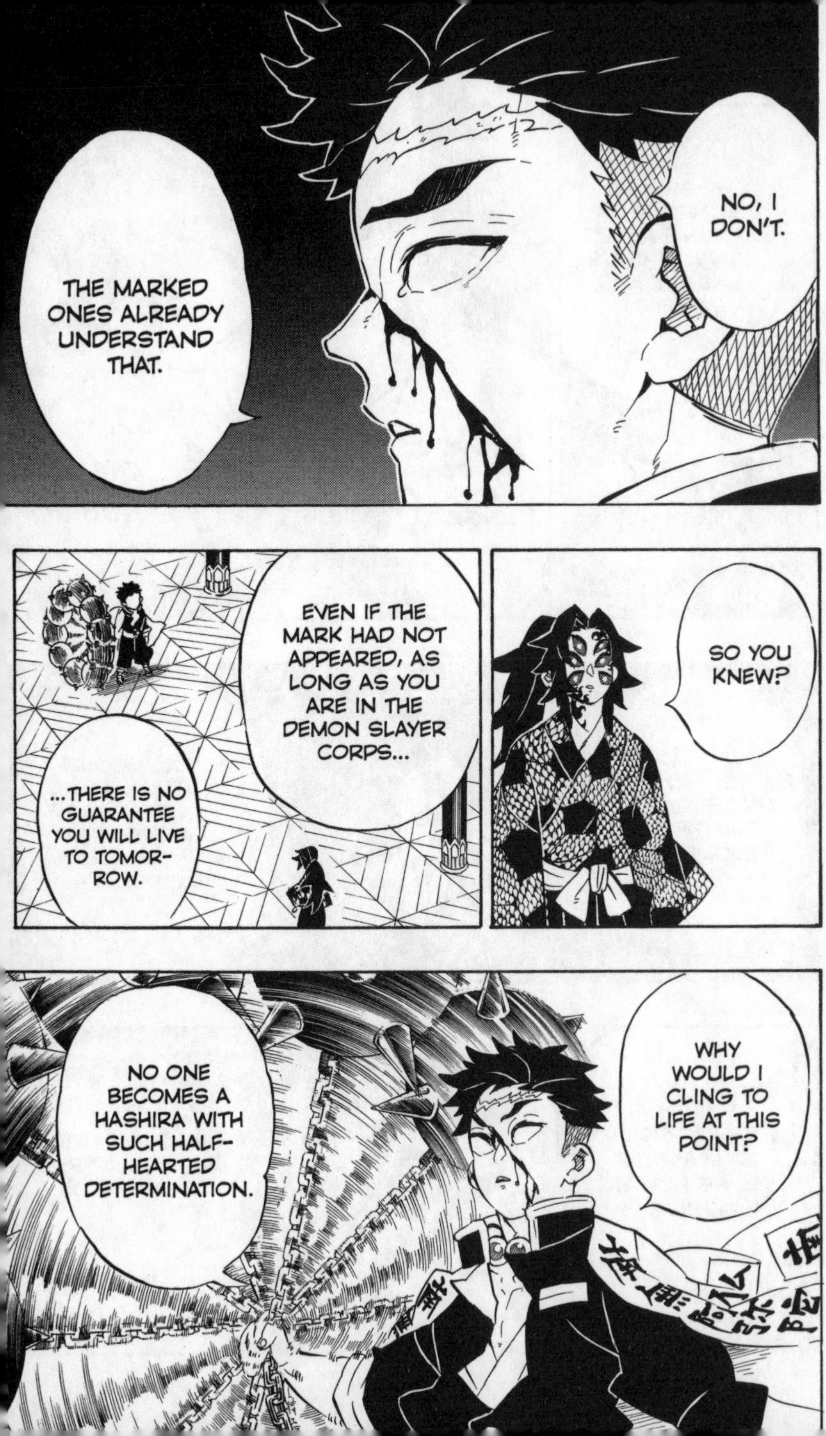
NO, I DON'T.
THE MARKED ONES ALREADY UNDERSTAND THAT.
SO YOU KNEW?
EVEN IF THE MARK HAD NOT APPEARED, AS LONG AS YOU ARE IN THE DEMON SLAYER CORPS...
...THERE IS NO GUARANTEE YOU WILL LIVE TO TOMOR-ROW.
WHY WOULD I CLING TO LIFE AT THIS POINT?
NO ONE BECOMES A HASHIRA WITH SUCH HALF-HEARTED DETERMINATION.

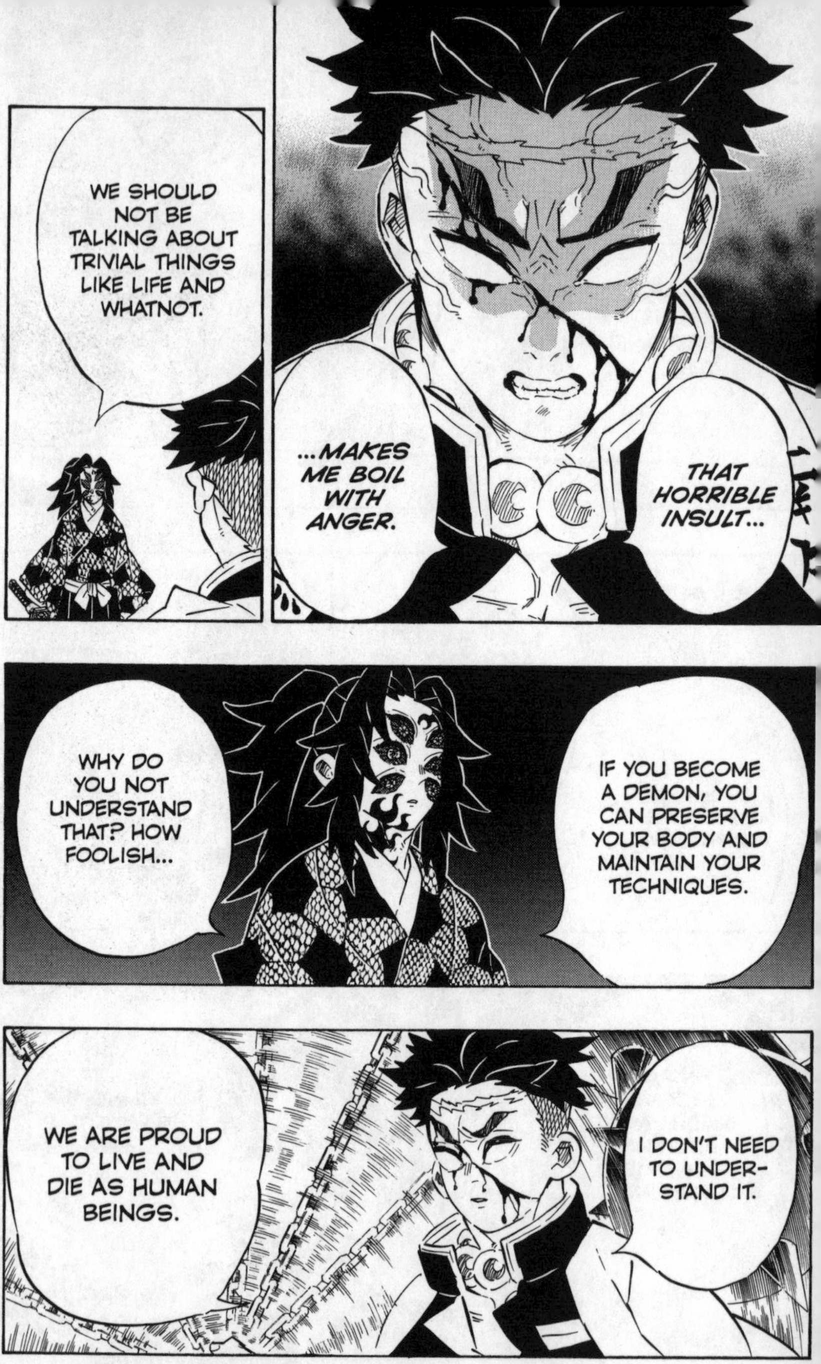
THAT HORRIBLE INSULT...
...MAKES ME BOIL WITH ANGER.
WE SHOULD NOT BE TALKING ABOUT TRIVIAL THINGS LIKE LIFE AND WHATNOT.
IF YOU BECOME A DEMON, YOU CAN PRESERVE YOUR BODY AND MAINTAIN YOUR TECHNIQUES.
WHY DO YOU NOT UNDERSTAND THAT? HOW FOOLISH...
I DON'T NEED TO UNDER-STAND IT.
WE ARE PROUD TO LIVE AND DIE AS HUMAN BEINGS.

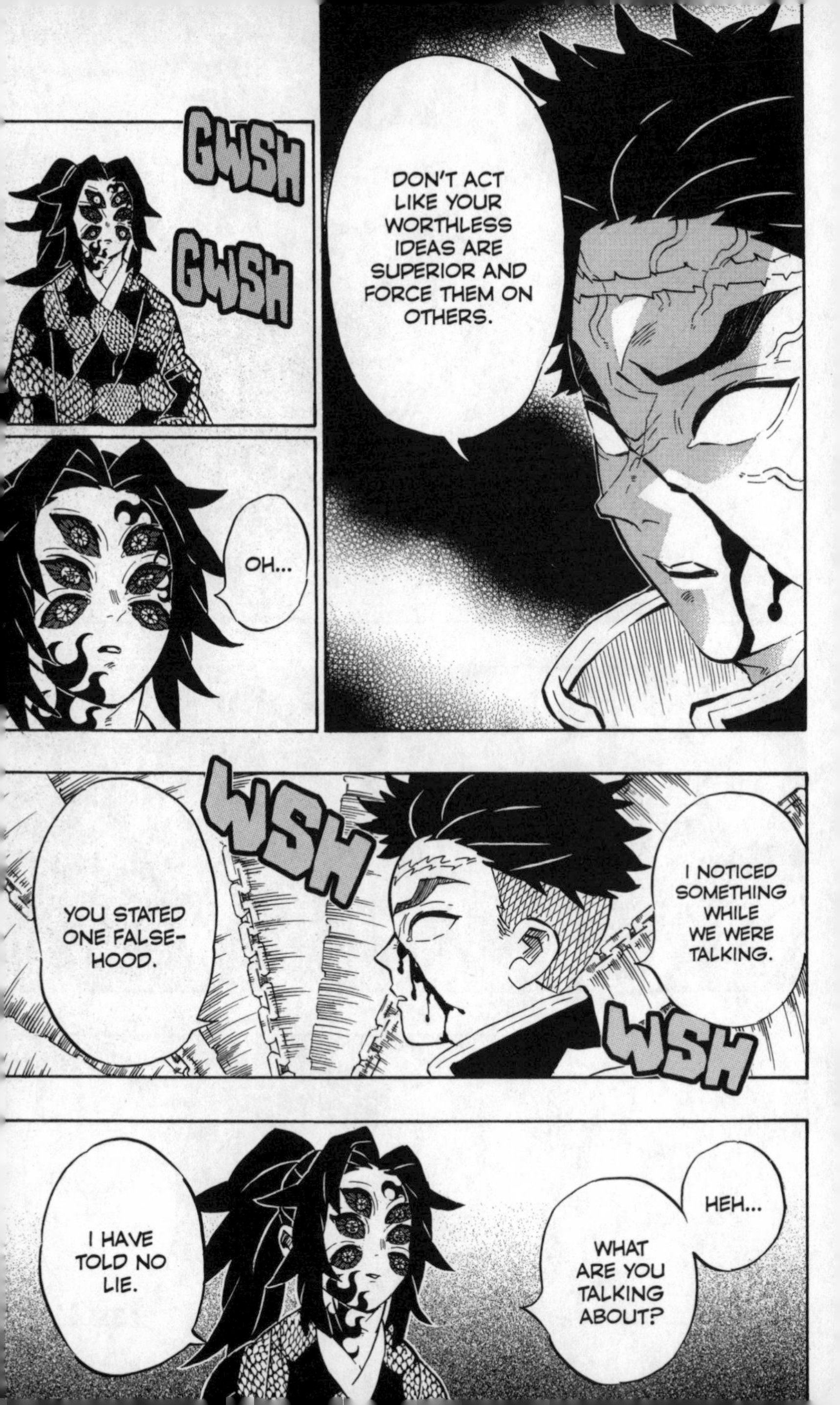
DON'T ACT LIKE YOUR WORTHLESS IDEAS ARE SUPERIOR AND FORCE THEM ON OTHERS.
GWSH
GWSH
OH...
I NOTICED SOMETHING WHILE WE WERE TALKING.
WSH
WSH
YOU STATED ONE FALSE-HOOD.
HEH...
WHAT ARE YOU TALKING ABOUT?
I HAVE TOLD NO LIE.

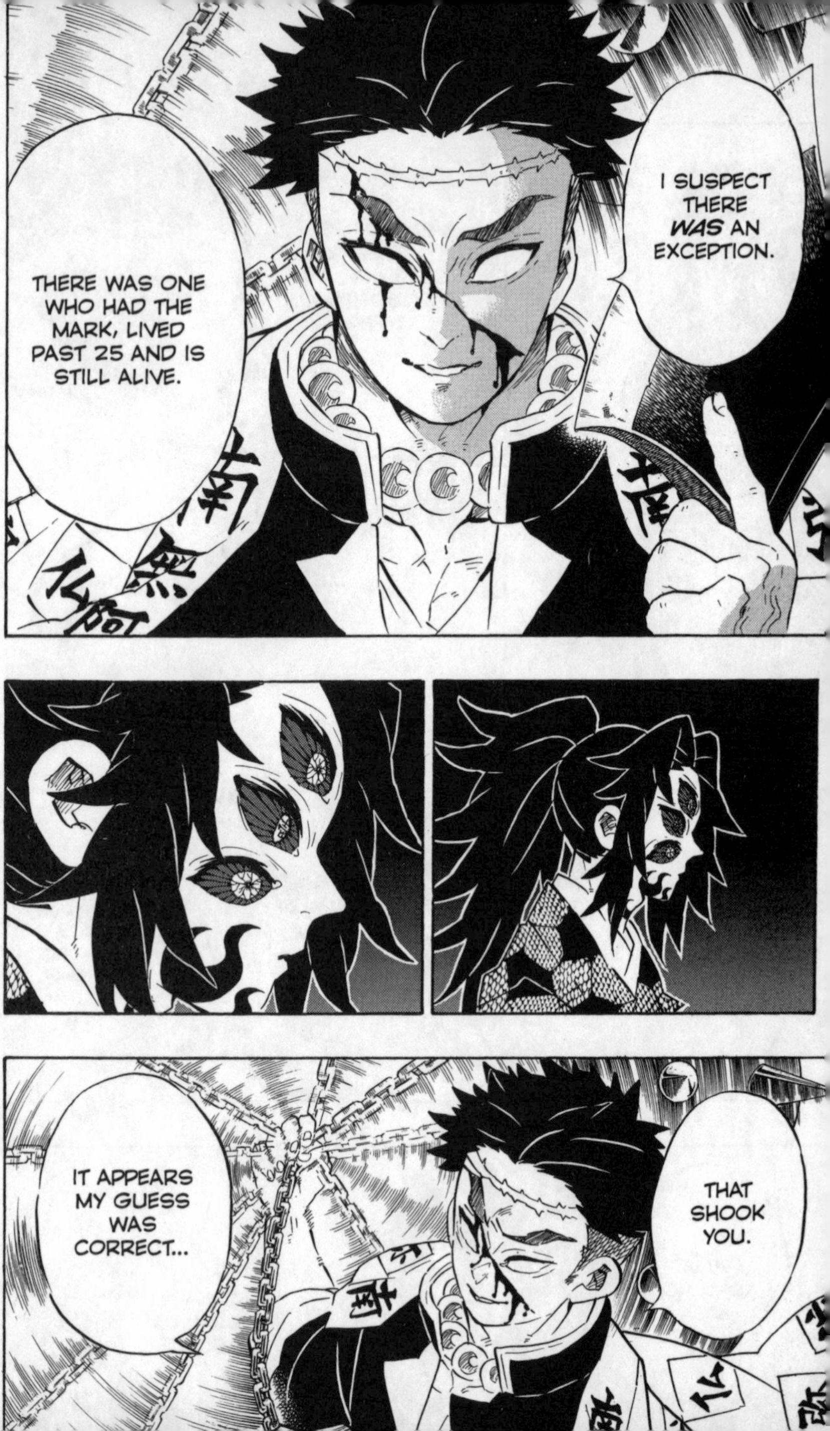
I SUSPECT THERE *WAS* AN EXCEPTION.
THERE WAS ONE WHO HAD THE MARK, LIVED PAST 25 AND IS STILL ALIVE.
THAT SHOOK YOU.
IT APPEARS MY GUESS WAS CORRECT...

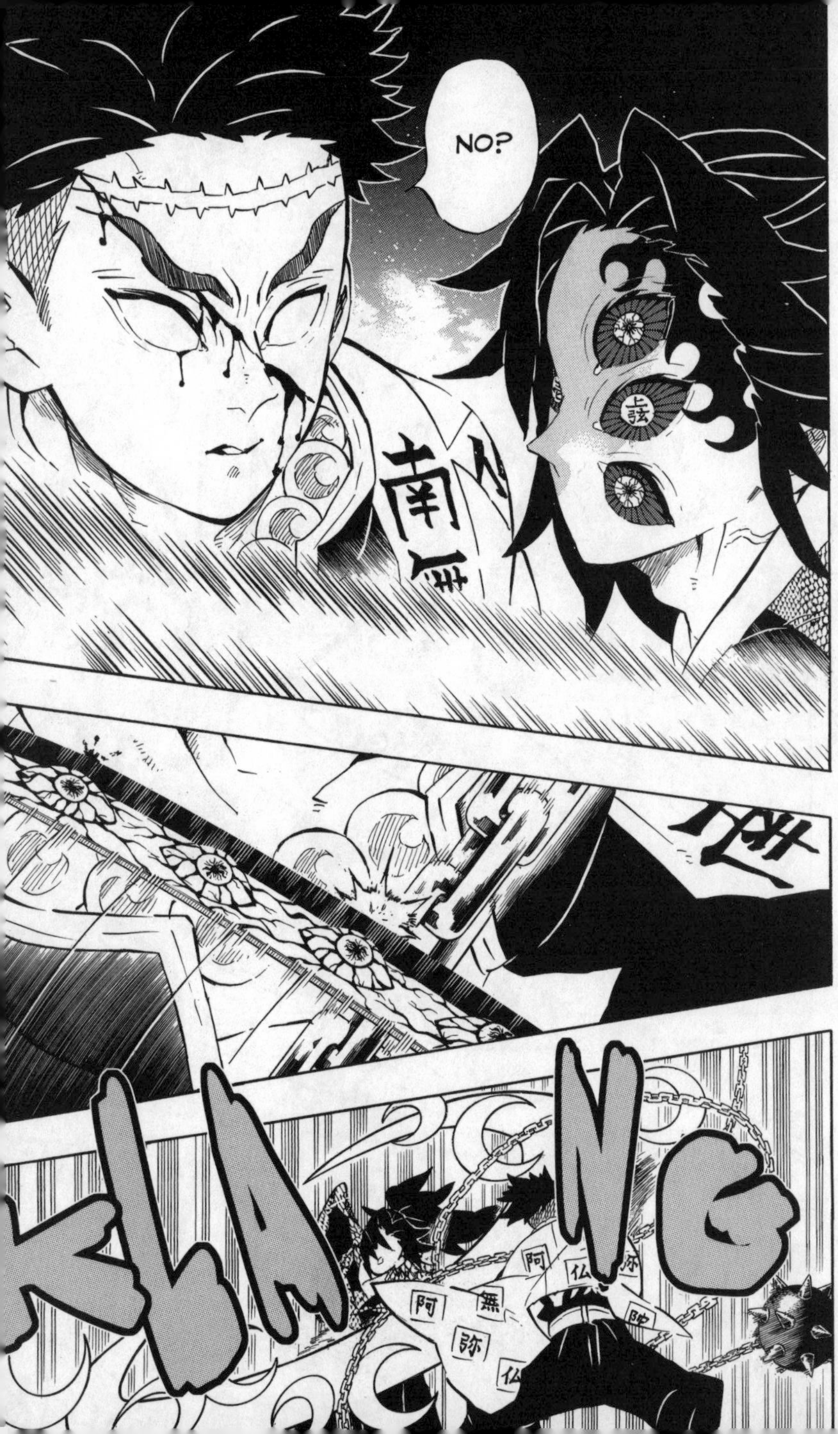
NO?
KLANG

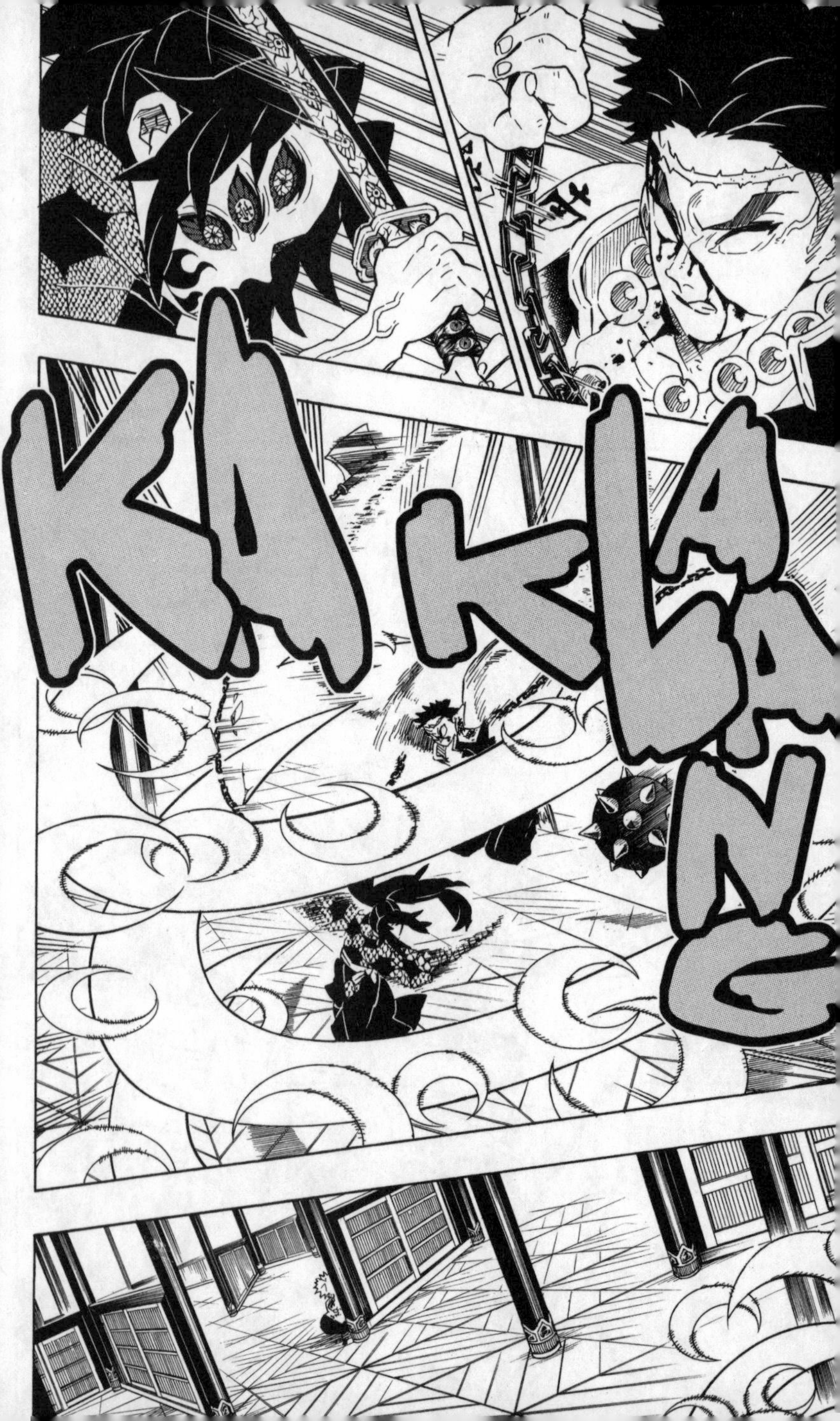
KA-KLANG

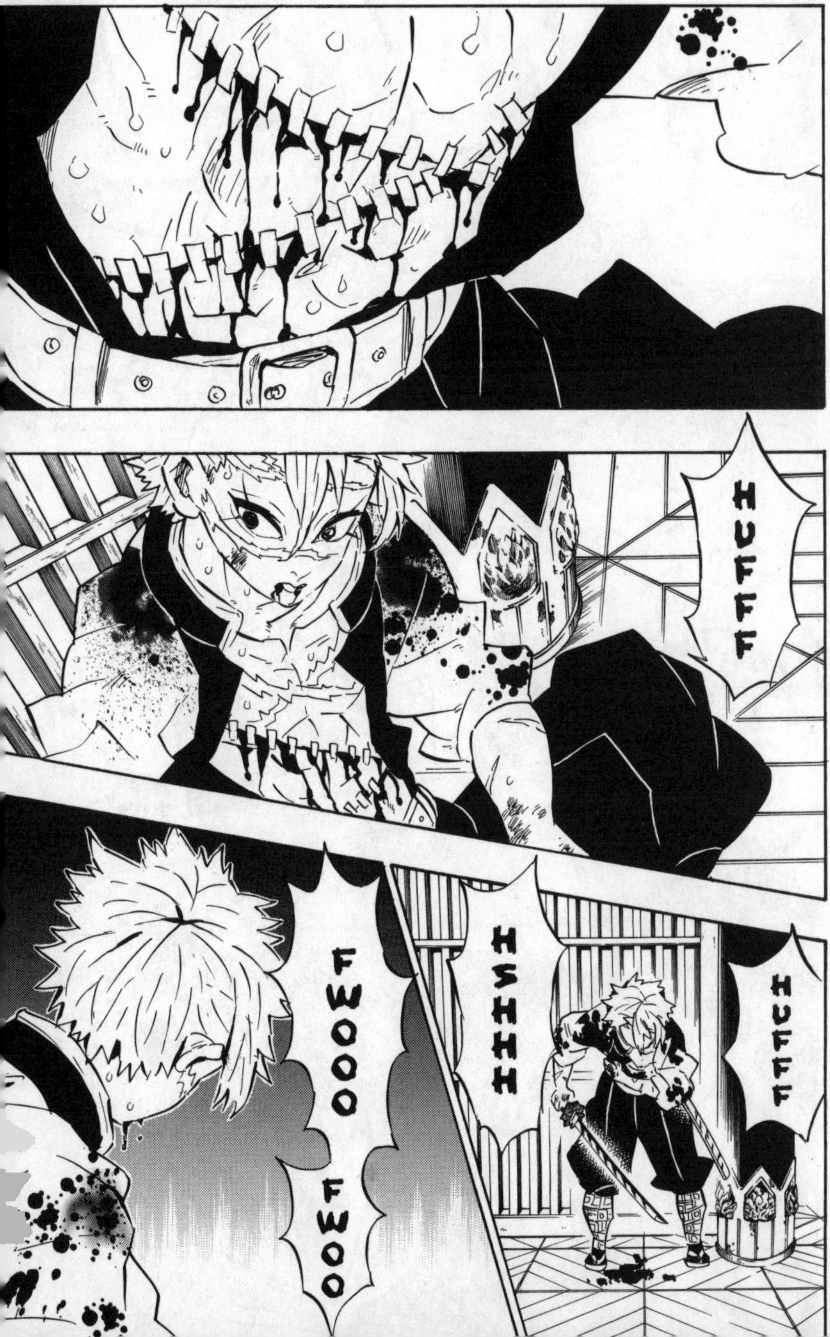
HUFFF
HUFFF
HSHHH
FWOOO
FWOO

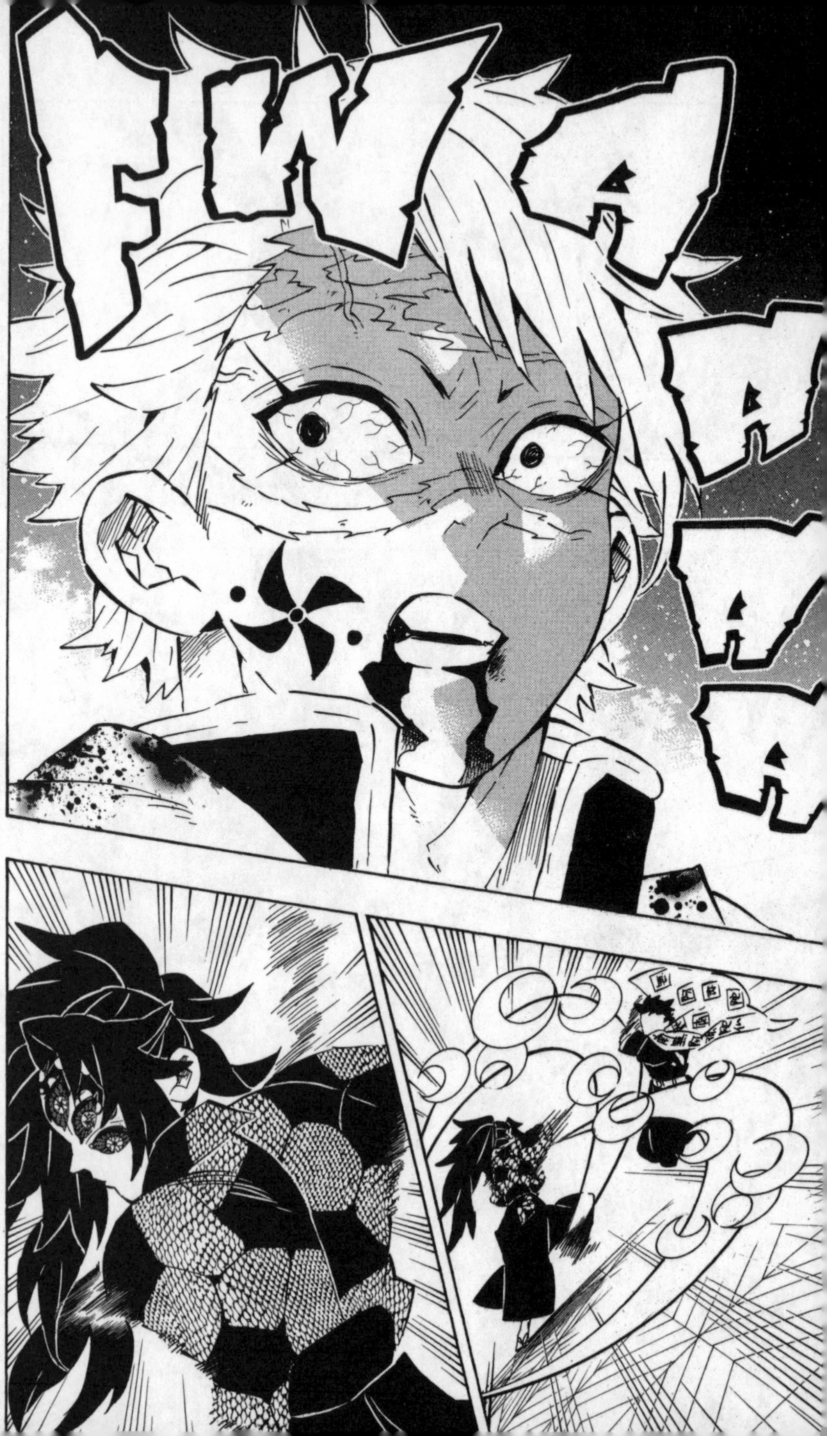
FWAAAA

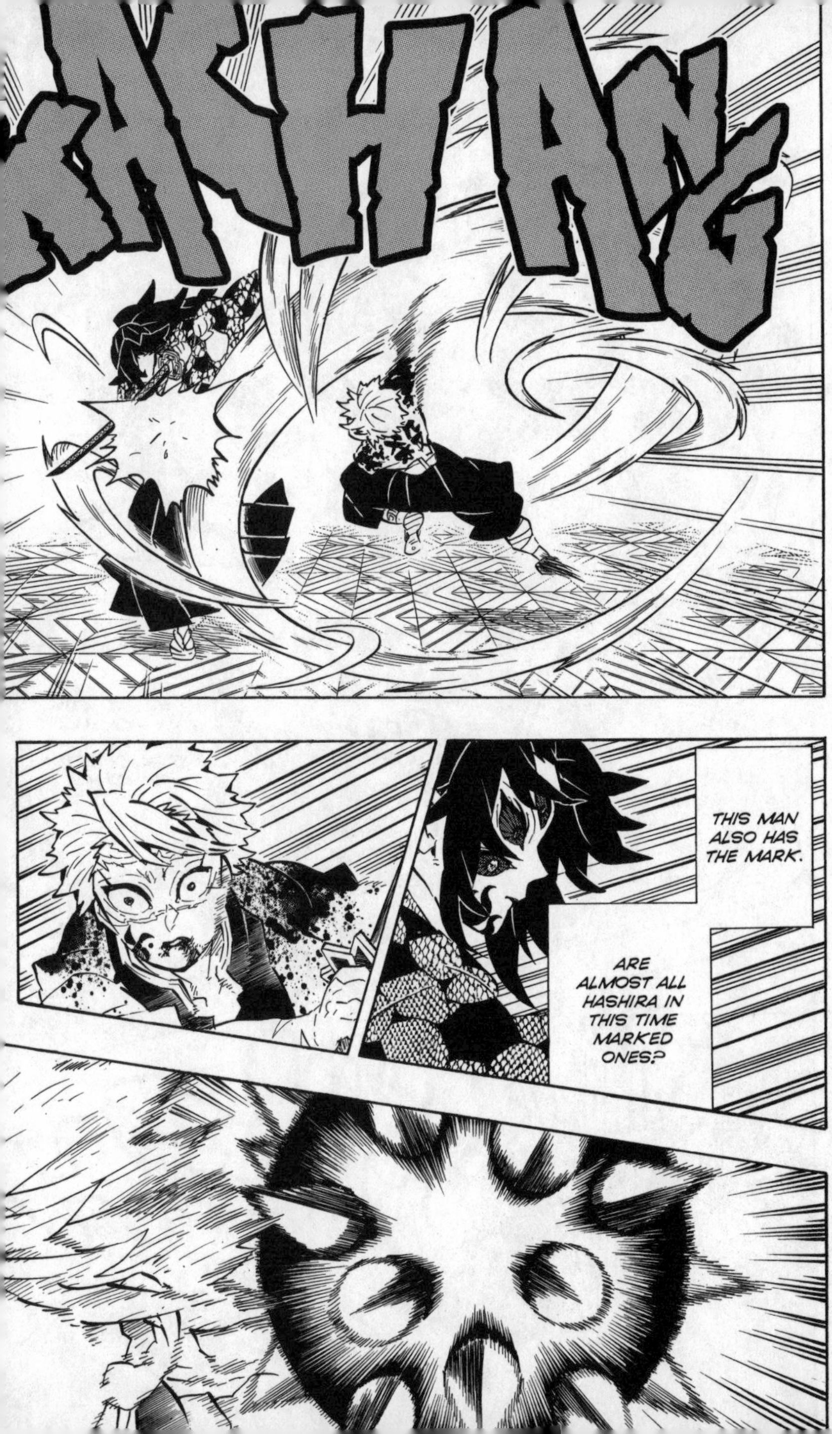

KAHANG
THIS MAN ALSO HAS THE MARK.
ARE ALMOST ALL HASHIRA IN THIS TIME MARKED ONES?

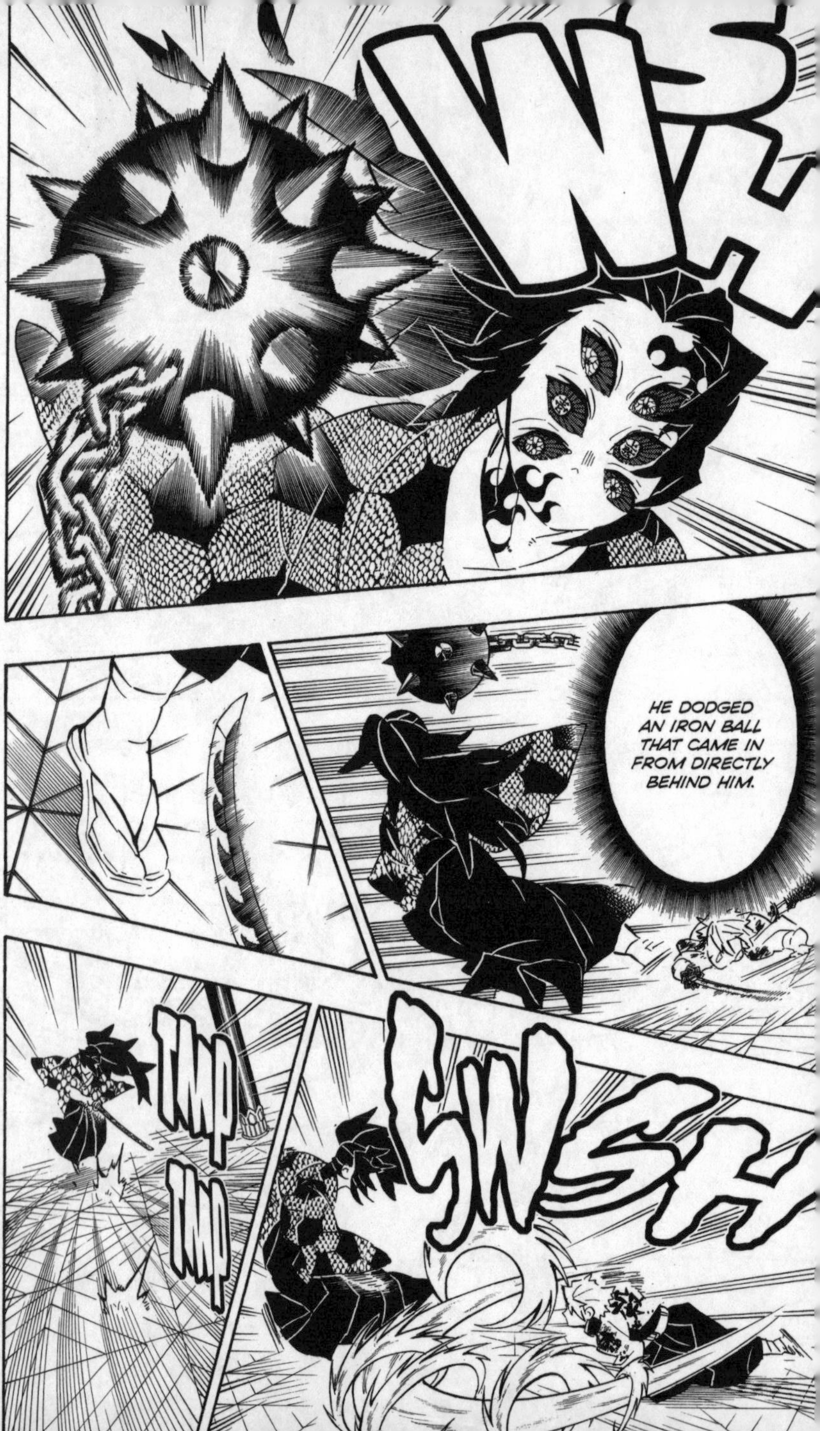
WH
HE DODGED AN IRON BALL THAT CAME IN FROM DIRECTLY BEHIND HIM.
SWSH
TMP TMP

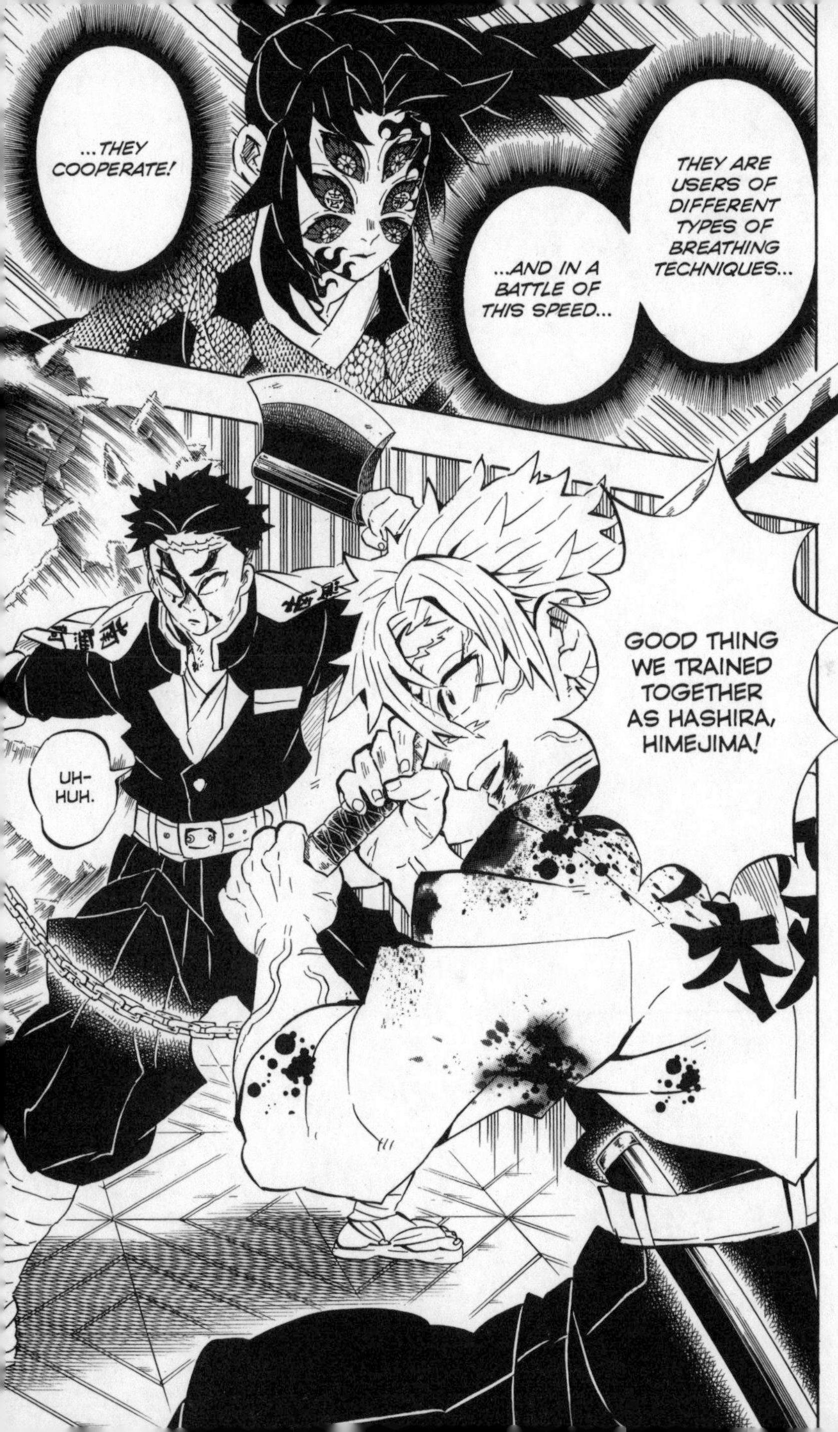
THEY ARE USERS OF DIFFERENT TYPES OF BREATHING TECHNIQUES...
...AND IN A BATTLE OF THIS SPEED...
...THEY COOPERATE!
GOOD THING WE TRAINED TOGETHER AS HASHIRA, HIMEJIMA!
UH-HUH.

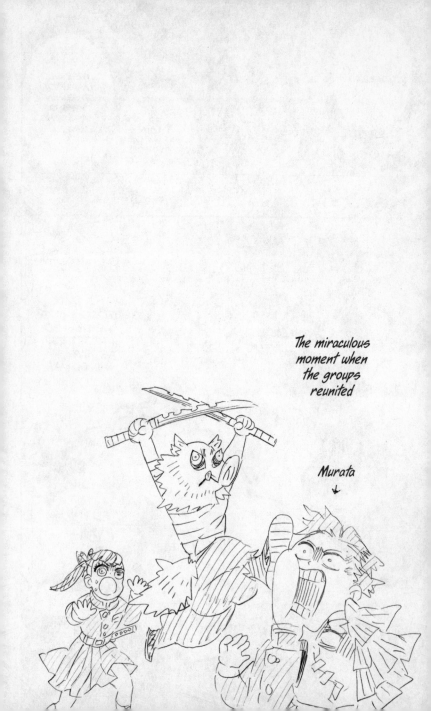

The miraculous
moment when
the groups
reunited

Murata
↓

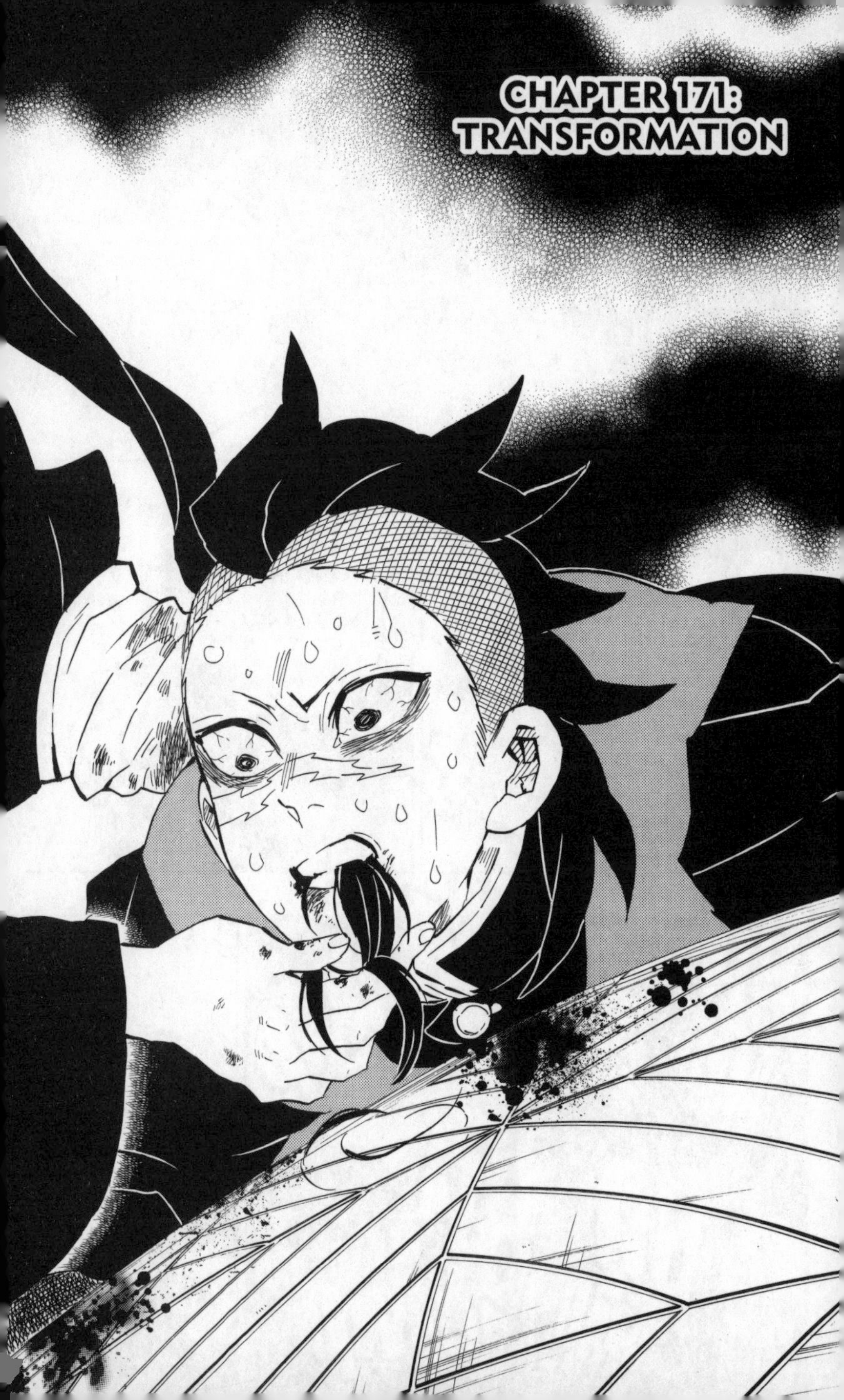
CHAPTER 171:
TRANSFORMATION

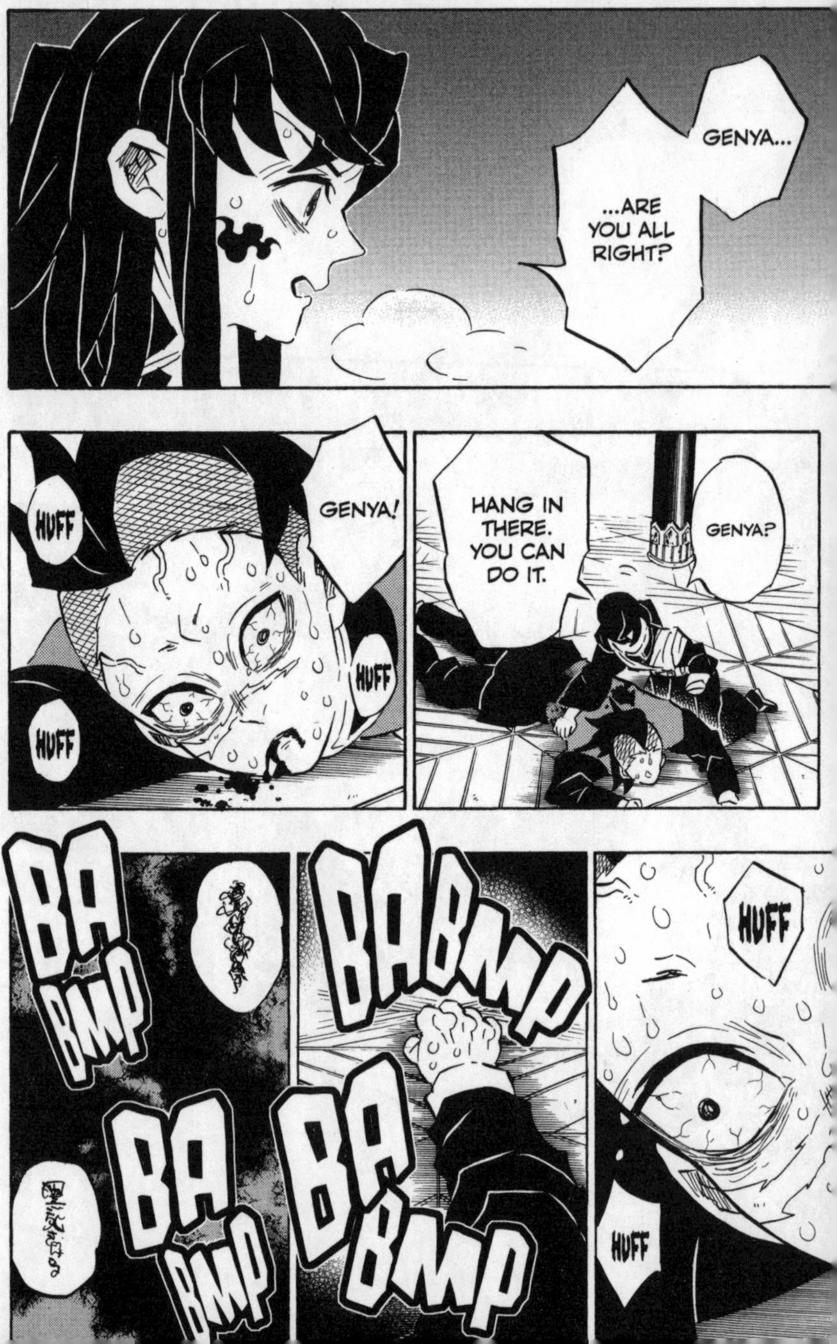
GENYA...
...ARE YOU ALL RIGHT?
GENYA?
HANG IN THERE. YOU CAN DO IT.
GENYA!
HUFF
HUFF
HUFF
HUFF
HUFF
BABMP
BA BMP
BA BMP
BA BMP

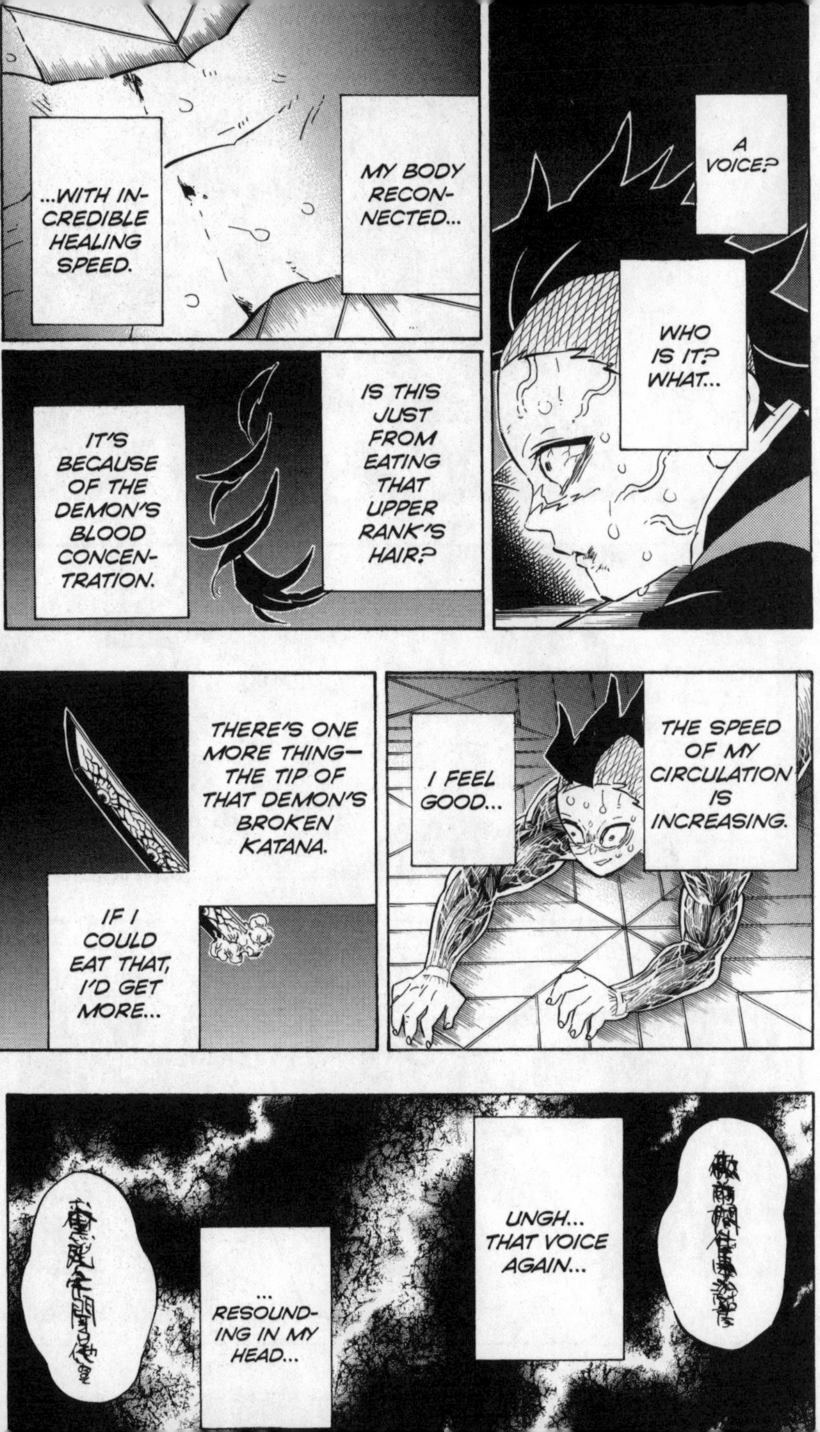

A VOICE?
WHO IS IT? WHAT...
MY BODY RECONNECTED...
...WITH INCREDIBLE HEALING SPEED.
IS THIS JUST FROM EATING THAT UPPER RANK'S HAIR?
IT'S BECAUSE OF THE DEMON'S BLOOD CONCENTRATION.
THE SPEED OF MY CIRCULATION IS INCREASING.
I FEEL GOOD...
THERE'S ONE MORE THING— THE TIP OF THAT DEMON'S BROKEN KATANA.
IF I COULD EAT THAT, I'D GET MORE...
UNGH... THAT VOICE AGAIN...
...RESOUNDING IN MY HEAD...

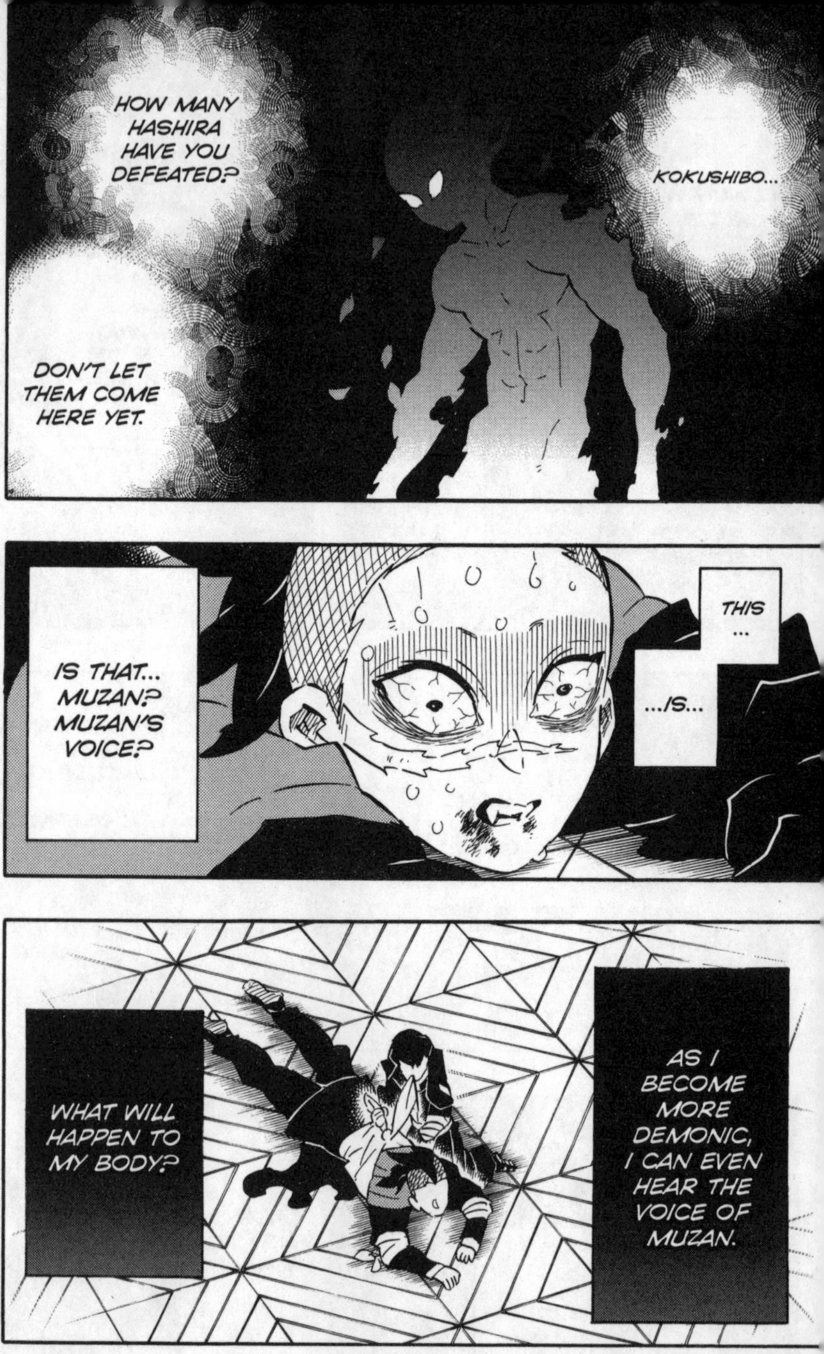
KOKUSHIBO...
HOW MANY HASHIRA HAVE YOU DEFEATED?
DON'T LET THEM COME HERE YET.
THIS ...
...IS...
IS THAT... MUZAN? MUZAN'S VOICE?
AS I BECOME MORE DEMONIC, I CAN EVEN HEAR THE VOICE OF MUZAN.
WHAT WILL HAPPEN TO MY BODY?

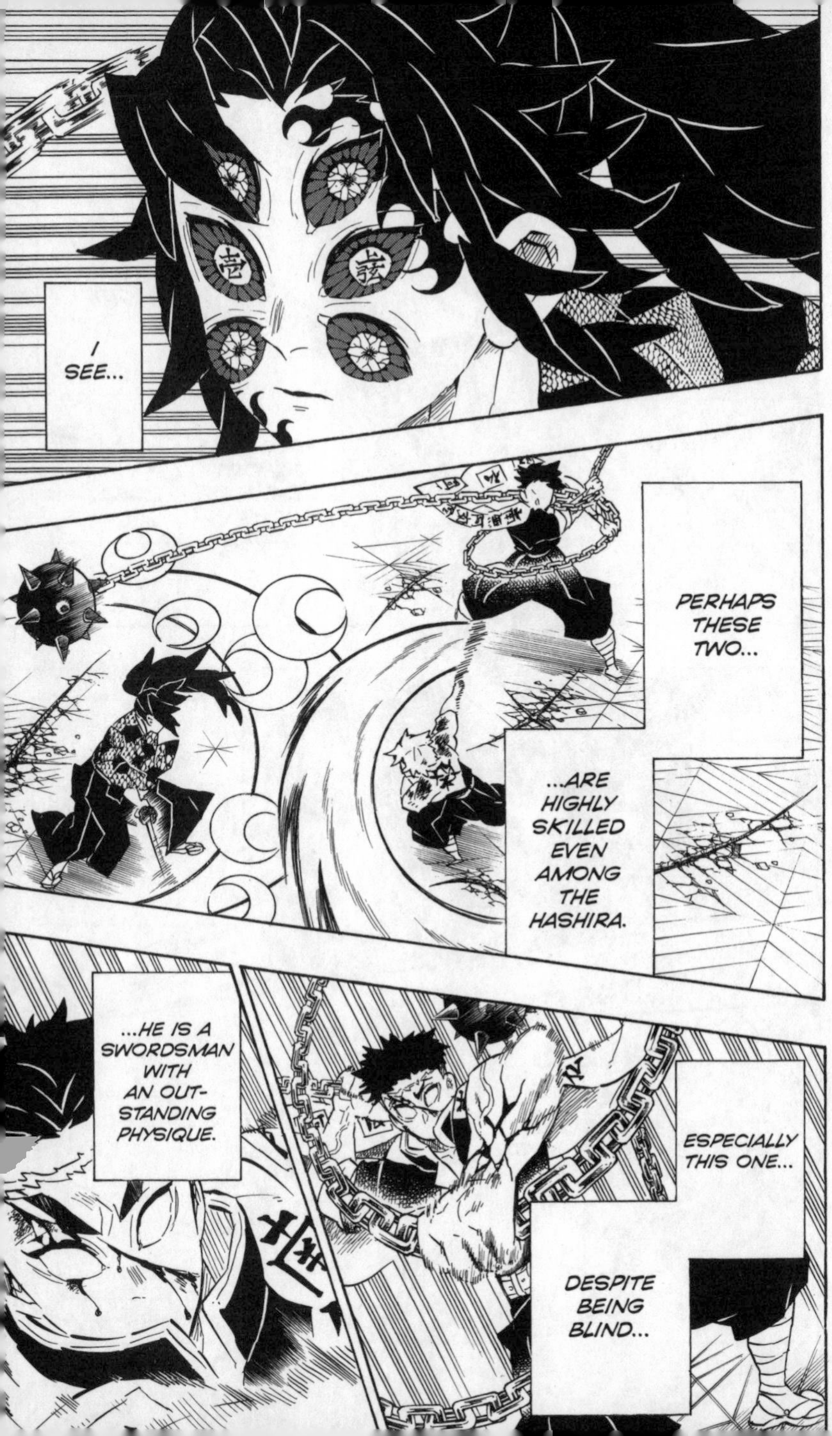
I SEE...
PERHAPS THESE TWO...
...ARE HIGHLY SKILLED EVEN AMONG THE HASHIRA.
ESPECIALLY THIS ONE...
DESPITE BEING BLIND...
...HE IS A SWORDSMAN WITH AN OUT-STANDING PHYSIQUE.

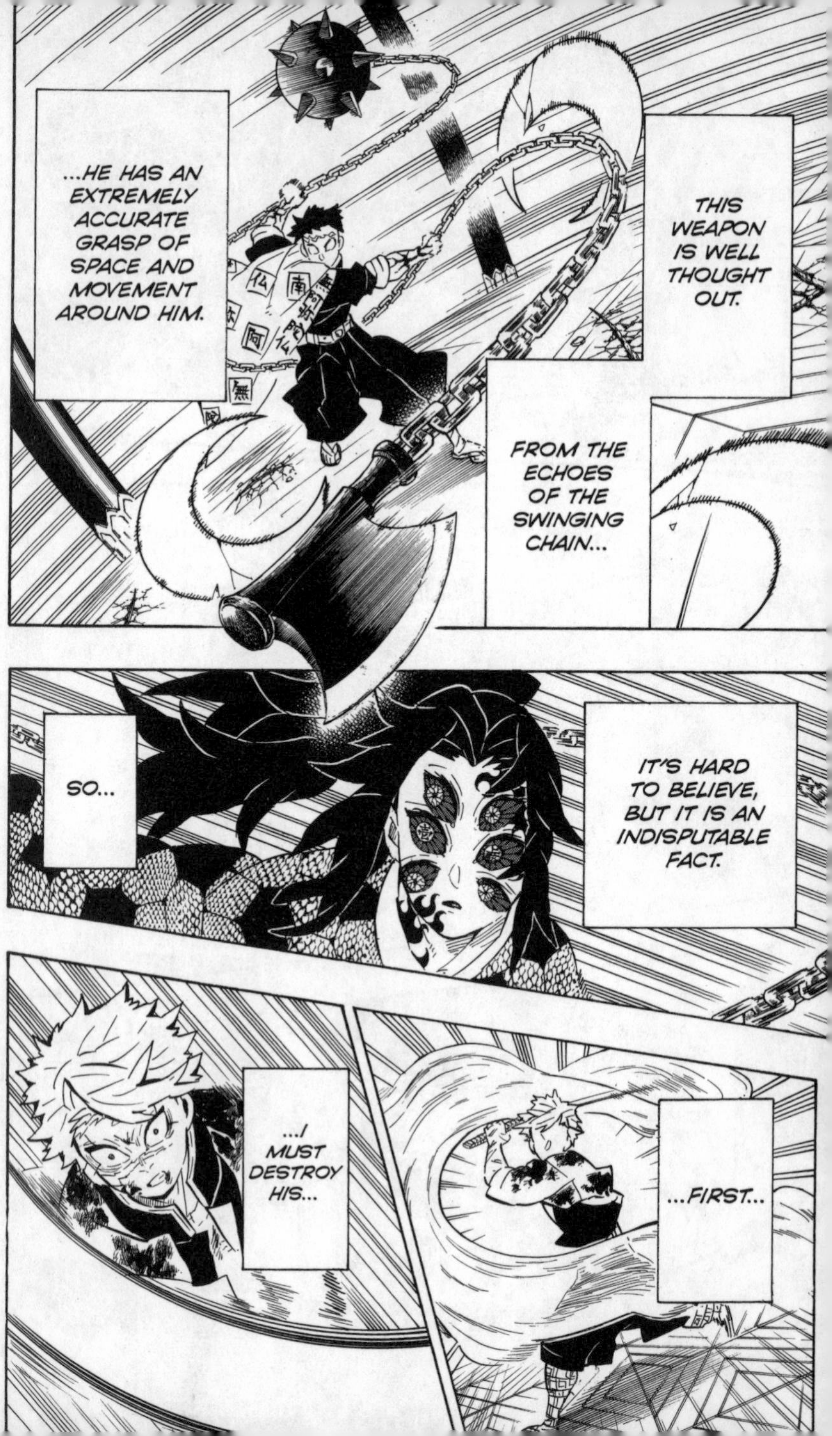
THIS WEAPON IS WELL THOUGHT OUT.
FROM THE ECHOES OF THE SWINGING CHAIN...
...HE HAS AN EXTREMELY ACCURATE GRASP OF SPACE AND MOVEMENT AROUND HIM.
IT'S HARD TO BELIEVE, BUT IT IS AN INDISPUTABLE FACT.
SO...
...FIRST...
...I MUST DESTROY HIS...

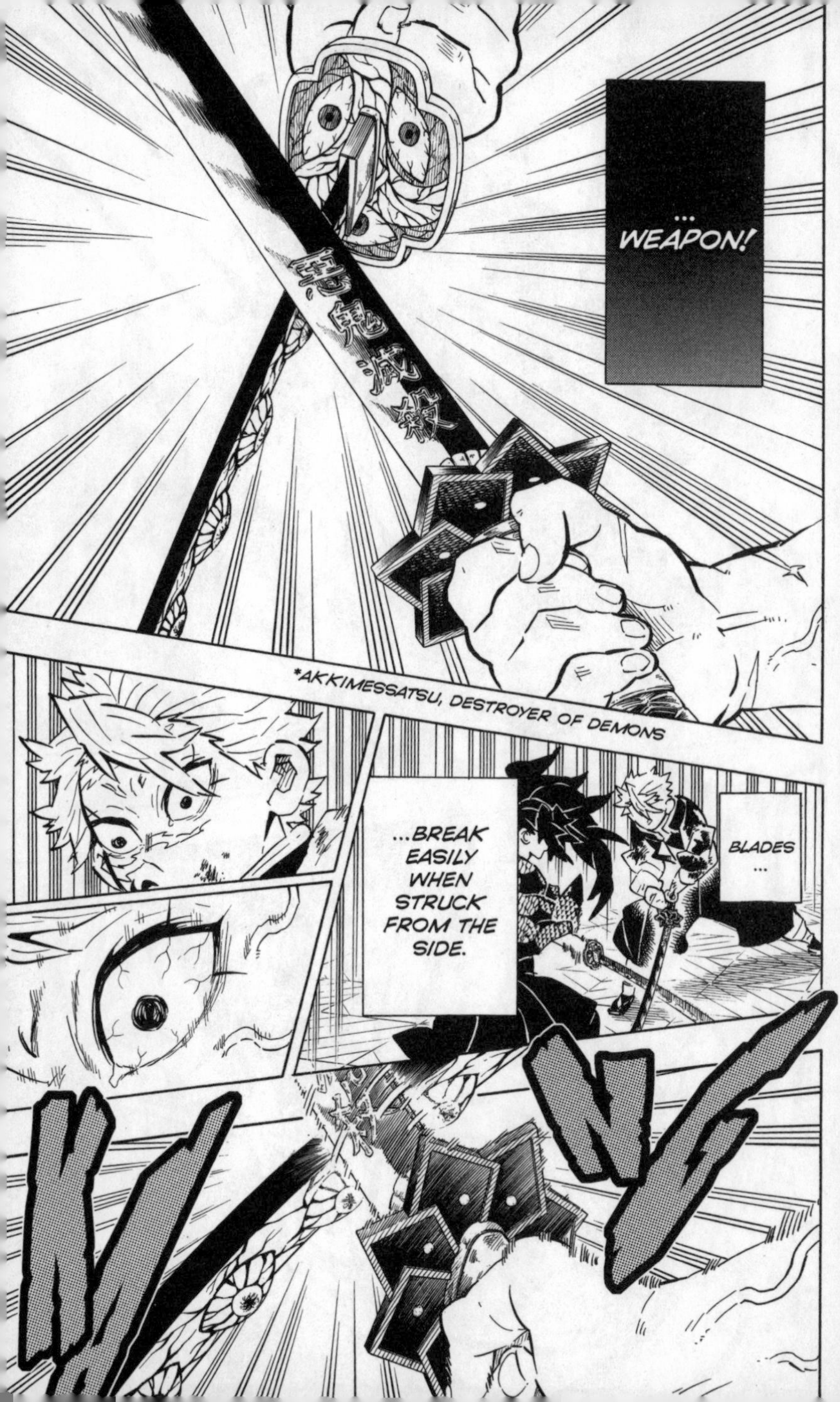
...WEAPON!
悪鬼滅殺
*AKKIMESSATSU, DESTROYER OF DEMONS
BLADES ...
...BREAK EASILY WHEN STRUCK FROM THE SIDE.

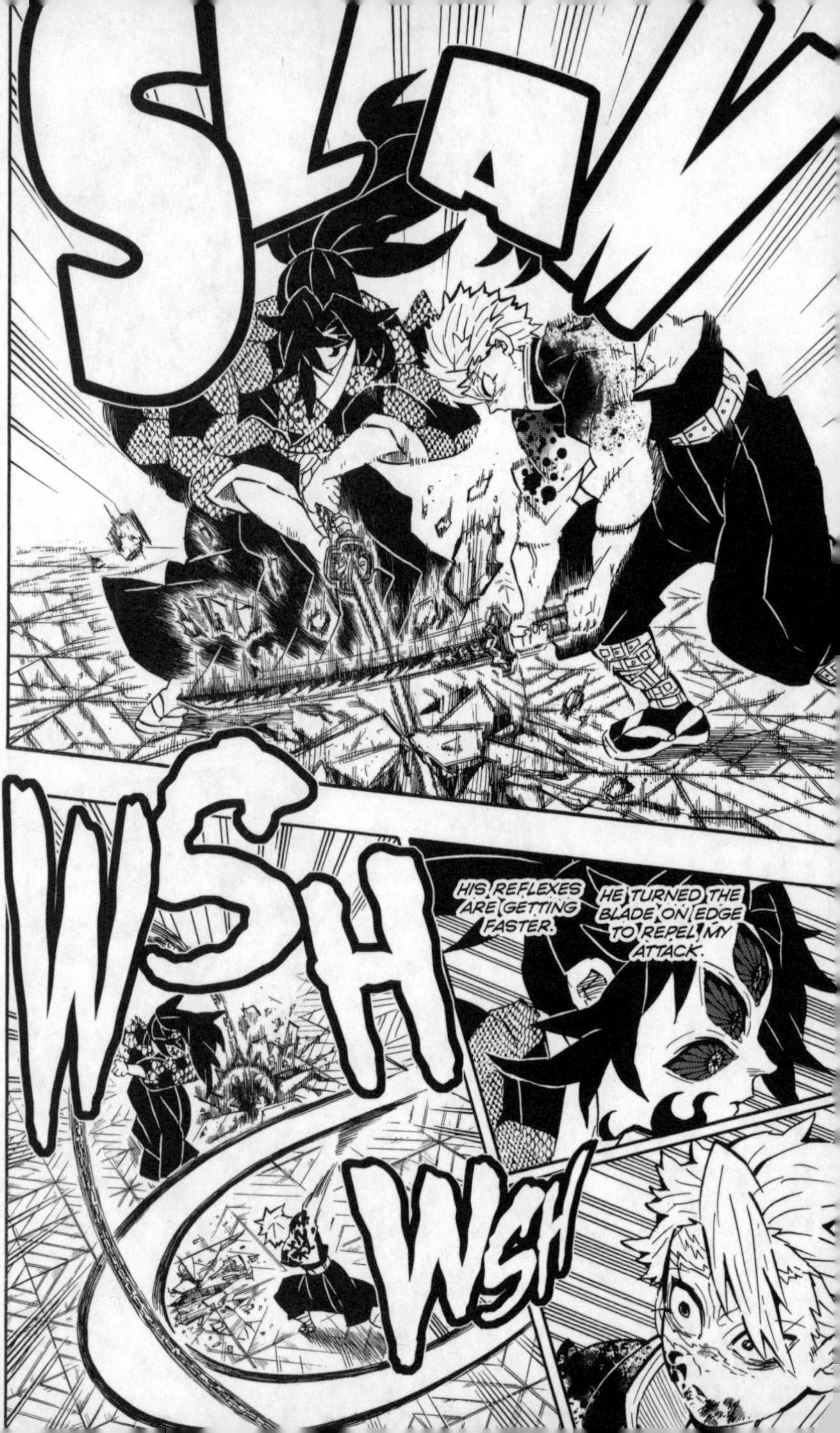
SLAM
HE TURNED THE BLADE ON EDGE TO REPEL MY ATTACK.
HIS REFLEXES ARE GETTING FASTER.
WSH
WSH

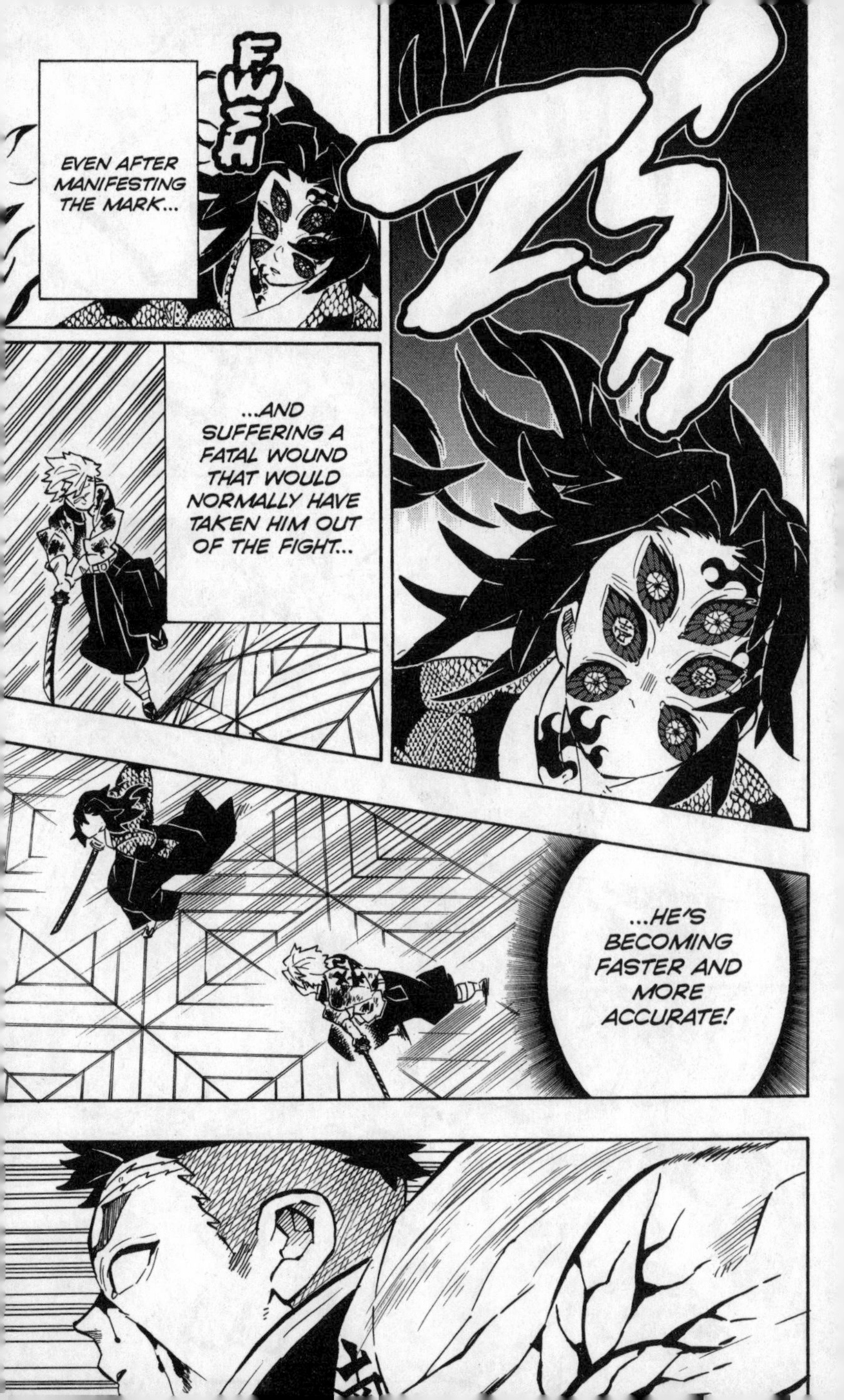
FWSH
EVEN AFTER MANIFESTING THE MARK...
...AND SUFFERING A FATAL WOUND THAT WOULD NORMALLY HAVE TAKEN HIM OUT OF THE FIGHT...
...HE'S BECOMING FASTER AND MORE ACCURATE!

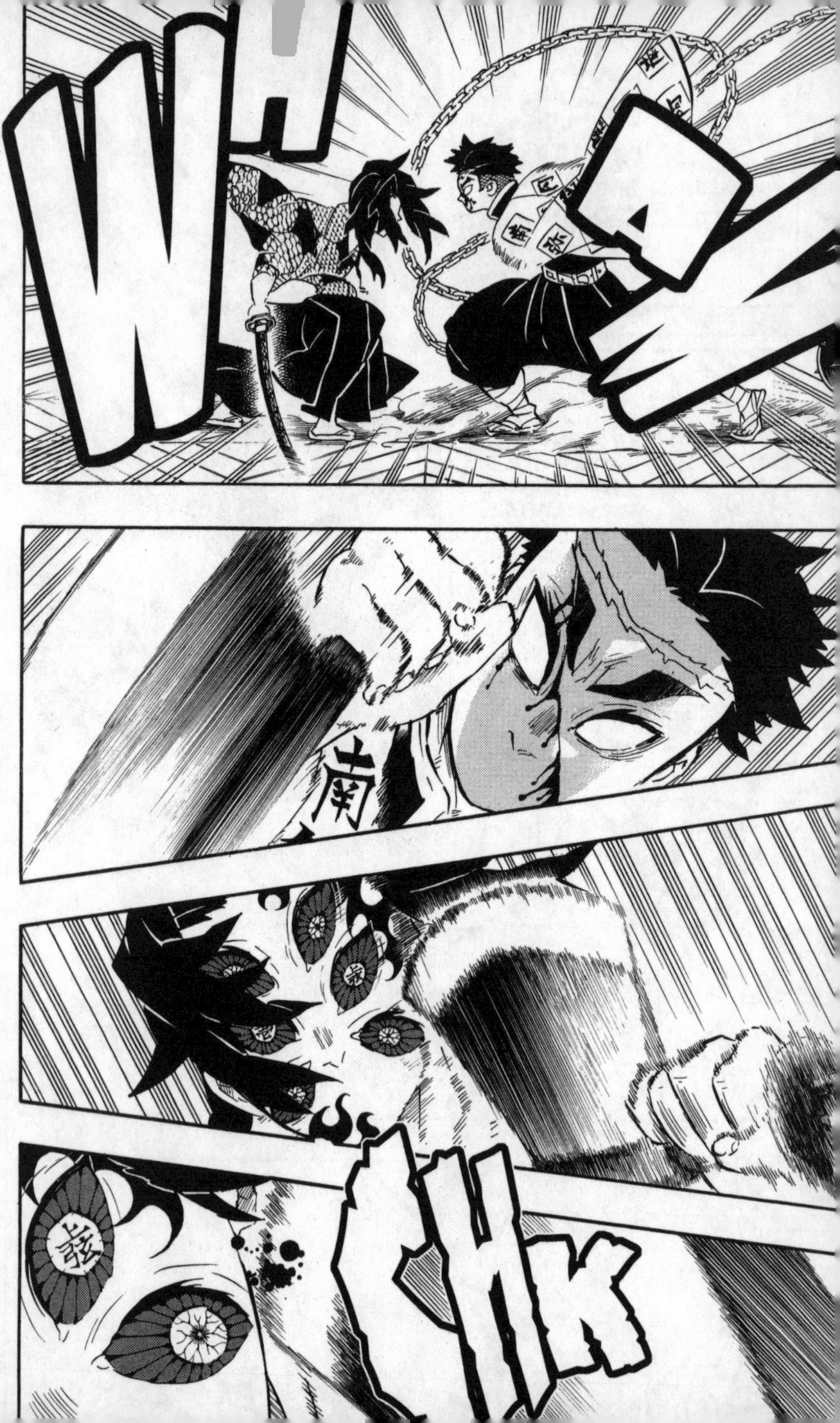
WHAM
CHK

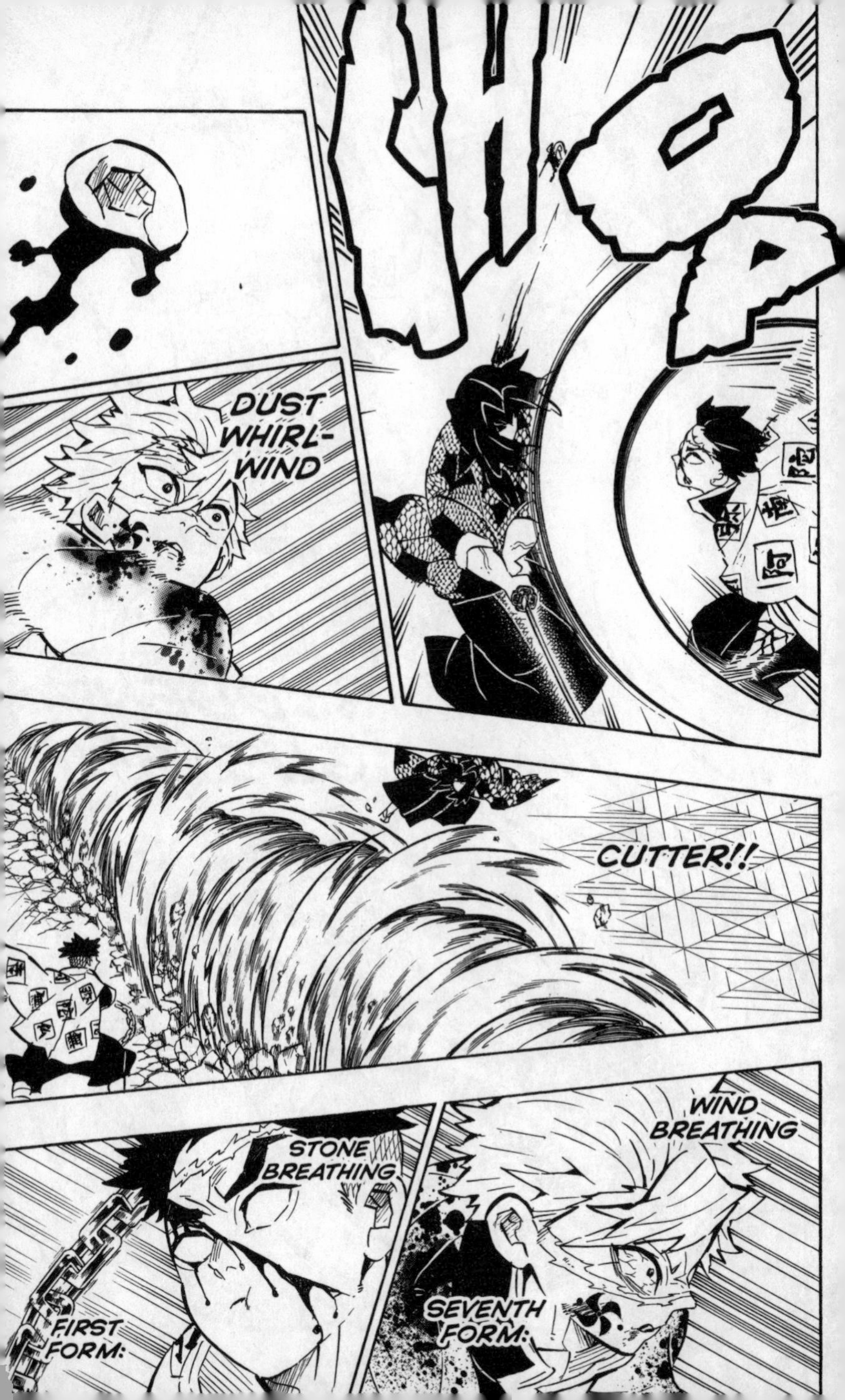
CHOP
DUST WHIRL-WIND
CUTTER!!
WIND BREATHING
SEVENTH FORM:
STONE BREATHING
FIRST FORM:

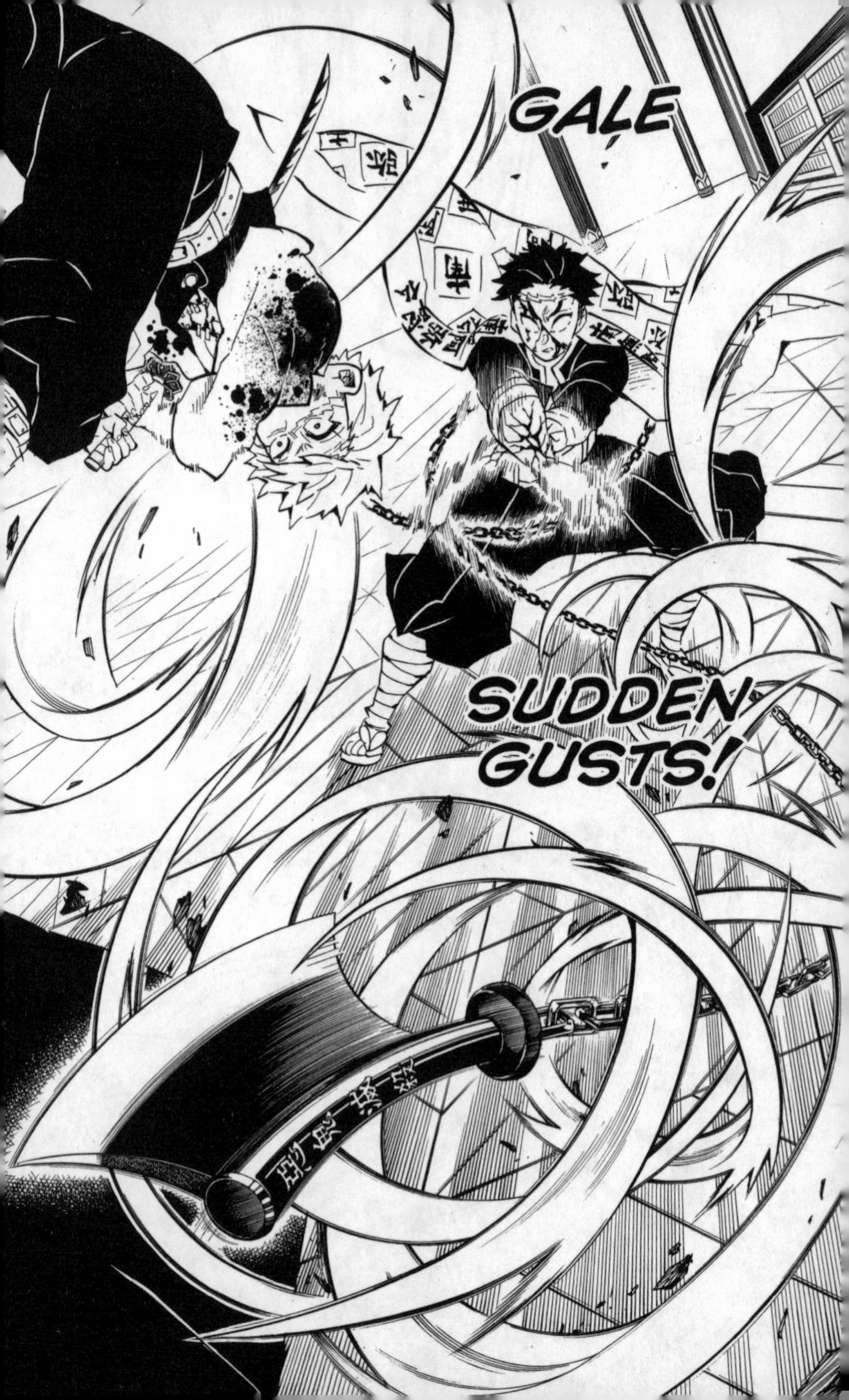
GALE
SUDDEN GUSTS!

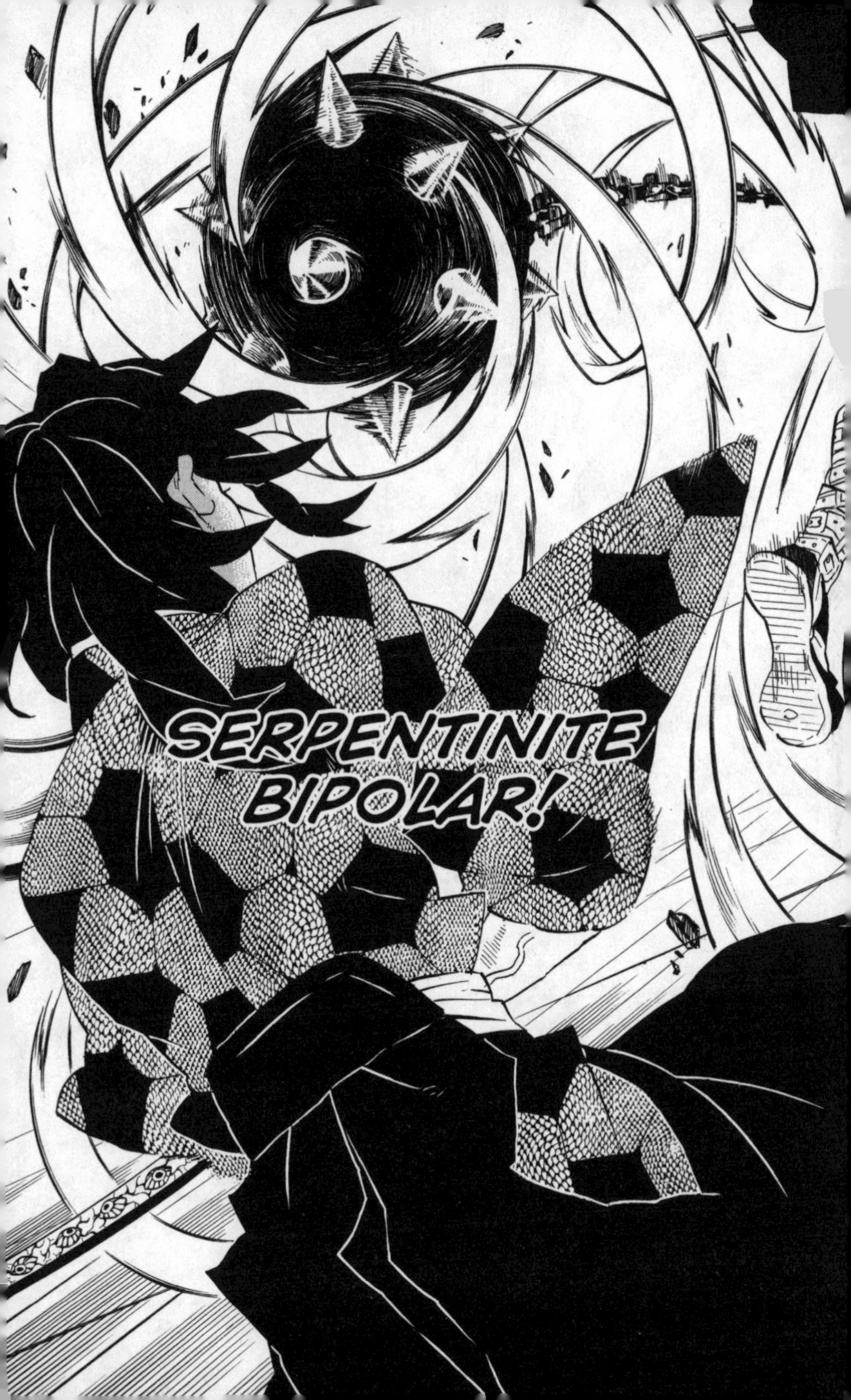
SERPENTINITE BIPOLAR!

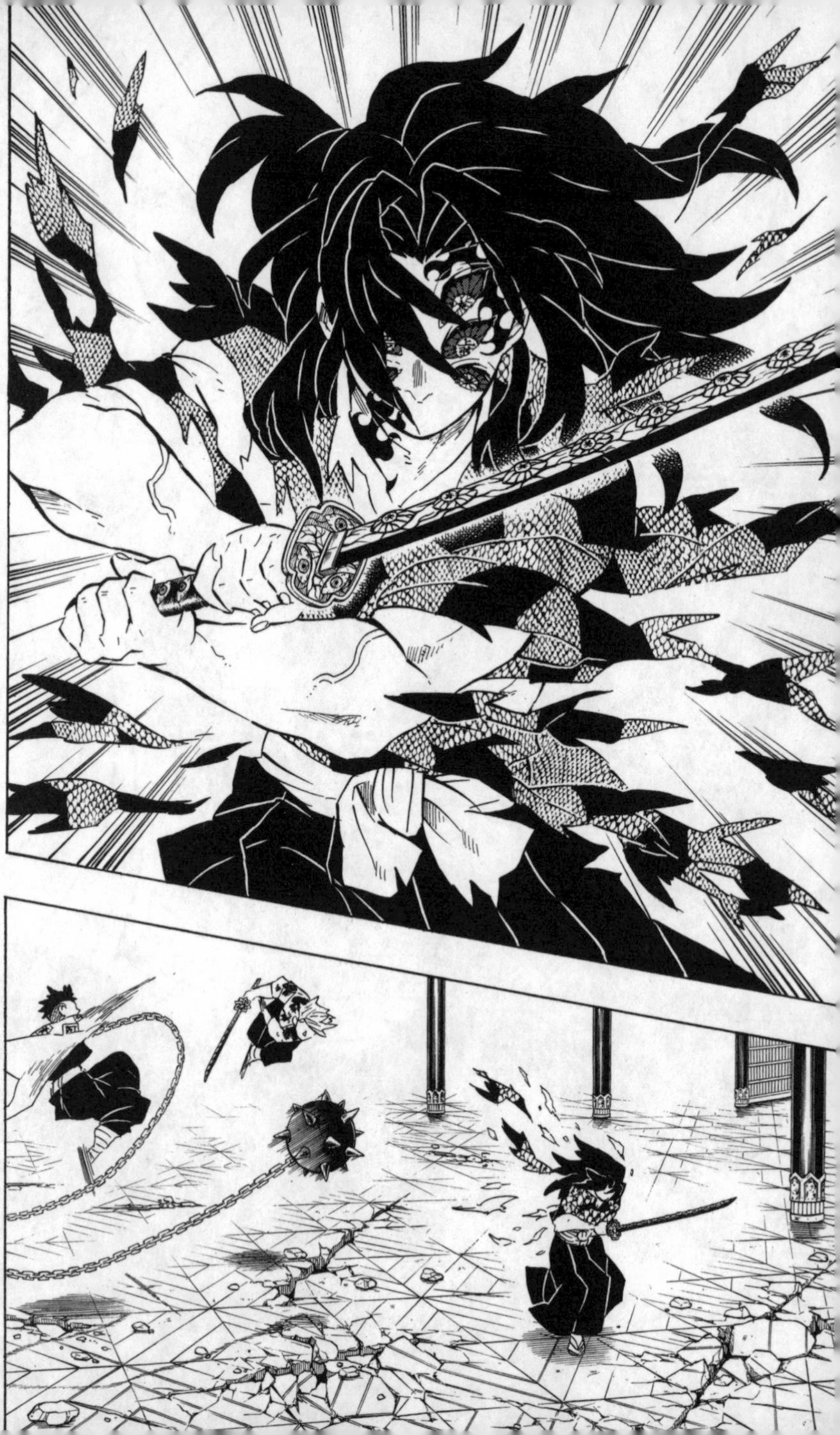

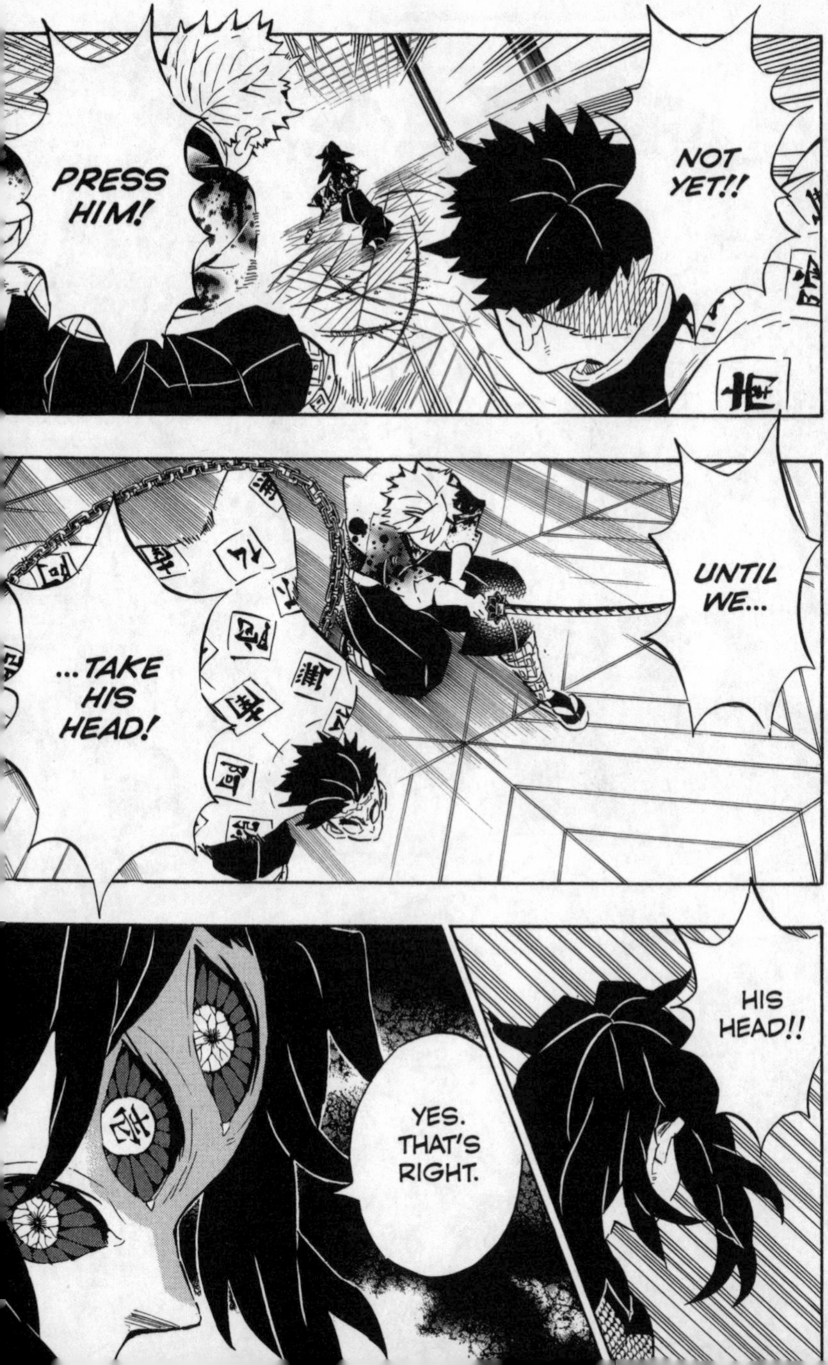
NOT YET!!
PRESS HIM!
UNTIL WE...
...TAKE HIS HEAD!
HIS HEAD!!
YES. THAT'S RIGHT.

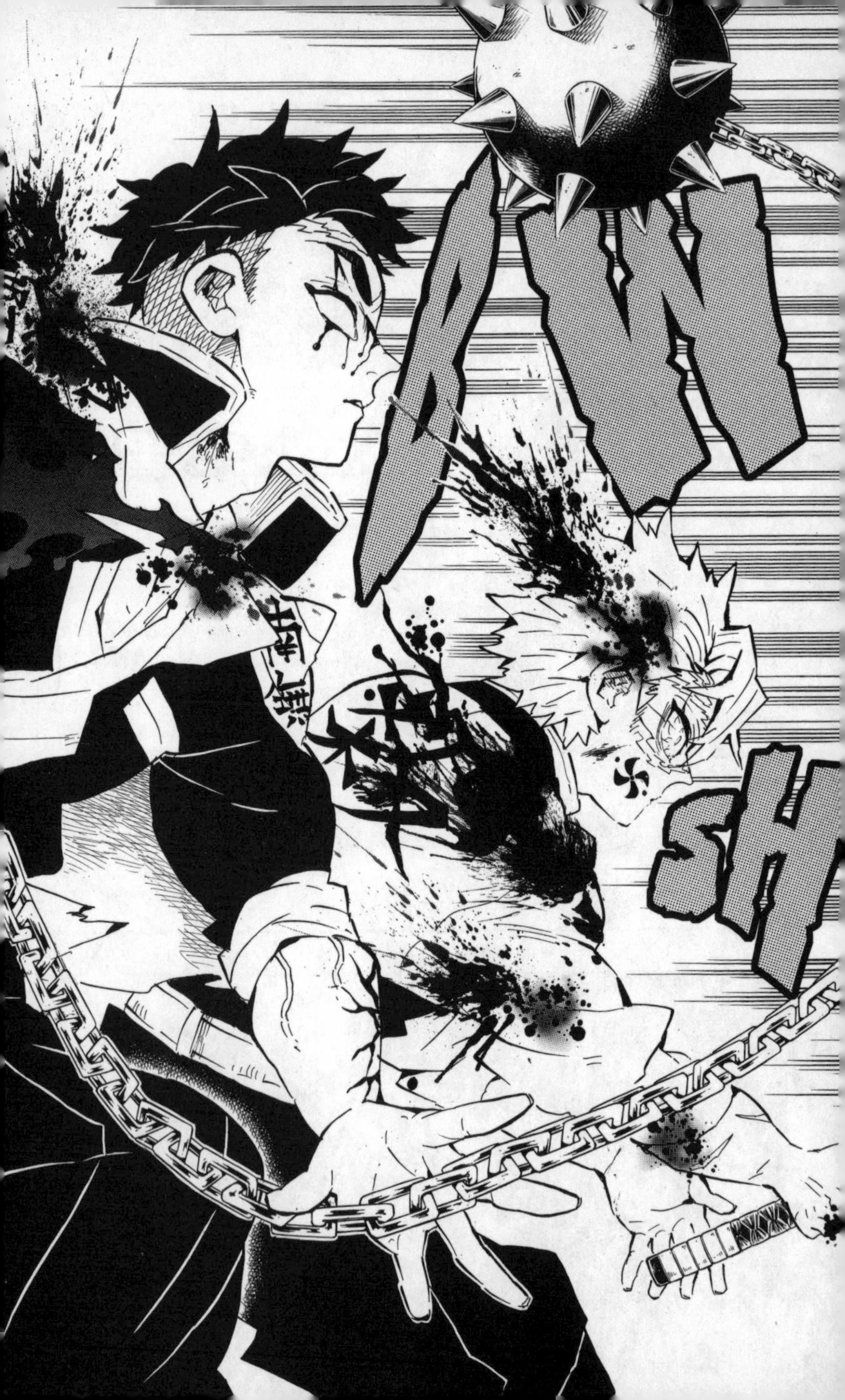
SH

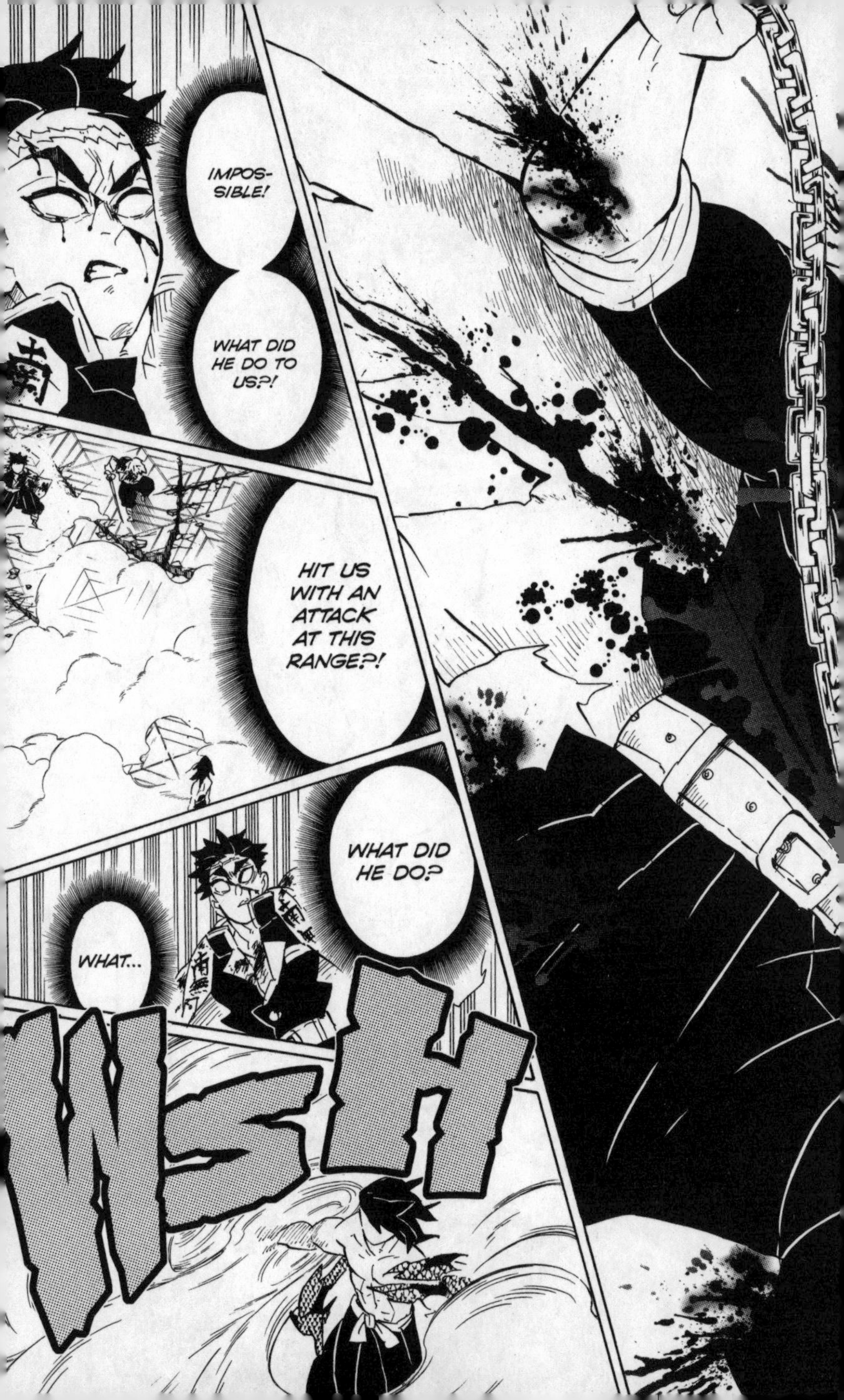
IMPOSSIBLE!
WHAT DID HE DO TO US?!
HIT US WITH AN ATTACK AT THIS RANGE?!
WHAT DID HE DO?
WHAT...
WSH

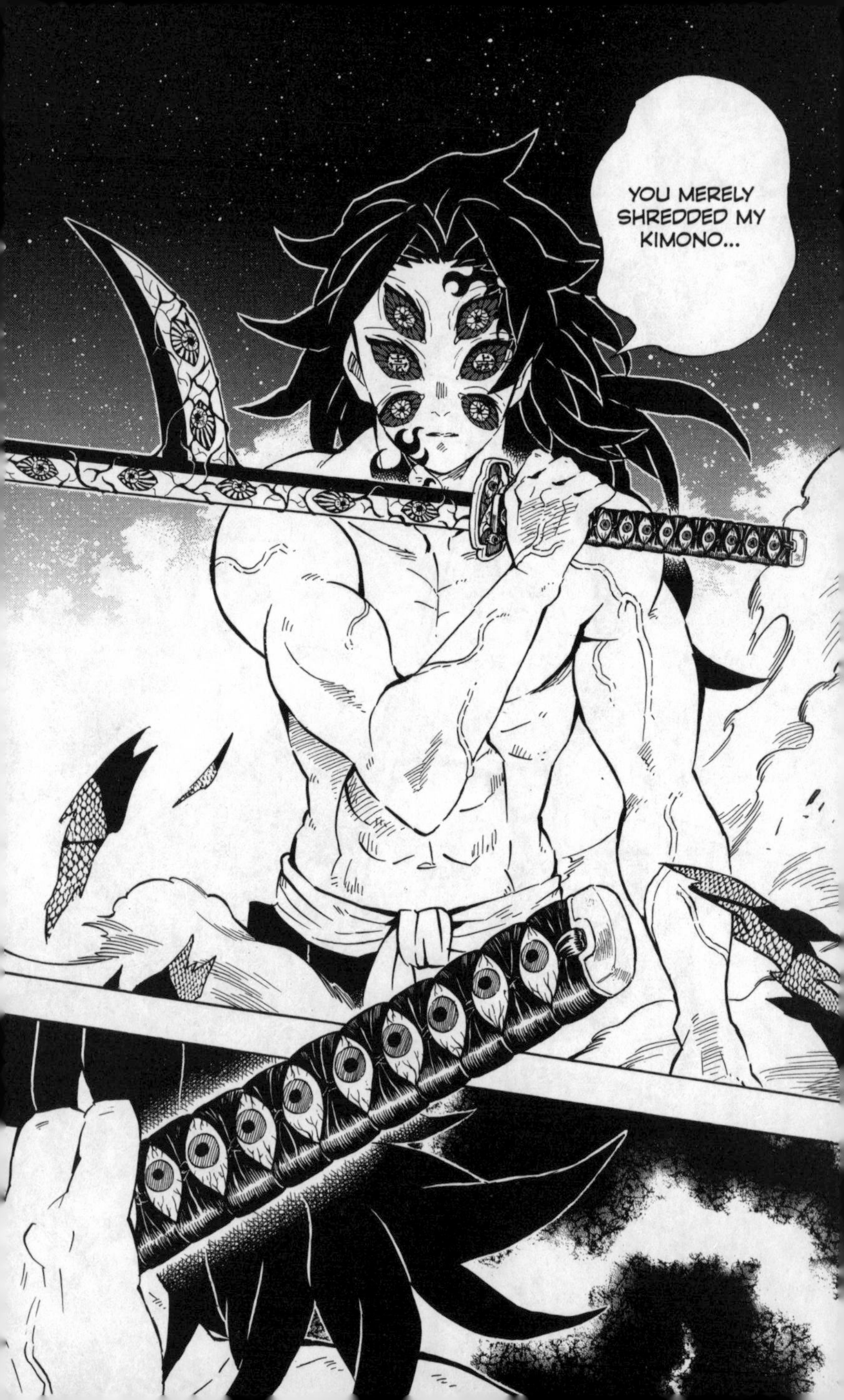
YOU MERELY SHREDDED MY KIMONO...

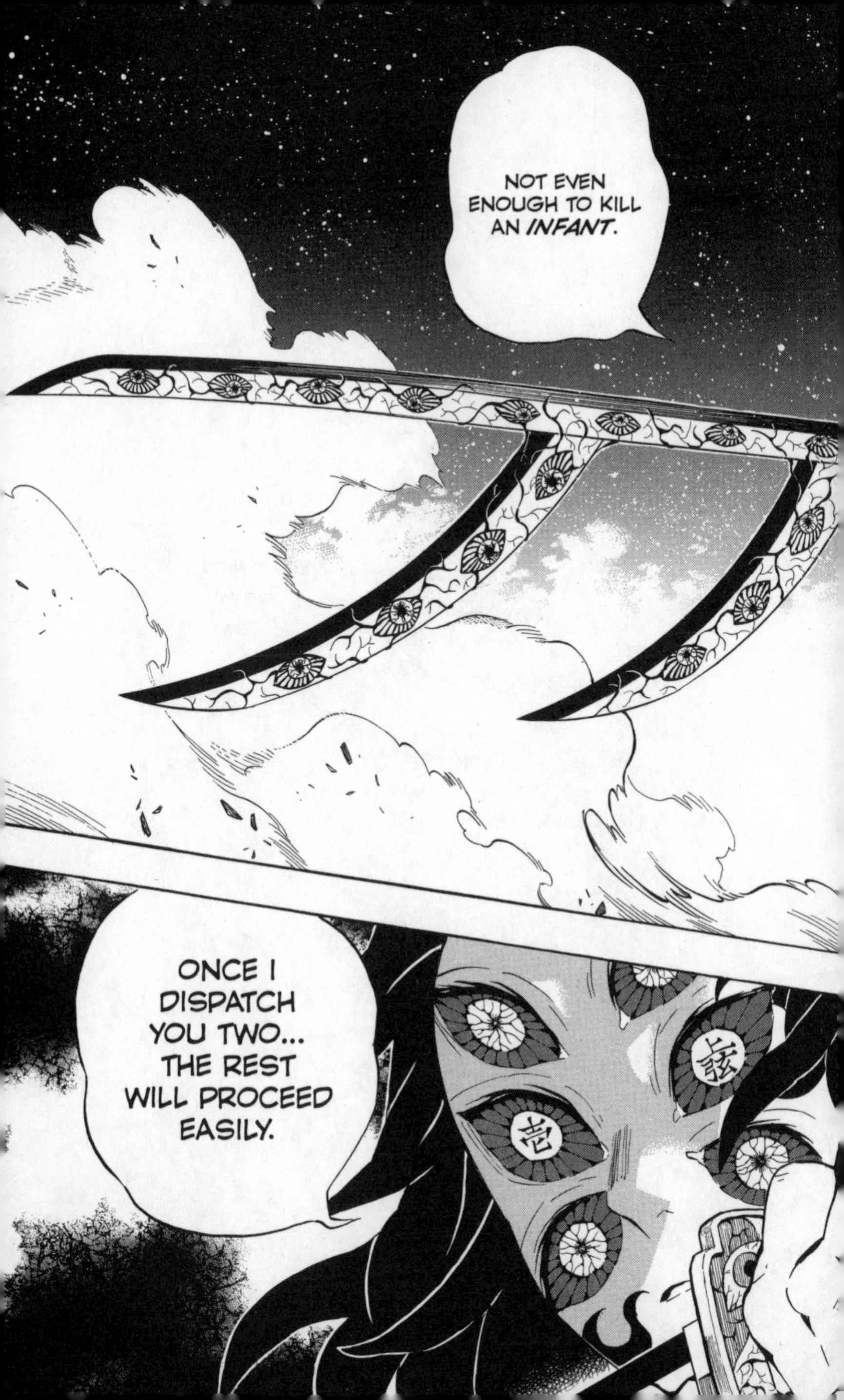
NOT EVEN ENOUGH TO KILL AN *INFANT*.
ONCE I DISPATCH YOU TWO... THE REST WILL PROCEED EASILY.

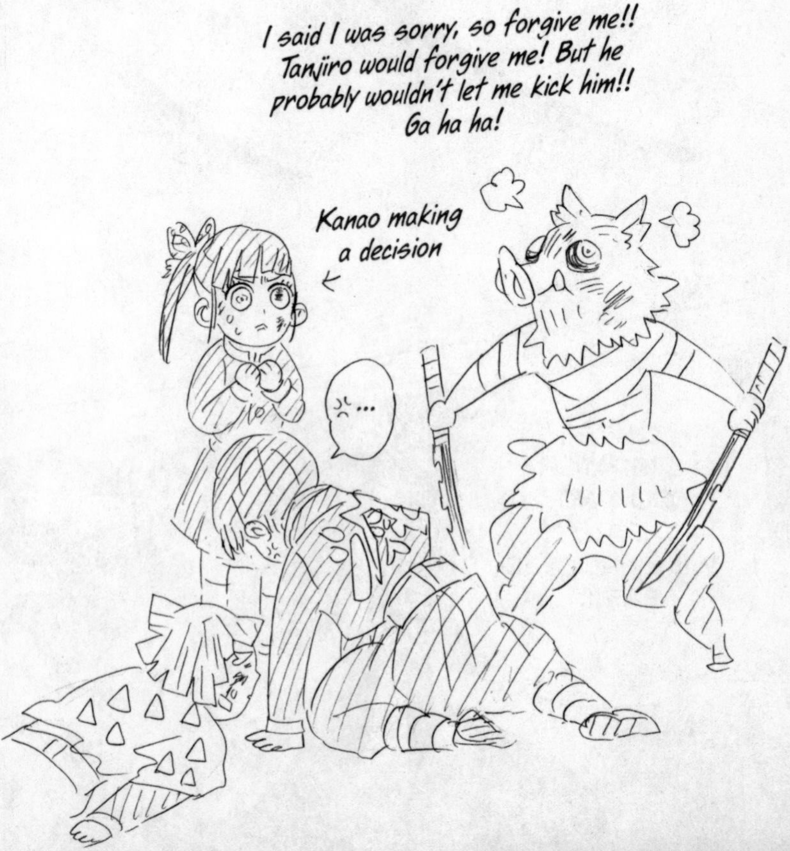
I said I was sorry, so forgive me!! Tanjiro would forgive me! But he probably wouldn't let me kick him!! Ga ha ha!
Kanao making a decision
...

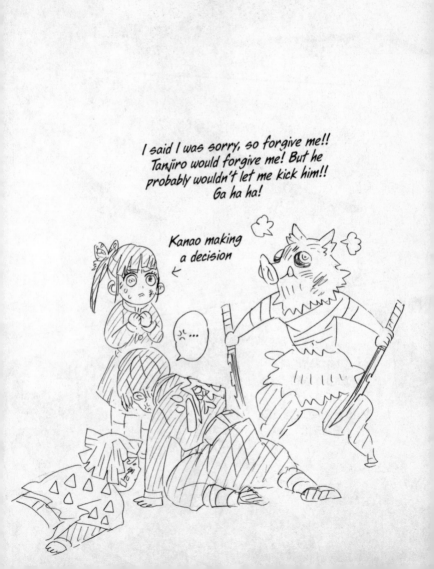

CHAPTER 172: A WEAKLING'S POTENTIAL

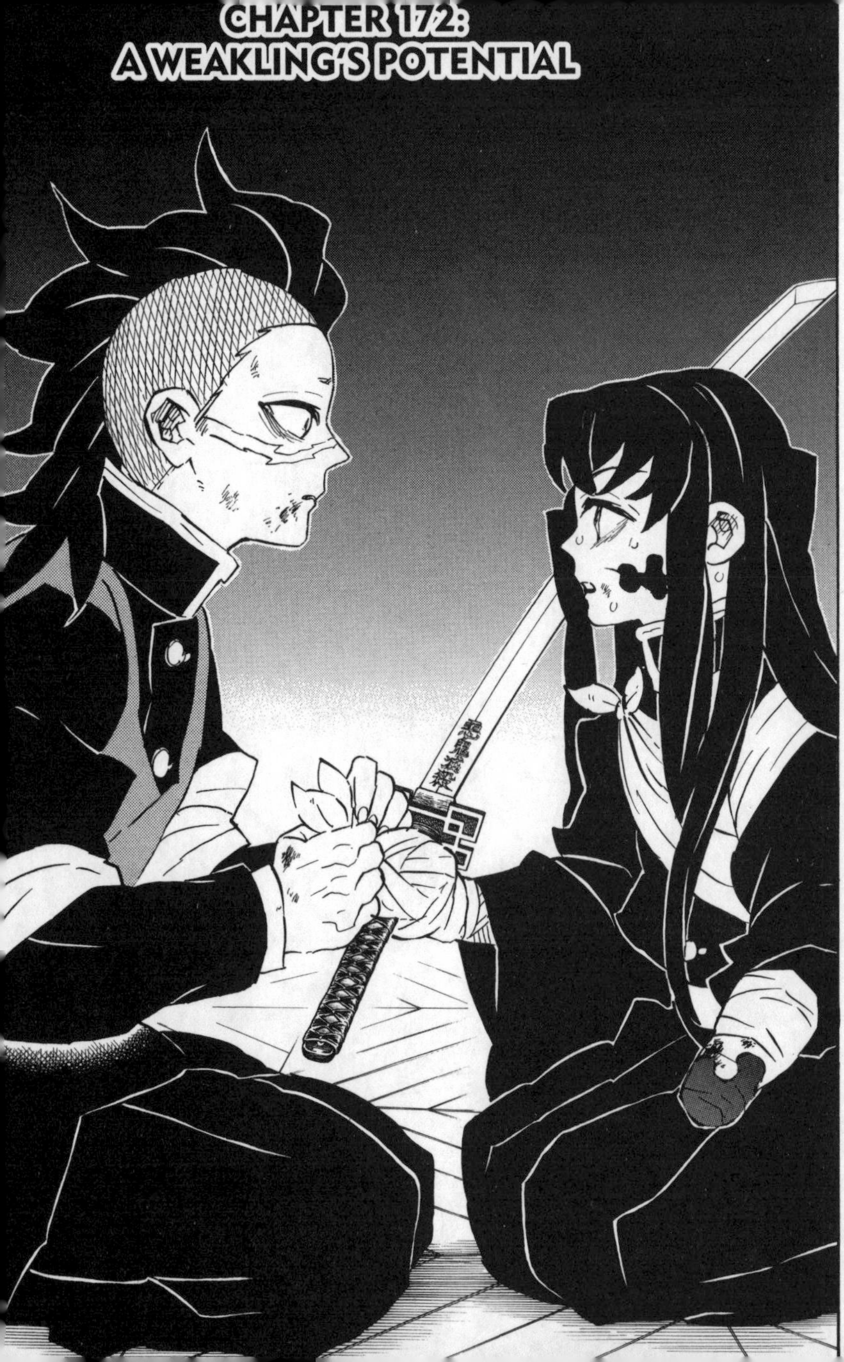

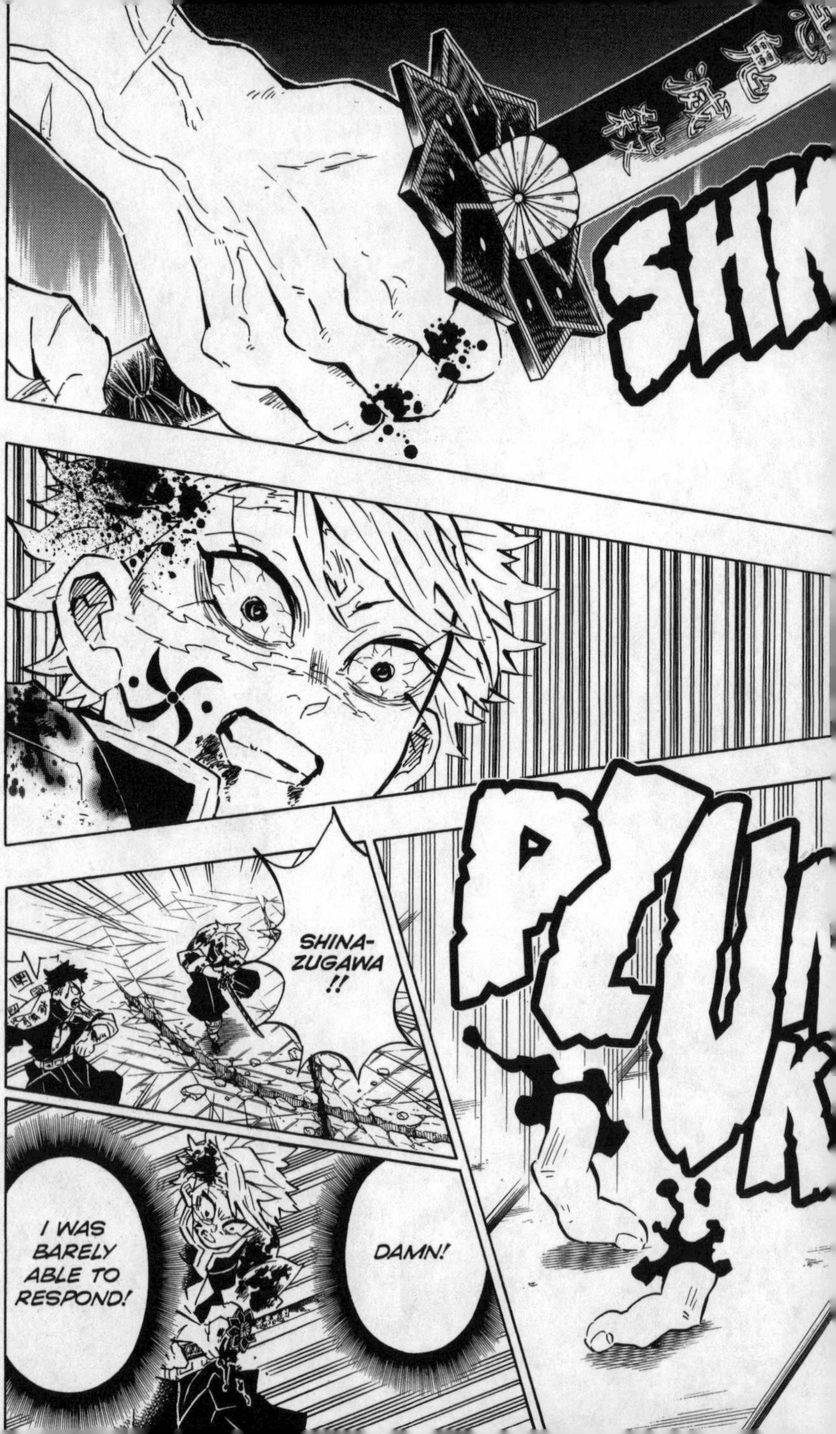
SHINA-
ZUGAWA
!!
DAMN!
I WAS BARELY ABLE TO RESPOND!

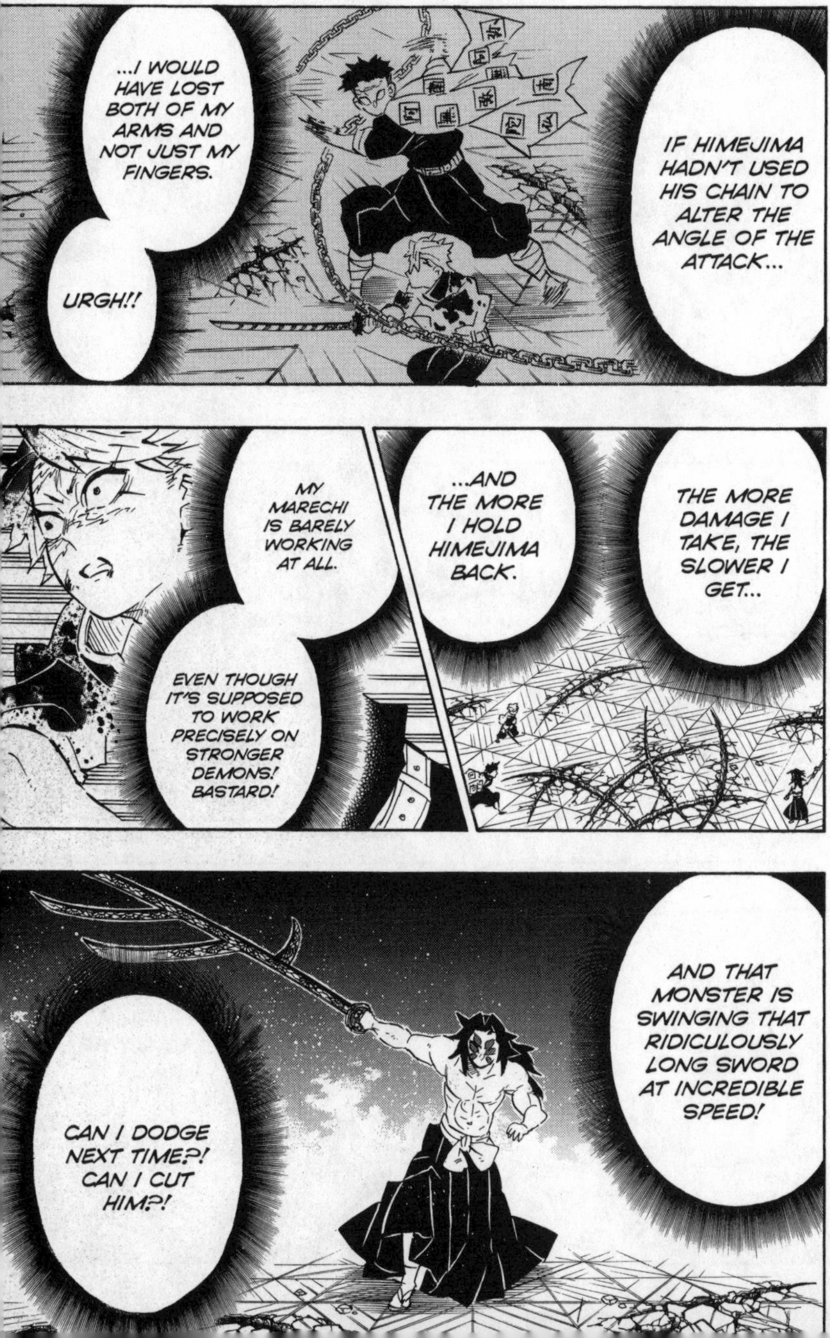
IF HIMEJIMA HADN'T USED HIS CHAIN TO ALTER THE ANGLE OF THE ATTACK...
...I WOULD HAVE LOST BOTH OF MY ARMS AND NOT JUST MY FINGERS.
URGH!!
THE MORE DAMAGE I TAKE, THE SLOWER I GET...
...AND THE MORE I HOLD HIMEJIMA BACK.
MY MARECHI IS BARELY WORKING AT ALL.
EVEN THOUGH IT'S SUPPOSED TO WORK PRECISELY ON STRONGER DEMONS! BASTARD!
AND THAT MONSTER IS SWINGING THAT RIDICULOUSLY LONG SWORD AT INCREDIBLE SPEED!
CAN I DODGE NEXT TIME?! CAN I CUT HIM?!

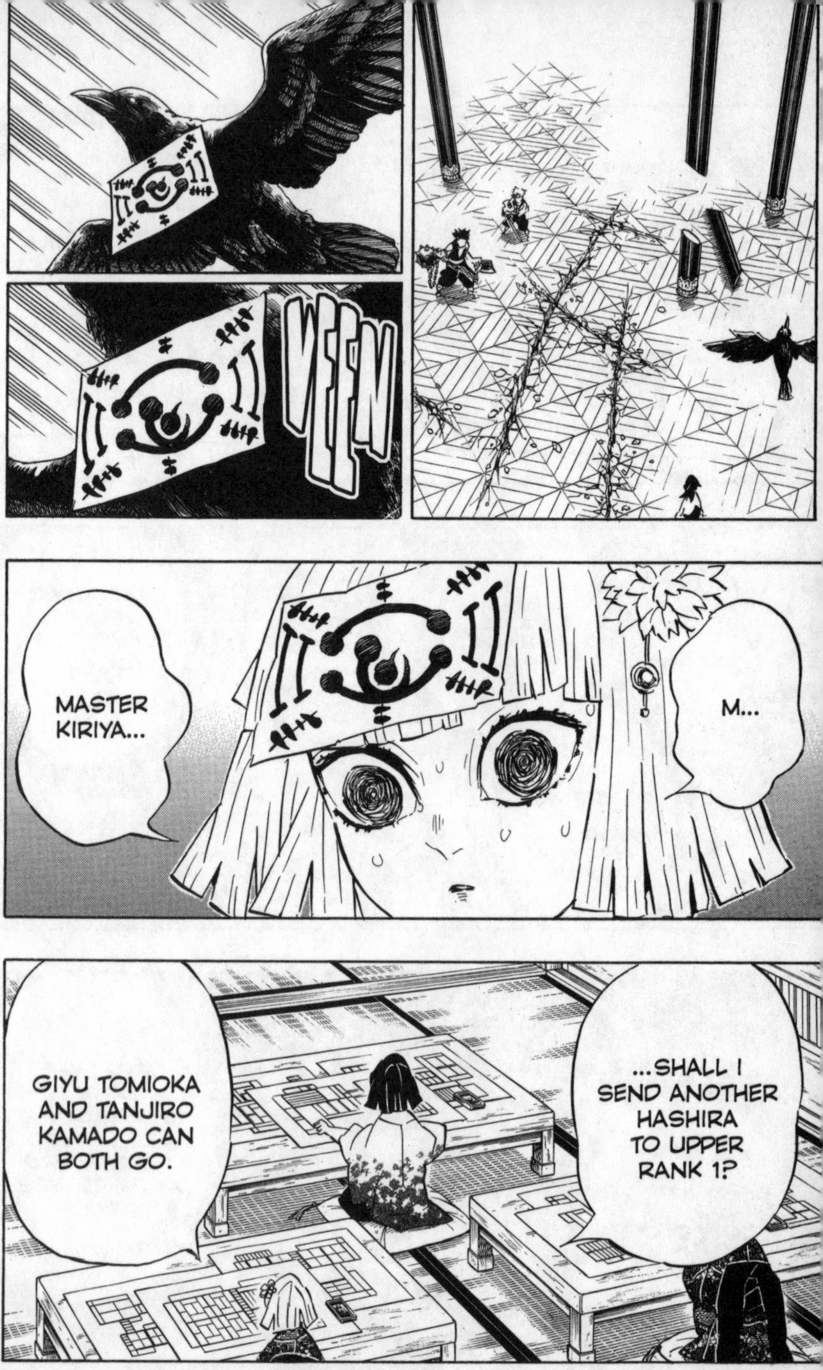
VEEN
M...
MASTER KIRIYA...
...SHALL I SEND ANOTHER HASHIRA TO UPPER RANK 1?
GIYU TOMIOKA AND TANJIRO KAMADO CAN BOTH GO.

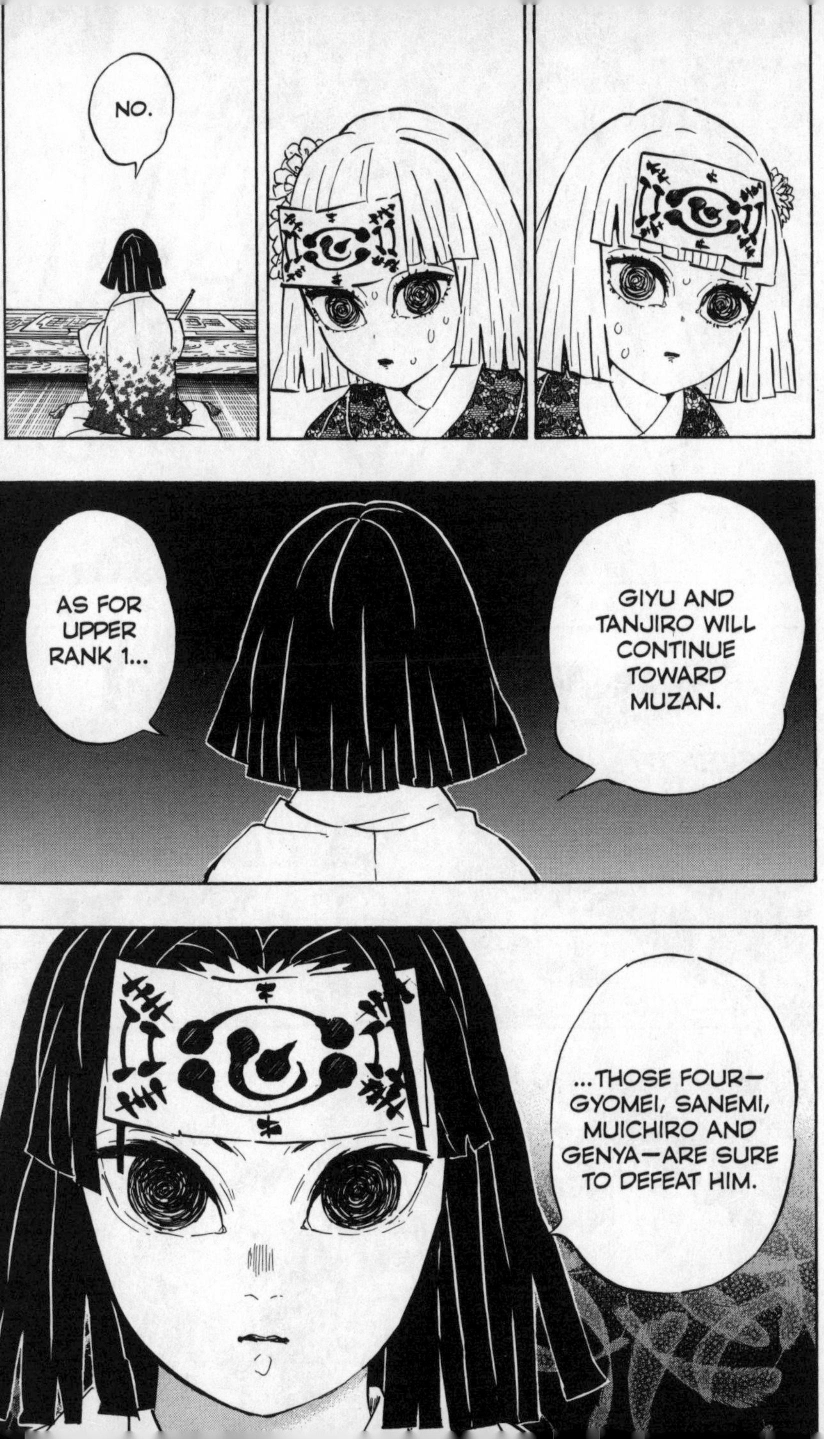
NO.
GIYU AND TANJIRO WILL CONTINUE TOWARD MUZAN.
AS FOR UPPER RANK 1...
...THOSE FOUR—GYOMEI, SANEMI, MUICHIRO AND GENYA—ARE SURE TO DEFEAT HIM.

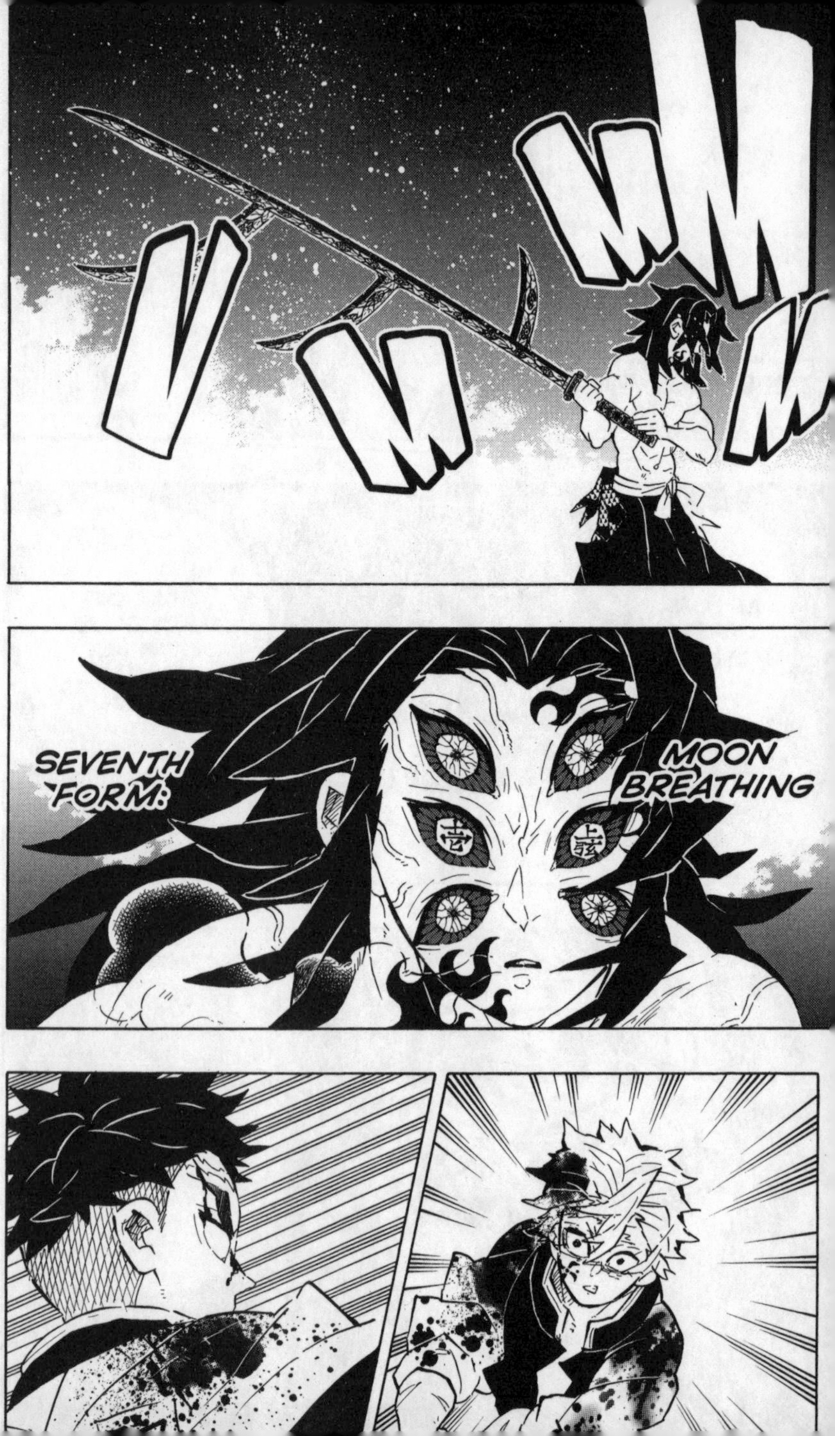
VMMMM
MOON BREATHING
SEVENTH FORM:

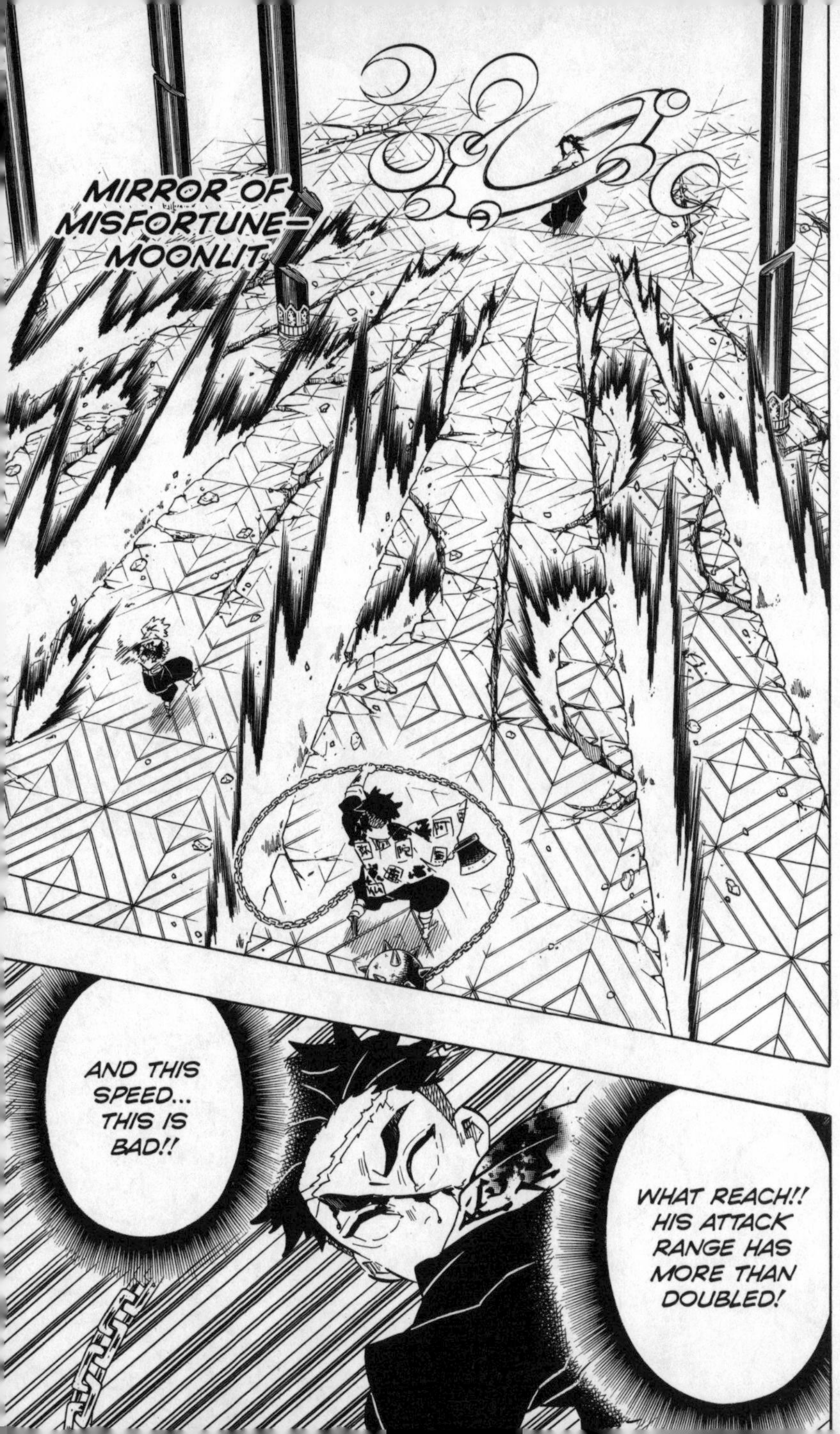
MIRROR OF MISFORTUNE— MOONLIT
WHAT REACH!! HIS ATTACK RANGE HAS MORE THAN DOUBLED!
AND THIS SPEED... THIS IS BAD!!

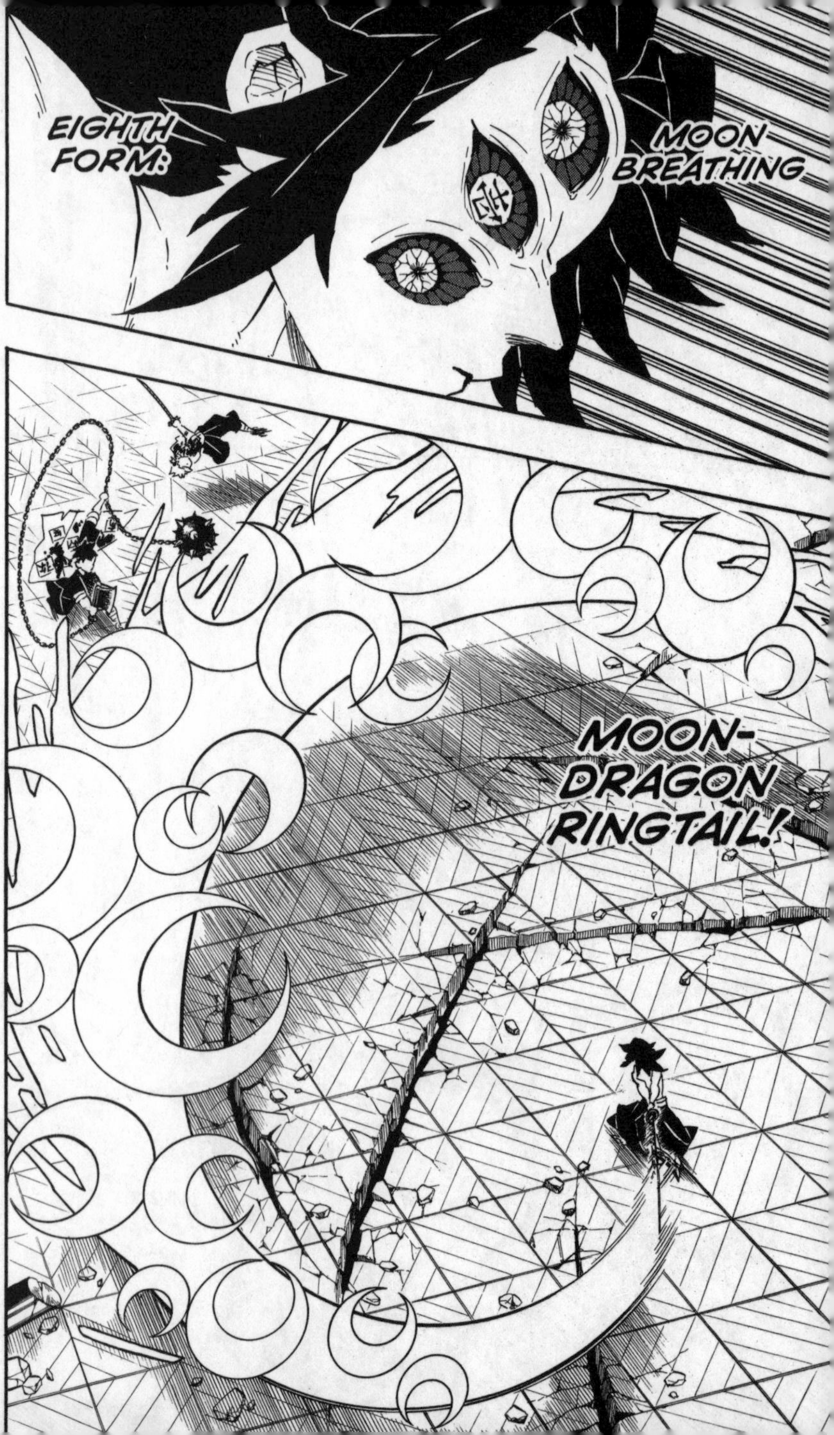
MOON BREATHING
EIGHTH FORM:
MOON-DRAGON RINGTAIL!

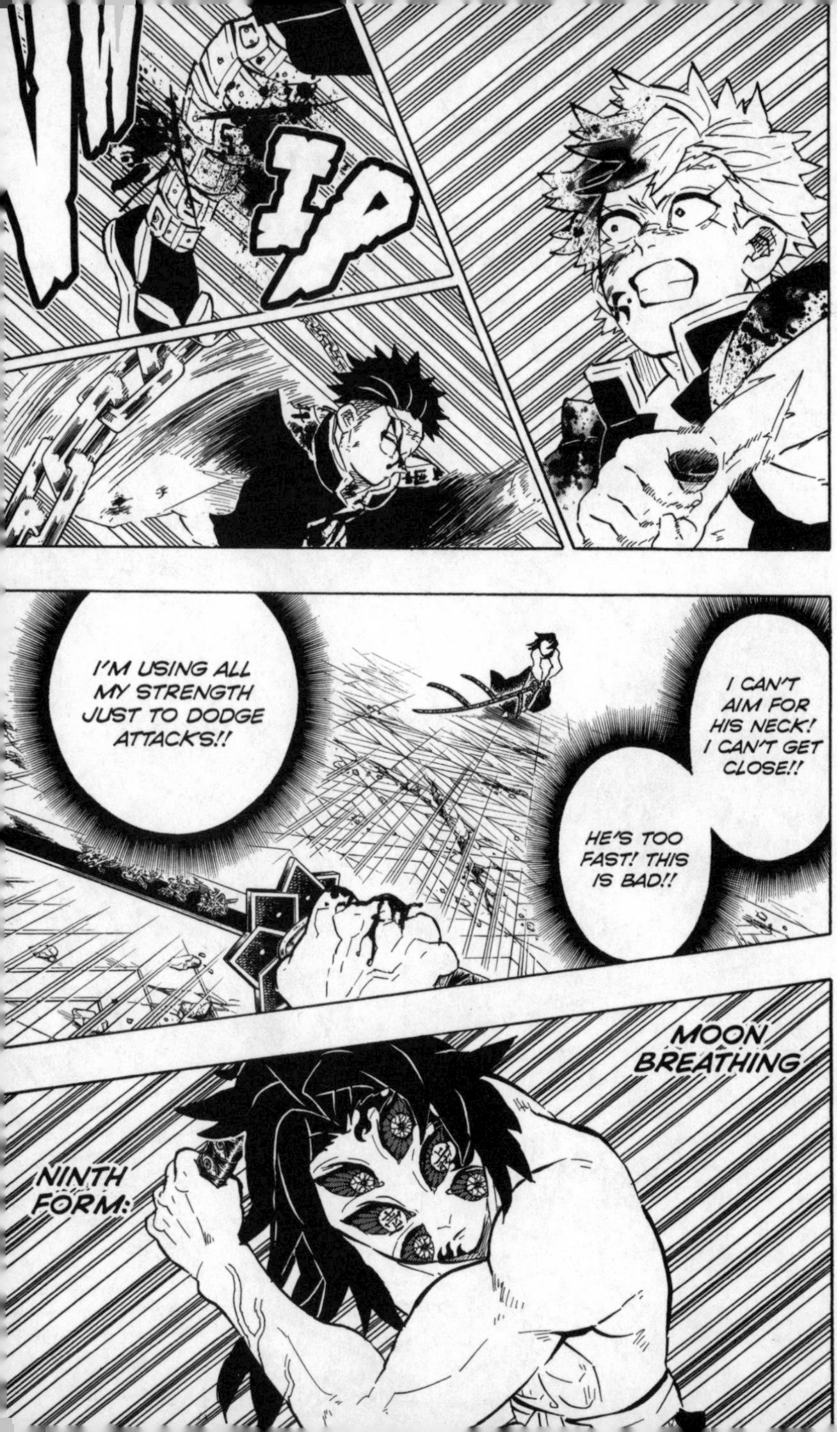
I CAN'T AIM FOR HIS NECK! I CAN'T GET CLOSE!!
HE'S TOO FAST! THIS IS BAD!!
I'M USING ALL MY STRENGTH JUST TO DODGE ATTACKS!!
MOON BREATHING
NINTH FORM:

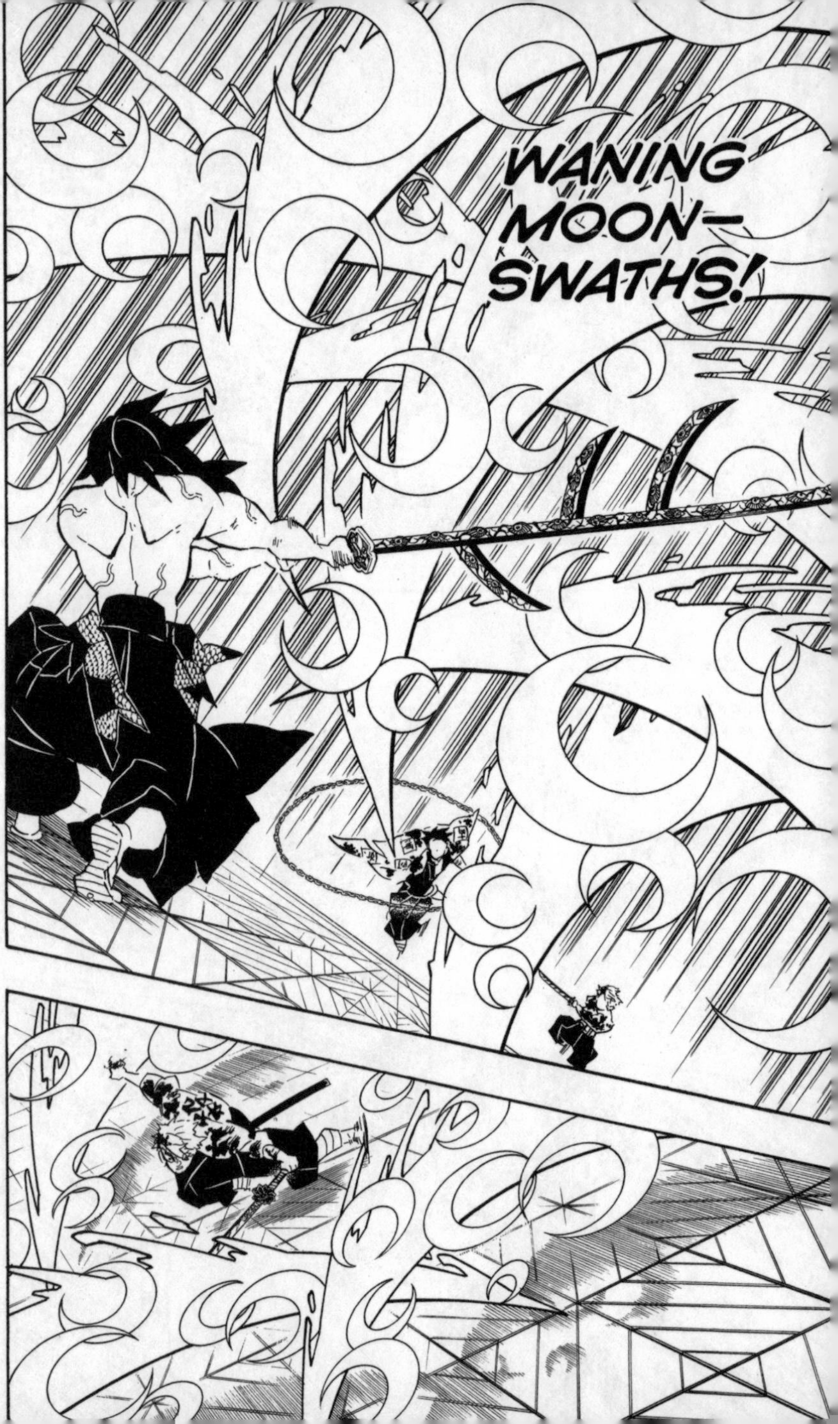
WANING MOON-SWATHS!

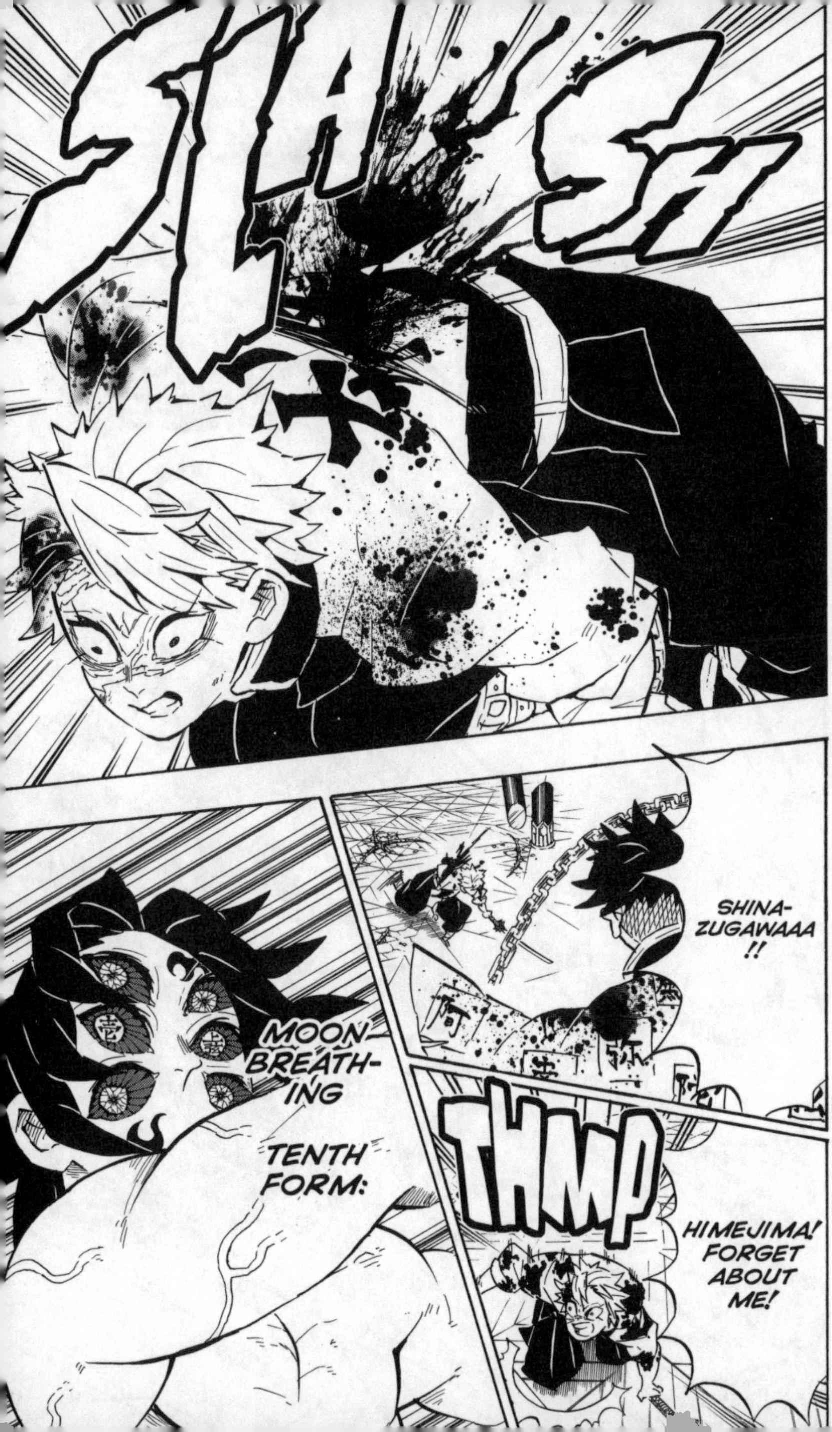
SLASH
SHINA-ZUGAWAAA !!
THMP
HIMEJIMA! FORGET ABOUT ME!
MOON-BREATH-ING
TENTH FORM:

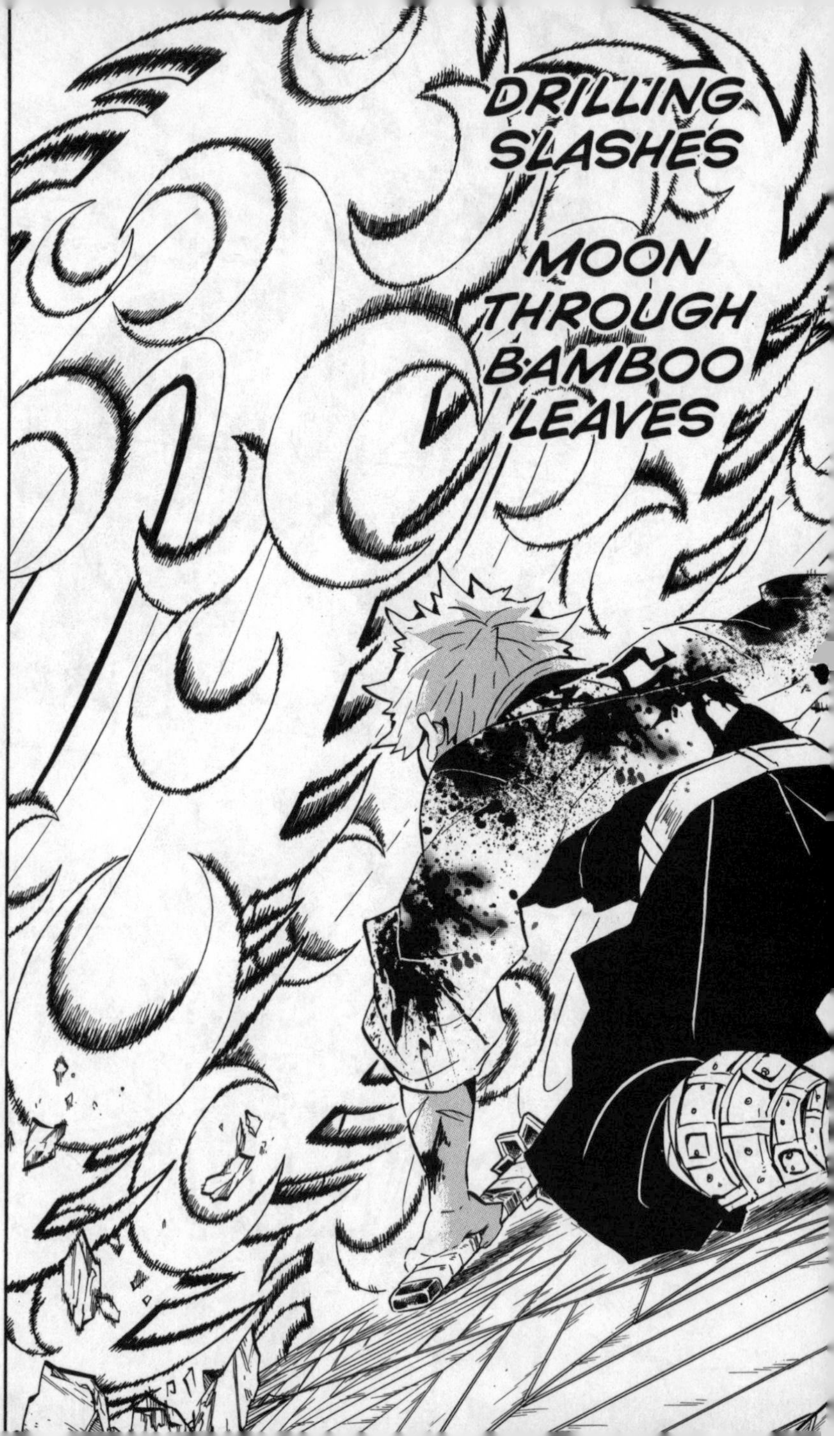
DRILLING SLASHES
MOON THROUGH BAMBOO LEAVES

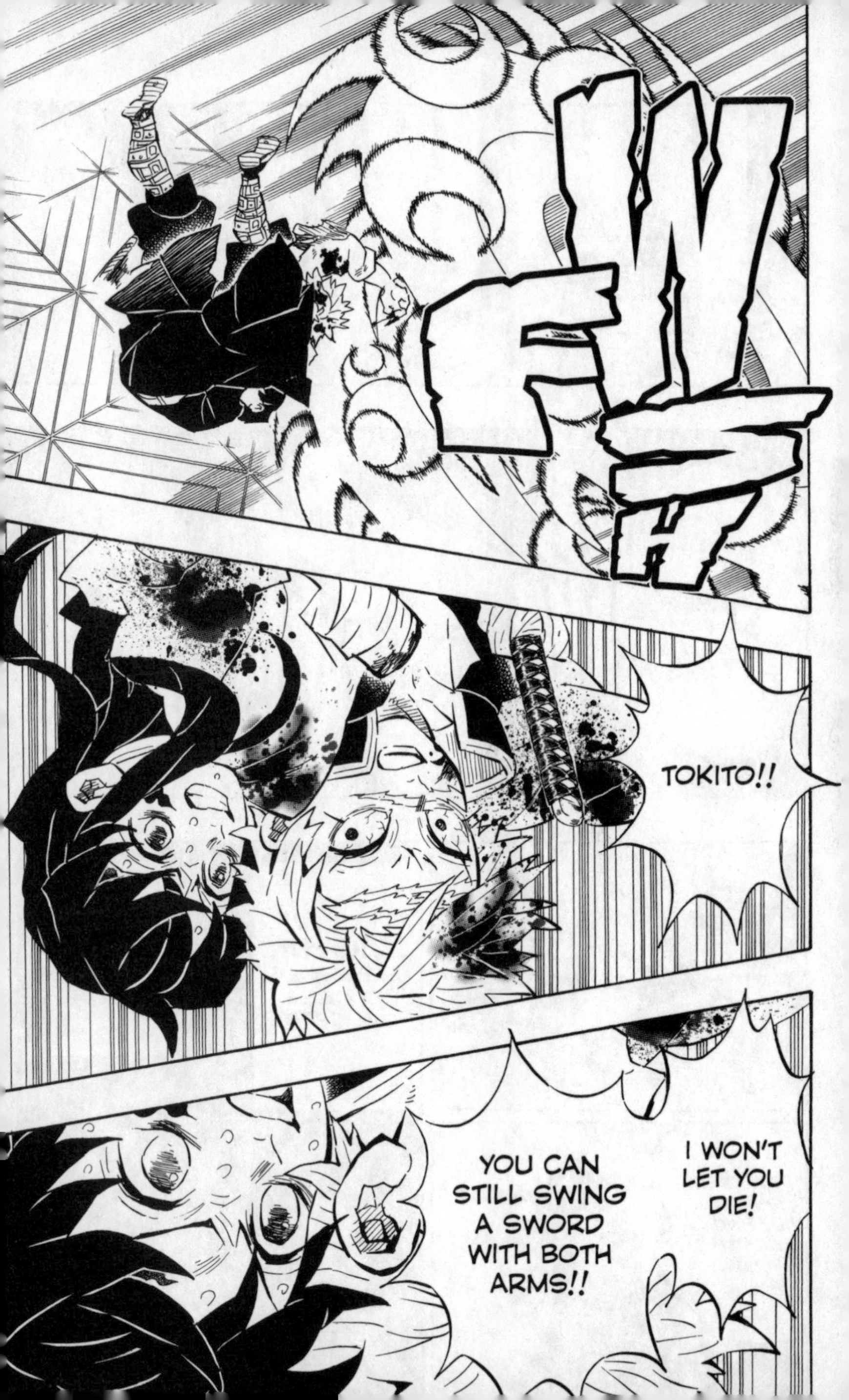
FWSH
TOKITO!!
I WON'T LET YOU DIE!
YOU CAN STILL SWING A SWORD WITH BOTH ARMS!!

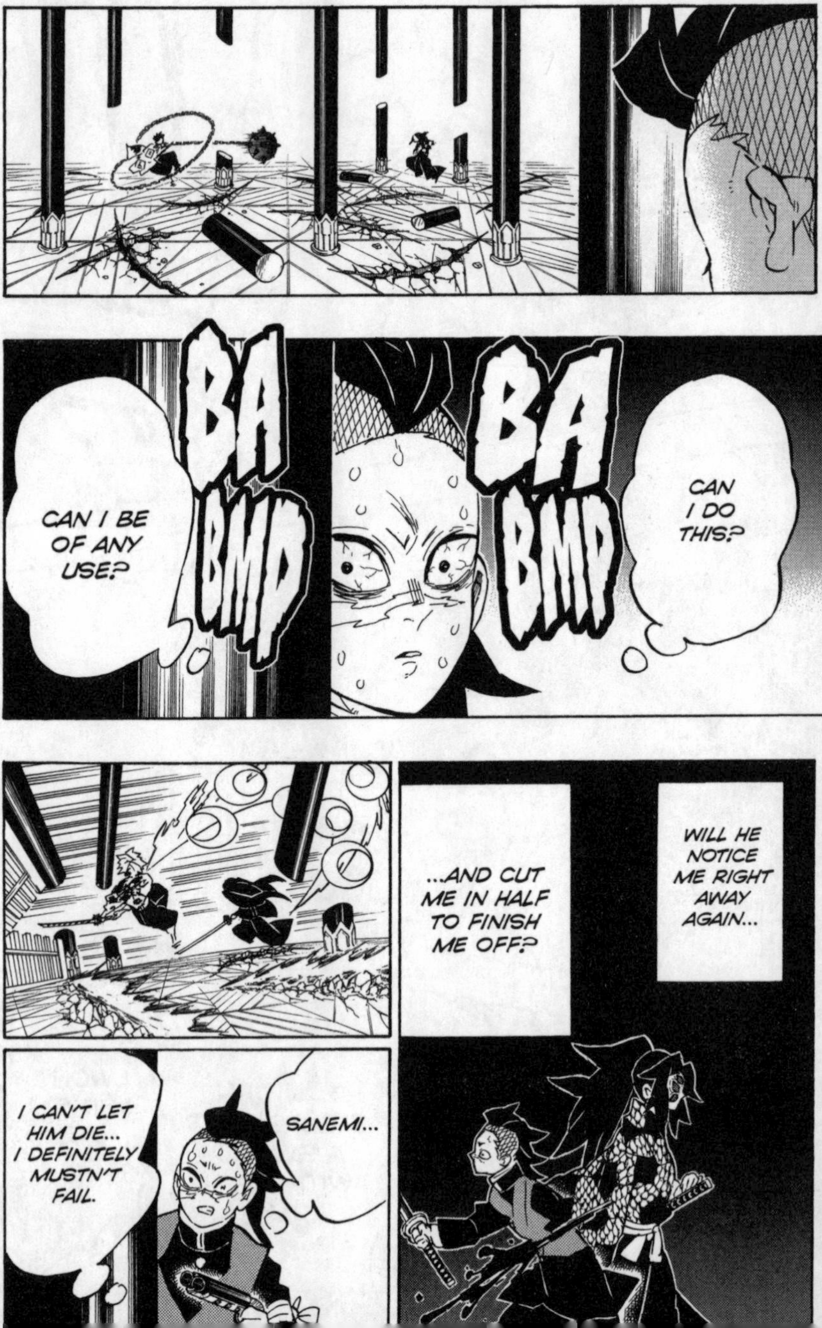
CAN I DO THIS?
BA BMP
BA BMP
CAN I BE OF ANY USE?
WILL HE NOTICE ME RIGHT AWAY AGAIN...
...AND CUT ME IN HALF TO FINISH ME OFF?
SANEMI...
I CAN'T LET HIM DIE... I DEFINITELY MUSTN'T FAIL.

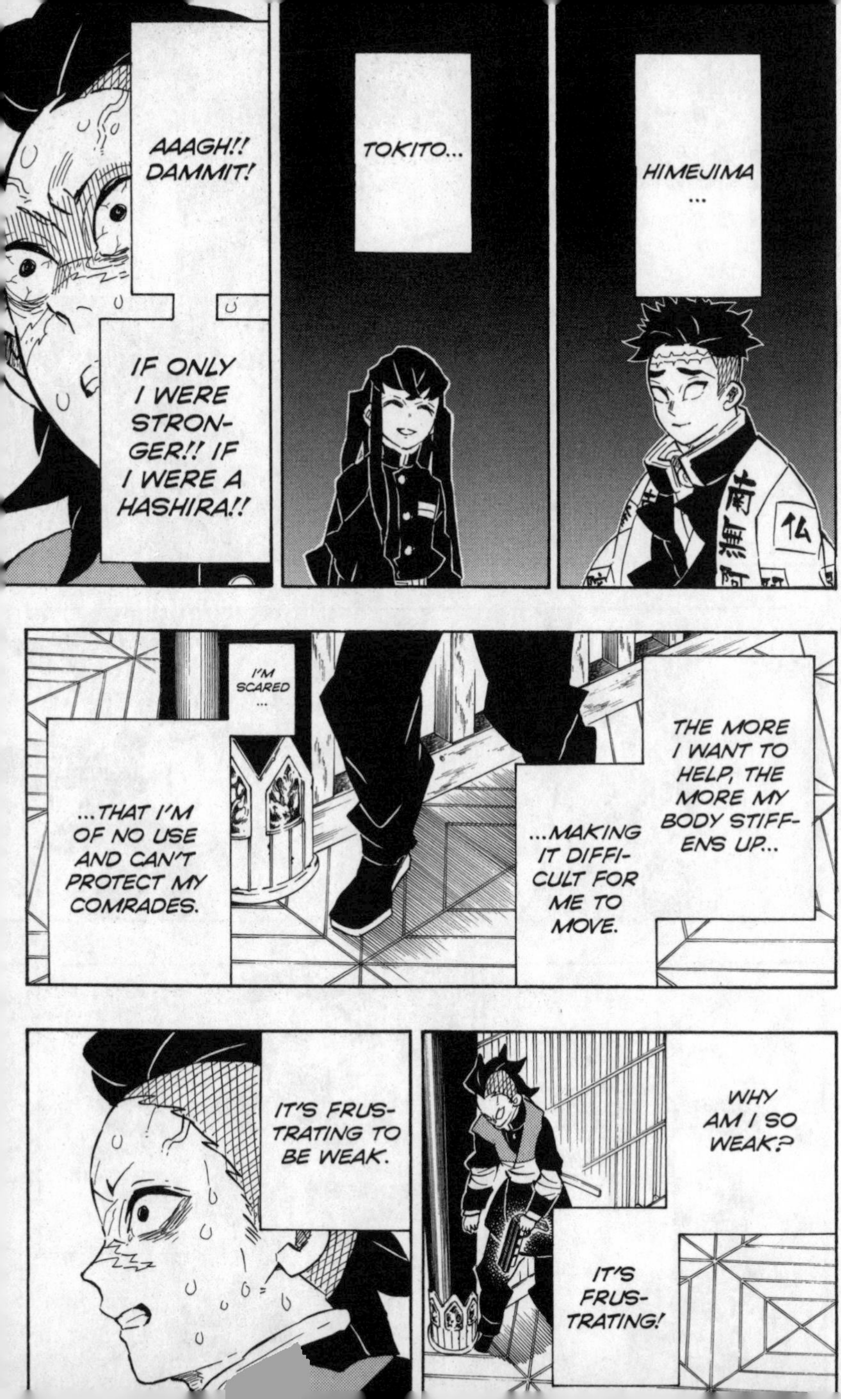
HIMEJIMA...
TOKITO...
AAAGH!! DAMMIT!
IF ONLY I WERE STRONGER!! IF I WERE A HASHIRA!!
THE MORE I WANT TO HELP, THE MORE MY BODY STIFFENS UP...
...MAKING IT DIFFICULT FOR ME TO MOVE.
I'M SCARED...
...THAT I'M OF NO USE AND CAN'T PROTECT MY COMRADES.
WHY AM I SO WEAK?
IT'S FRUSTRATING!
IT'S FRUSTRATING TO BE WEAK.

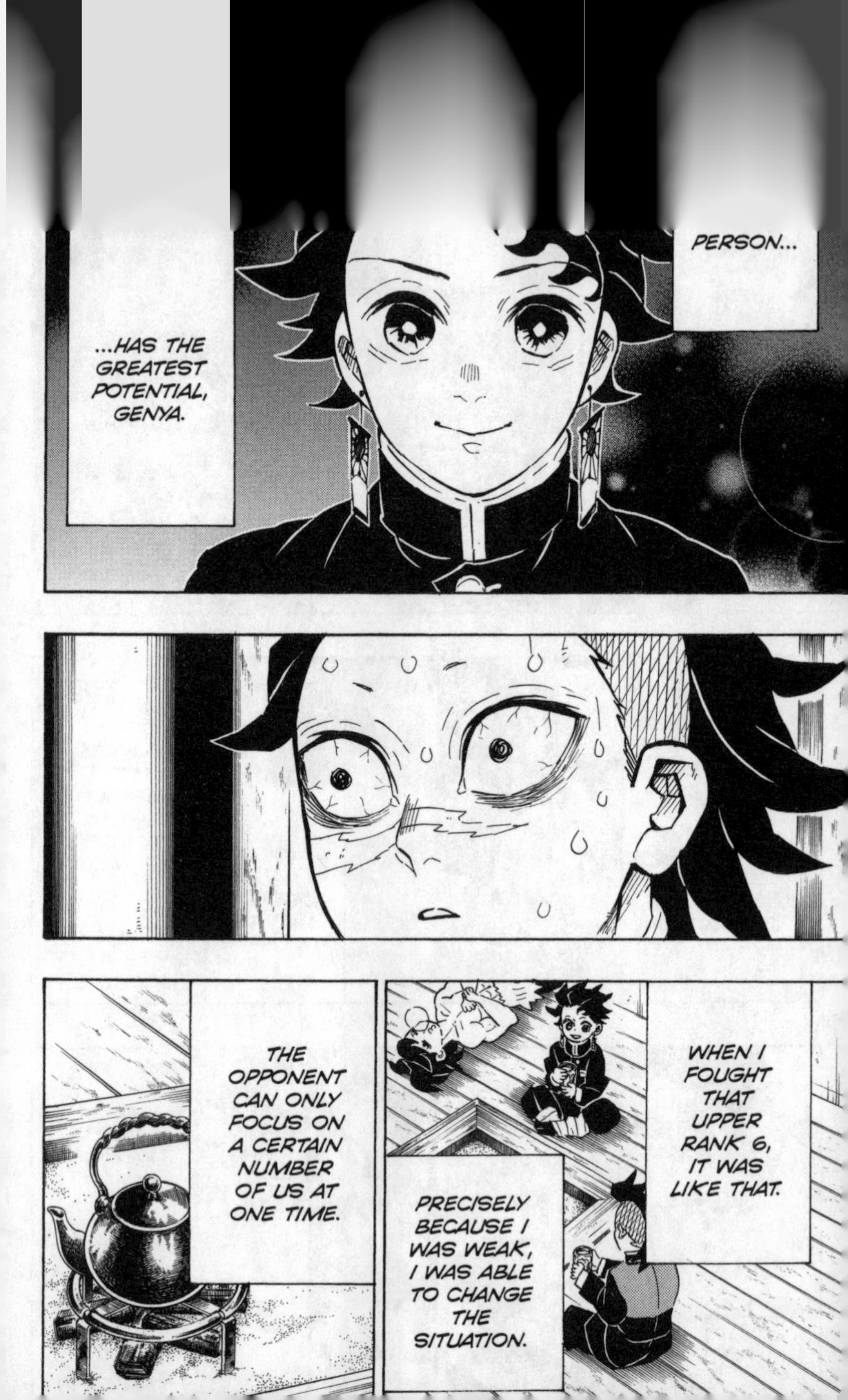
PERSON...
...HAS THE GREATEST POTENTIAL, GENYA.
WHEN I FOUGHT THAT UPPER RANK 6, IT WAS LIKE THAT.
PRECISELY BECAUSE I WAS WEAK, I WAS ABLE TO CHANGE THE SITUATION.
THE OPPONENT CAN ONLY FOCUS ON A CERTAIN NUMBER OF US AT ONE TIME.

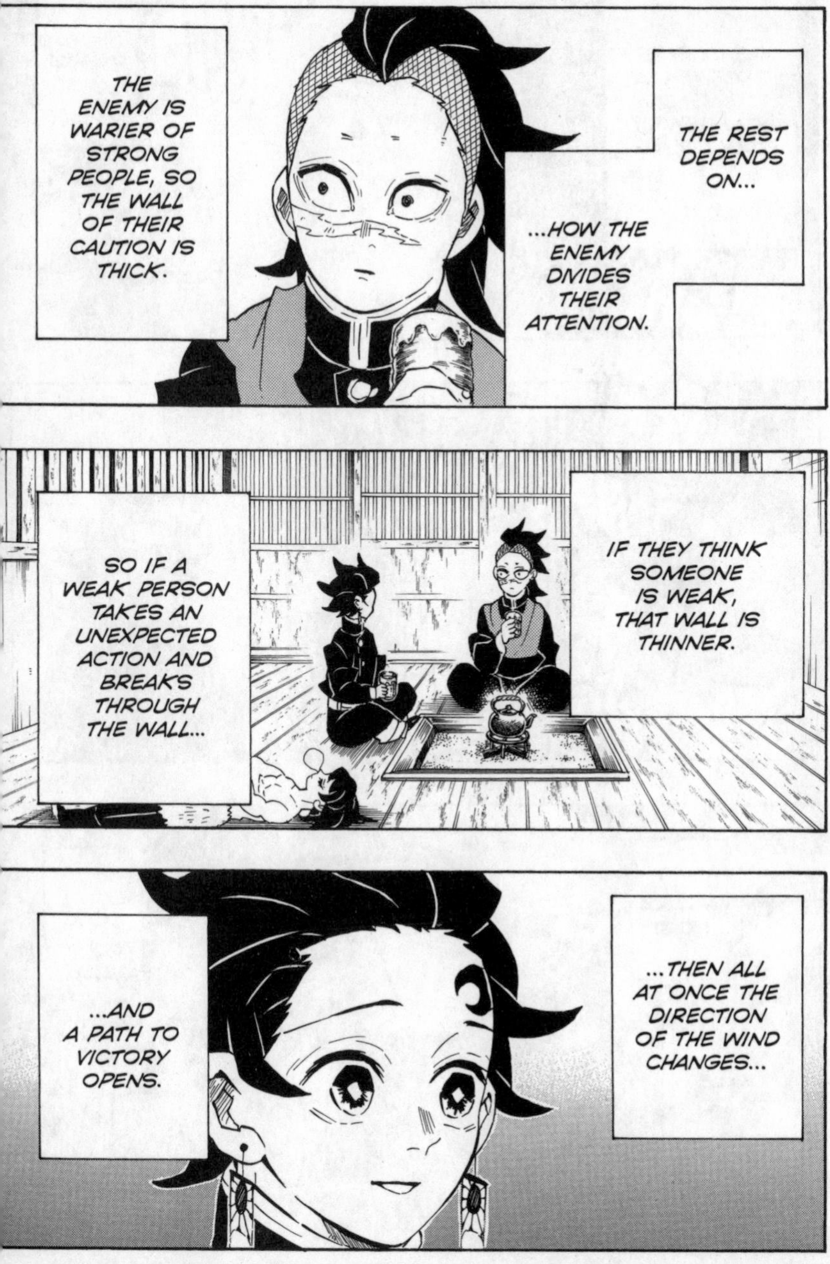
THE REST DEPENDS ON...
...HOW THE ENEMY DIVIDES THEIR ATTENTION.
THE ENEMY IS WARIER OF STRONG PEOPLE, SO THE WALL OF THEIR CAUTION IS THICK.
IF THEY THINK SOMEONE IS WEAK, THAT WALL IS THINNER.
SO IF A WEAK PERSON TAKES AN UNEXPECTED ACTION AND BREAKS THROUGH THE WALL...
...THEN ALL AT ONCE THE DIRECTION OF THE WIND CHANGES...
...AND A PATH TO VICTORY OPENS.

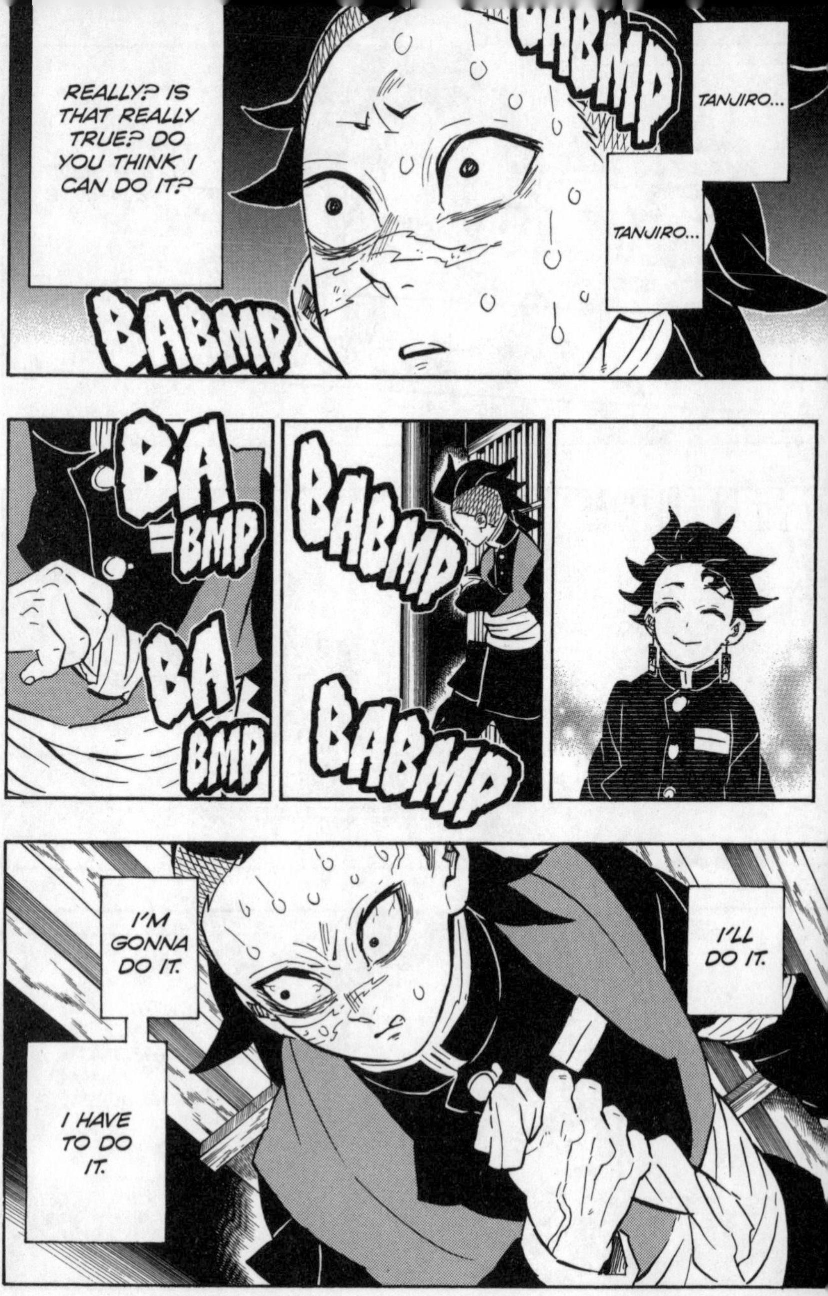
TANJIRO...
TANJIRO...
REALLY? IS THAT REALLY TRUE? DO YOU THINK I CAN DO IT?
BABMP
BABMP
BABMP
BA-BMP
BA-BMP
I'LL DO IT.
I'M GONNA DO IT.
I HAVE TO DO IT.

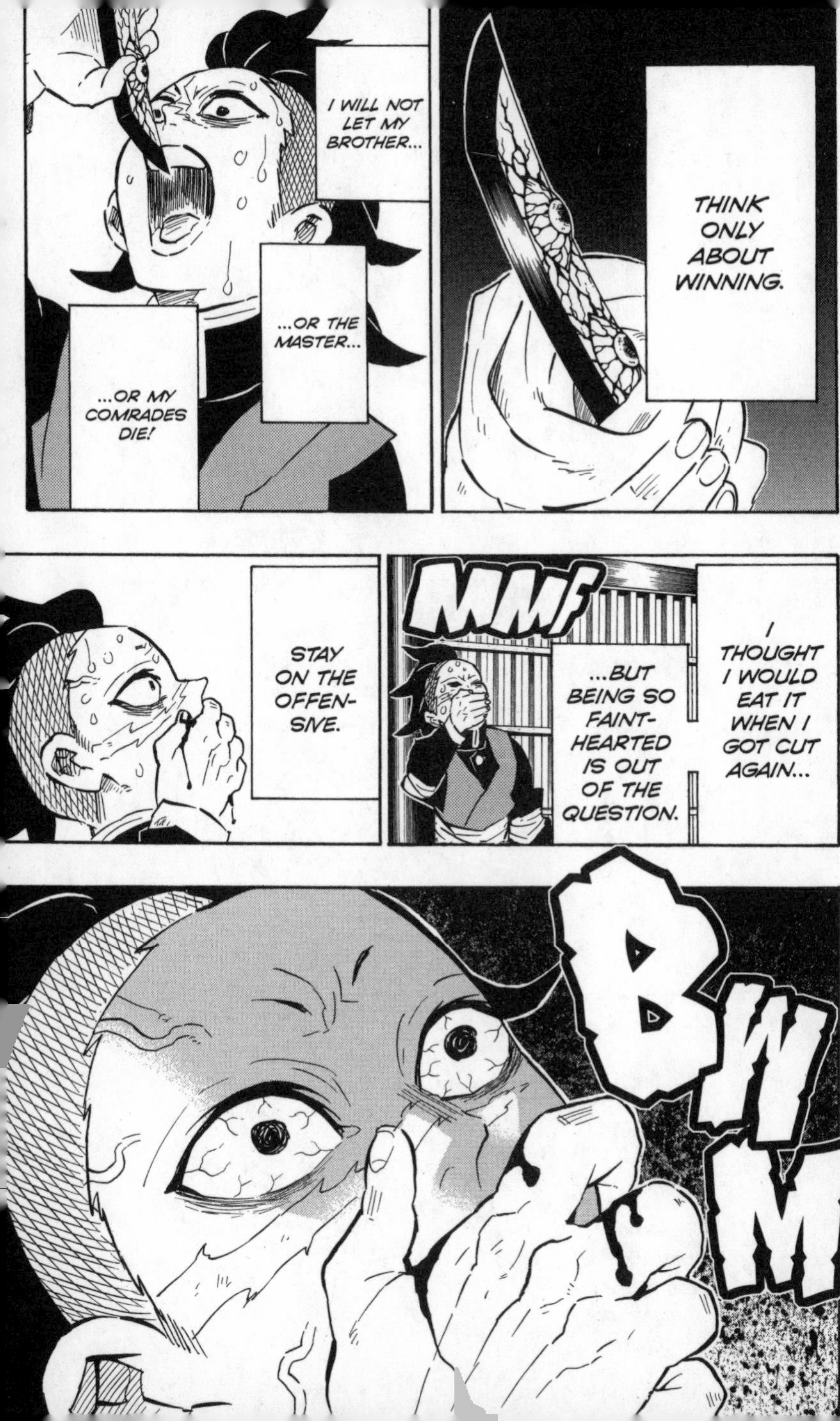
THINK ONLY ABOUT WINNING.
I WILL NOT LET MY BROTHER...
...OR THE MASTER...
...OR MY COMRADES DIE!
I THOUGHT I WOULD EAT IT WHEN I GOT CUT AGAIN...
...BUT BEING SO FAINT-HEARTED IS OUT OF THE QUESTION.
MMF
STAY ON THE OFFEN-SIVE.
BWM

Aoi's recommended disciplinary method: spanking

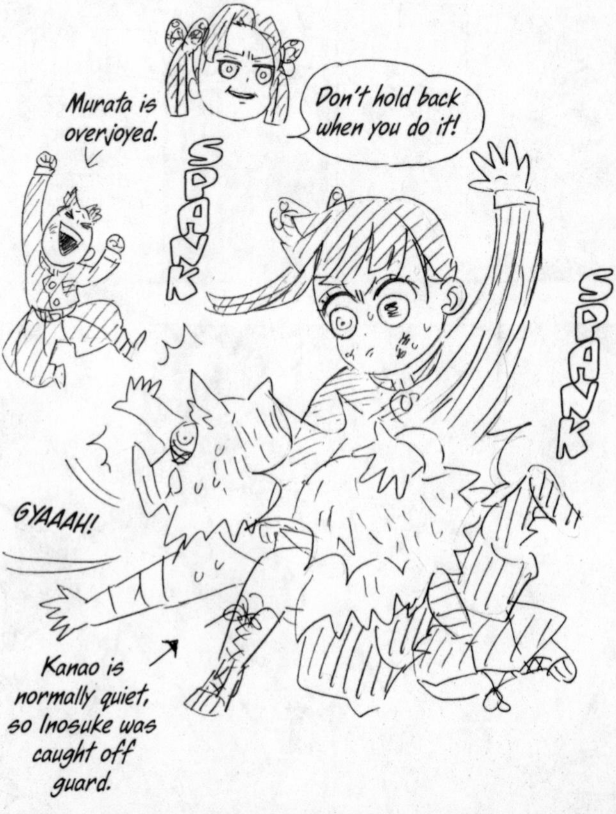
Don't hold back when you do it!
SPANK
Murata is overjoyed.
SPANK
GYAAAH!
Kanao is normally quiet, so Inosuke was caught off guard.

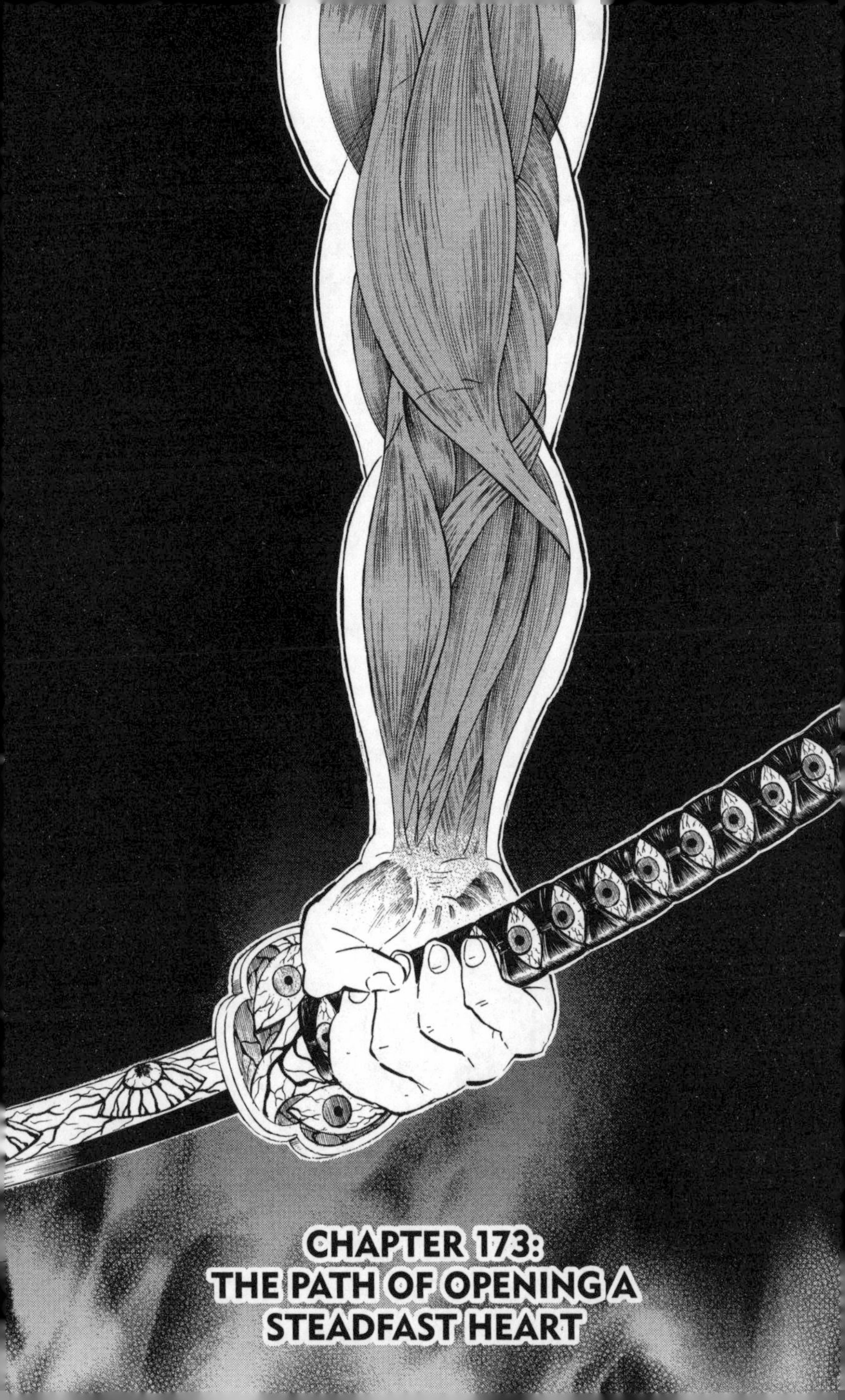
CHAPTER 173:
THE PATH OF OPENING A
STEADFAST HEART

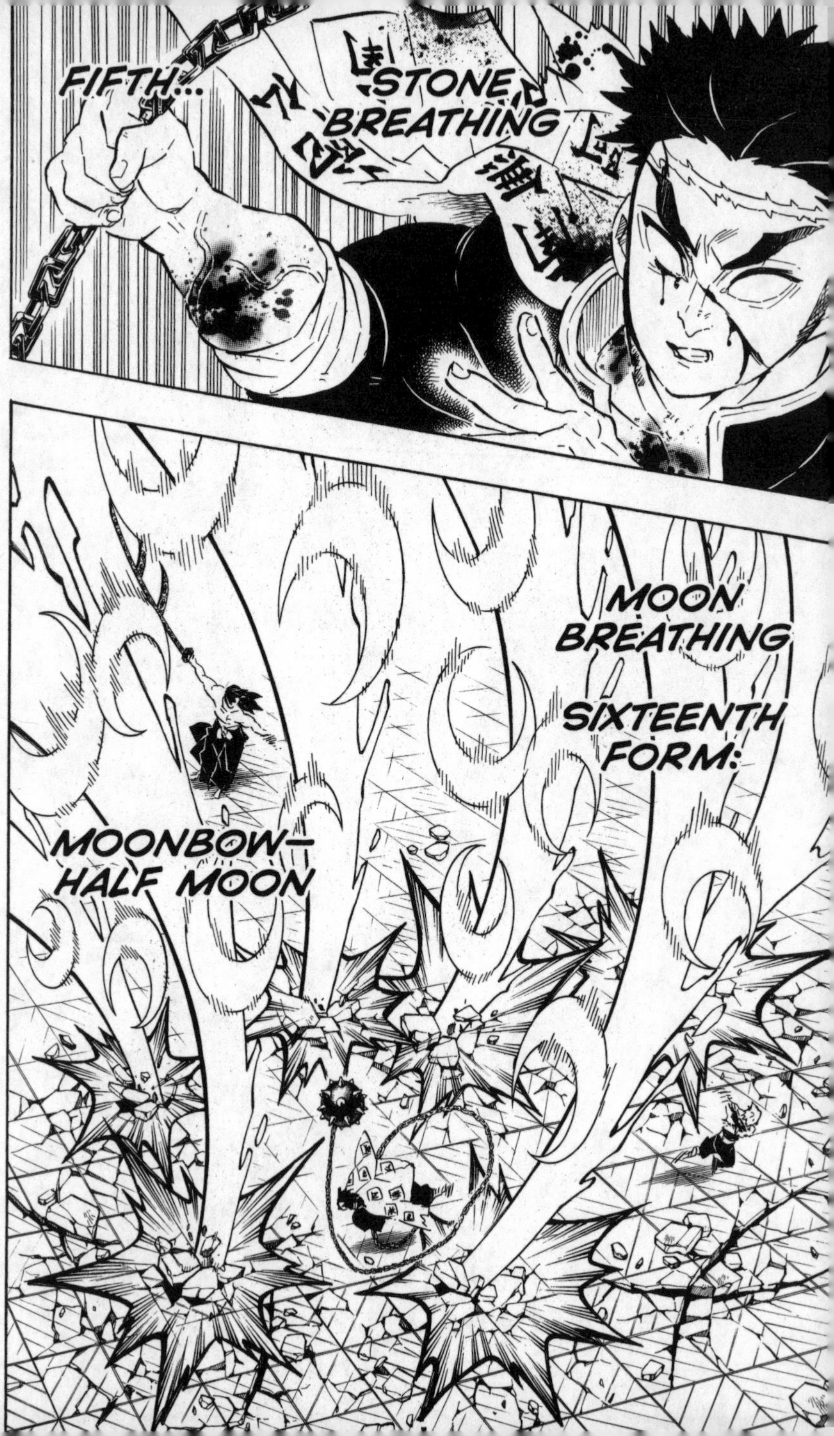
STONE BREATHING
FIFTH...
MOON BREATHING
SIXTEENTH FORM:
MOONBOW—HALF MOON

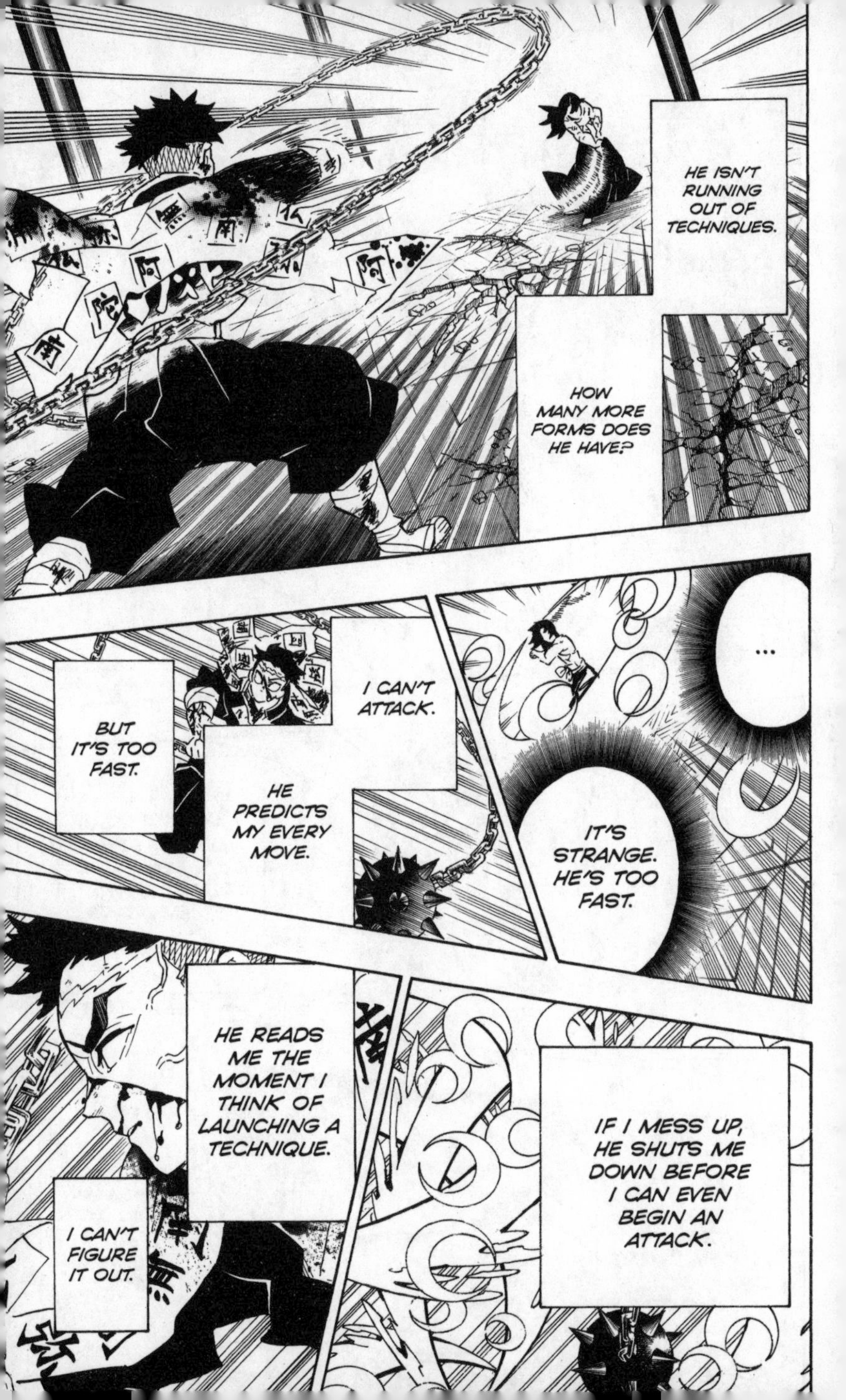
HE ISN'T RUNNING OUT OF TECHNIQUES.
HOW MANY MORE FORMS DOES HE HAVE?
...
IT'S STRANGE. HE'S TOO FAST.
I CAN'T ATTACK.
HE PREDICTS MY EVERY MOVE.
BUT IT'S TOO FAST.
IF I MESS UP, HE SHUTS ME DOWN BEFORE I CAN EVEN BEGIN AN ATTACK.
HE READS ME THE MOMENT I THINK OF LAUNCHING A TECHNIQUE.
I CAN'T FIGURE IT OUT.

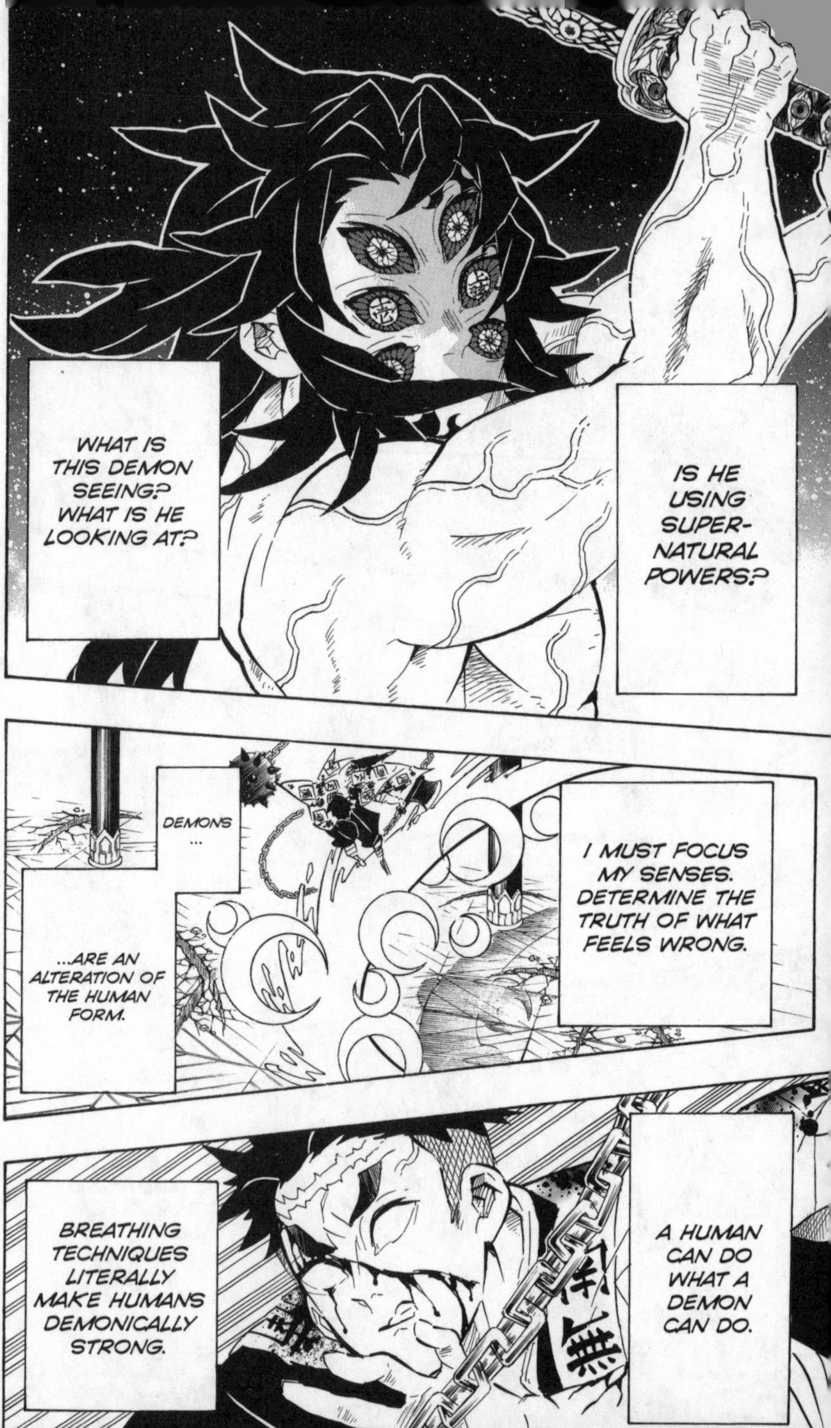
IS HE USING SUPER-NATURAL POWERS?
WHAT IS THIS DEMON SEEING? WHAT IS HE LOOKING AT?
I MUST FOCUS MY SENSES. DETERMINE THE TRUTH OF WHAT FEELS WRONG.
DEMONS ...
...ARE AN ALTERATION OF THE HUMAN FORM.
A HUMAN CAN DO WHAT A DEMON CAN DO.
BREATHING TECHNIQUES LITERALLY MAKE HUMANS DEMONICALLY STRONG.

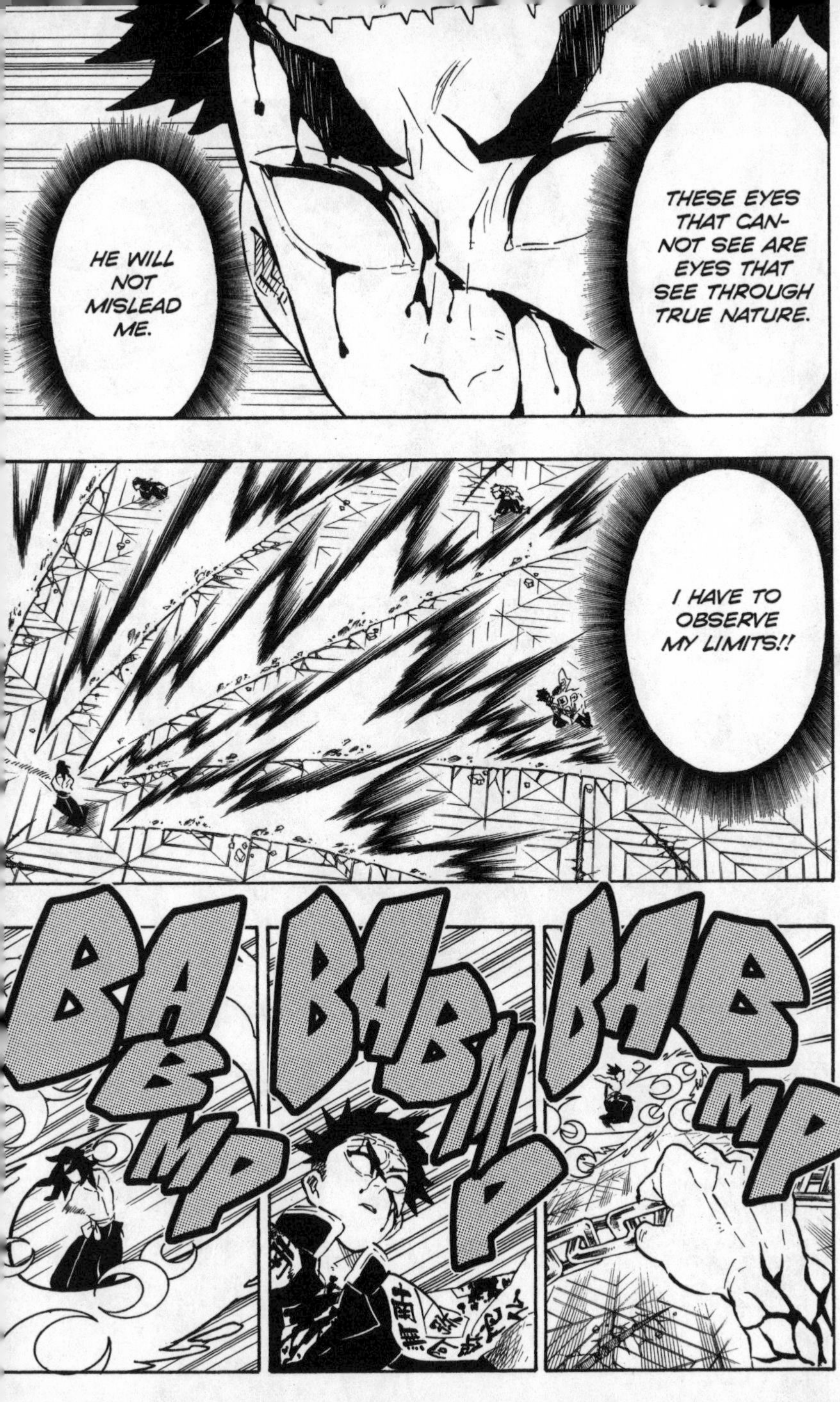
THESE EYES THAT CAN-NOT SEE ARE EYES THAT SEE THROUGH TRUE NATURE.
HE WILL NOT MISLEAD ME.
I HAVE TO OBSERVE MY LIMITS!!
BABMP
BABMP
BABMP

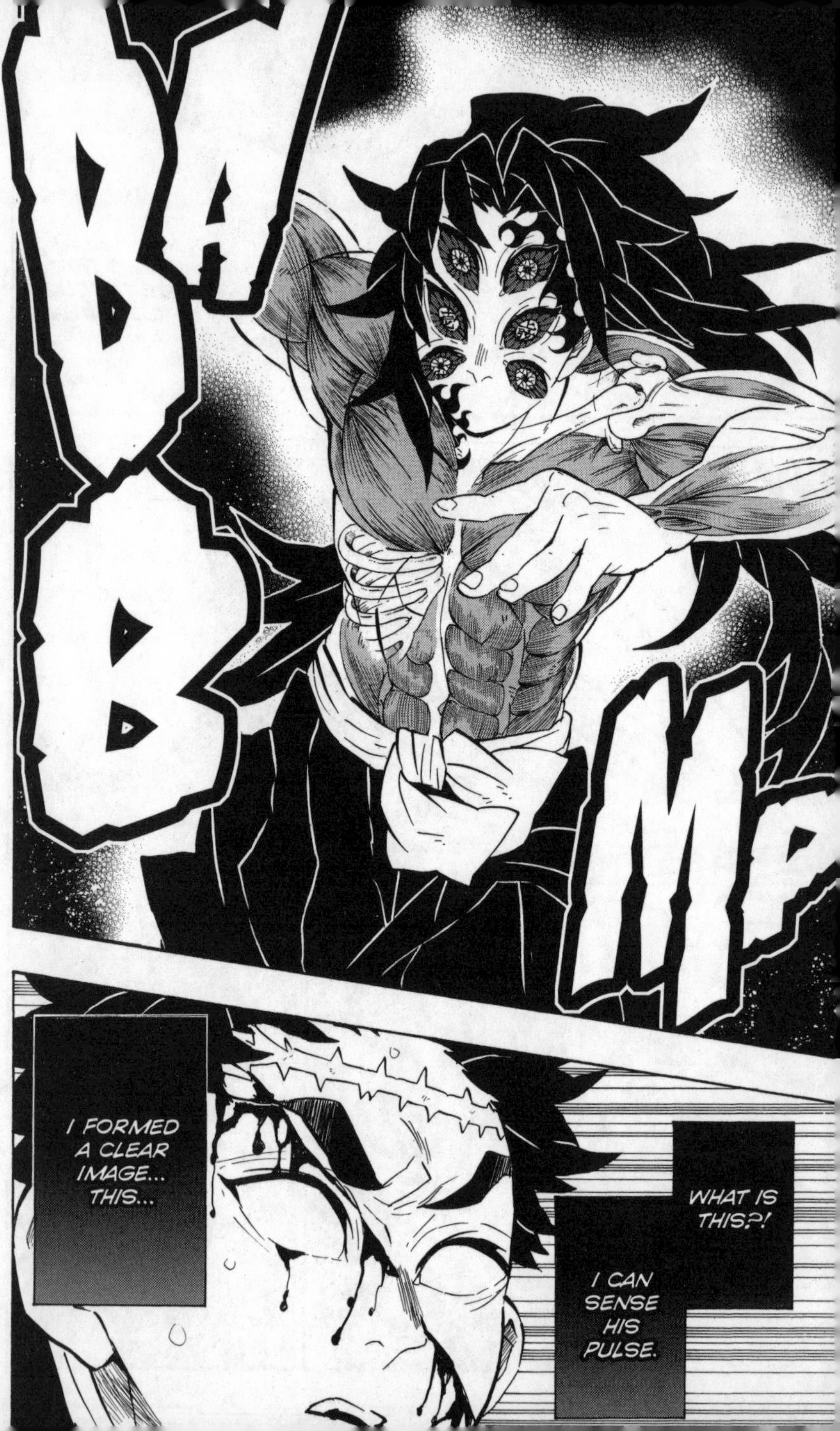
BA
B
MP
I FORMED A CLEAR IMAGE... THIS...
WHAT IS THIS?!
I CAN SENSE HIS PULSE.

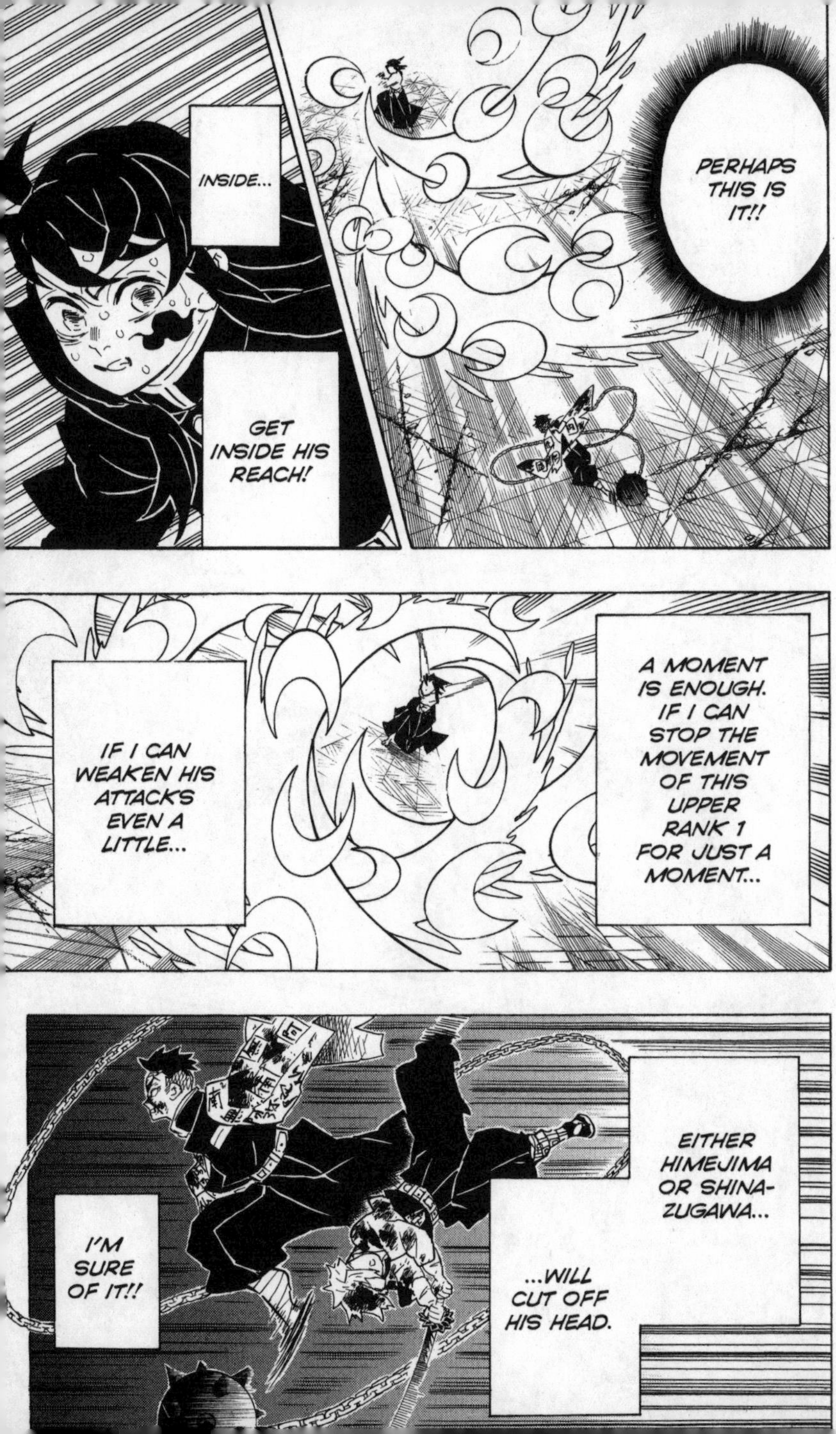
PERHAPS THIS IS IT!!
INSIDE...
GET INSIDE HIS REACH!
A MOMENT IS ENOUGH. IF I CAN STOP THE MOVEMENT OF THIS UPPER RANK 1 FOR JUST A MOMENT...
IF I CAN WEAKEN HIS ATTACKS EVEN A LITTLE...
EITHER HIMEJIMA OR SHINA-ZUGAWA...
...WILL CUT OFF HIS HEAD.
I'M SURE OF IT!!

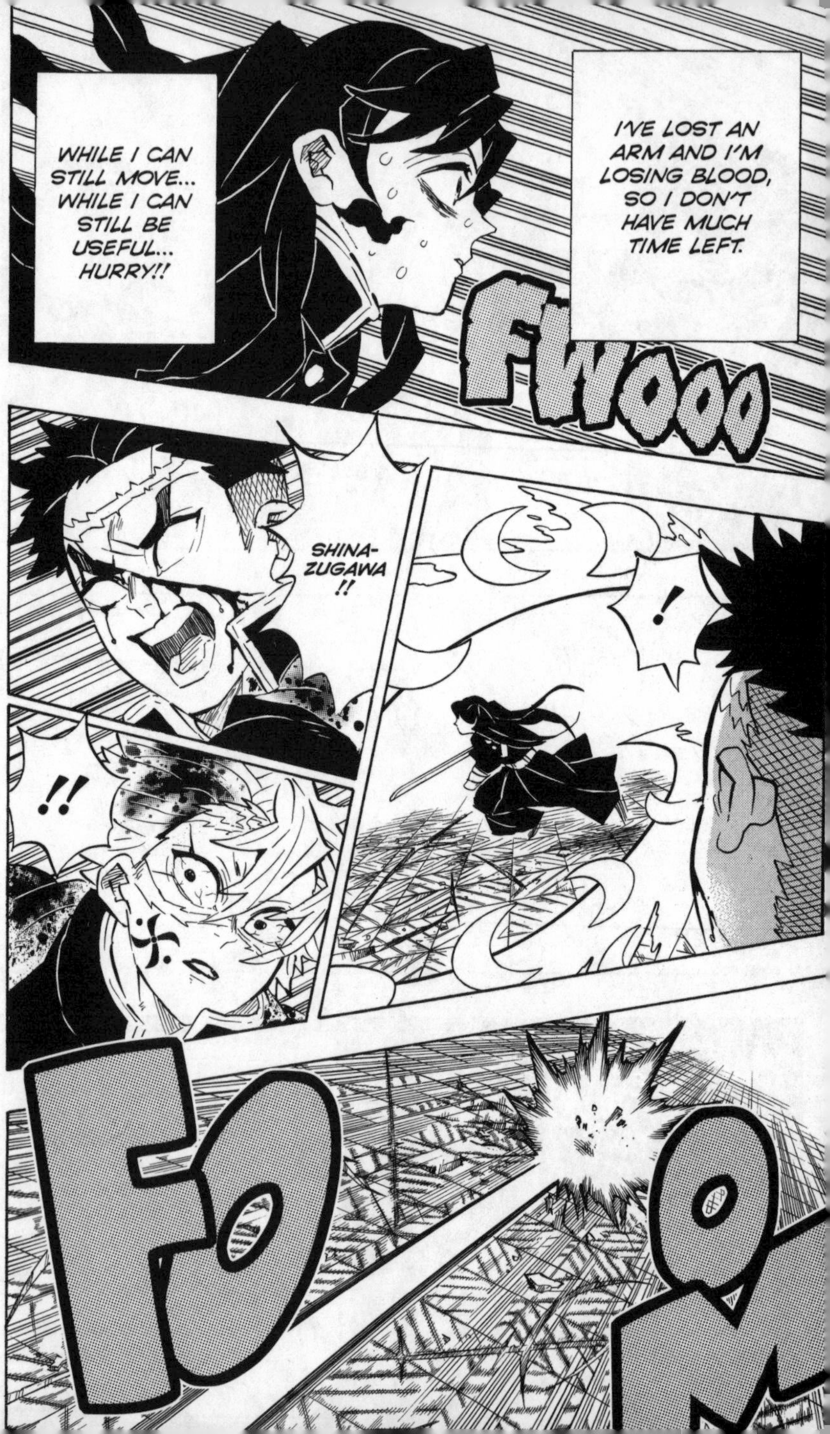
I'VE LOST AN ARM AND I'M LOSING BLOOD, SO I DON'T HAVE MUCH TIME LEFT.
WHILE I CAN STILL MOVE... WHILE I CAN STILL BE USEFUL... HURRY!!
FWOOO
!
SHINA-ZUGAWA!!
!!
FOOM

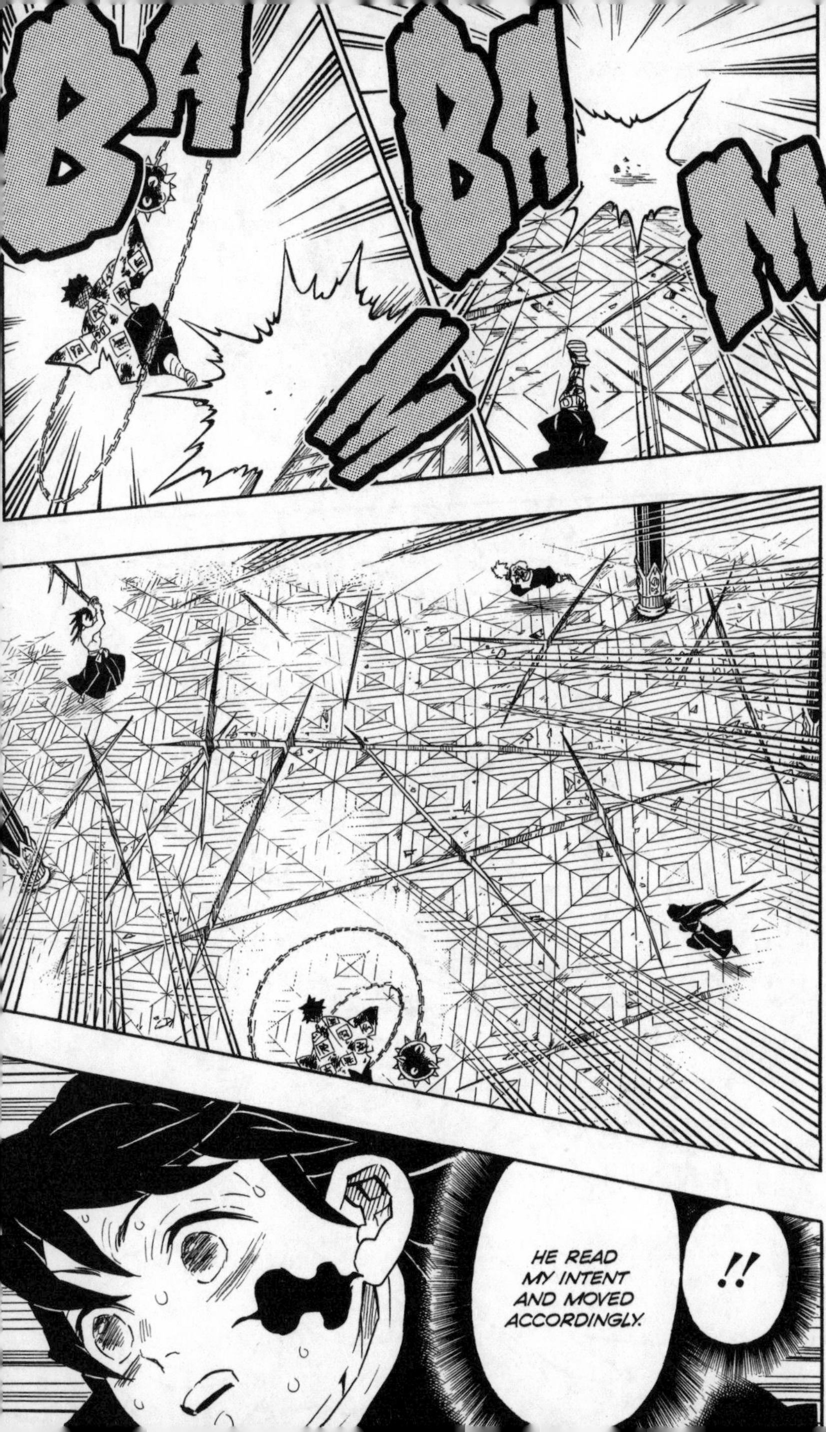
BA BA MM
!!
HE READ MY INTENT AND MOVED ACCORDINGLY.

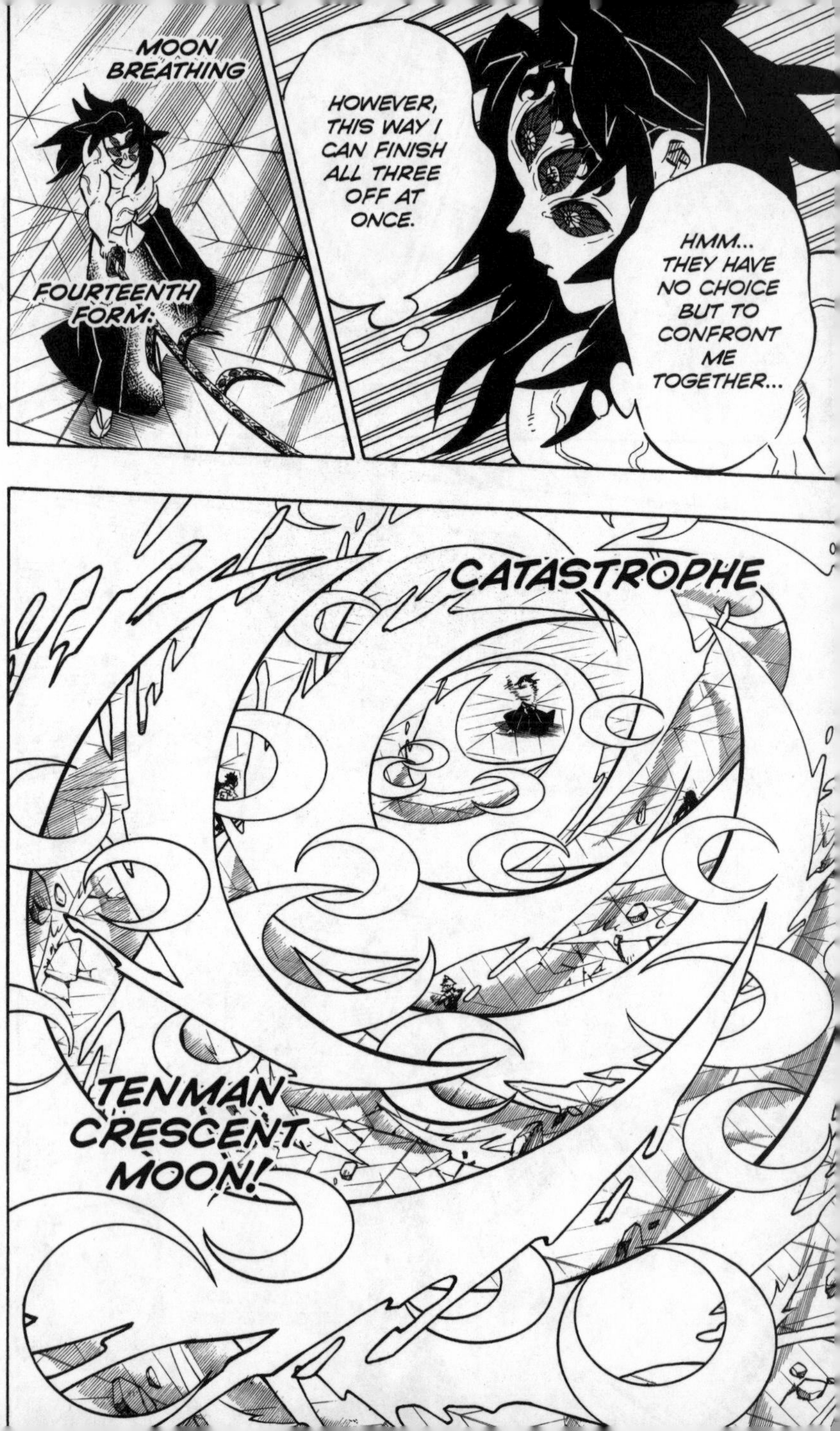
HMM... THEY HAVE NO CHOICE BUT TO CONFRONT ME TOGETHER...
HOWEVER, THIS WAY I CAN FINISH ALL THREE OFF AT ONCE.
MOON BREATHING
FOURTEENTH FORM:
CATASTROPHE
TENMAN CRESCENT MOON!

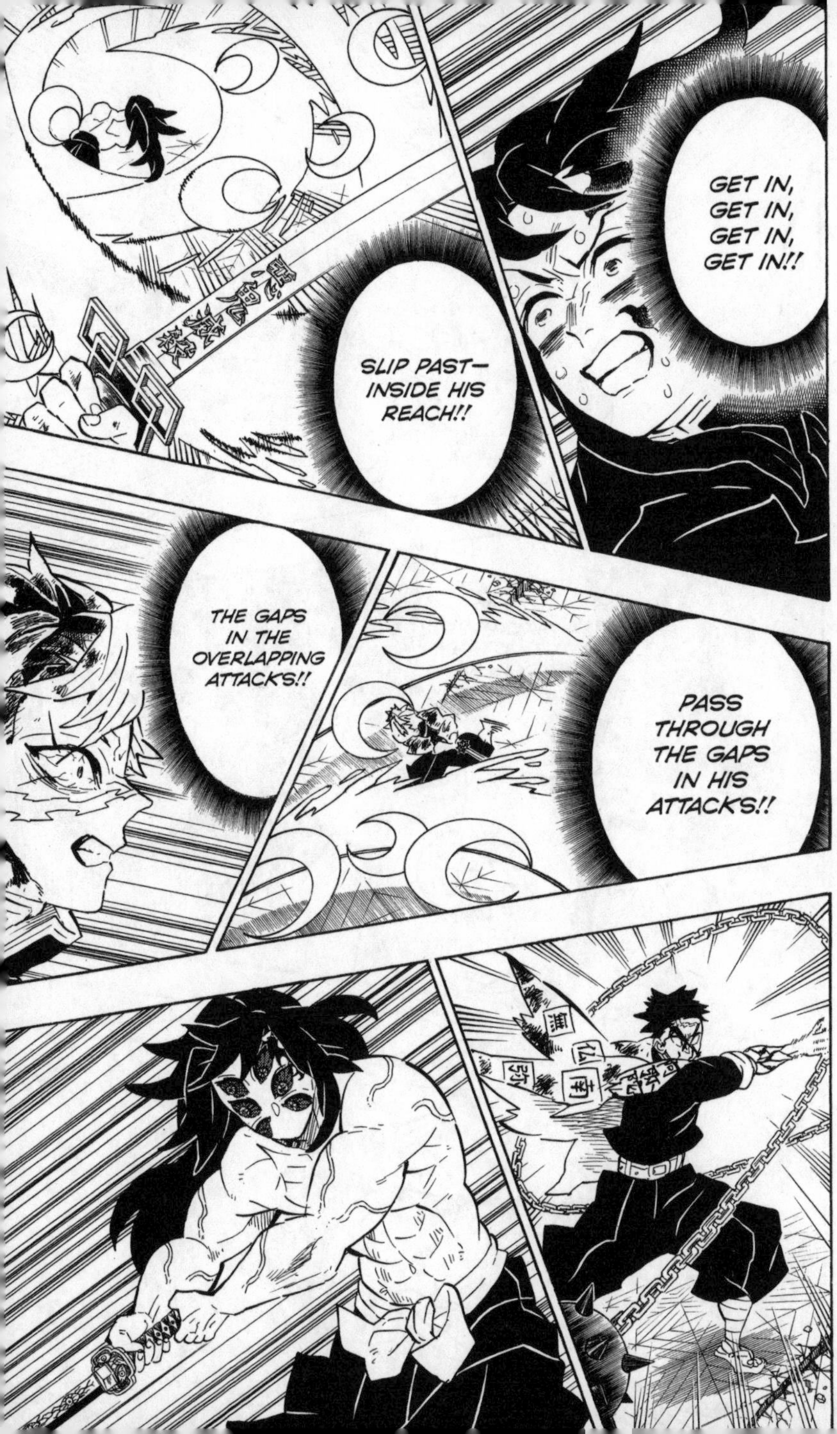
GET IN, GET IN, GET IN, GET IN!!
SLIP PAST— INSIDE HIS REACH!!
PASS THROUGH THE GAPS IN HIS ATTACKS!!
THE GAPS IN THE OVERLAPPING ATTACKS!!

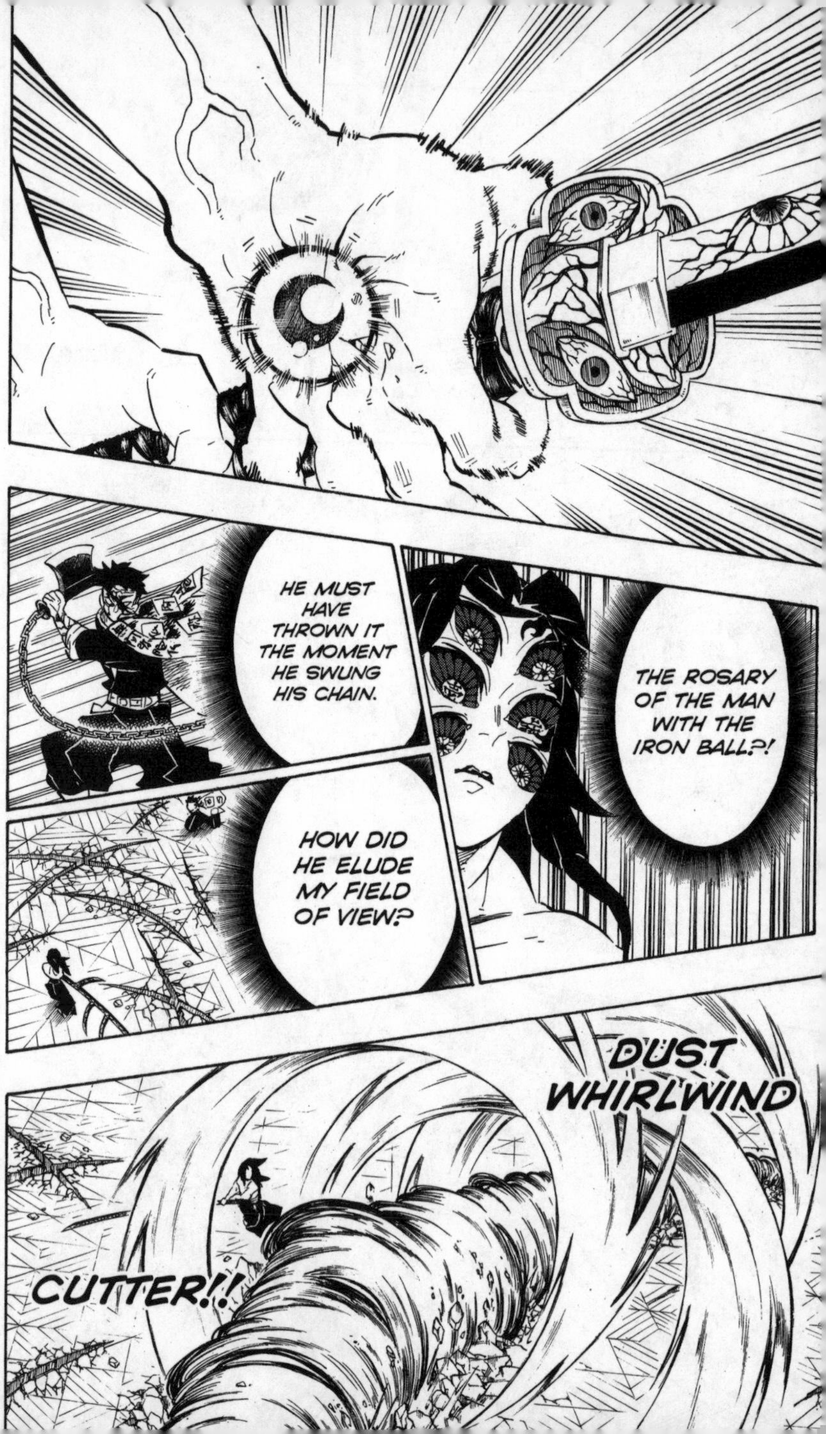
THE ROSARY OF THE MAN WITH THE IRON BALL?!
HE MUST HAVE THROWN IT THE MOMENT HE SWUNG HIS CHAIN.
HOW DID HE ELUDE MY FIELD OF VIEW?
DUST WHIRLWIND
CUTTER!!

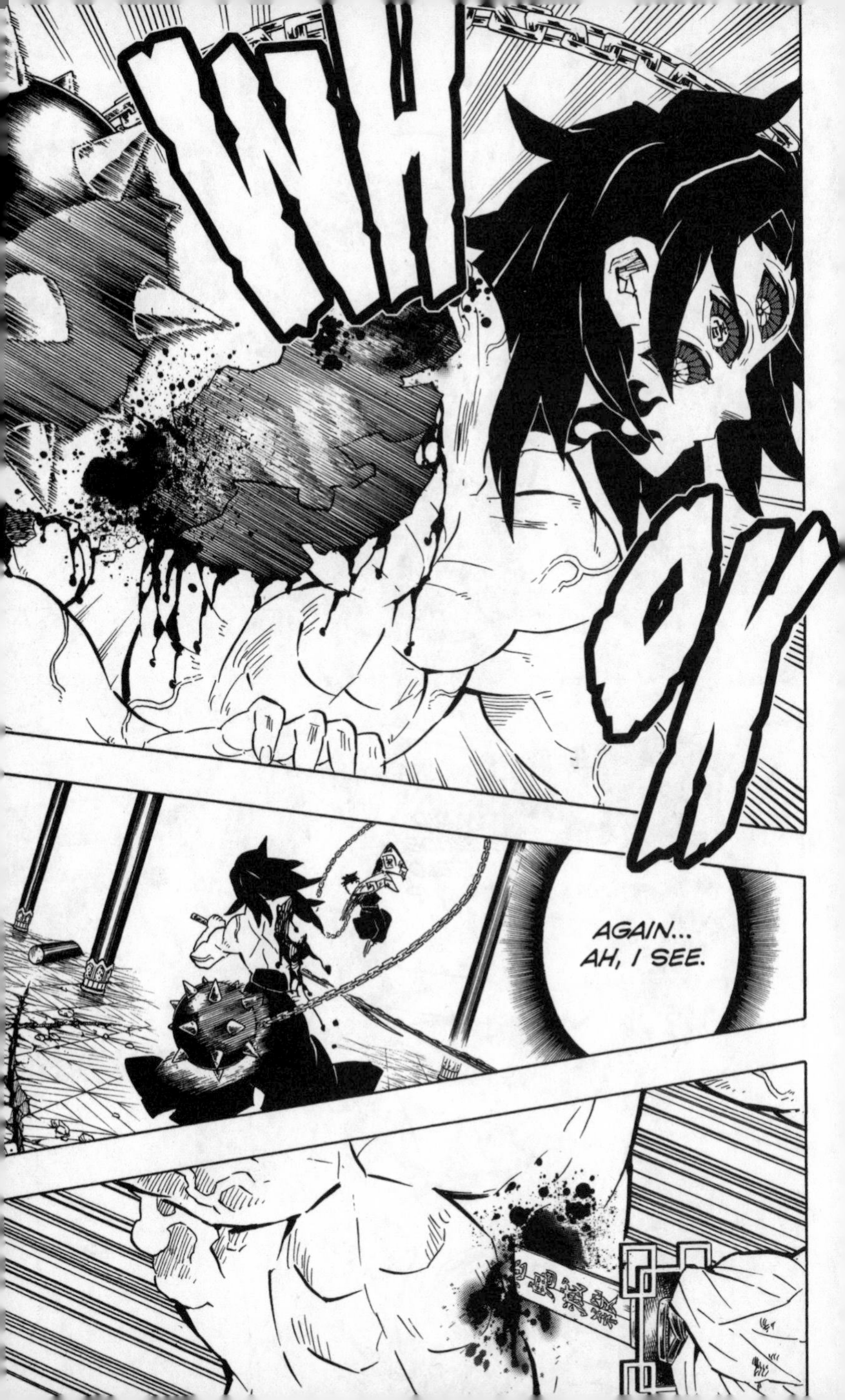
WHOK
AGAIN...
AH, I SEE.

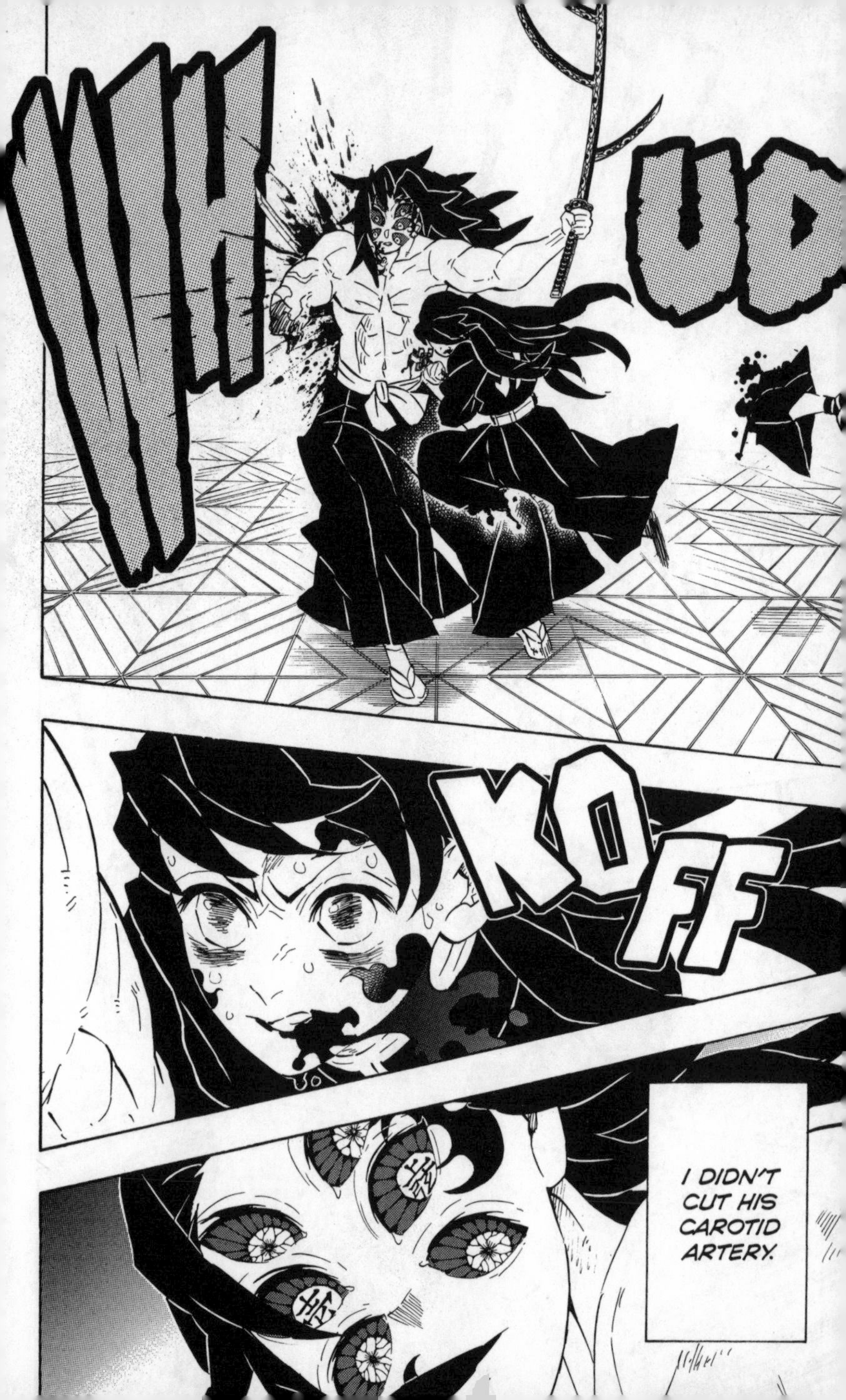
WHUD
KOFF
I DIDN'T CUT HIS CAROTID ARTERY.

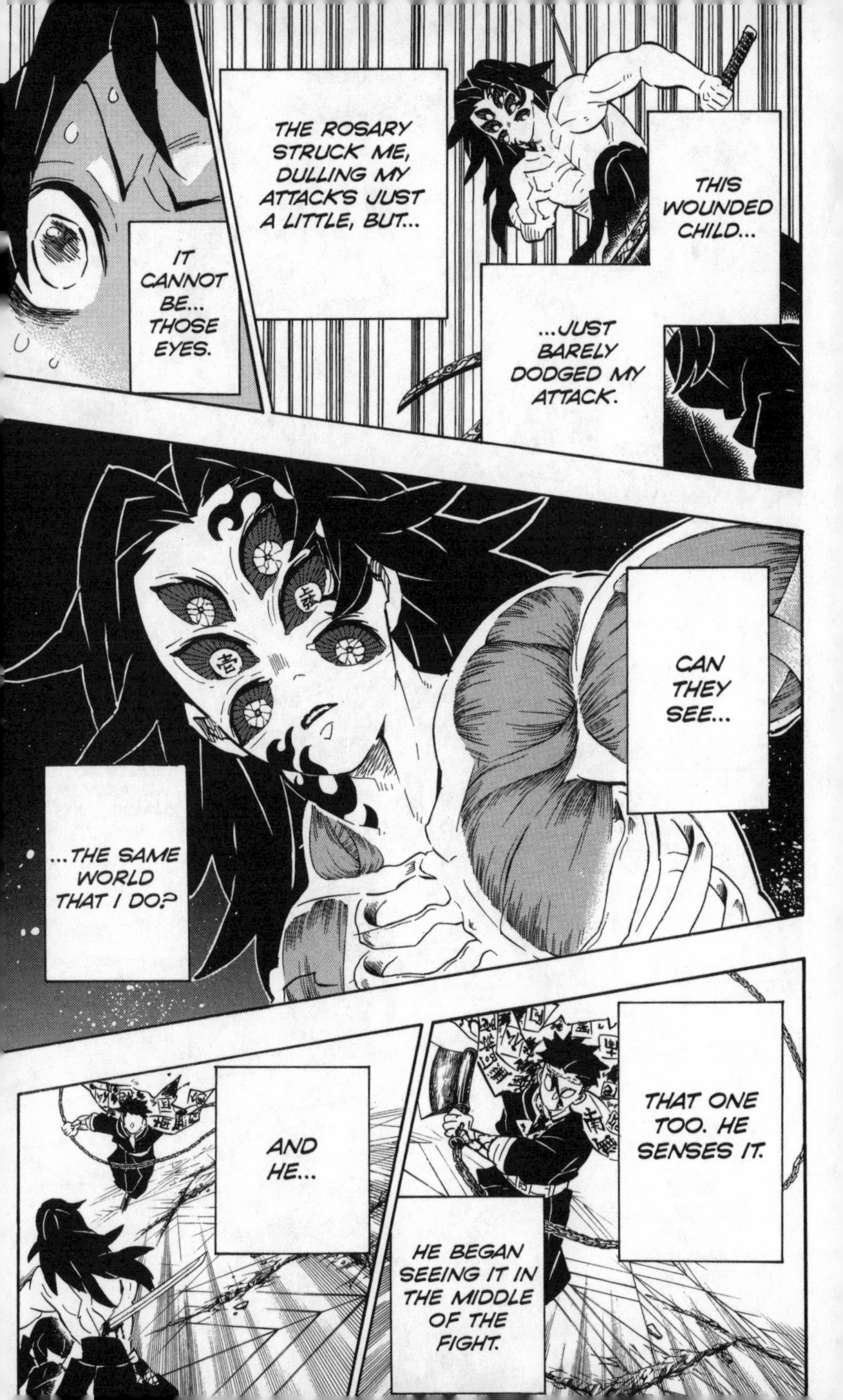
THE ROSARY STRUCK ME, DULLING MY ATTACK'S JUST A LITTLE, BUT...
THIS WOUNDED CHILD...
...JUST BARELY DODGED MY ATTACK.
IT CANNOT BE... THOSE EYES.
CAN THEY SEE...
...THE SAME WORLD THAT I DO?
THAT ONE TOO. HE SENSES IT.
HE BEGAN SEEING IT IN THE MIDDLE OF THE FIGHT.
AND HE...

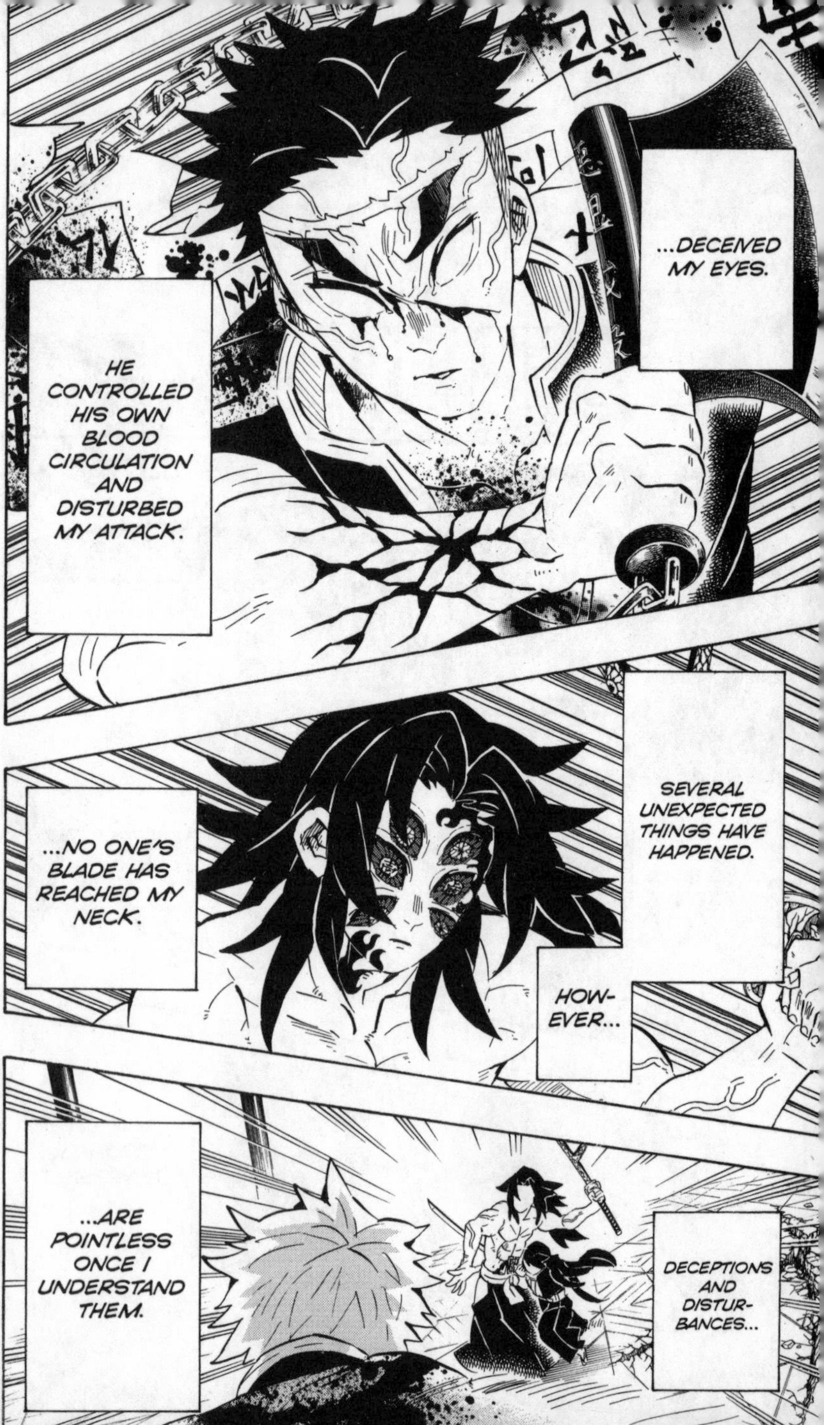

...DECEIVED MY EYES.
HE CONTROLLED HIS OWN BLOOD CIRCULATION AND DISTURBED MY ATTACK.
SEVERAL UNEXPECTED THINGS HAVE HAPPENED.
HOW-EVER...
...NO ONE'S BLADE HAS REACHED MY NECK.
DECEPTIONS AND DISTUR-BANCES...
...ARE POINTLESS ONCE I UNDERSTAND THEM.

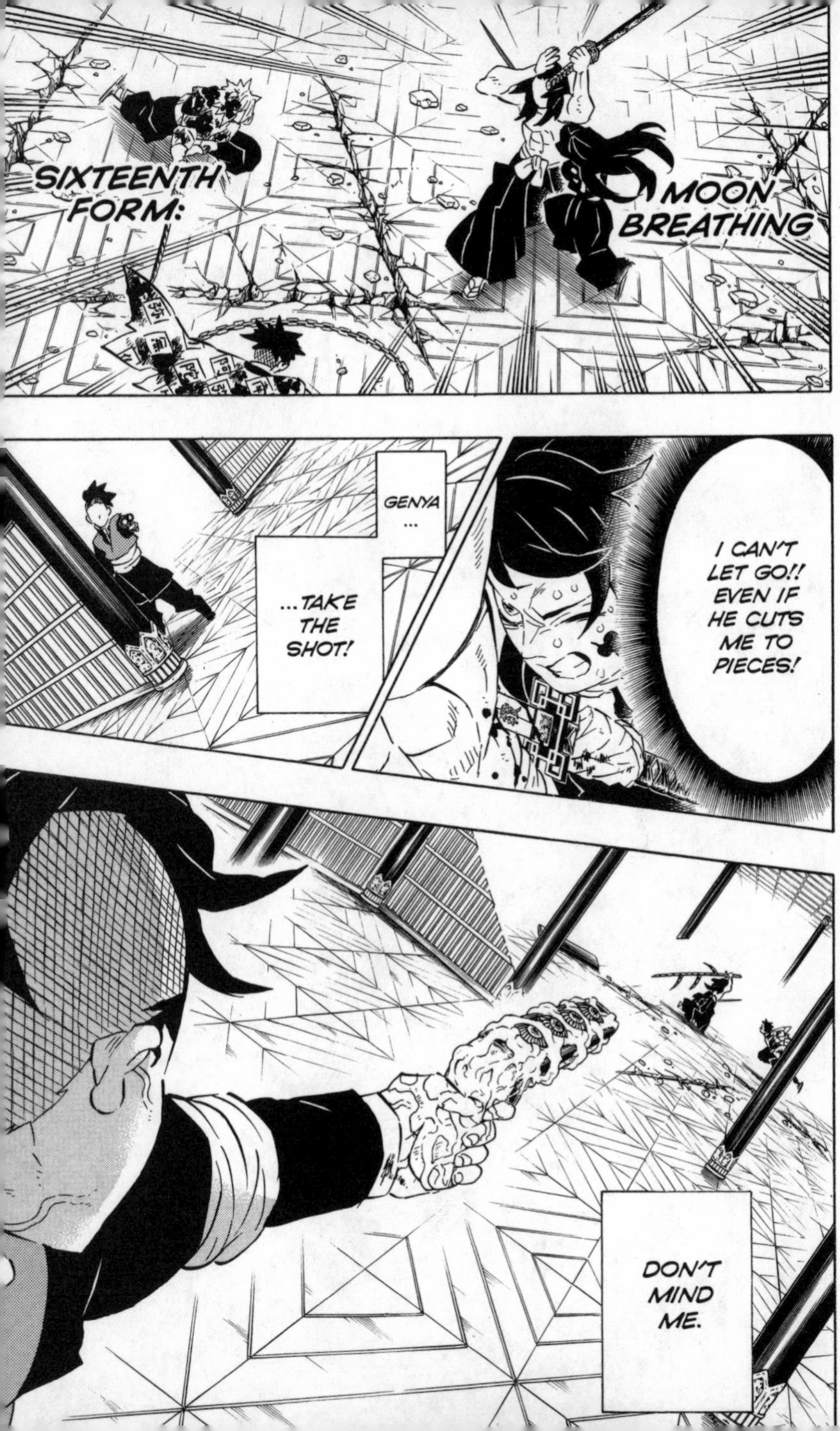
MOON BREATHING
SIXTEENTH FORM:
I CAN'T LET GO!! EVEN IF HE CUTS ME TO PIECES!
GENYA...
...TAKE THE SHOT!
DON'T MIND ME.

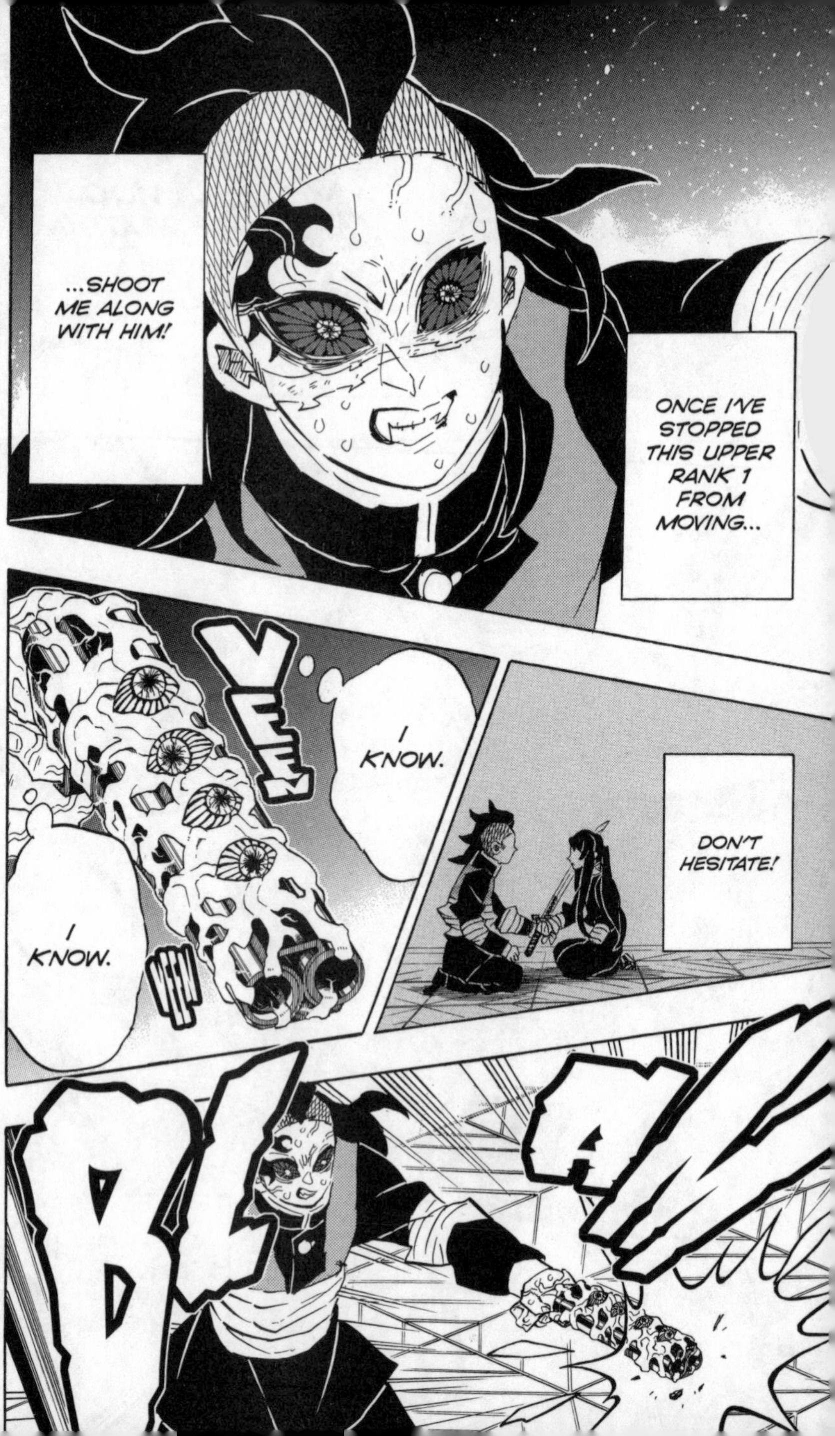
ONCE I'VE STOPPED THIS UPPER RANK 1 FROM MOVING...
...SHOOT ME ALONG WITH HIM!
DON'T HESITATE!
I KNOW.
VEEN
I KNOW.
VEEN
BLAM

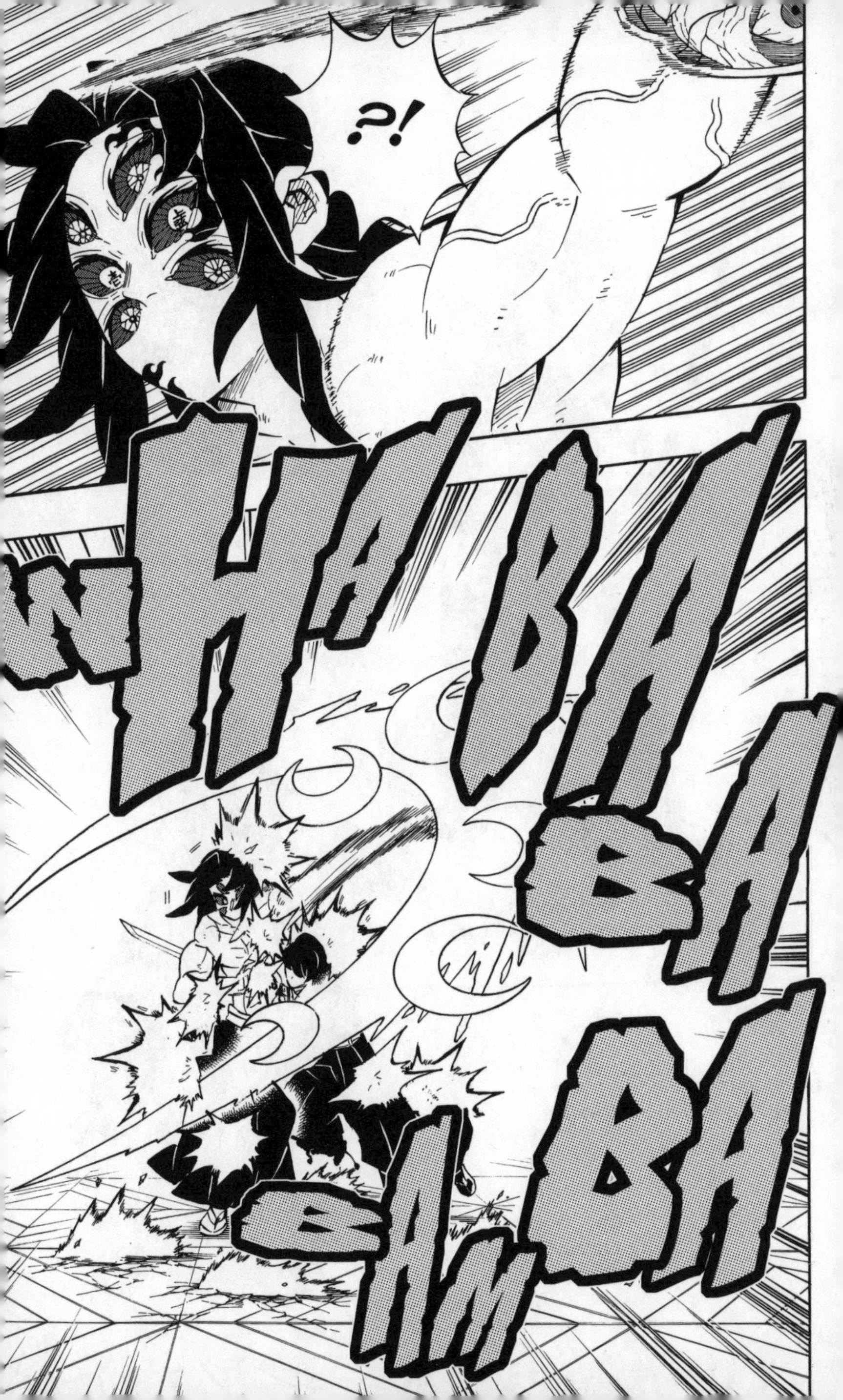
?!

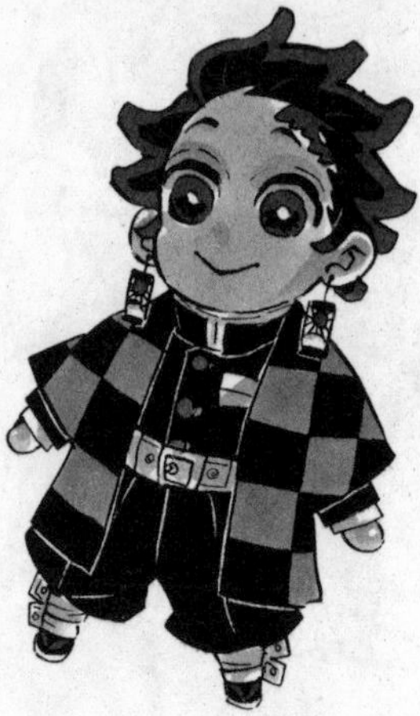

From *Weekly Shonen Jump*,
combined issue No. 45, 2019

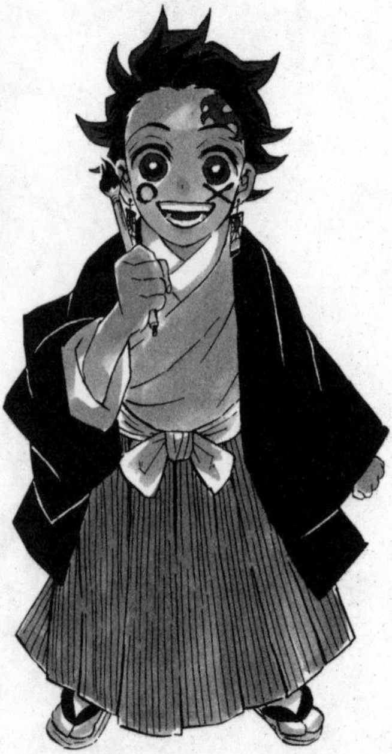

From *Weekly Shonen Jump*,
combined issue No. 6–7, 2019

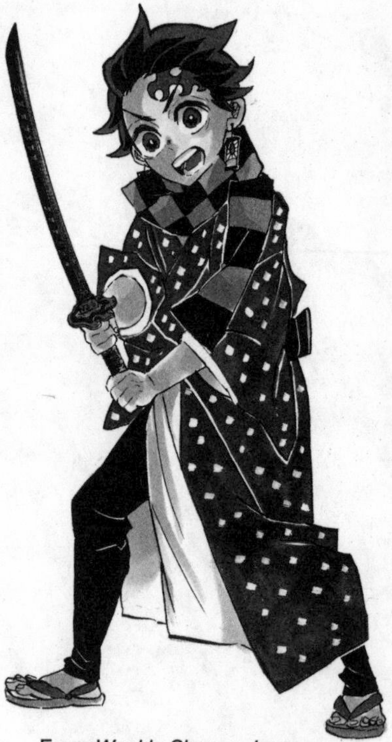

From *Weekly Shonen Jump*,
combined issue No. 22–23, 2019

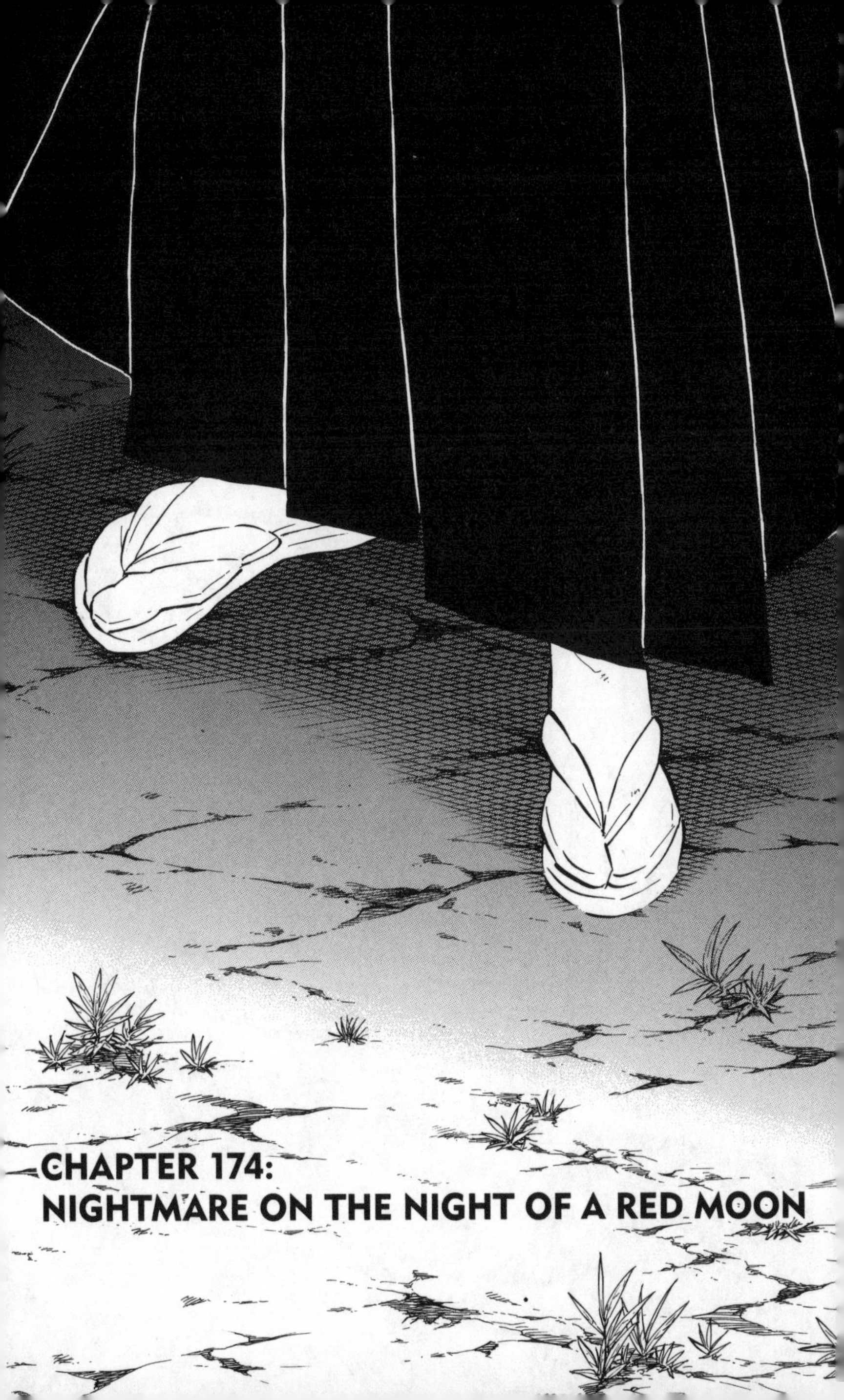
CHAPTER 174:
NIGHTMARE ON THE NIGHT OF A RED MOON

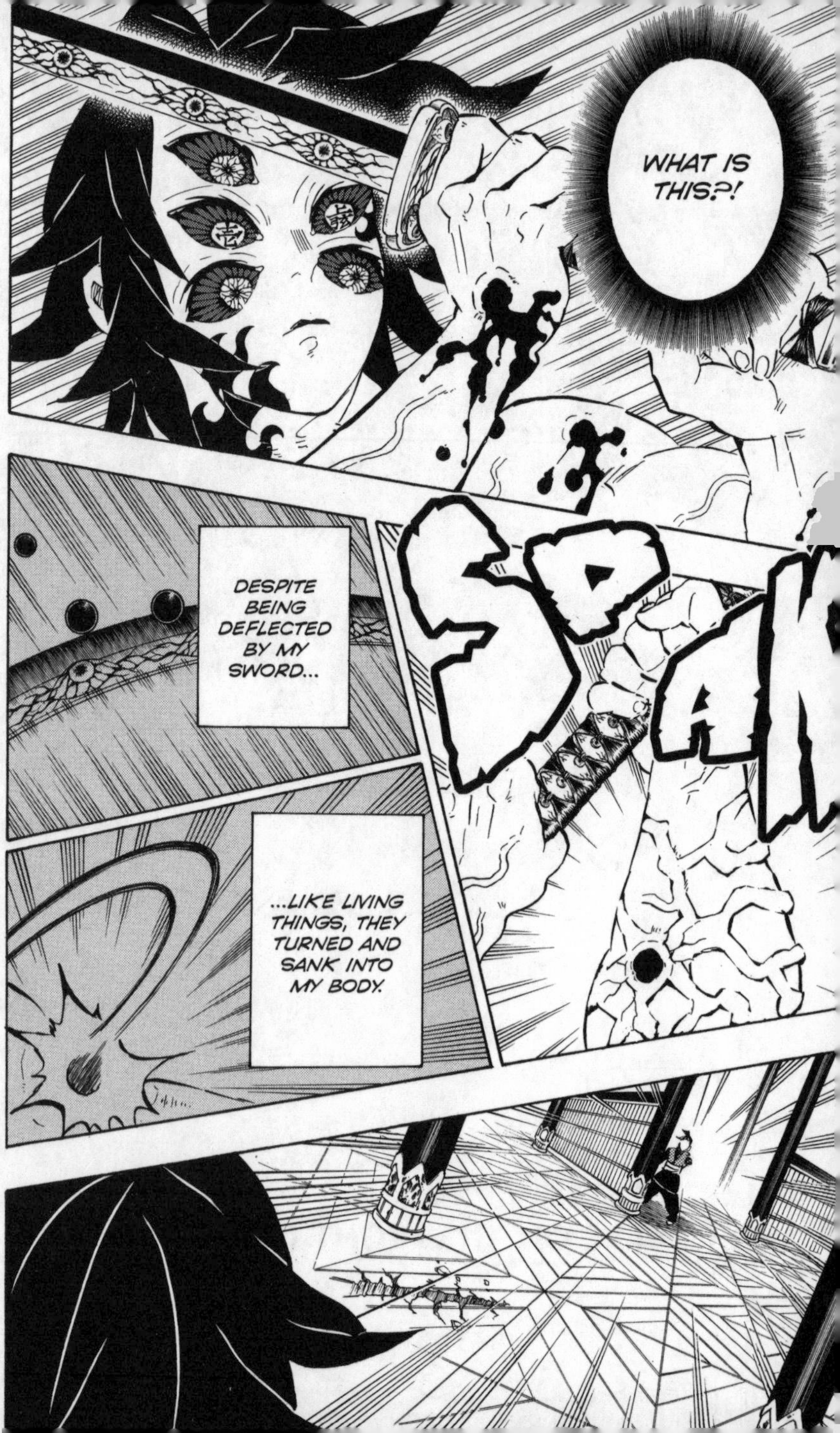
WHAT IS THIS?!
SPAK
DESPITE BEING DEFLECTED BY MY SWORD...
...LIKE LIVING THINGS, THEY TURNED AND SANK INTO MY BODY.

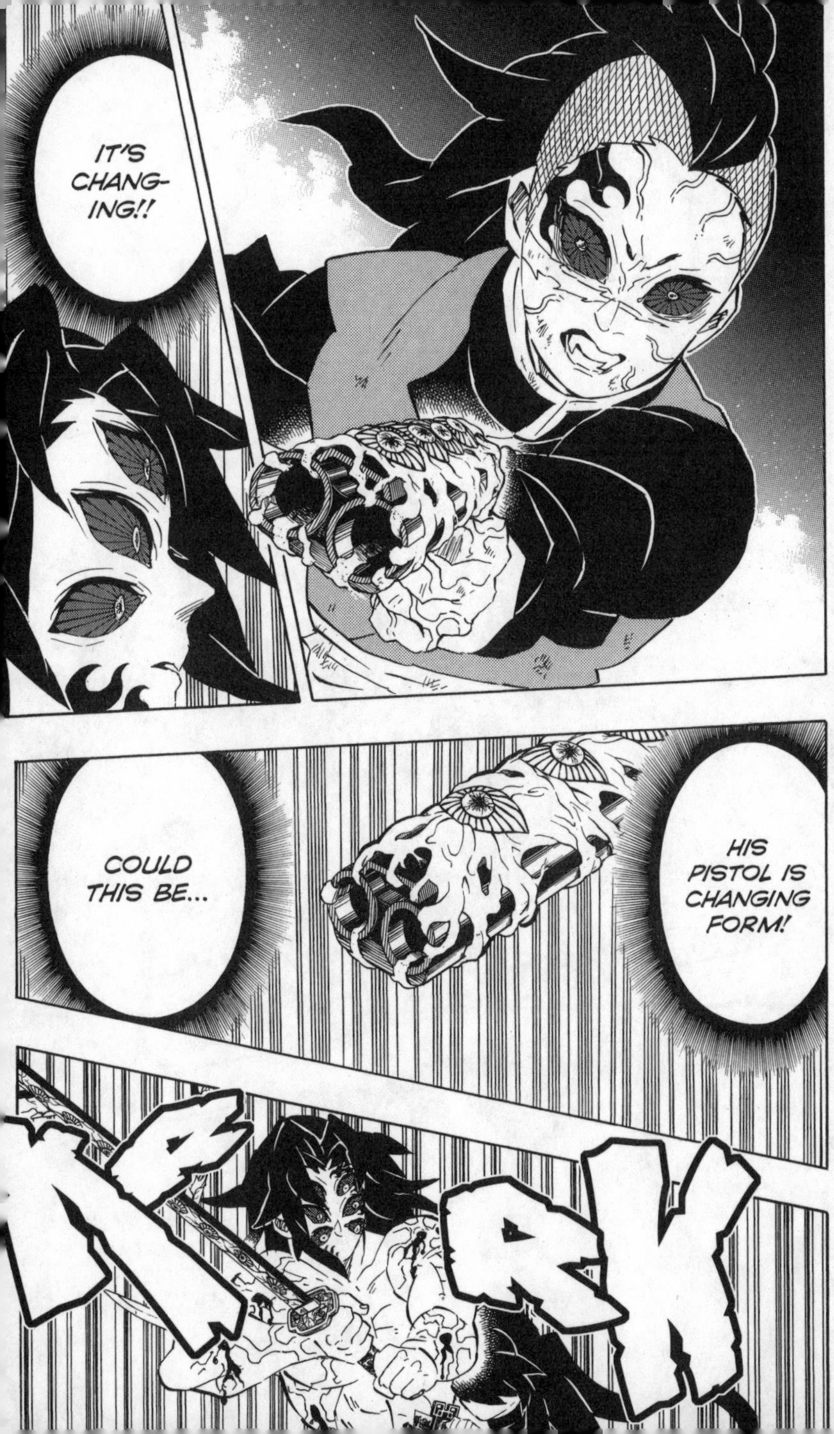
IT'S CHANGING!!
HIS PISTOL IS CHANGING FORM!
COULD THIS BE...

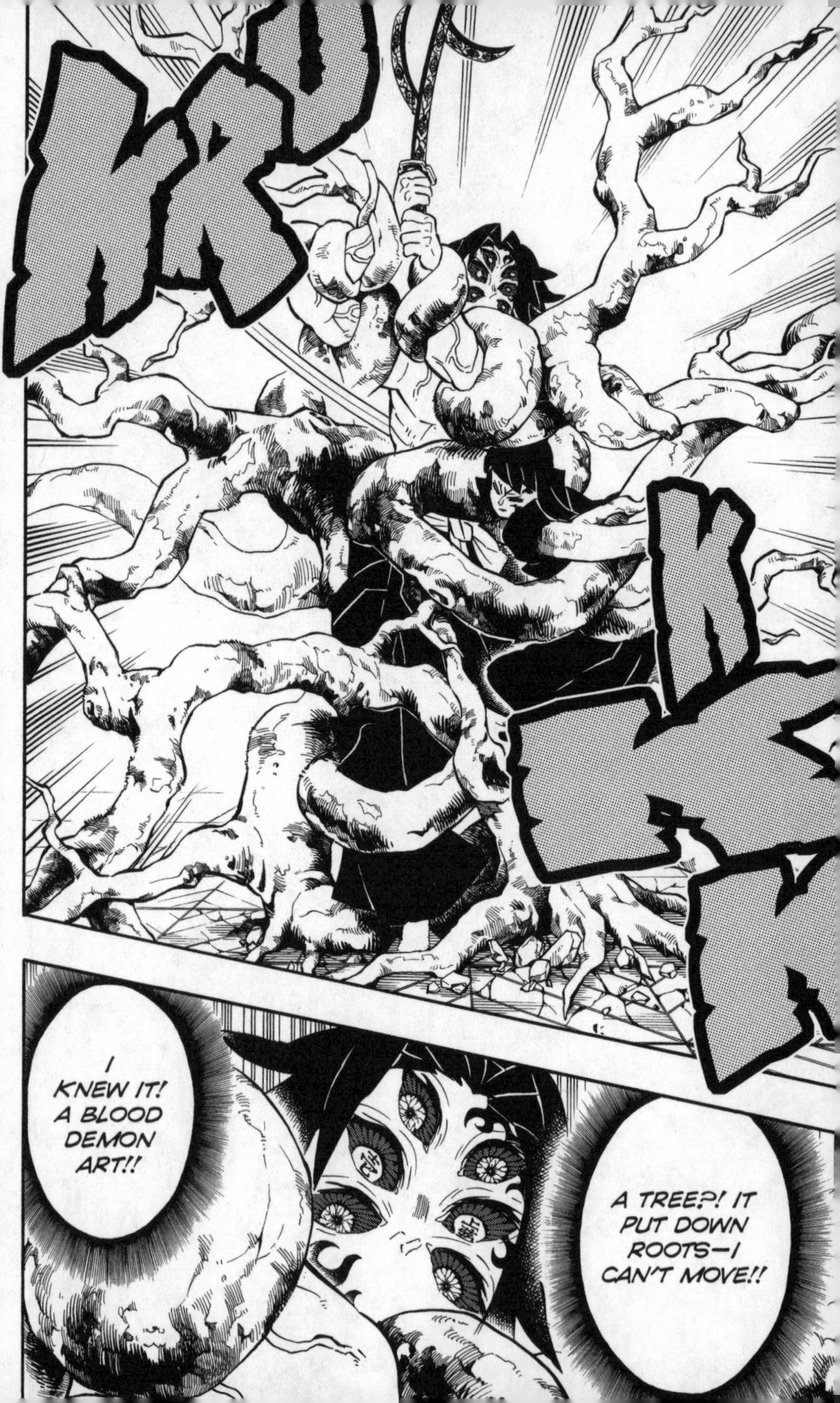
A TREE?! IT PUT DOWN ROOTS—I CAN'T MOVE!!
I KNEW IT! A BLOOD DEMON ART!!

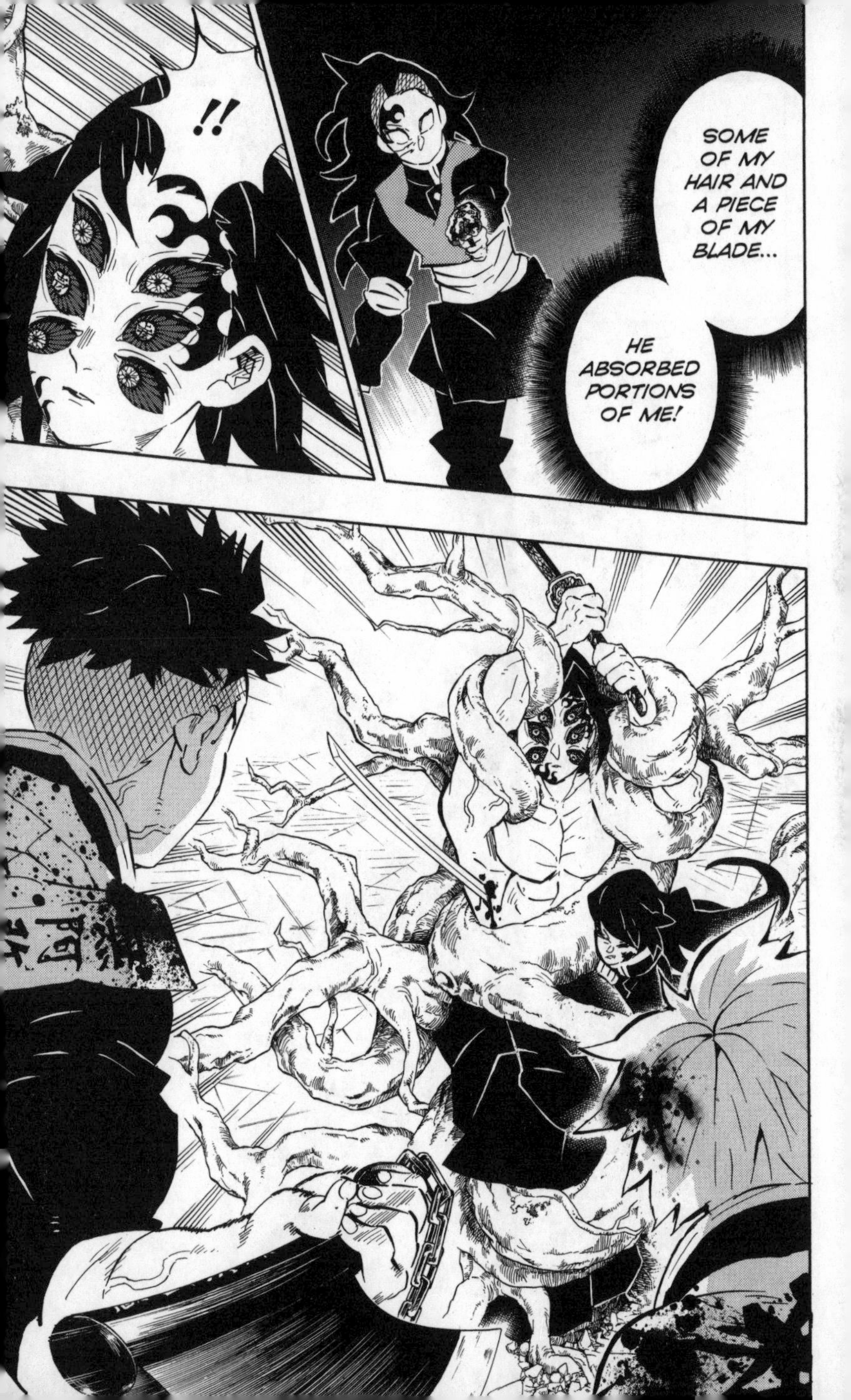
SOME OF MY HAIR AND A PIECE OF MY BLADE...
HE ABSORBED PORTIONS OF ME!
!!

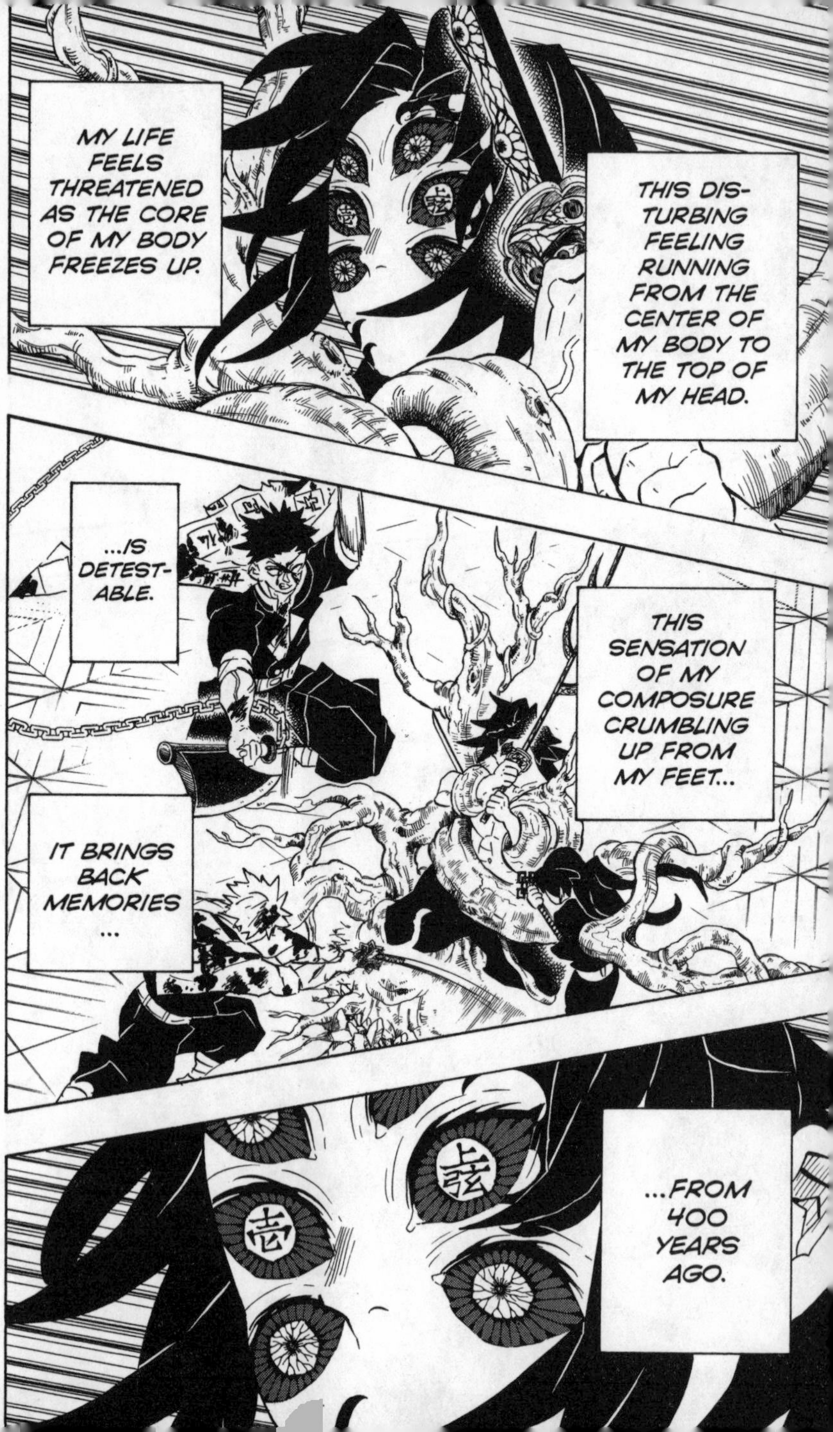
THIS DIS-
TURBING
FEELING
RUNNING
FROM THE
CENTER OF
MY BODY TO
THE TOP OF
MY HEAD.
MY LIFE
FEELS
THREATENED
AS THE CORE
OF MY BODY
FREEZES UP.
THIS
SENSATION
OF MY
COMPOSURE
CRUMBLING
UP FROM
MY FEET...
...IS
DETEST-
ABLE.
IT BRINGS
BACK
MEMORIES
...
上弦
壱
...FROM
400
YEARS
AGO.

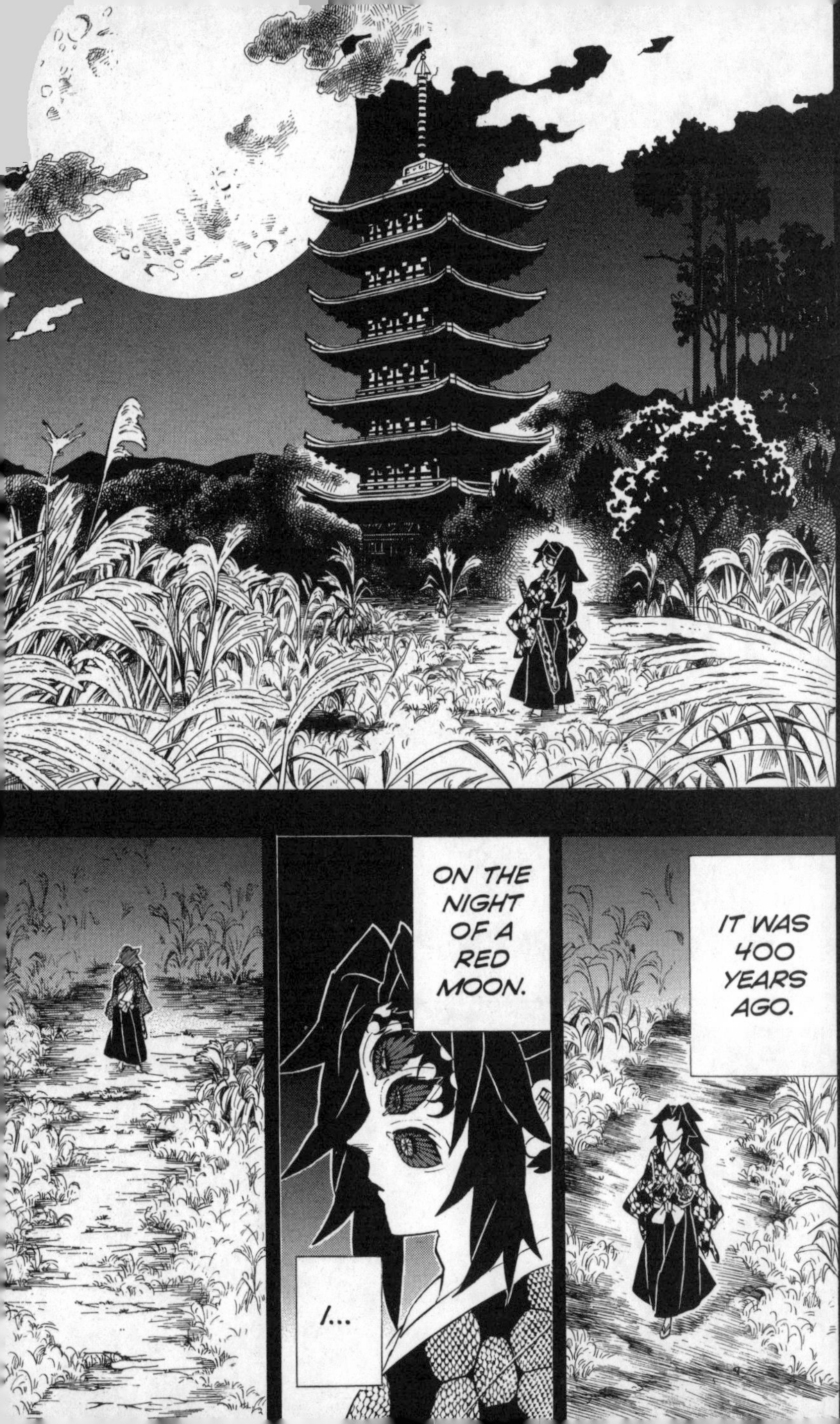
IT WAS 400 YEARS AGO.
ON THE NIGHT OF A RED MOON.
I...

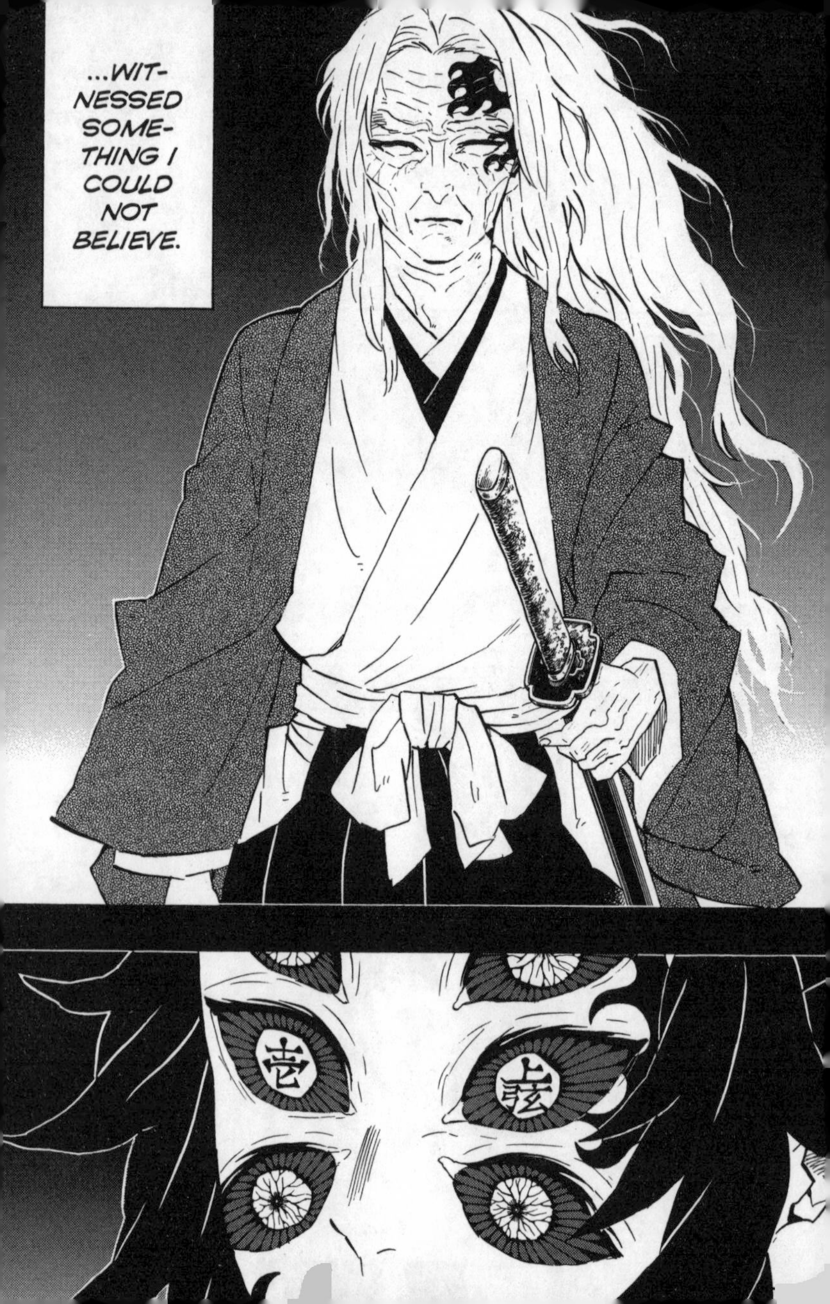
...WIT-NESSED SOME-THING I COULD NOT BELIEVE.
上弦
壱

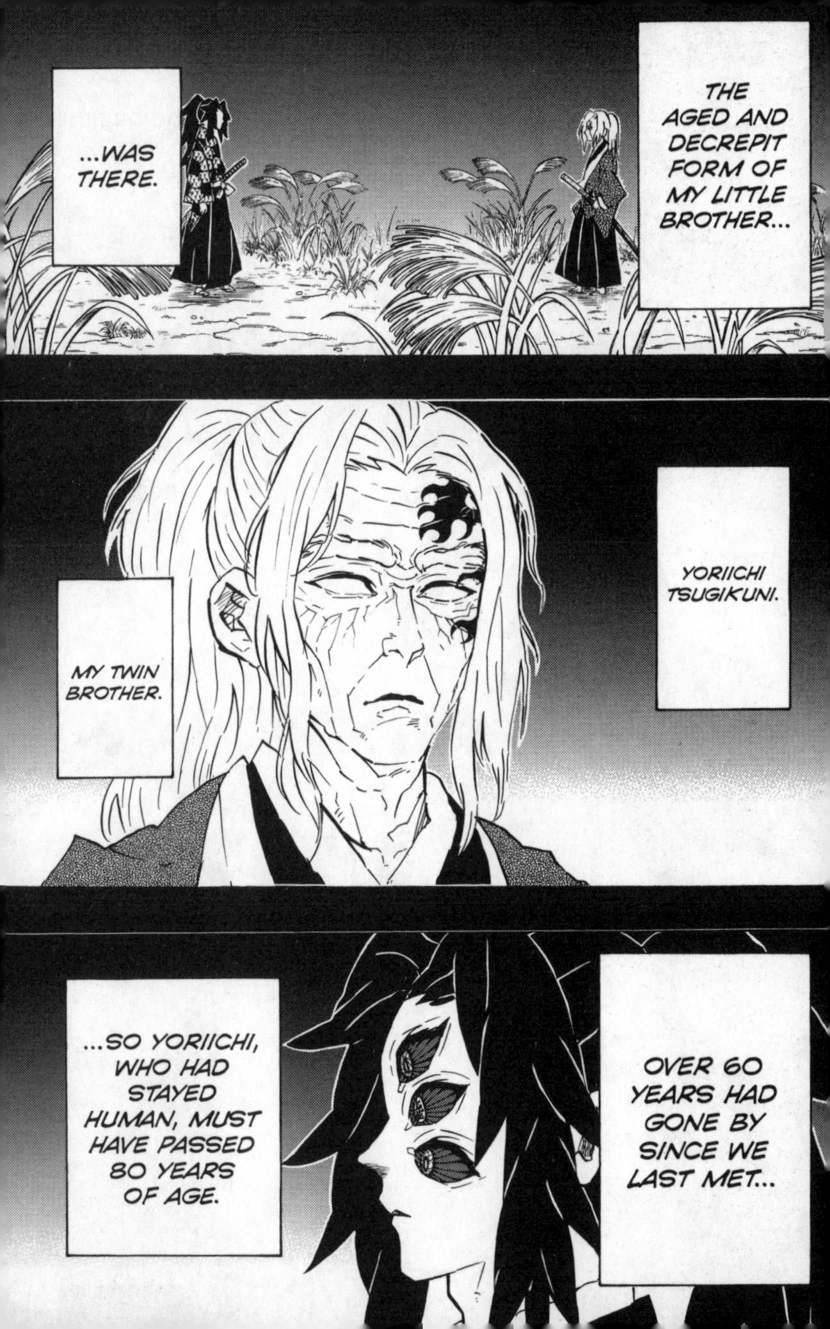
THE AGED AND DECREPIT FORM OF MY LITTLE BROTHER...
...WAS THERE.
YORIICHI TSUGIKUNI.
MY TWIN BROTHER.
OVER 60 YEARS HAD GONE BY SINCE WE LAST MET...
...SO YORIICHI, WHO HAD STAYED HUMAN, MUST HAVE PASSED 80 YEARS OF AGE.

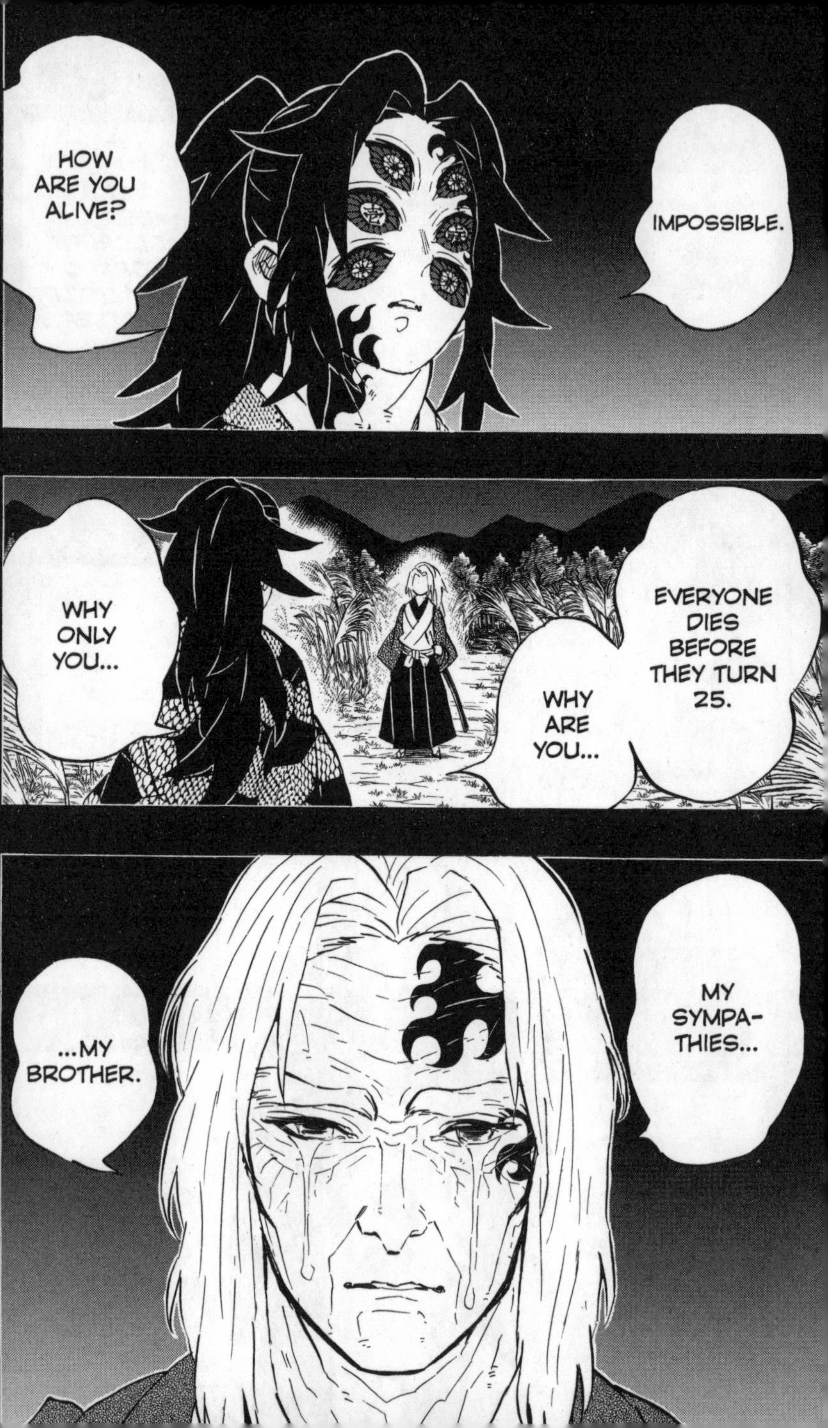
IMPOSSIBLE.
HOW ARE YOU ALIVE?
EVERYONE DIES BEFORE THEY TURN 25.
WHY ARE YOU...
WHY ONLY YOU...
MY SYMPA-THIES...
...MY BROTHER.

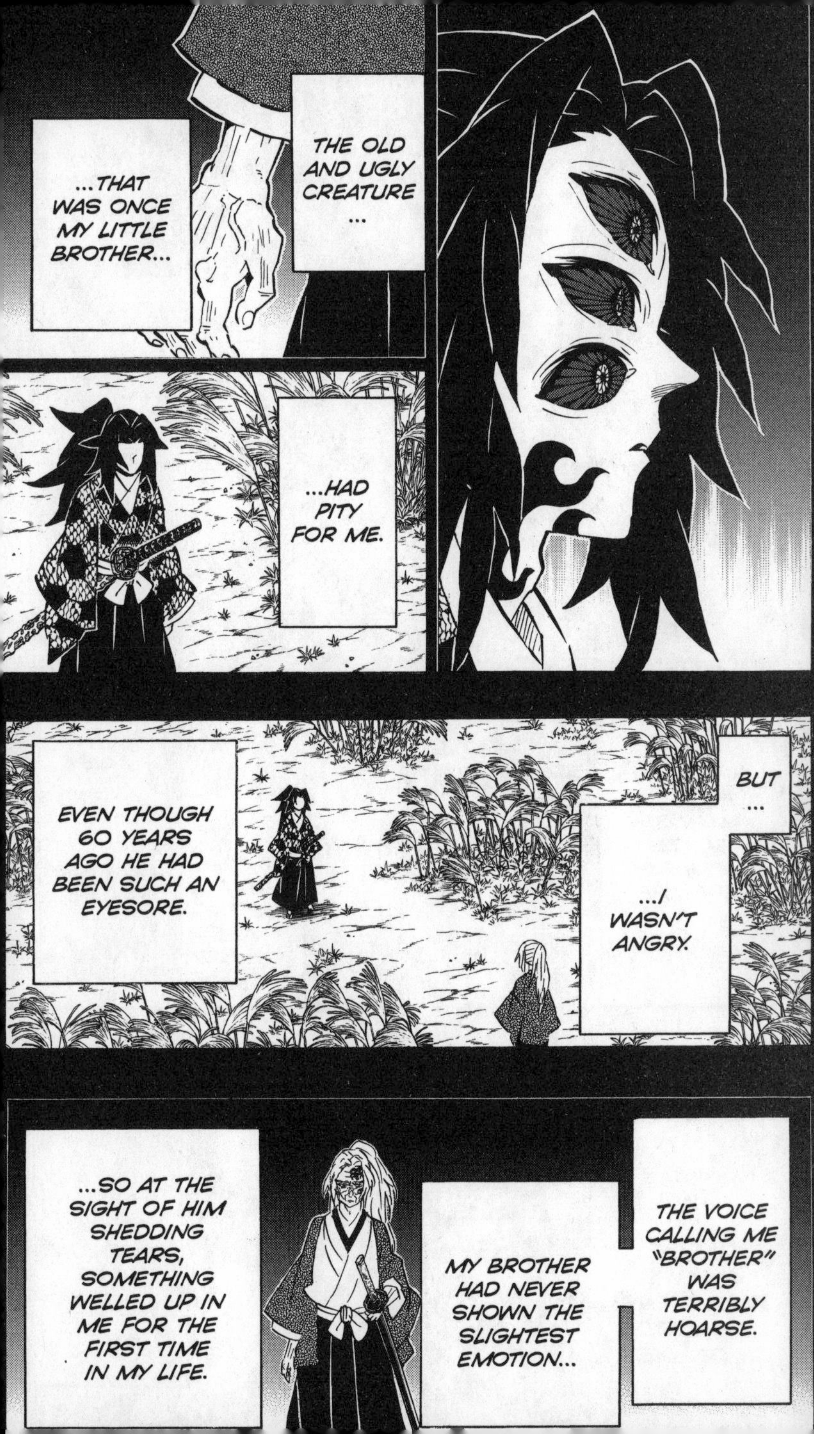
THE OLD AND UGLY CREATURE...
...THAT WAS ONCE MY LITTLE BROTHER...
...HAD PITY FOR ME.
BUT...
...I WASN'T ANGRY.
EVEN THOUGH 60 YEARS AGO HE HAD BEEN SUCH AN EYESORE.
THE VOICE CALLING ME "BROTHER" WAS TERRIBLY HOARSE.
MY BROTHER HAD NEVER SHOWN THE SLIGHTEST EMOTION...
...SO AT THE SIGHT OF HIM SHEDDING TEARS, SOMETHING WELLED UP IN ME FOR THE FIRST TIME IN MY LIFE.

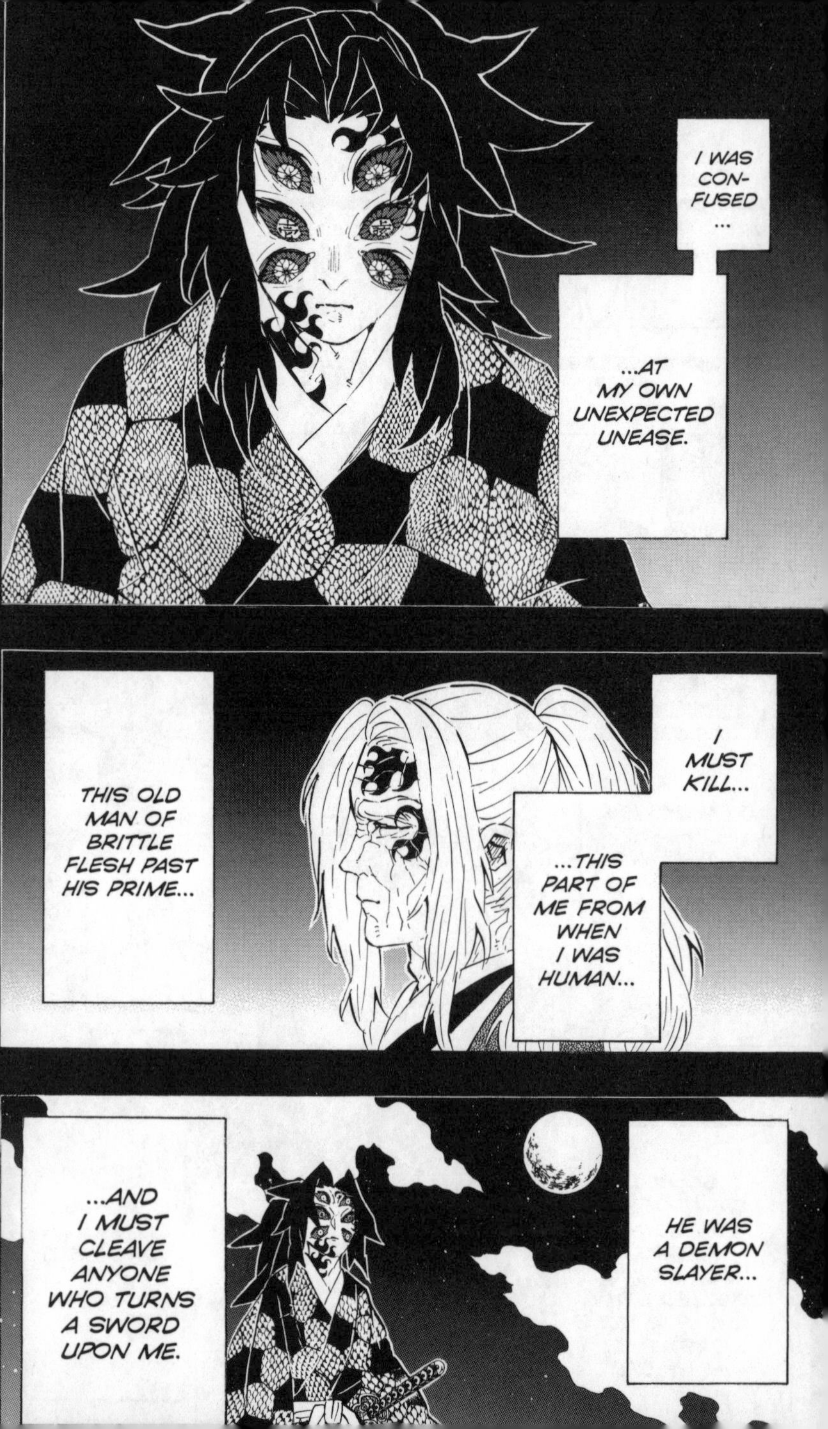
I WAS CON-FUSED ...
...AT MY OWN UNEXPECTED UNEASE.
I MUST KILL...
...THIS PART OF ME FROM WHEN I WAS HUMAN...
THIS OLD MAN OF BRITTLE FLESH PAST HIS PRIME...
HE WAS A DEMON SLAYER...
...AND I MUST CLEAVE ANYONE WHO TURNS A SWORD UPON ME.

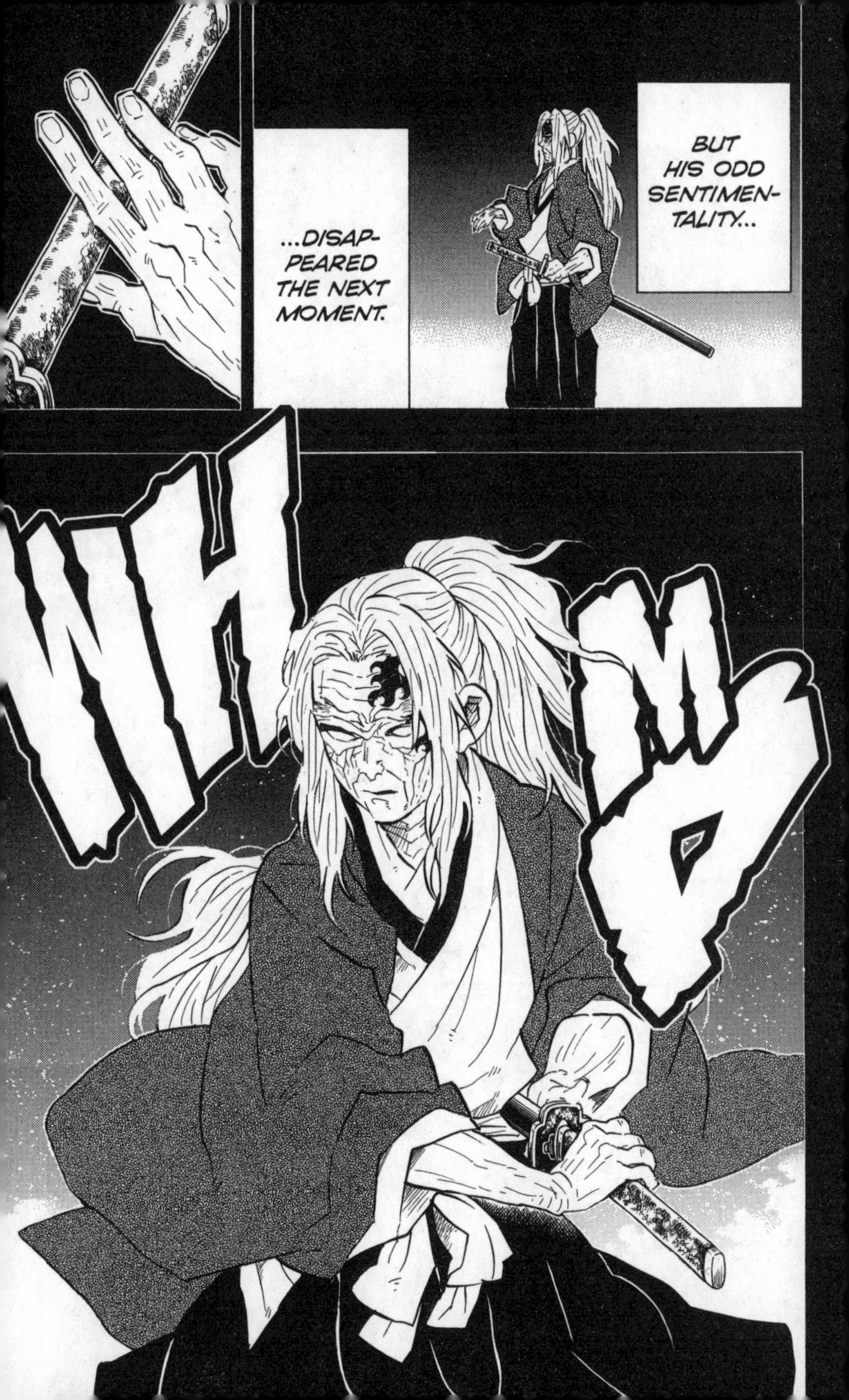
BUT HIS ODD SENTIMEN-TALITY...
...DISAP-PEARED THE NEXT MOMENT.

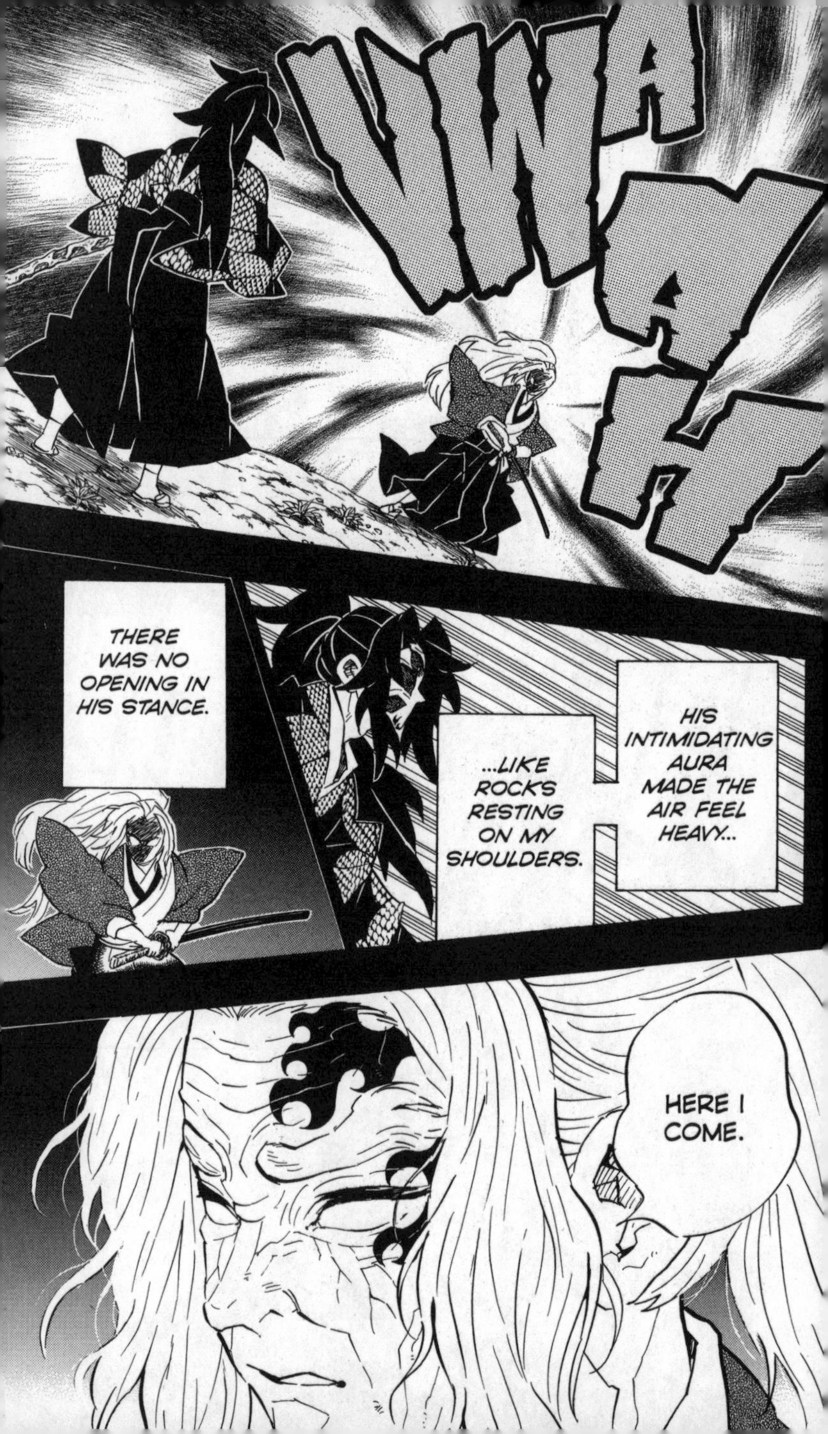
VWAAH
HIS INTIMIDATING AURA MADE THE AIR FEEL HEAVY...
...LIKE ROCKS RESTING ON MY SHOULDERS.
THERE WAS NO OPENING IN HIS STANCE.
HERE I COME.

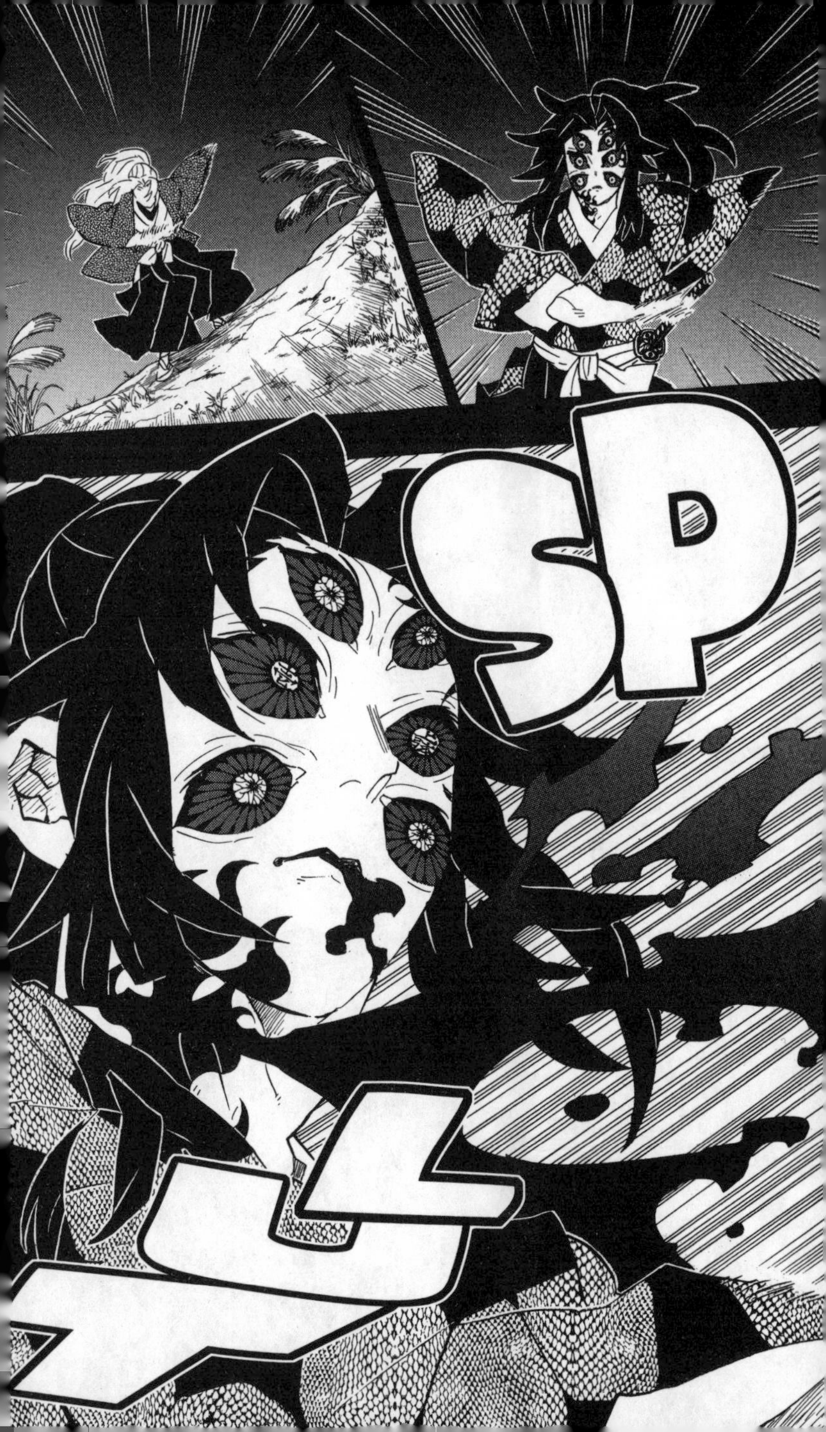
SP

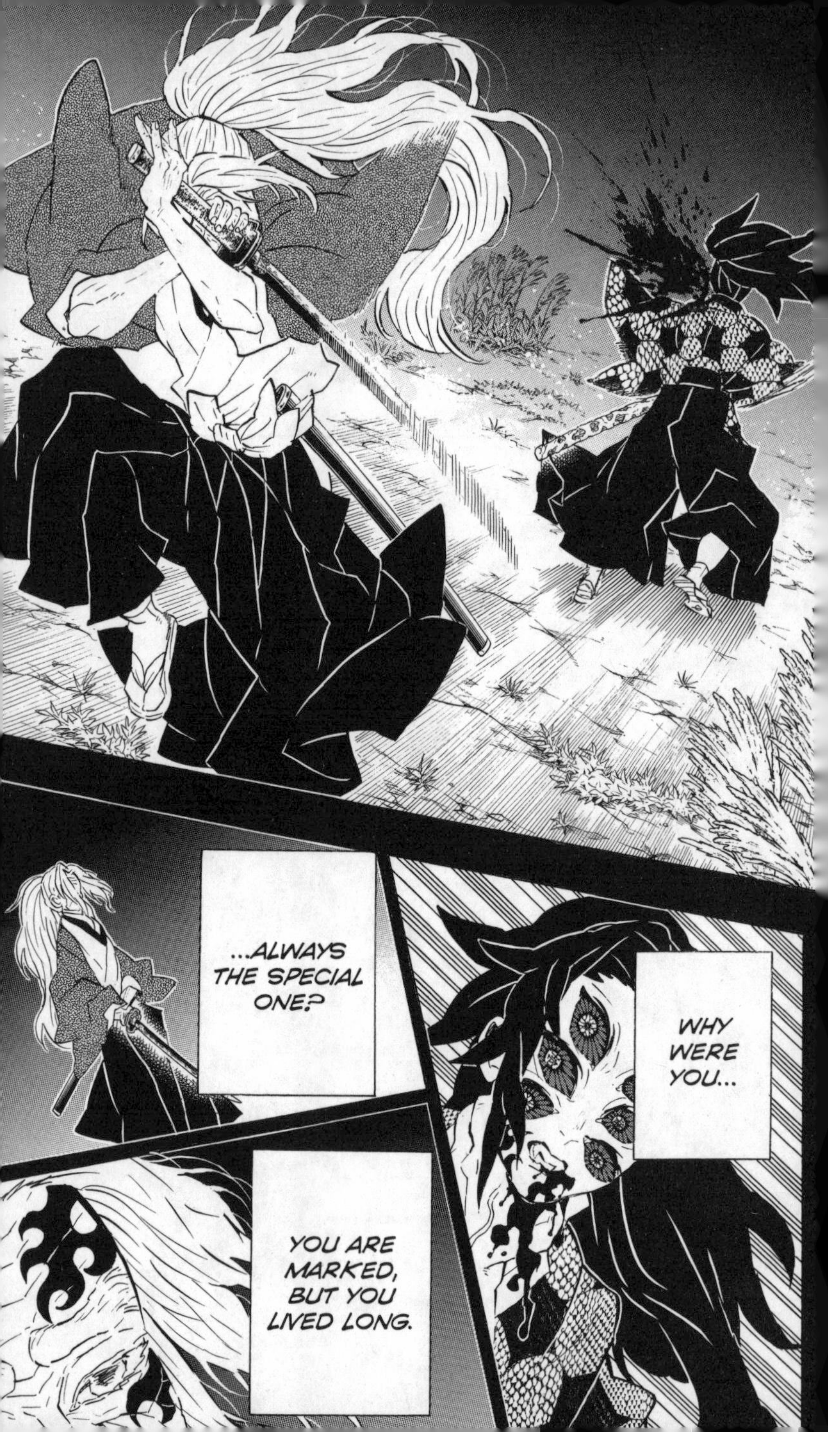
WHY WERE YOU...
...ALWAYS THE SPECIAL ONE?
YOU ARE MARKED, BUT YOU LIVED LONG.

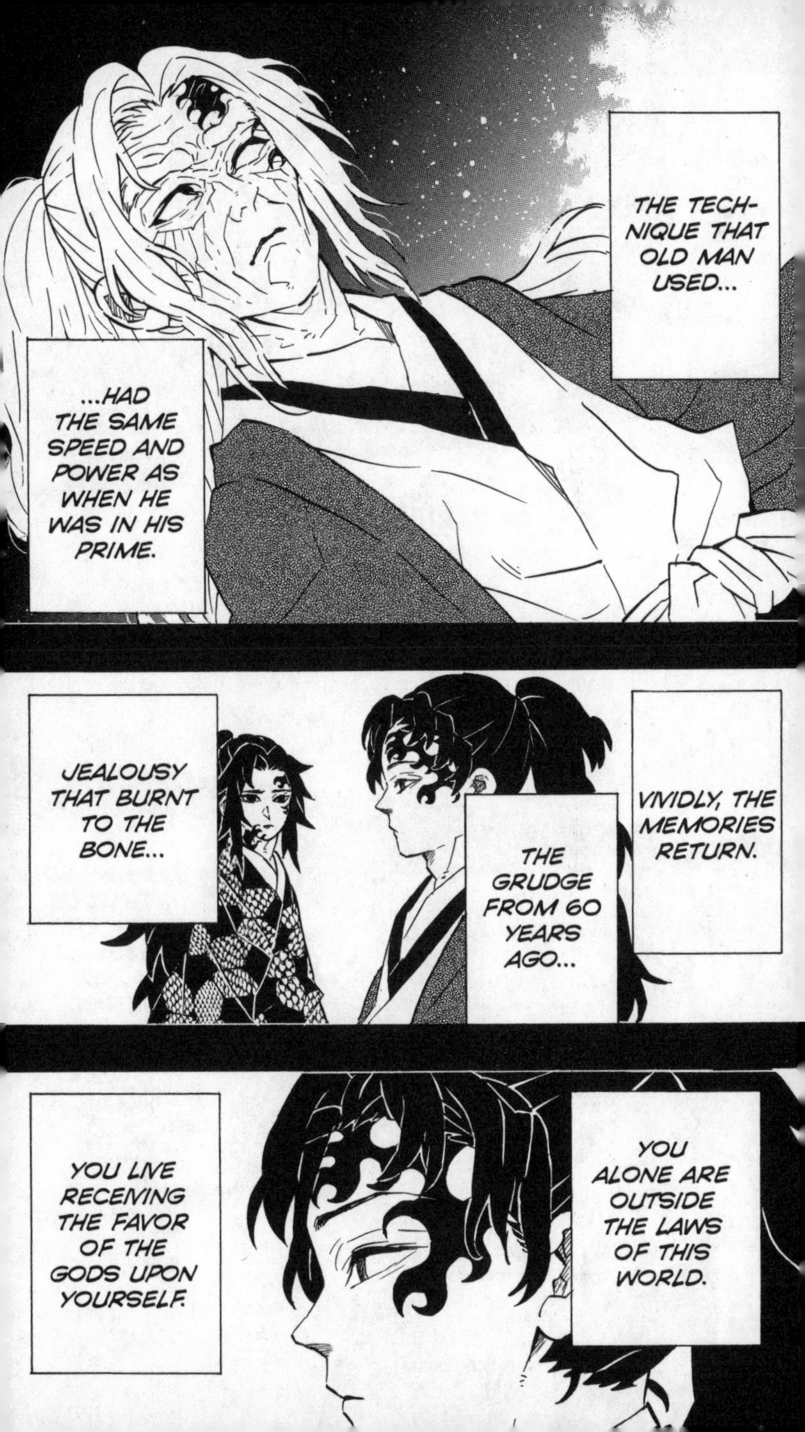
THE TECHNIQUE THAT OLD MAN USED...
...HAD THE SAME SPEED AND POWER AS WHEN HE WAS IN HIS PRIME.
VIVIDLY, THE MEMORIES RETURN.
THE GRUDGE FROM 60 YEARS AGO...
JEALOUSY THAT BURNT TO THE BONE...
YOU ALONE ARE OUTSIDE THE LAWS OF THIS WORLD.
YOU LIVE RECEIVING THE FAVOR OF THE GODS UPON YOURSELF.

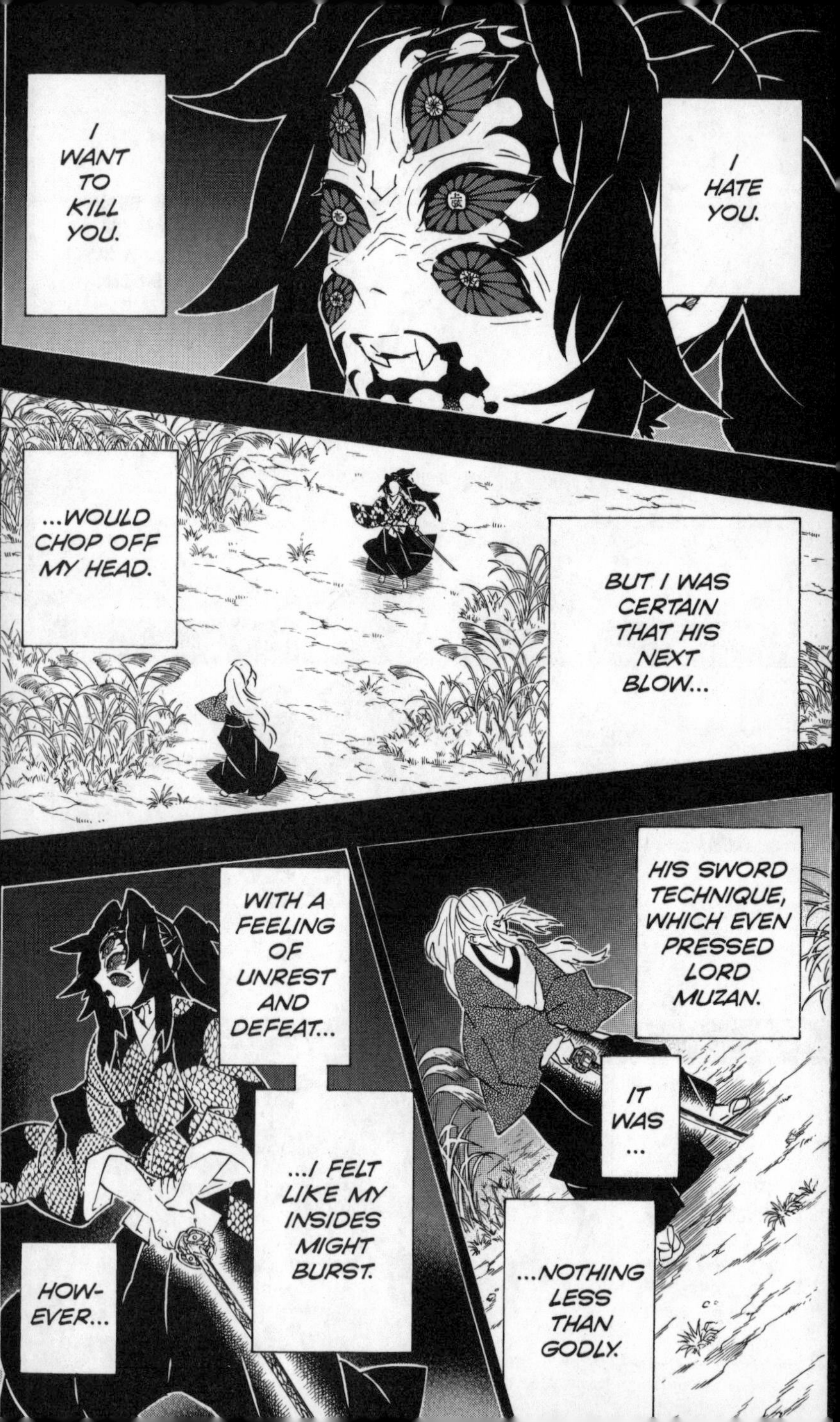
I HATE YOU.
I WANT TO KILL YOU.
BUT I WAS CERTAIN THAT HIS NEXT BLOW...
...WOULD CHOP OFF MY HEAD.
HIS SWORD TECHNIQUE, WHICH EVEN PRESSED LORD MUZAN.
IT WAS...
...NOTHING LESS THAN GODLY.
WITH A FEELING OF UNREST AND DEFEAT...
...I FELT LIKE MY INSIDES MIGHT BURST.
HOW-EVER...

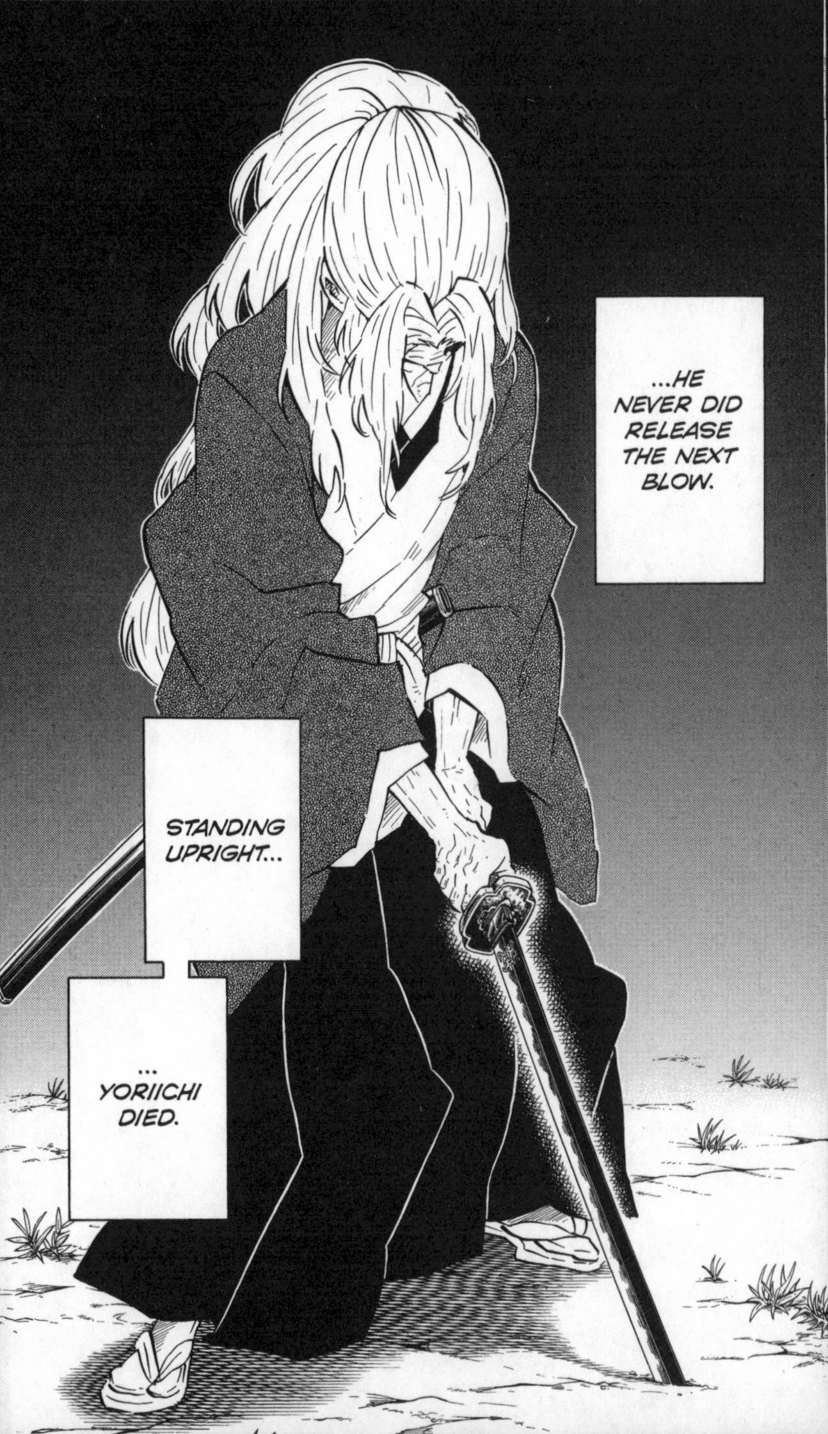
...HE NEVER DID RELEASE THE NEXT BLOW.
STANDING UPRIGHT...
... YORIICHI DIED.

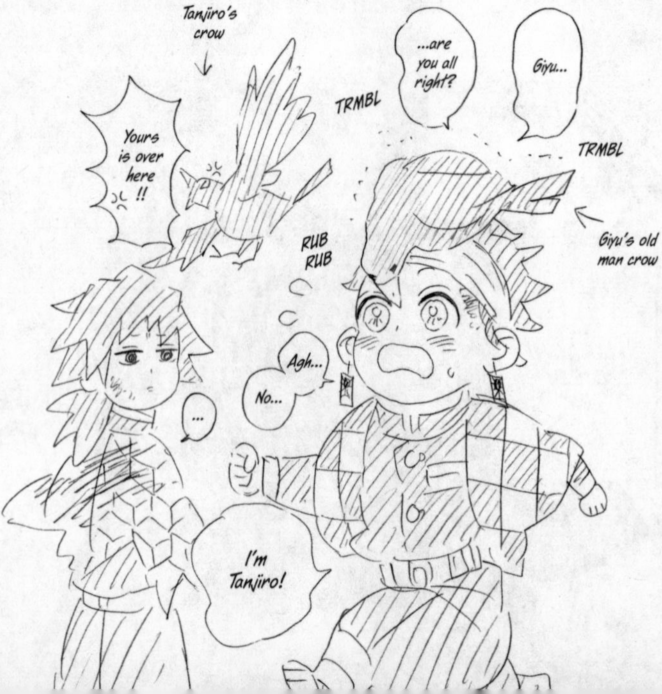
Giyu...
...are you all right?
TRMBL
TRMBL
Giyu's old man crow
Tanjiro's crow
Yours is over here!!
RUB RUB
Agh...
No...
...
I'm Tanjiro!

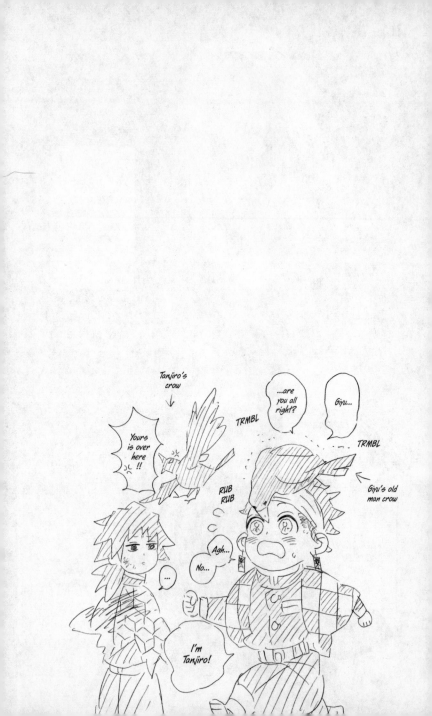

CHAPTER 175: RESPECT FOR FUTURE GENERATIONS

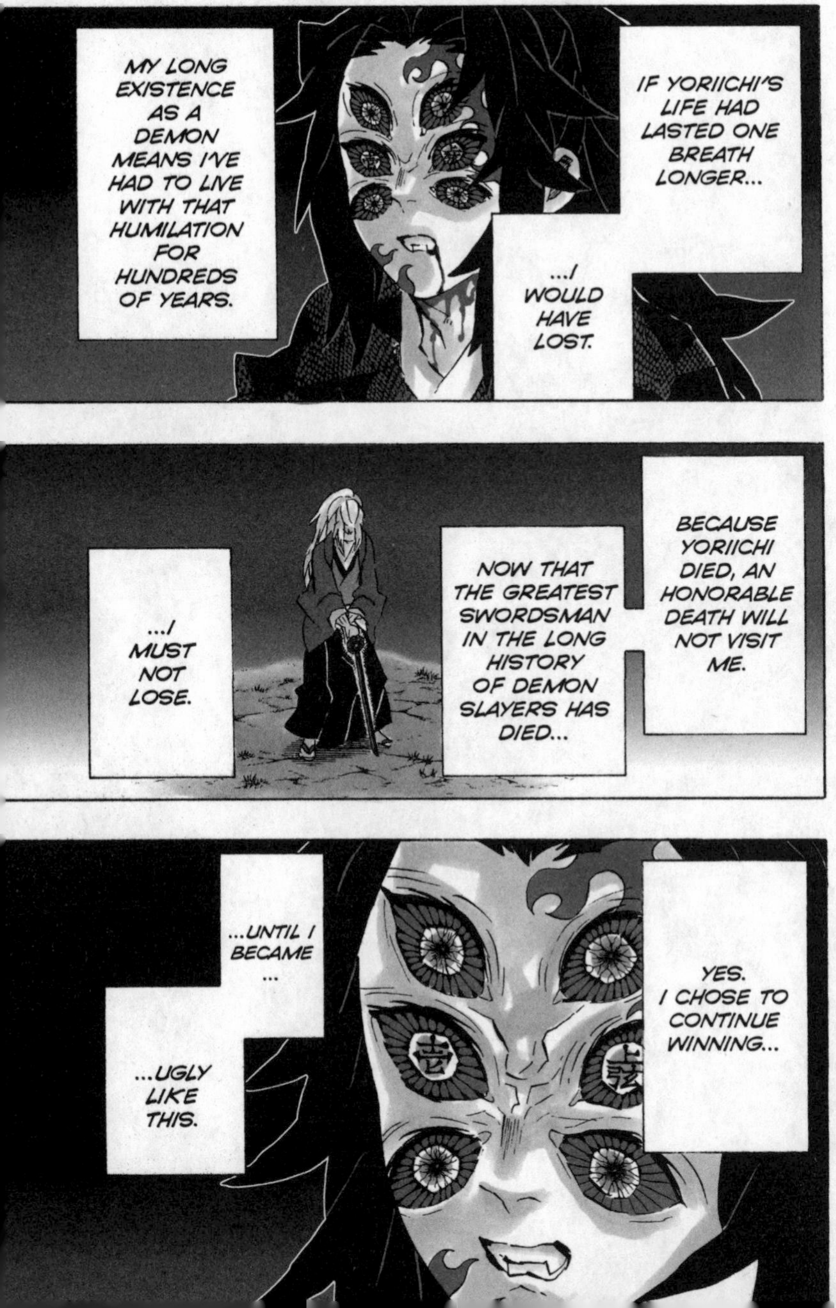
IF YORIICHI'S LIFE HAD LASTED ONE BREATH LONGER...
...I WOULD HAVE LOST.
MY LONG EXISTENCE AS A DEMON MEANS I'VE HAD TO LIVE WITH THAT HUMILATION FOR HUNDREDS OF YEARS.
BECAUSE YORIICHI DIED, AN HONORABLE DEATH WILL NOT VISIT ME.
NOW THAT THE GREATEST SWORDSMAN IN THE LONG HISTORY OF DEMON SLAYERS HAS DIED...
...I MUST NOT LOSE.
YES. I CHOSE TO CONTINUE WINNING...
...UNTIL I BECAME ...
...UGLY LIKE THIS.

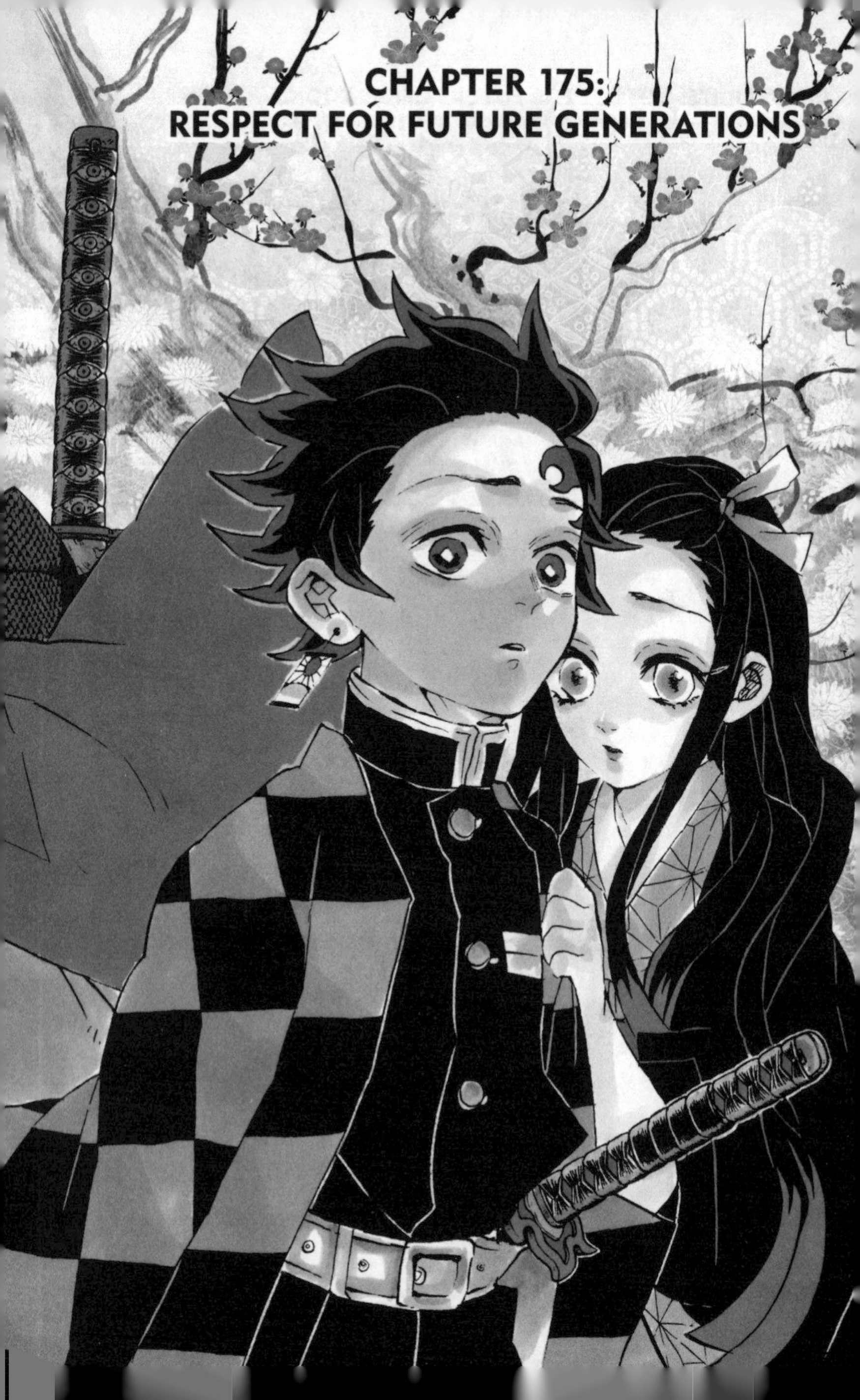
CHAPTER 175:
RESPECT FOR FUTURE GENERATIONS

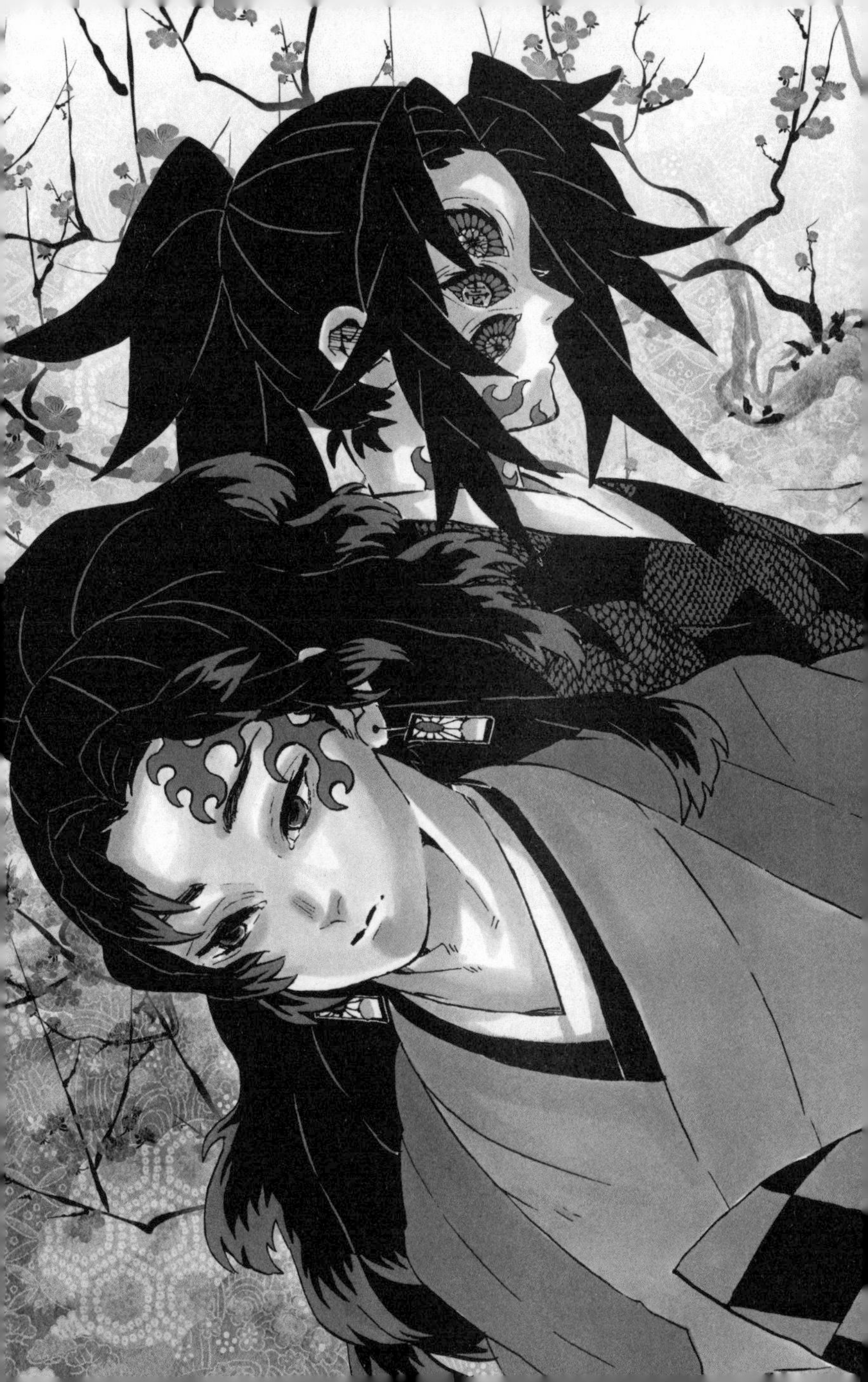

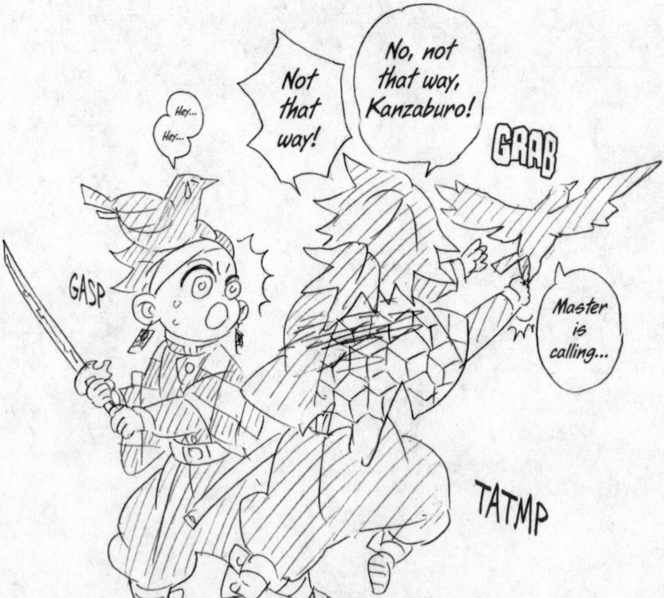
GRAB
No, not that way, Kanzaburo!
Not that way!
Hey... Hey...
Master is calling...
GASP
TATMP

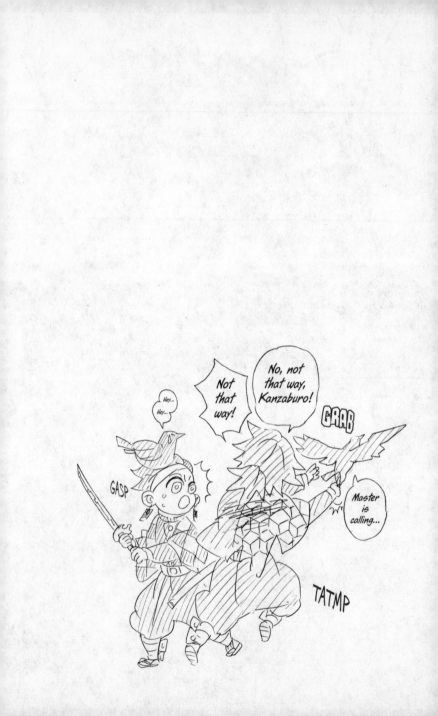

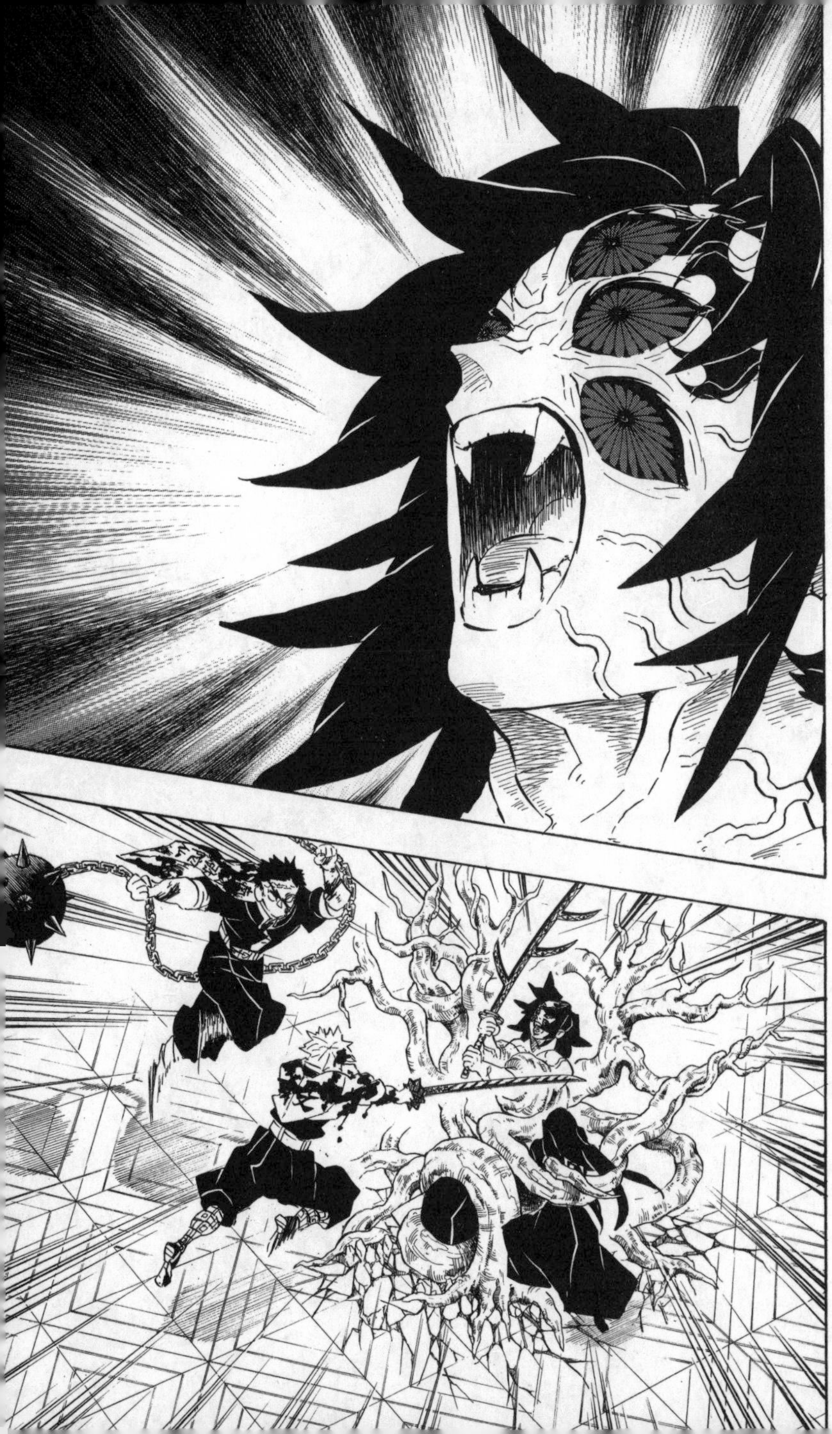

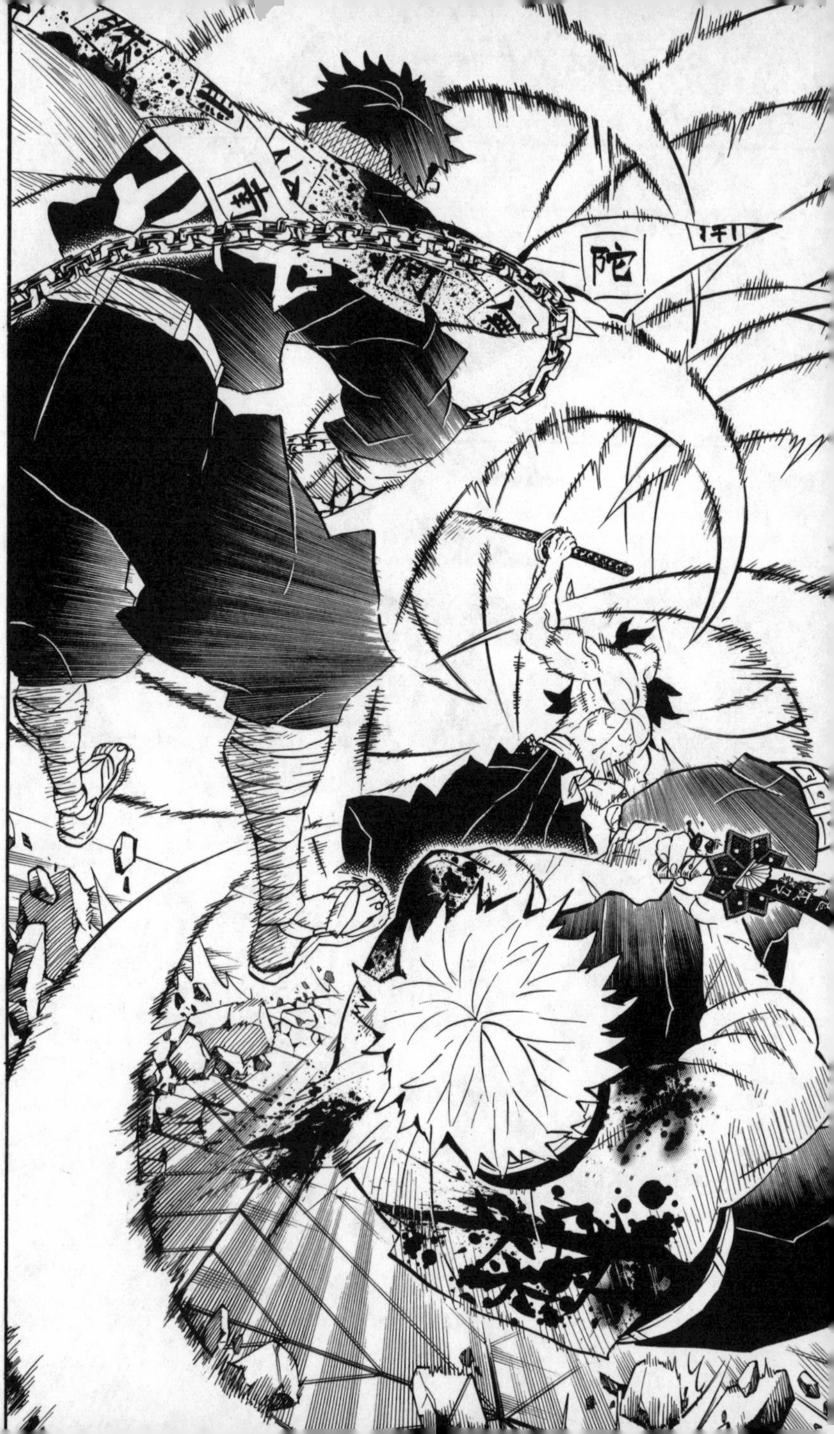
陀

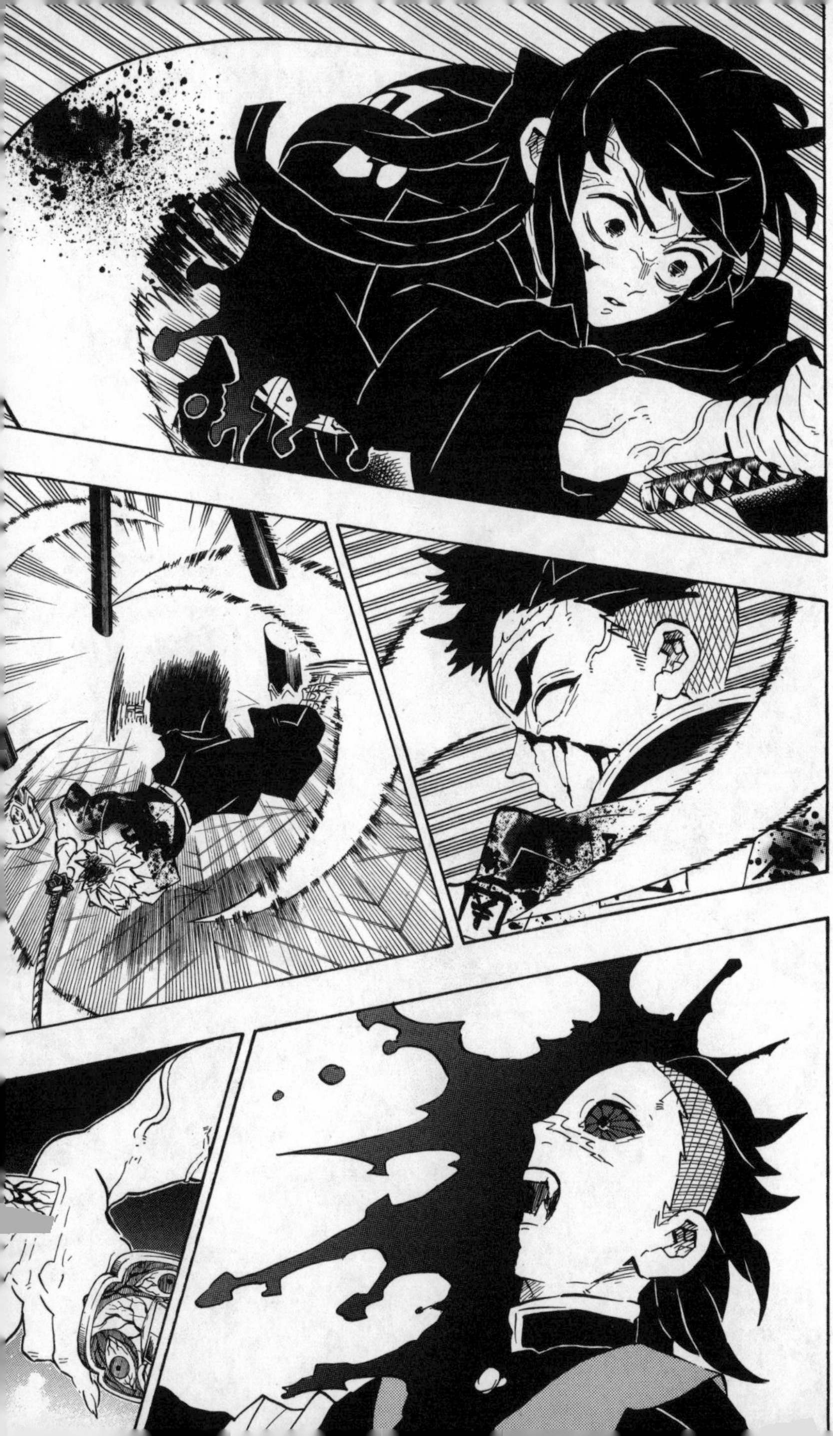

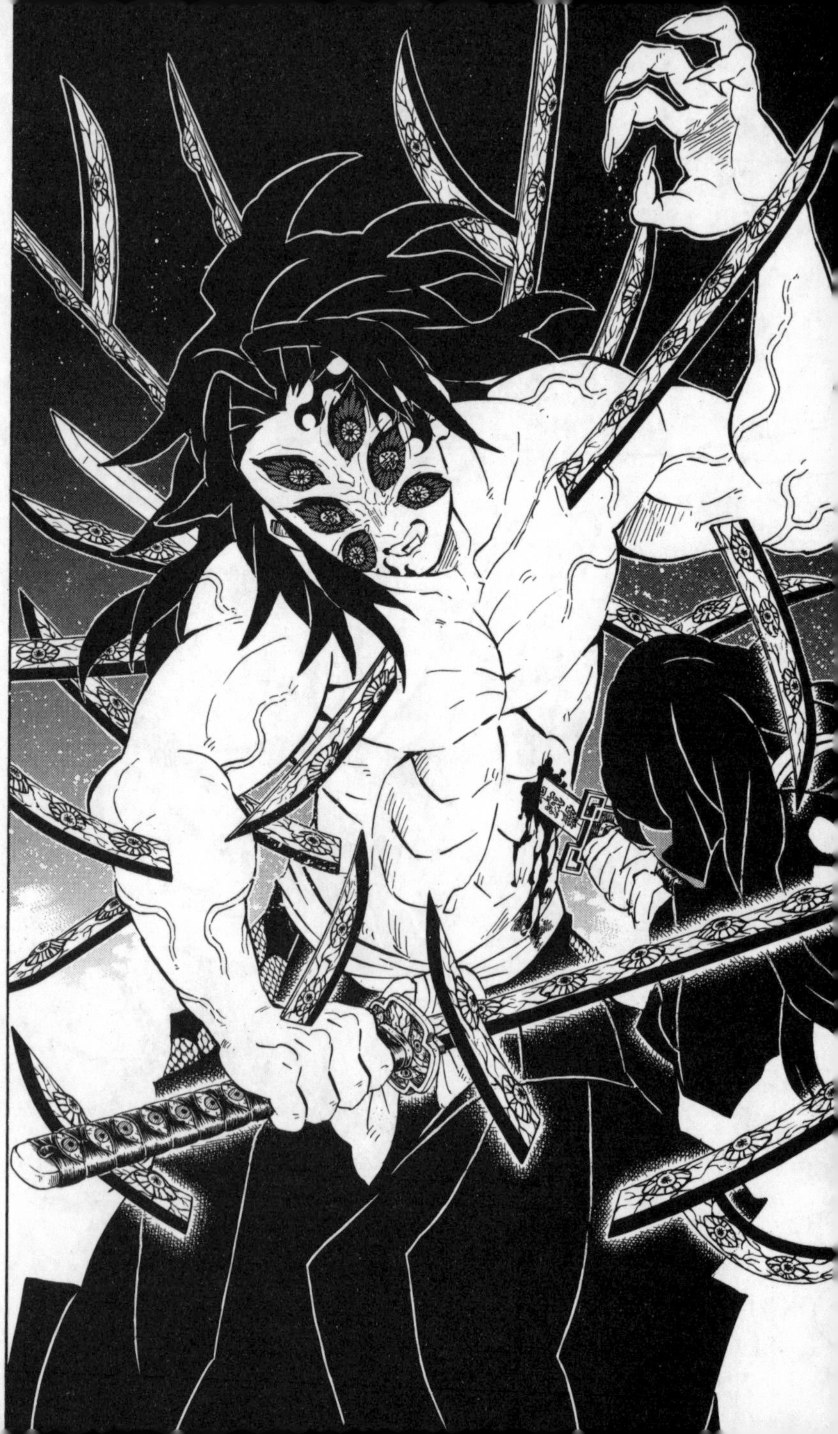

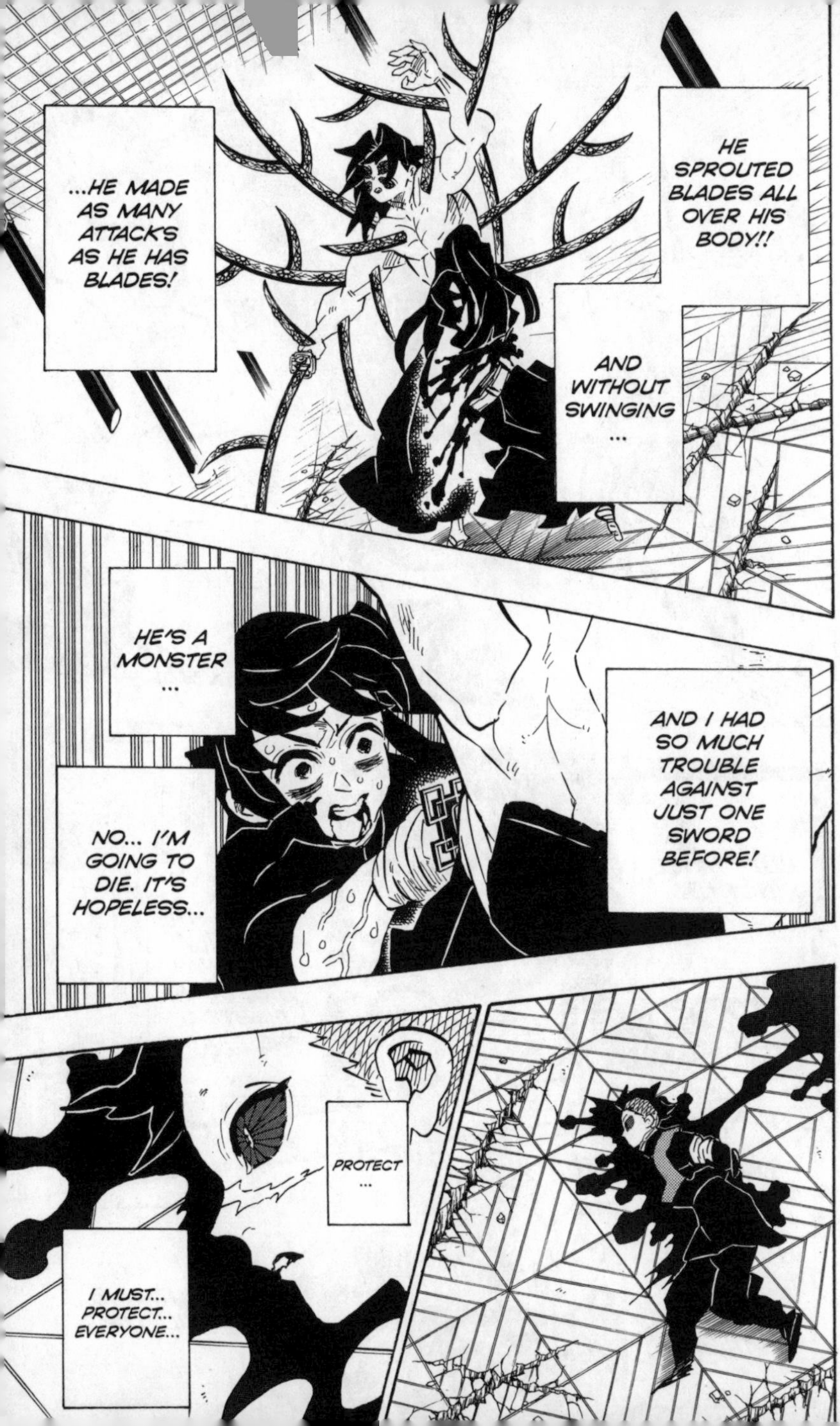
HE SPROUTED BLADES ALL OVER HIS BODY!!
AND WITHOUT SWINGING ...
...HE MADE AS MANY ATTACKS AS HE HAS BLADES!
AND I HAD SO MUCH TROUBLE AGAINST JUST ONE SWORD BEFORE!
HE'S A MONSTER ...
NO... I'M GOING TO DIE. IT'S HOPELESS...
PROTECT ...
I MUST... PROTECT... EVERYONE...

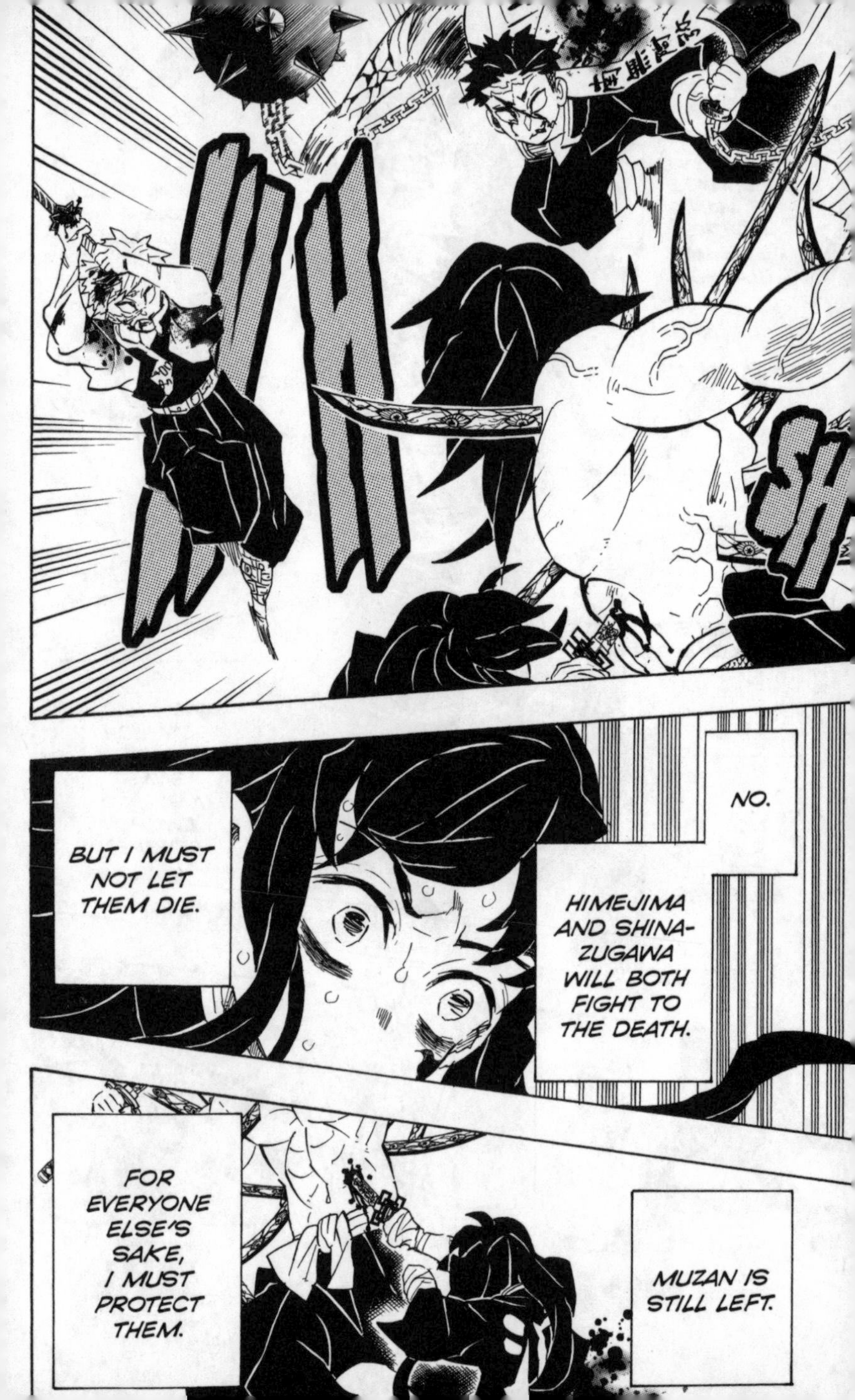
SH
WHA
NO.
HIMEJIMA AND SHINA-ZUGAWA WILL BOTH FIGHT TO THE DEATH.
BUT I MUST NOT LET THEM DIE.
MUZAN IS STILL LEFT.
FOR EVERYONE ELSE'S SAKE, I MUST PROTECT THEM.

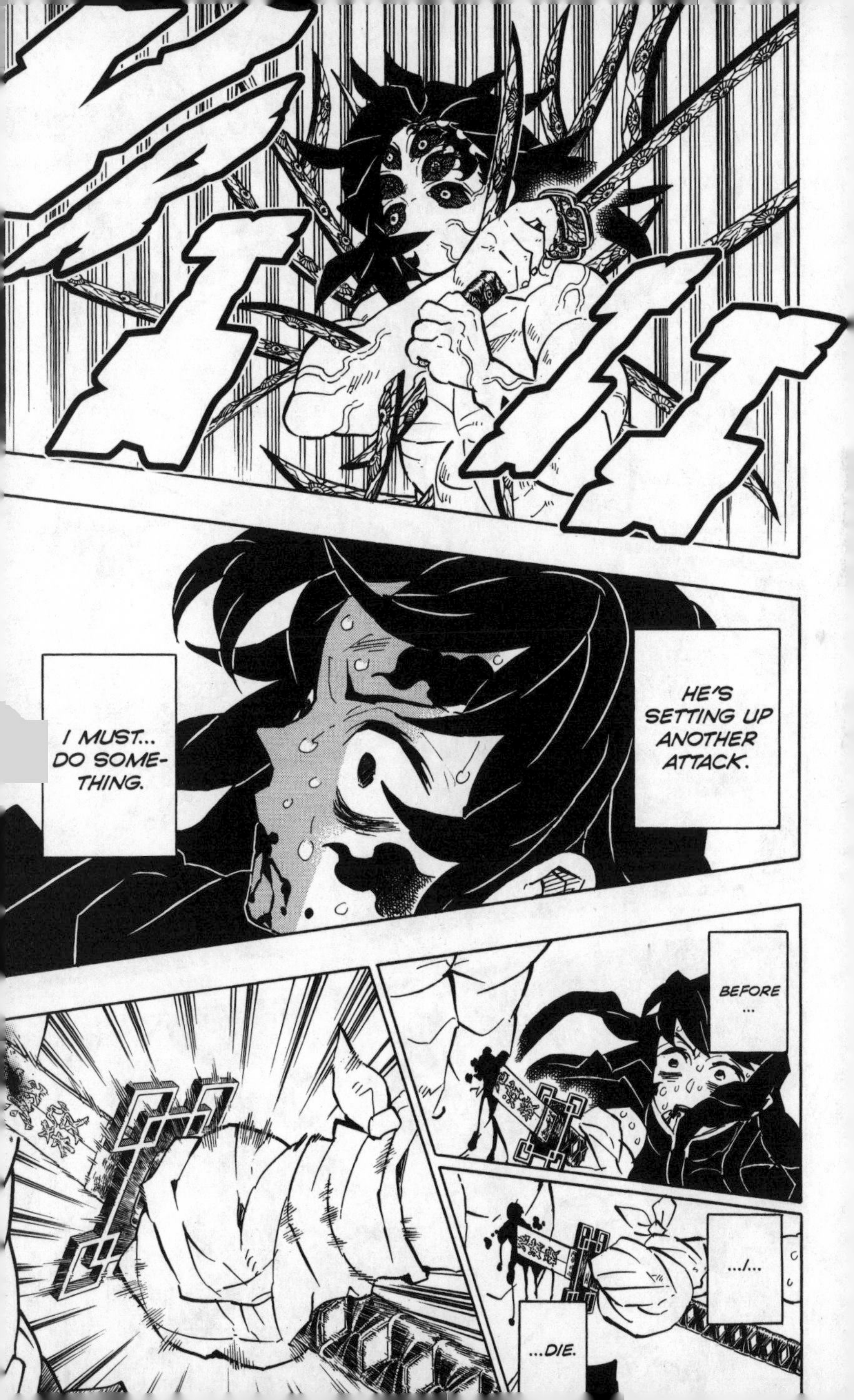
HE'S SETTING UP ANOTHER ATTACK.
I MUST... DO SOME-THING.
BEFORE ...
.../...
...DIE.

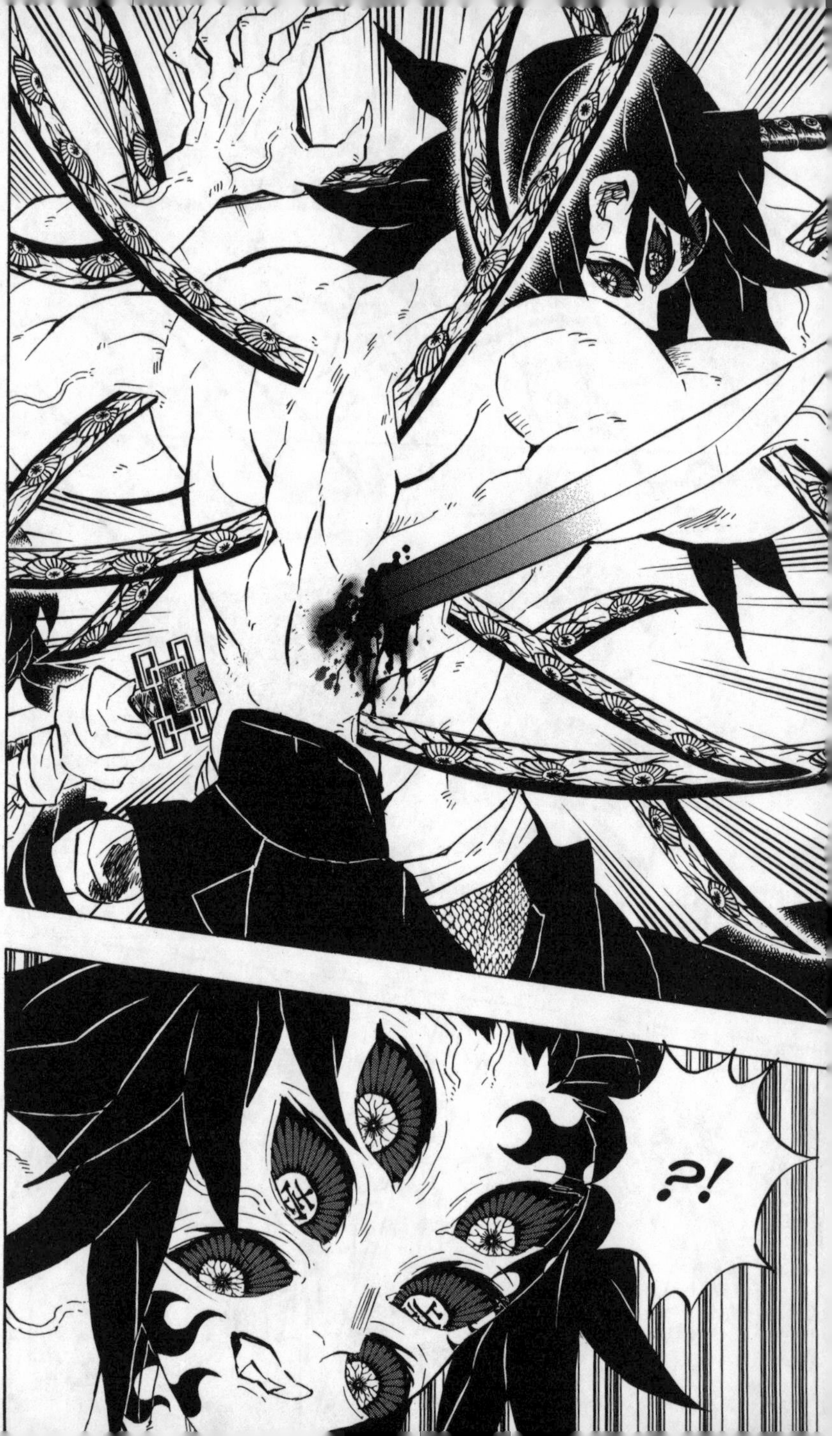
?!

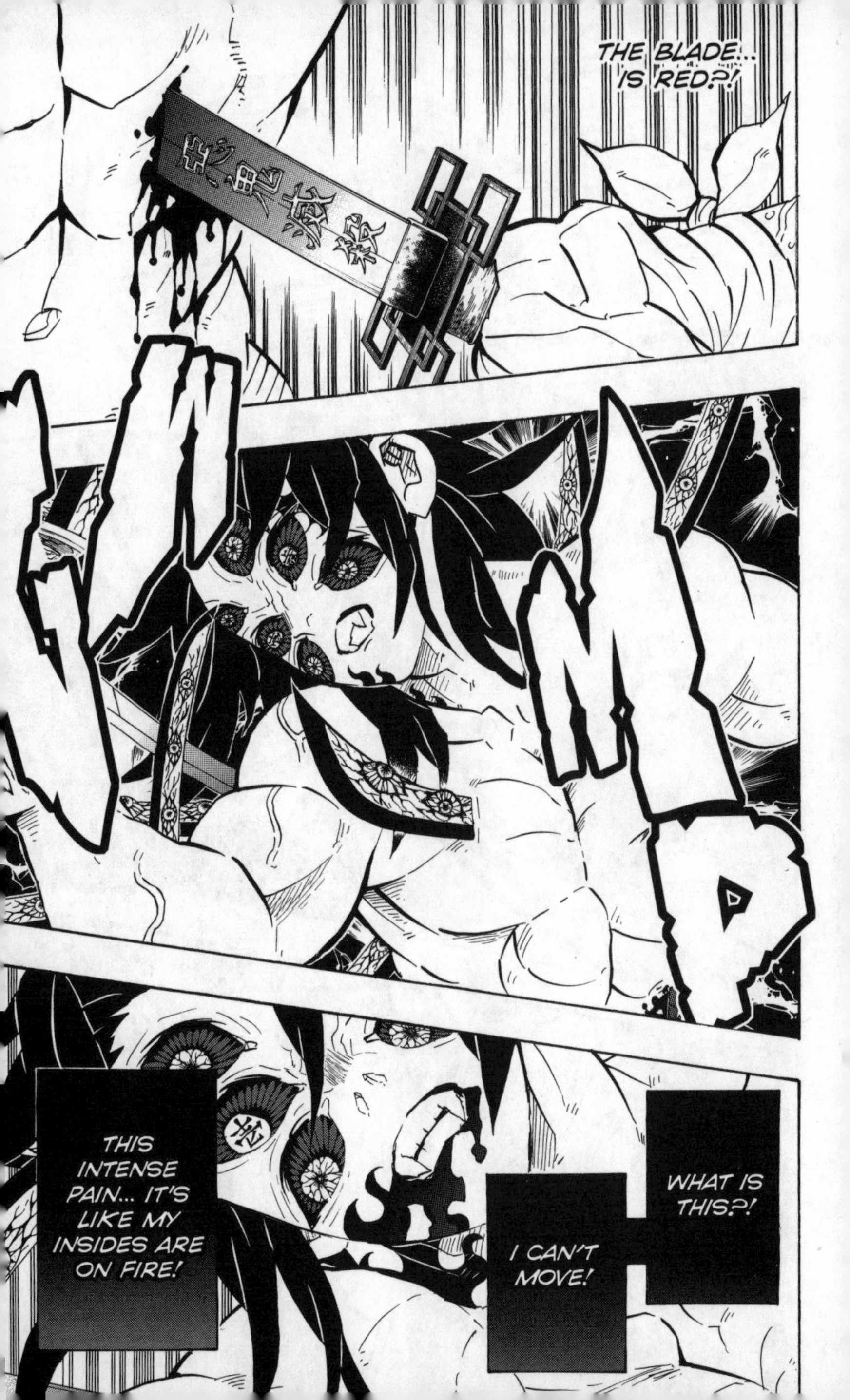
THE BLADE... IS RED?!
WHAT IS THIS?!
I CAN'T MOVE!
THIS INTENSE PAIN... IT'S LIKE MY INSIDES ARE ON FIRE!

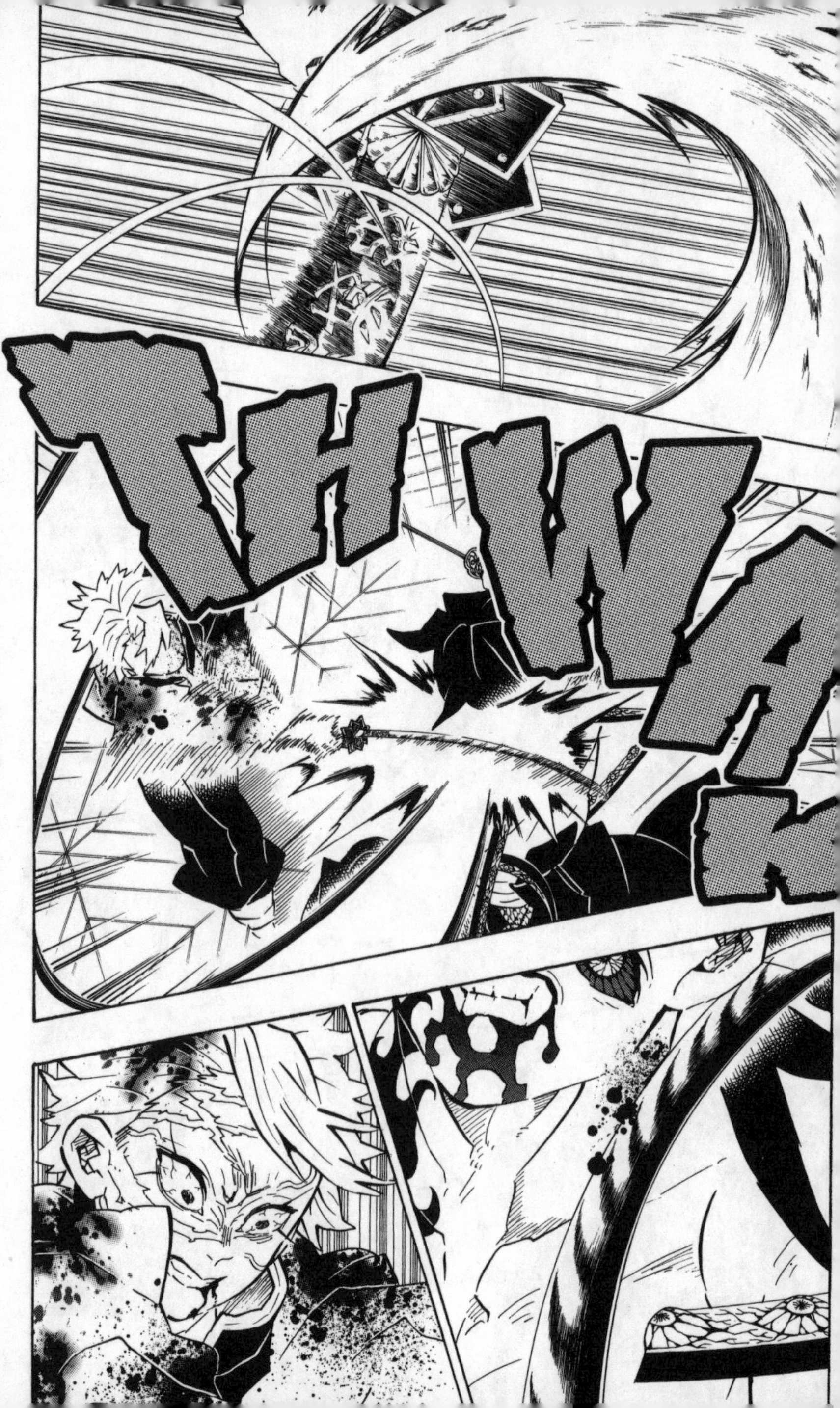
THWAK

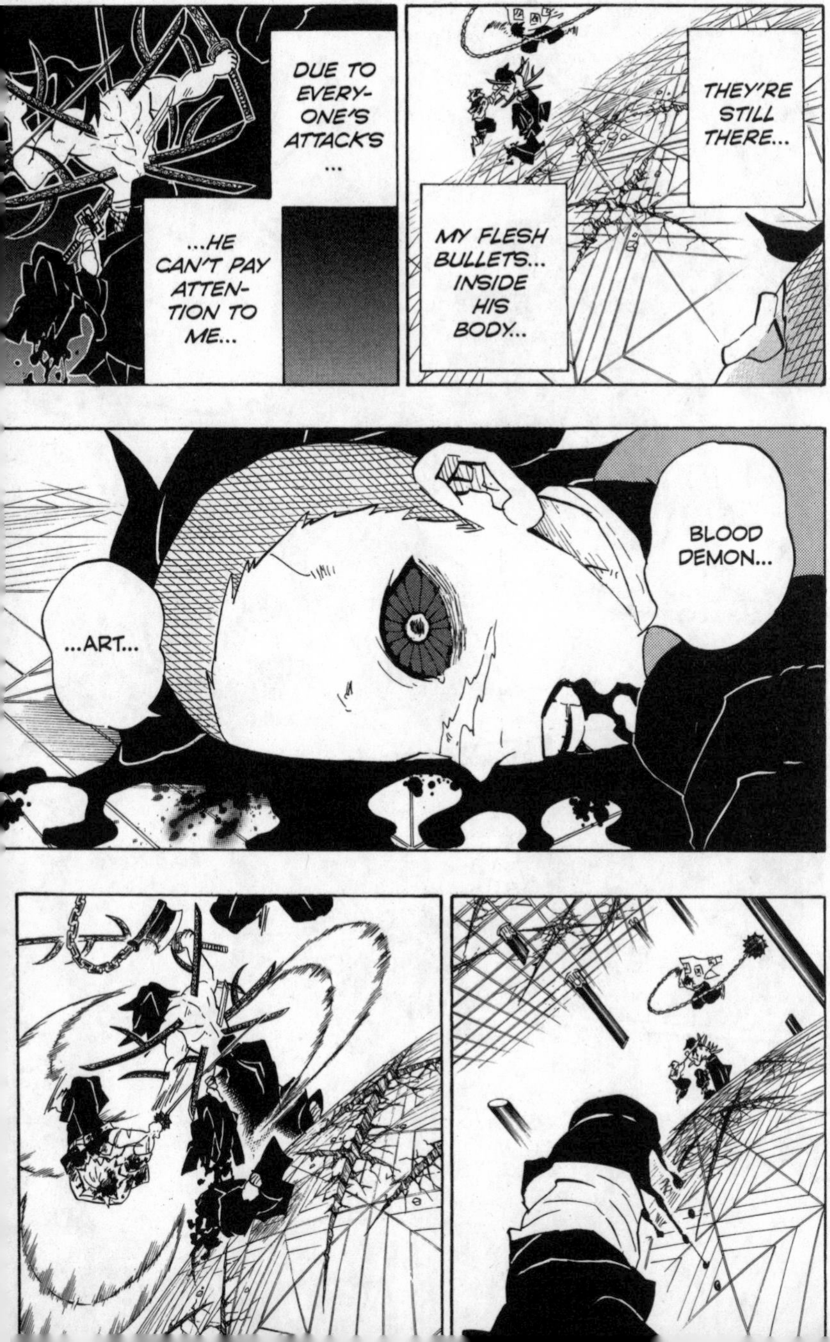
THEY'RE STILL THERE...
MY FLESH BULLETS... INSIDE HIS BODY...
DUE TO EVERYONE'S ATTACKS...
...HE CAN'T PAY ATTENTION TO ME...
BLOOD DEMON...
...ART...

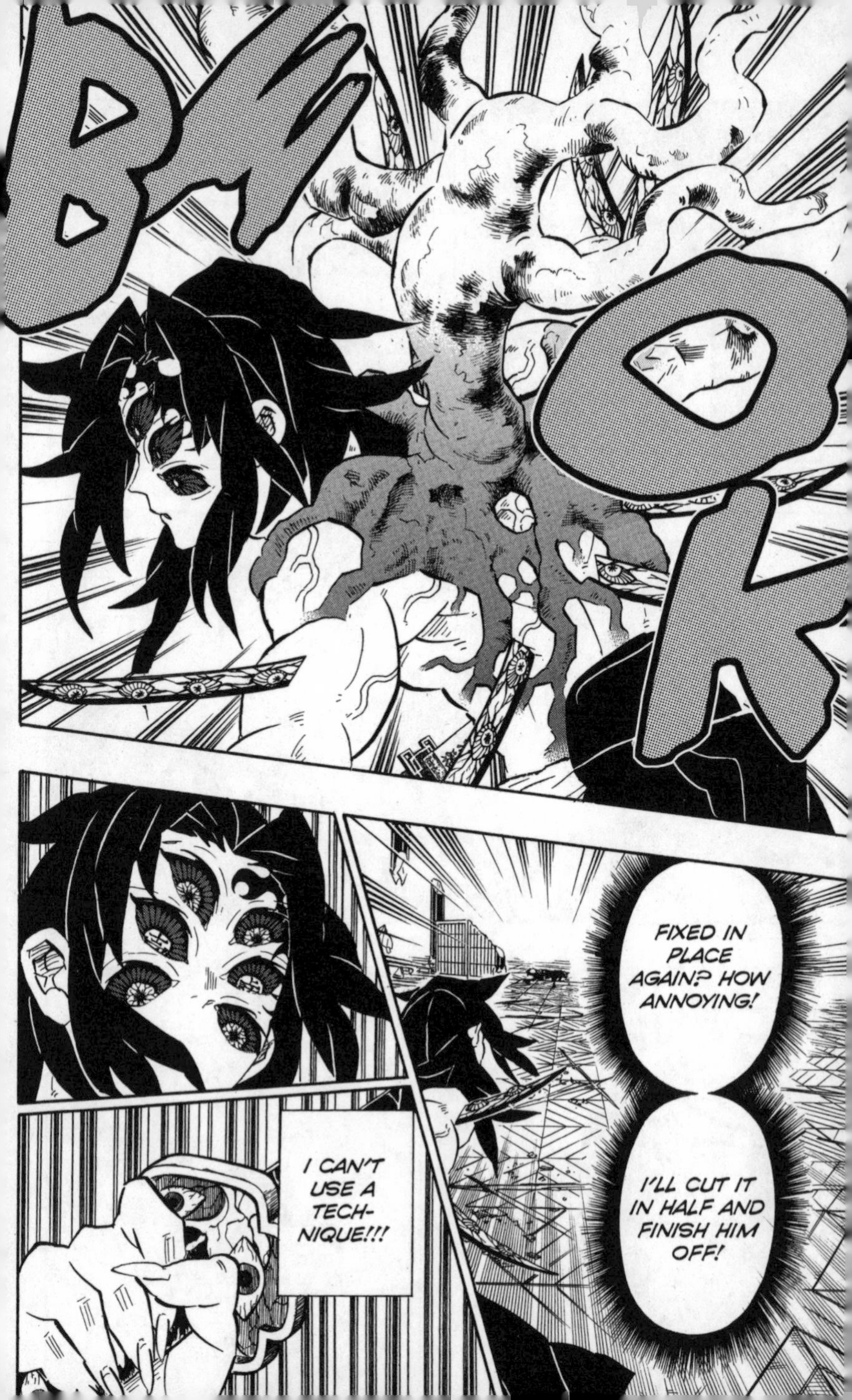
FIXED IN PLACE AGAIN? HOW ANNOYING!
I'LL CUT IT IN HALF AND FINISH HIM OFF!
I CAN'T USE A TECH-NIQUE!!!

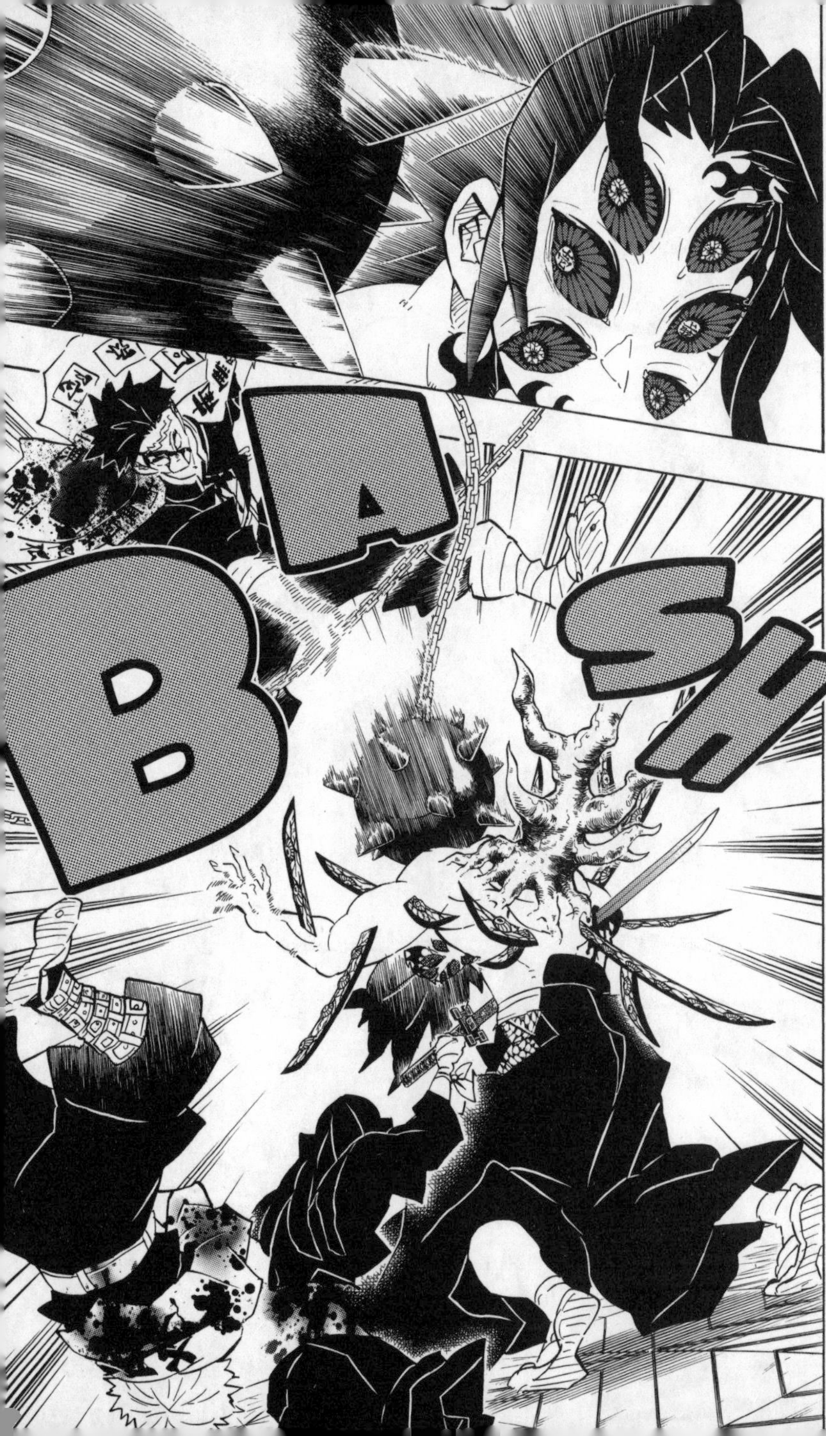
BASH

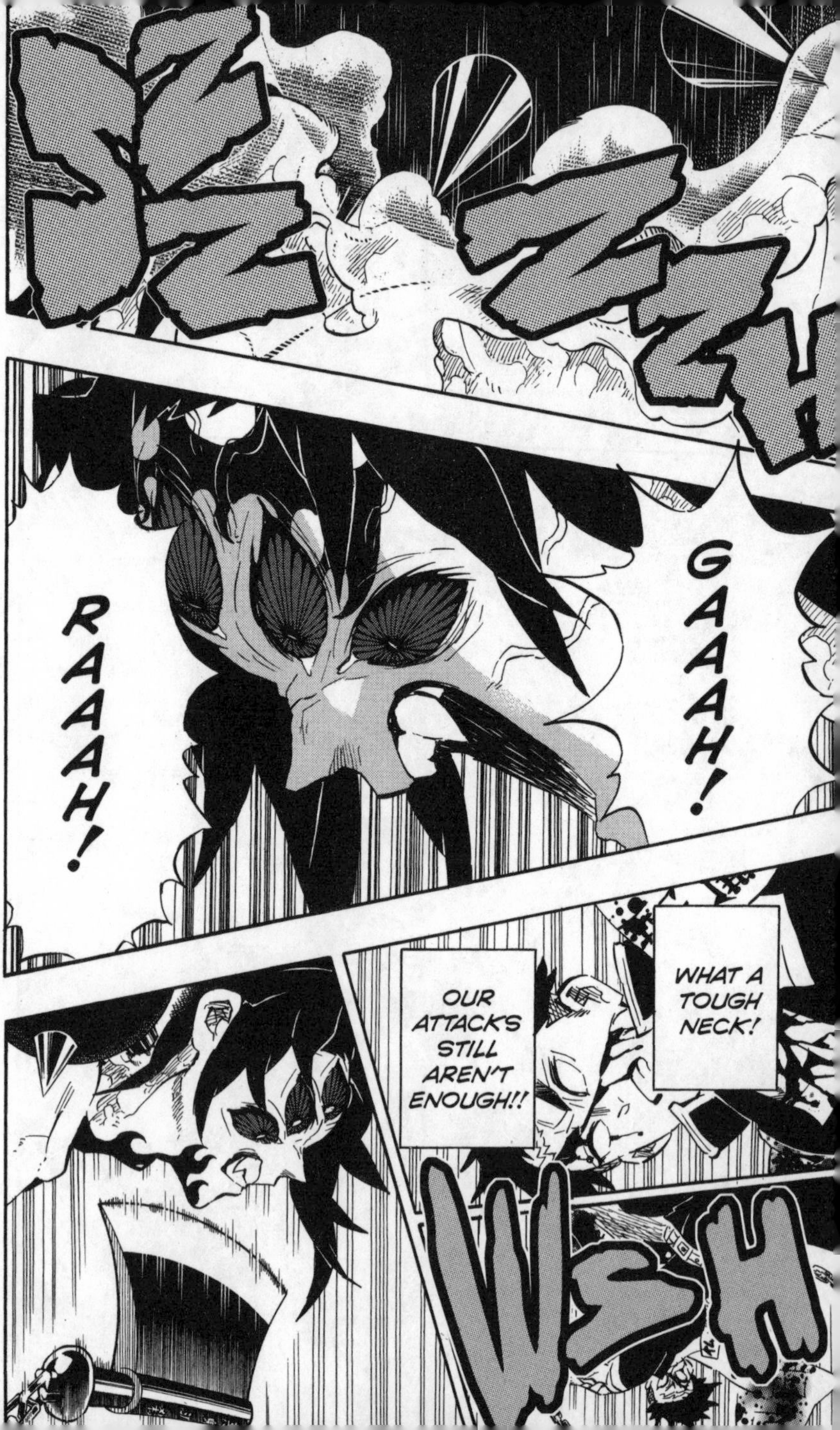
GAAAH!
RAAAH!
WHAT A TOUGH NECK!
OUR ATTACKS STILL AREN'T ENOUGH!!

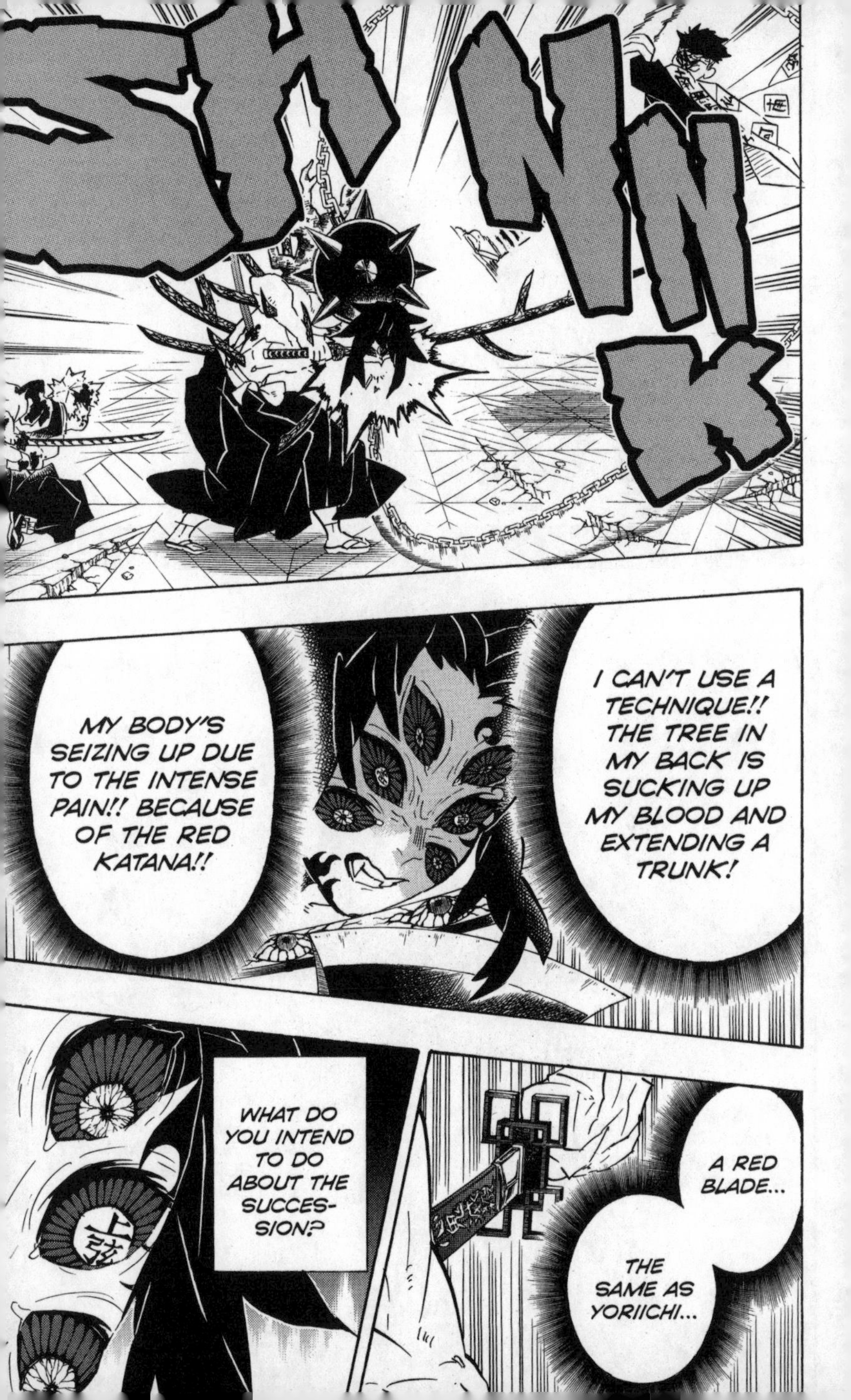
SHNNK
I CAN'T USE A TECHNIQUE!! THE TREE IN MY BACK IS SUCKING UP MY BLOOD AND EXTENDING A TRUNK!
MY BODY'S SEIZING UP DUE TO THE INTENSE PAIN!! BECAUSE OF THE RED KATANA!!
A RED BLADE...
THE SAME AS YORIICHI...
WHAT DO YOU INTEND TO DO ABOUT THE SUCCES-SION?
上弦

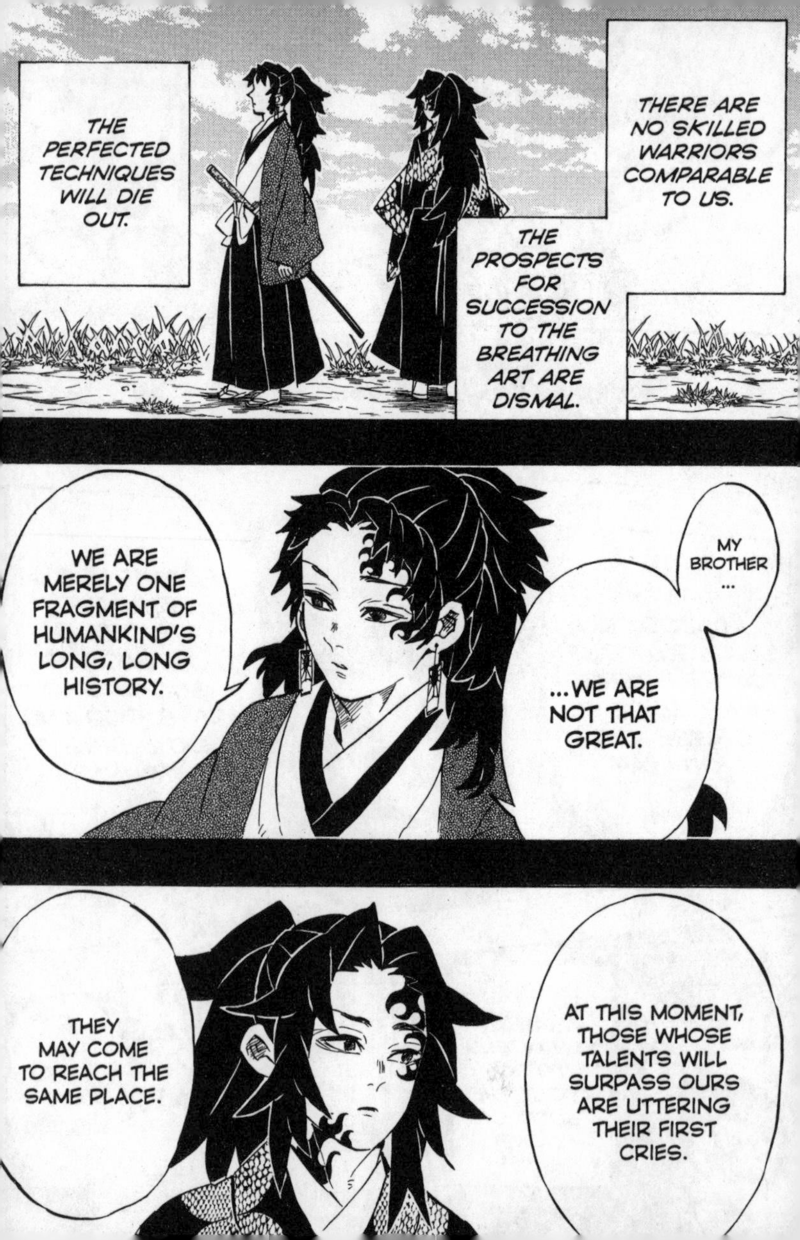
THERE ARE NO SKILLED WARRIORS COMPARABLE TO US.
THE PROSPECTS FOR SUCCESSION TO THE BREATHING ART ARE DISMAL.
THE PERFECTED TECHNIQUES WILL DIE OUT.
MY BROTHER ...
...WE ARE NOT THAT GREAT.
WE ARE MERELY ONE FRAGMENT OF HUMANKIND'S LONG, LONG HISTORY.
AT THIS MOMENT, THOSE WHOSE TALENTS WILL SURPASS OURS ARE UTTERING THEIR FIRST CRIES.
THEY MAY COME TO REACH THE SAME PLACE.

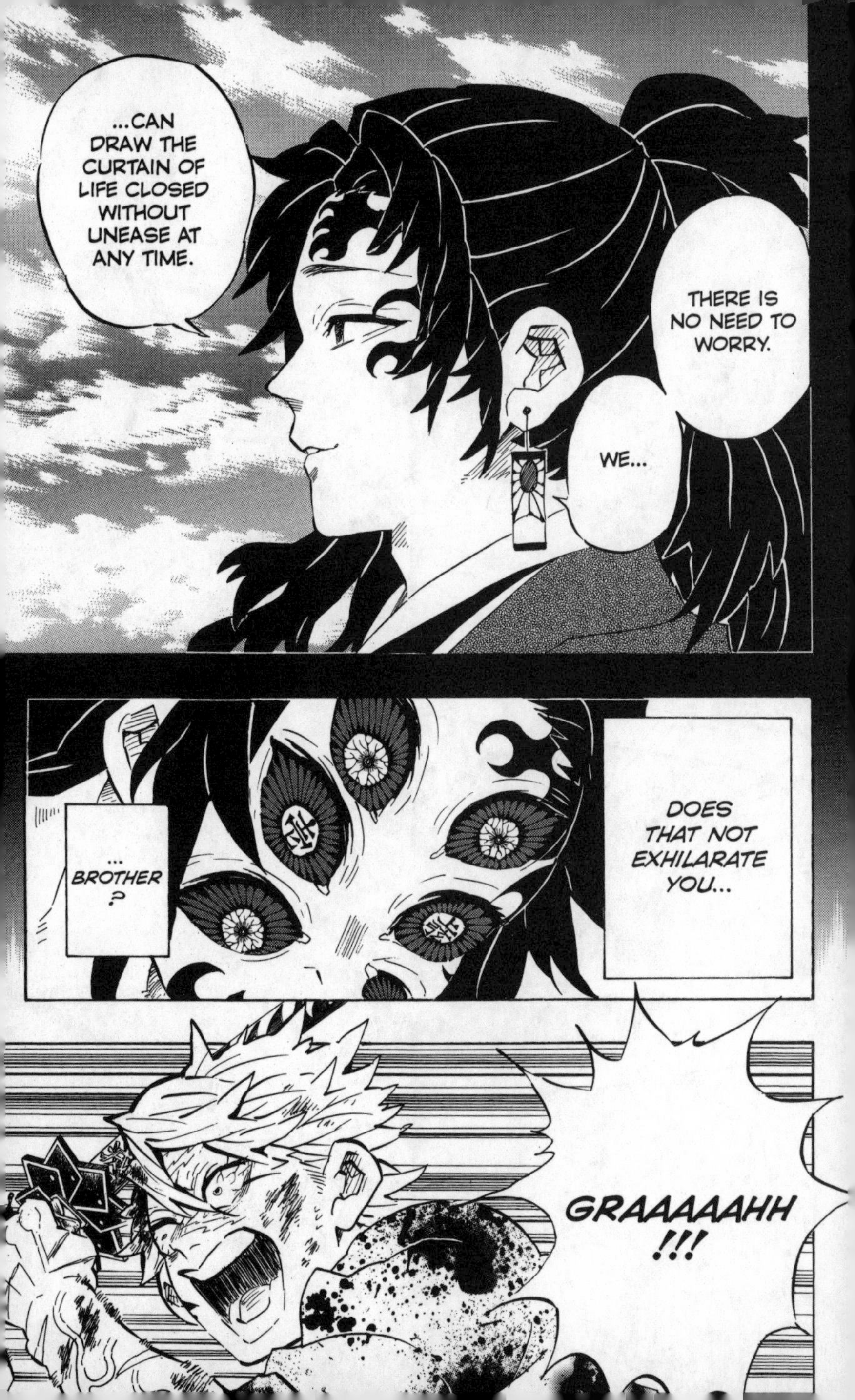
THERE IS NO NEED TO WORRY.
WE...
...CAN DRAW THE CURTAIN OF LIFE CLOSED WITHOUT UNEASE AT ANY TIME.
DOES THAT NOT EXHILARATE YOU...
...BROTHER?
GRAAAAAHH!!!

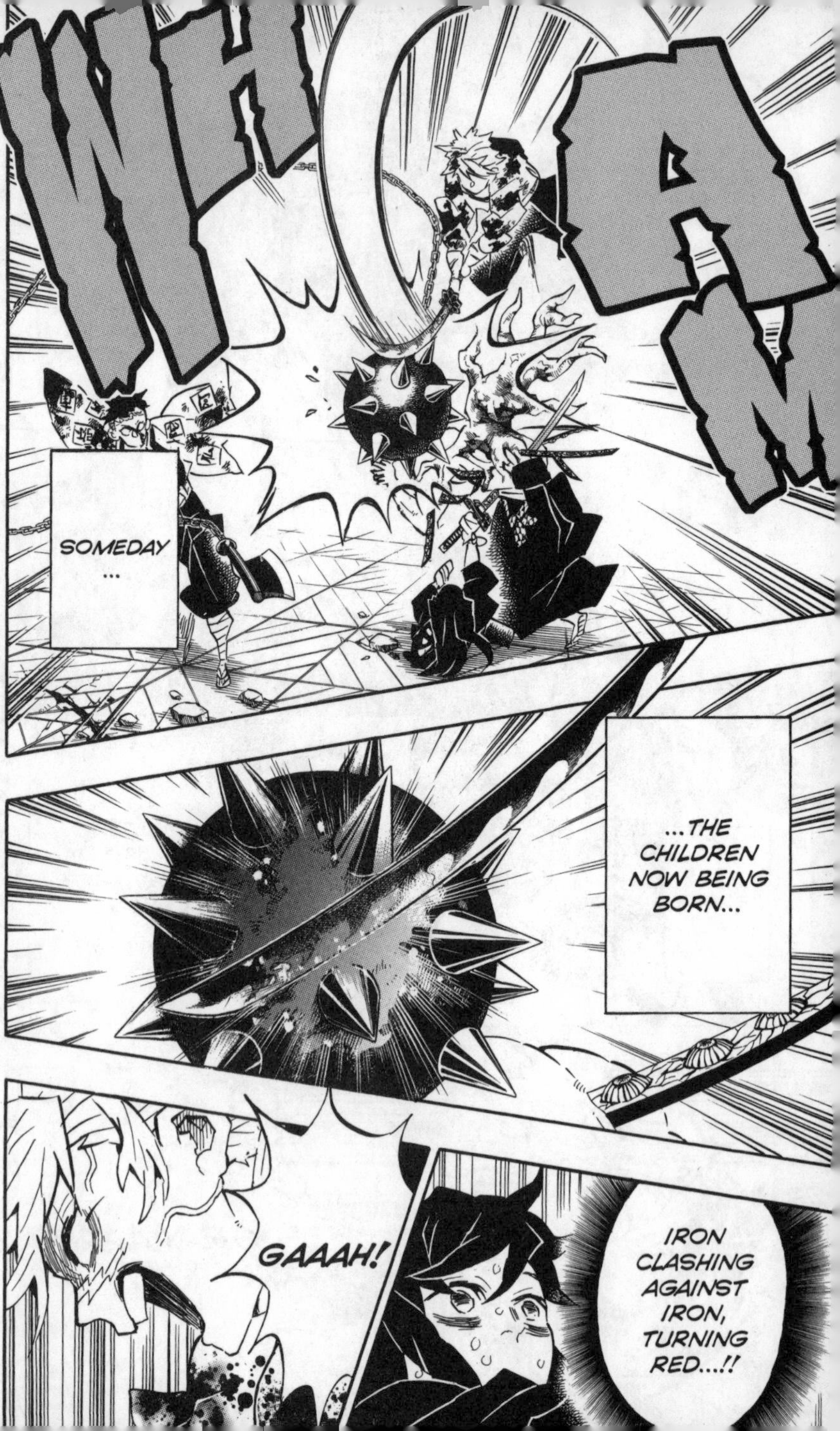WHAM
SOMEDAY ...
...THE CHILDREN NOW BEING BORN...
IRON CLASHING AGAINST IRON, TURNING RED...!!
GAAAH!

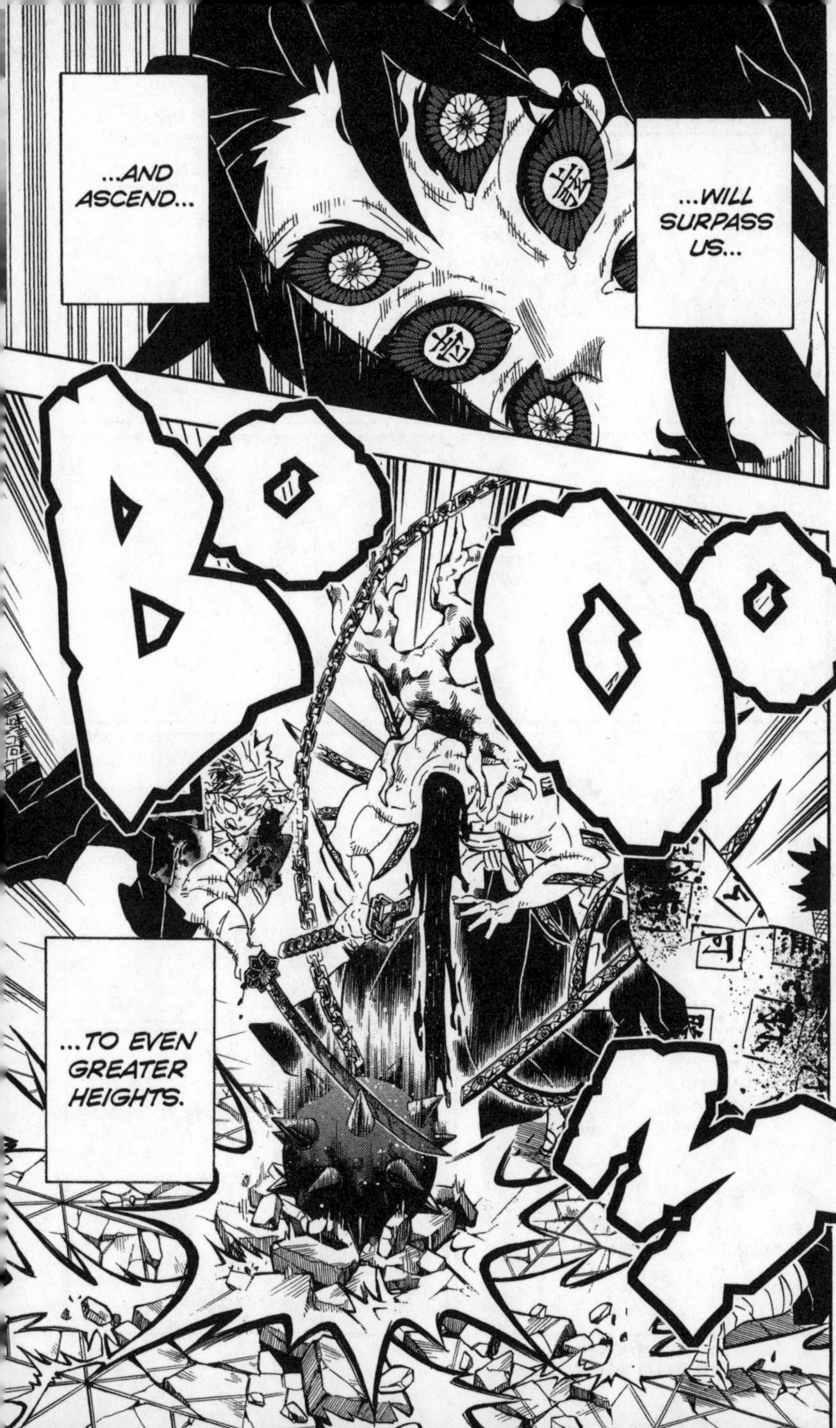
...WILL SURPASS US...
...AND ASCEND...
BOOOM
...TO EVEN GREATER HEIGHTS.

TANJIRO'S RESEARCH PROJECT

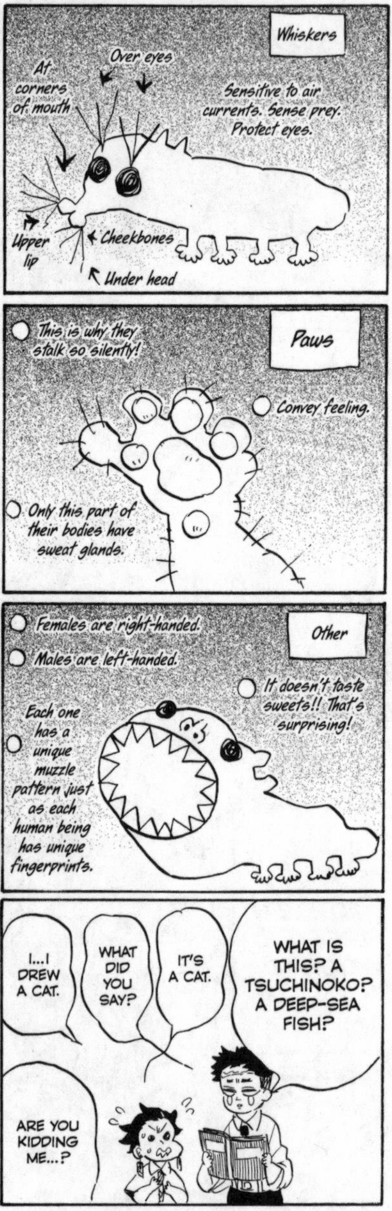
Whiskers
Sensitive to air currents. Sense prey. Protect eyes.
Over eyes
At corners of mouth
Cheekbones
Upper lip
Under head
Paws
Convey feeling.
This is why they stalk so silently!
Only this part of their bodies have sweat glands.
Other
Females are right-handed.
Males are left-handed.
It doesn't taste sweets!! That's surprising!
Each one has a unique muzzle pattern just as each human being has unique fingerprints.
WHAT IS THIS? A TSUCHINOKO? A DEEP-SEA FISH?
IT'S A CAT.
WHAT DID YOU SAY?
I...I DREW A CAT.
ARE YOU KIDDING ME...?

NEZUKO'S SWIMSUIT

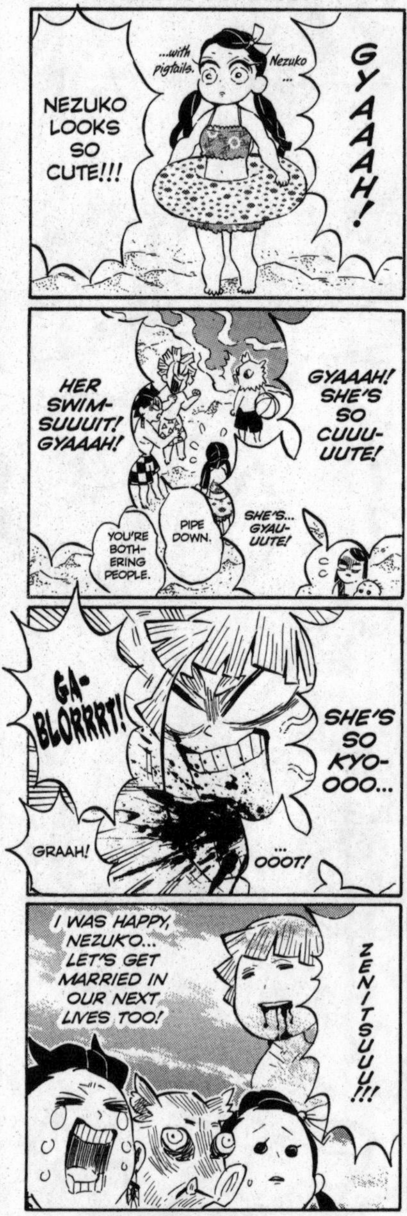
GYAAAH!
Nezuko...
...with pigtails.
NEZUKO LOOKS SO CUTE!!!
GYAAAH! SHE'S SO CUUUUUTE!
HER SWIM-SUUUIT! GYAAAH!
SHE'S... GYAUUTE!
PIPE DOWN.
YOU'RE BOTHERING PEOPLE.
SHE'S SO KYO-OOO...
GA-BLORRRT!
...OOOT!
GRAAH!
ZENITSUUUU!!!
I WAS HAPPY, NEZUKO... LET'S GET MARRIED IN OUR NEXT LIVES TOO!

FROM WEEKLY SHONEN JUMP, COMBINED ISSUE 36–37, 2019.

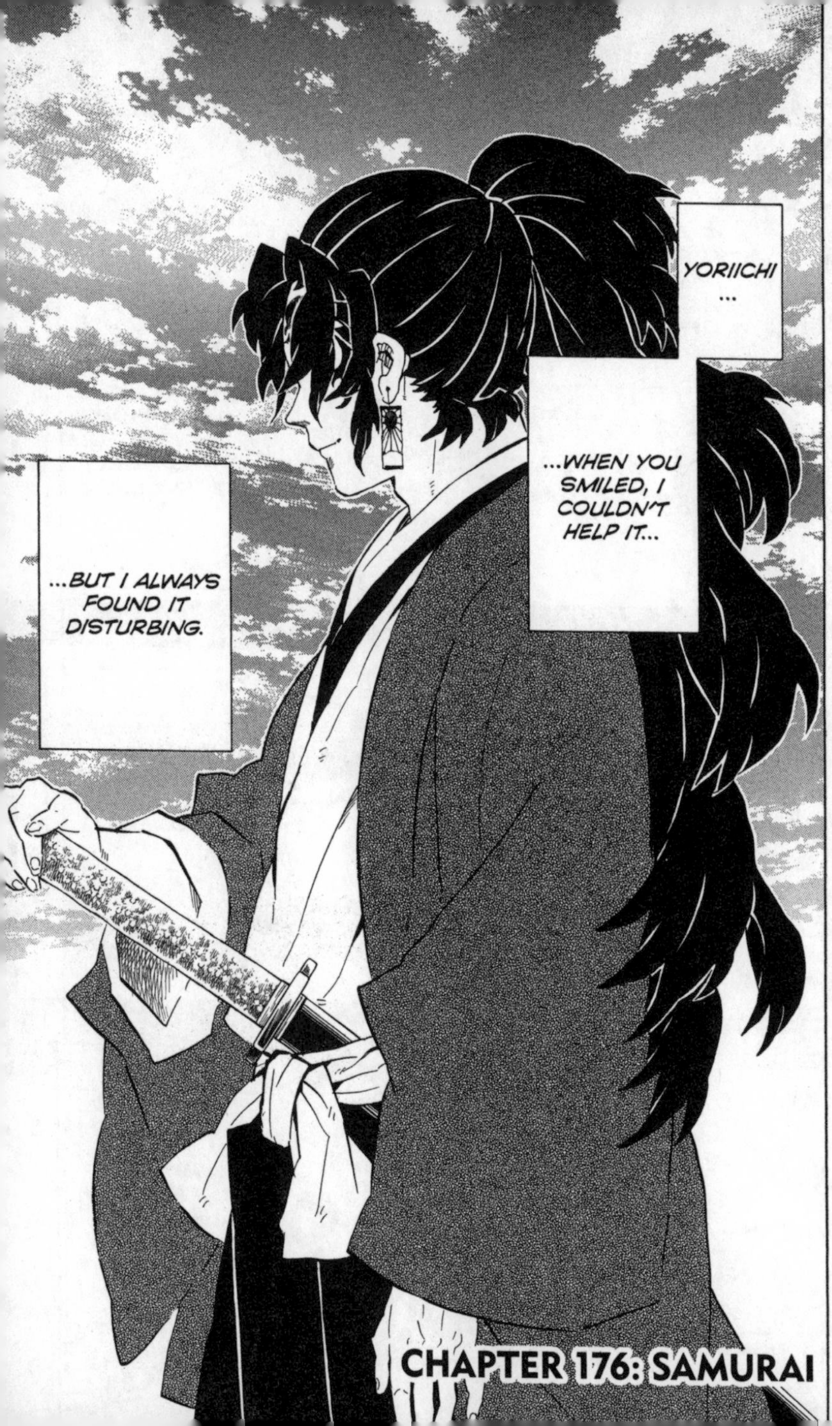
YORIICHI
...
...WHEN YOU SMILED, I COULDN'T HELP IT...
...BUT I ALWAYS FOUND IT DISTURBING.
CHAPTER 176: SAMURAI

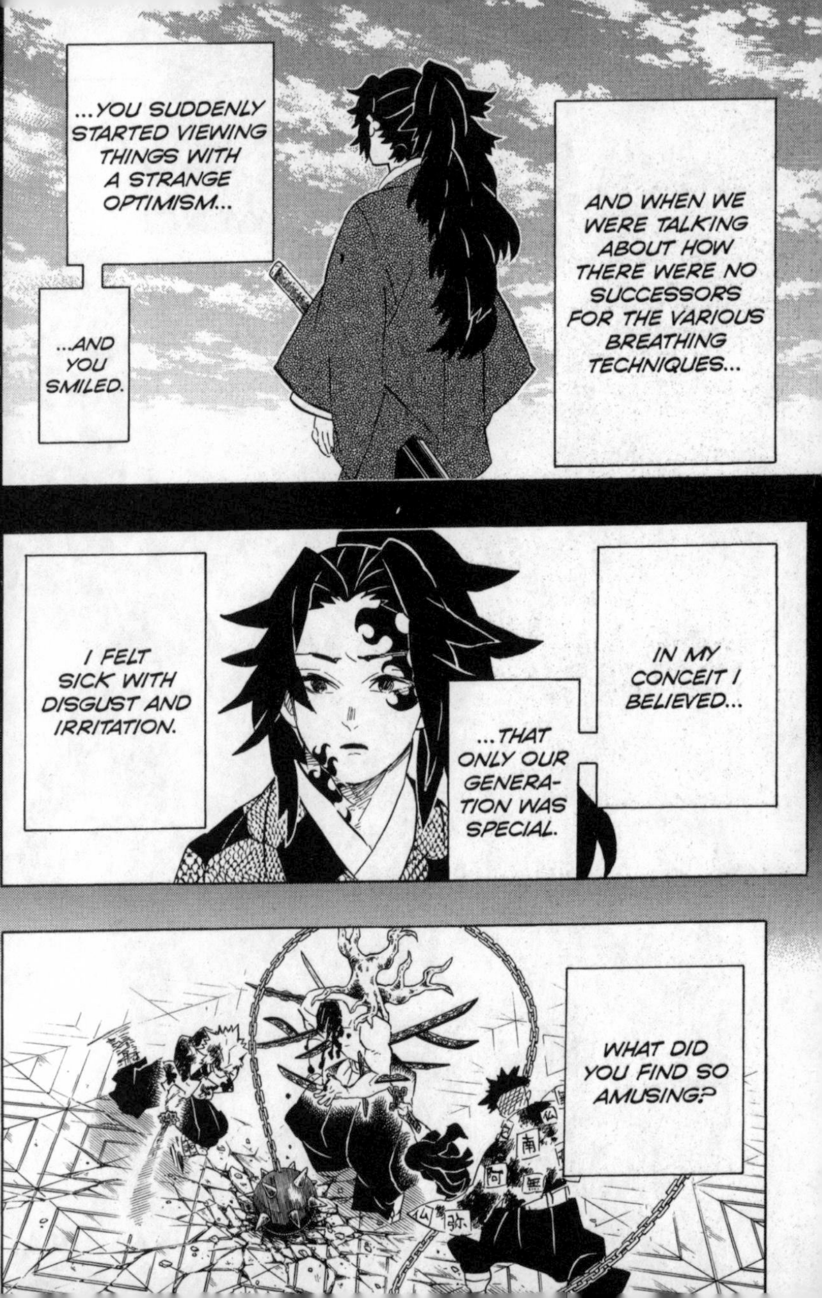
AND WHEN WE WERE TALKING ABOUT HOW THERE WERE NO SUCCESSORS FOR THE VARIOUS BREATHING TECHNIQUES...
...YOU SUDDENLY STARTED VIEWING THINGS WITH A STRANGE OPTIMISM...
...AND YOU SMILED.
IN MY CONCEIT I BELIEVED...
...THAT ONLY OUR GENERA-TION WAS SPECIAL.
I FELT SICK WITH DISGUST AND IRRITATION.
WHAT DID YOU FIND SO AMUSING?

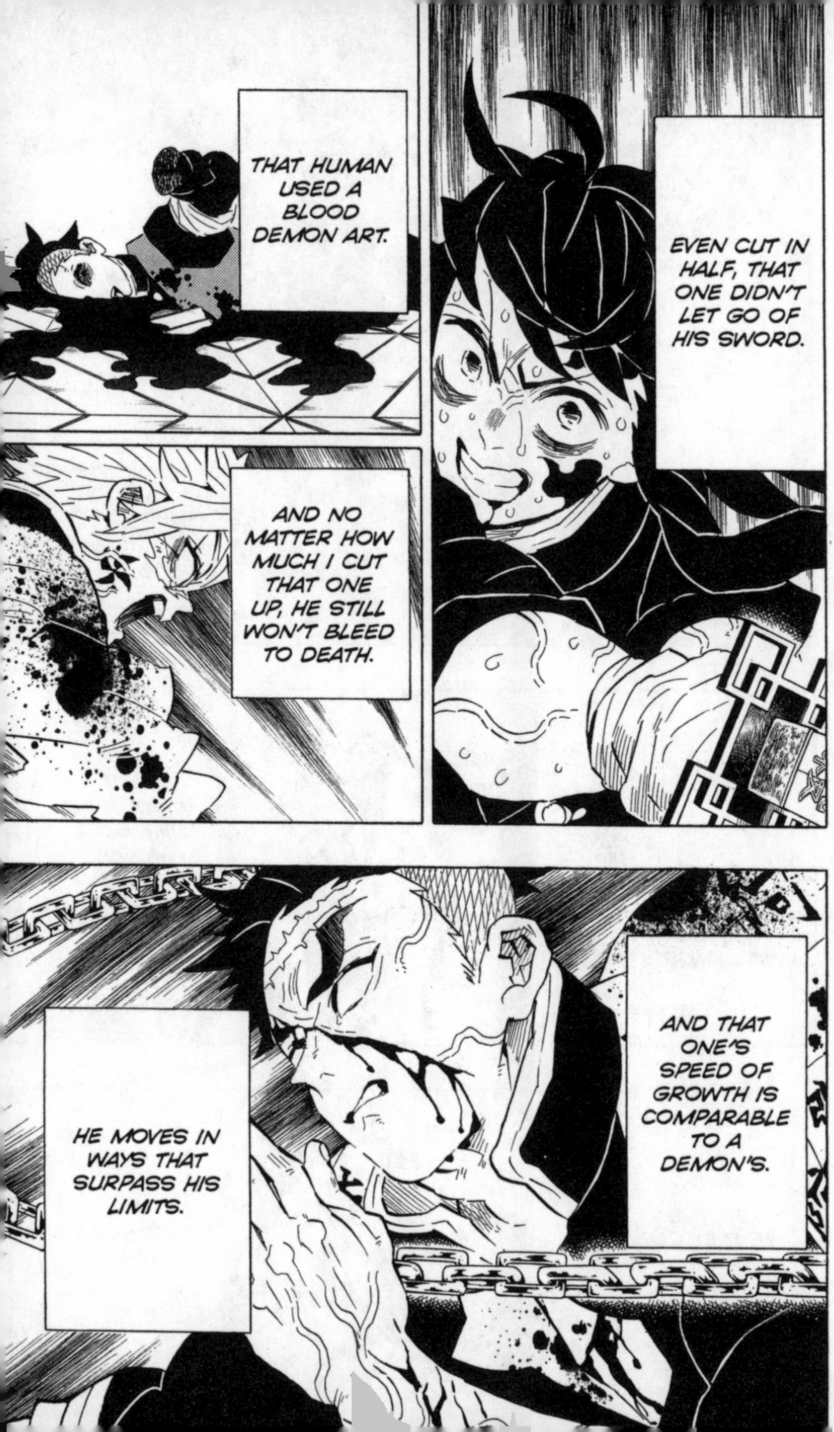
EVEN CUT IN HALF, THAT ONE DIDN'T LET GO OF HIS SWORD.
THAT HUMAN USED A BLOOD DEMON ART.
AND NO MATTER HOW MUCH I CUT THAT ONE UP, HE STILL WON'T BLEED TO DEATH.
AND THAT ONE'S SPEED OF GROWTH IS COMPARABLE TO A DEMON'S.
HE MOVES IN WAYS THAT SURPASS HIS LIMITS.

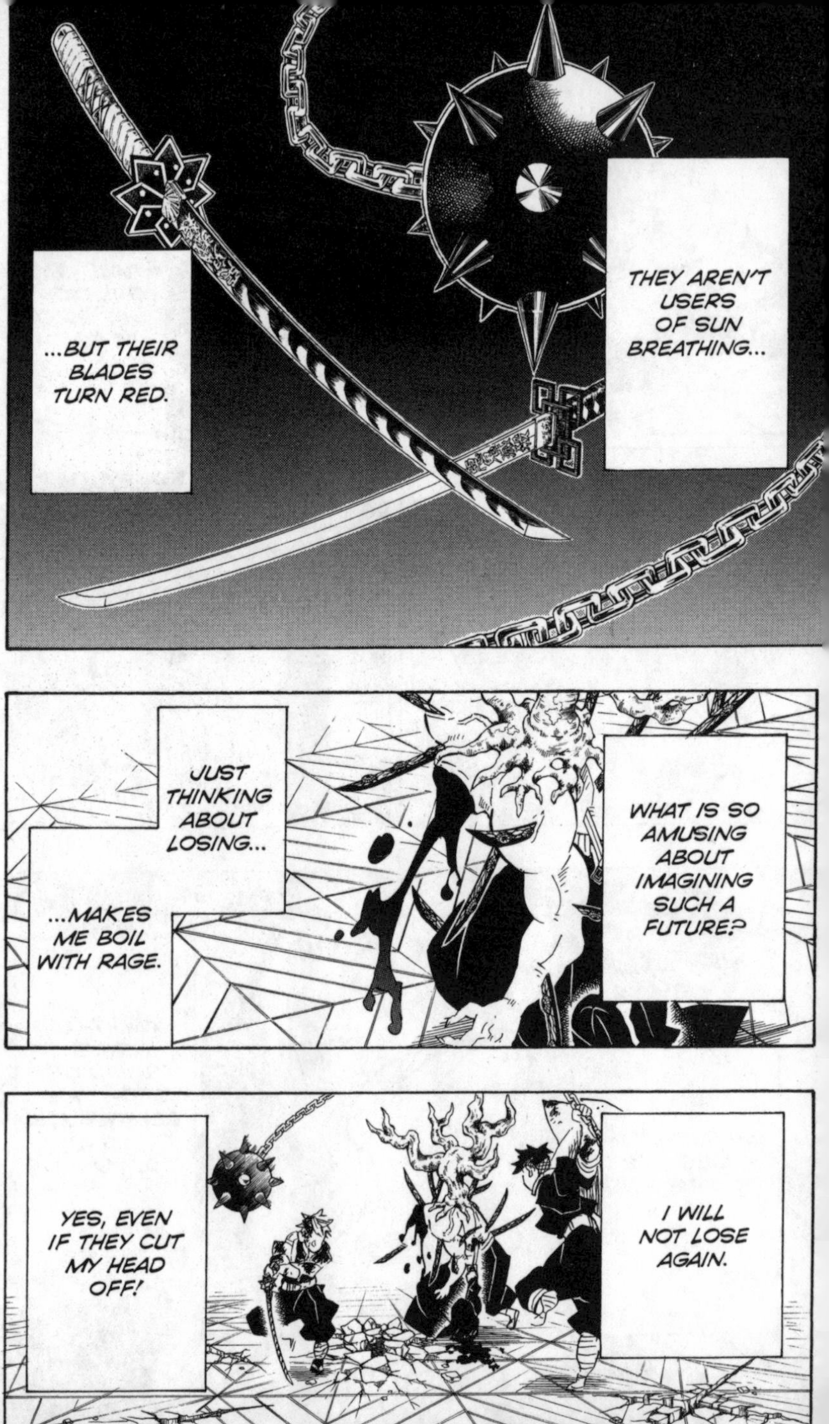
THEY AREN'T USERS OF SUN BREATHING...
...BUT THEIR BLADES TURN RED.
WHAT IS SO AMUSING ABOUT IMAGINING SUCH A FUTURE?
JUST THINKING ABOUT LOSING...
...MAKES ME BOIL WITH RAGE.
I WILL NOT LOSE AGAIN.
YES, EVEN IF THEY CUT MY HEAD OFF!

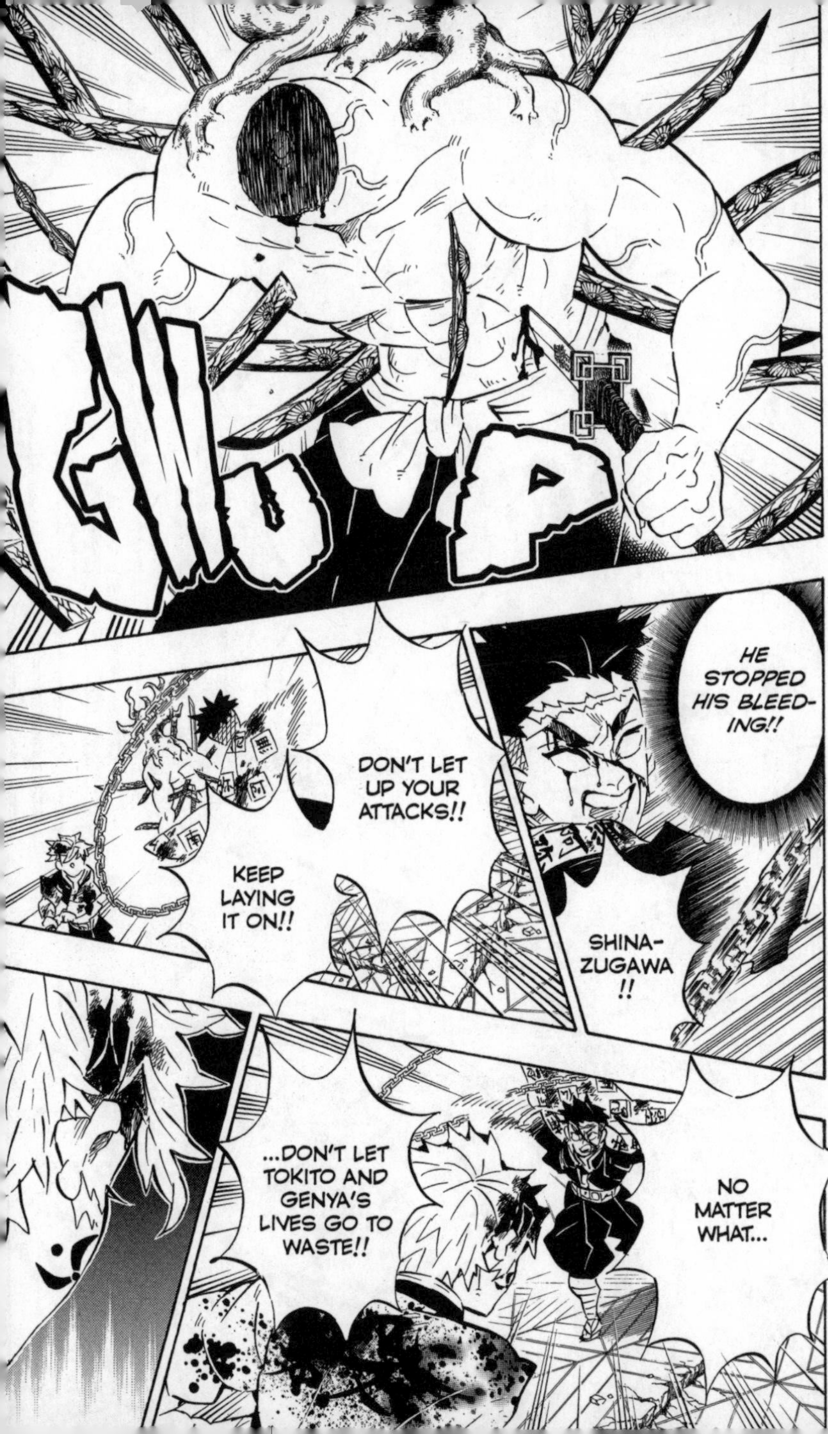
HE STOPPED HIS BLEED-ING!!
SHINA-ZUGAWA!!
DON'T LET UP YOUR ATTACKS!!
KEEP LAYING IT ON!!
NO MATTER WHAT...
...DON'T LET TOKITO AND GENYA'S LIVES GO TO WASTE!!

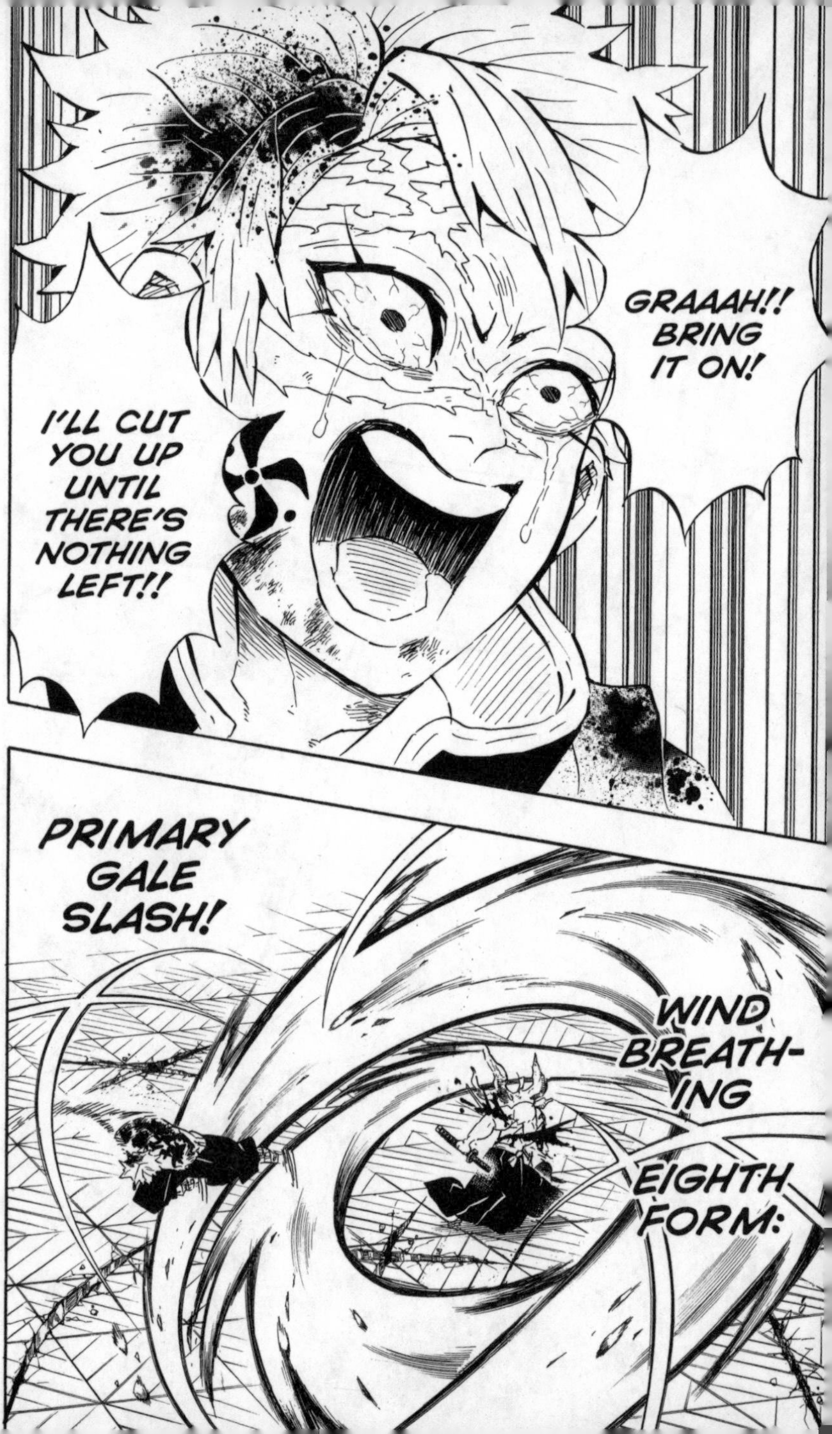
GRAAAH!! BRING IT ON!
I'LL CUT YOU UP UNTIL THERE'S NOTHING LEFT!!
WIND BREATHING EIGHTH FORM:
PRIMARY GALE SLASH!

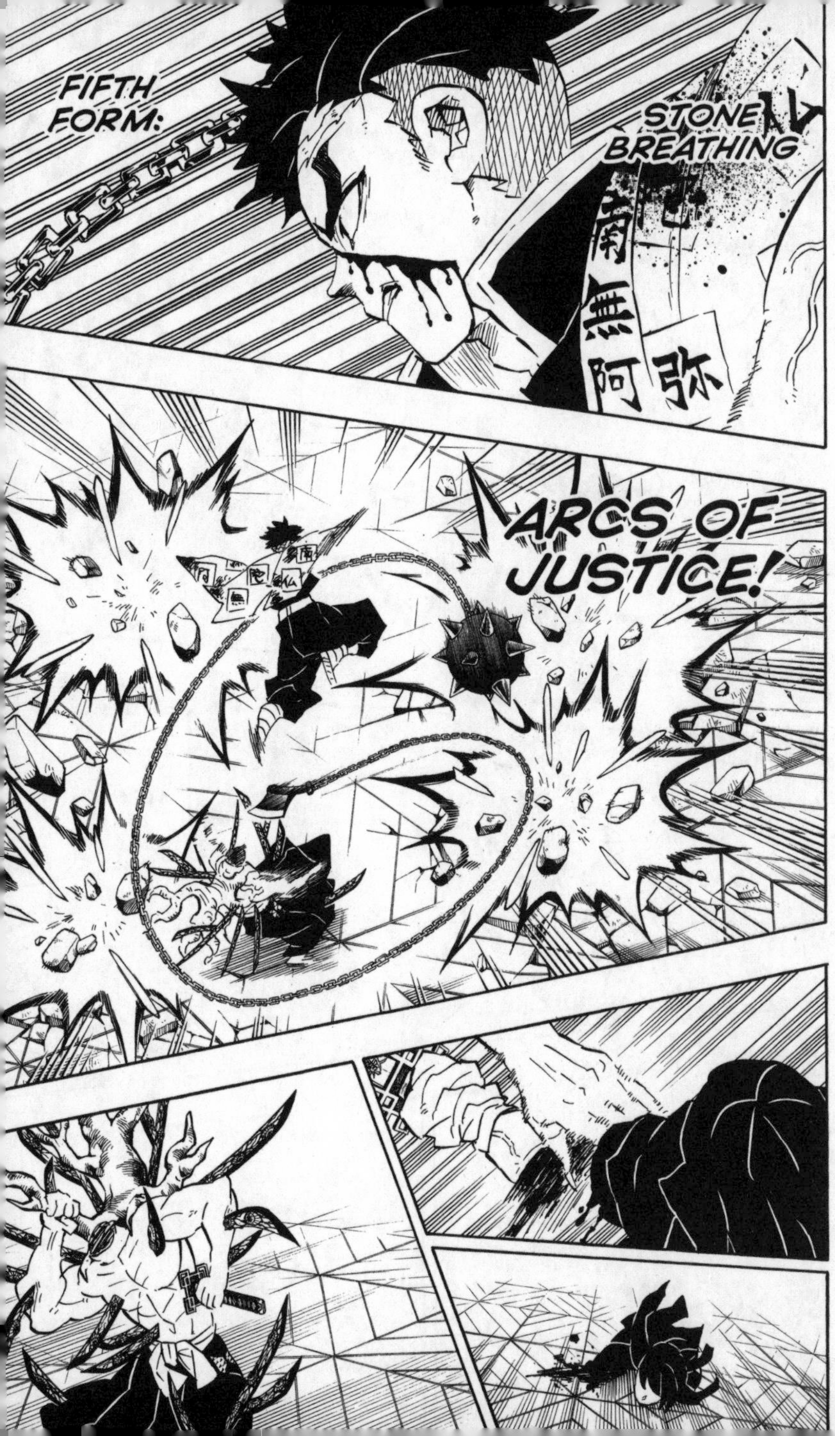
STONE BREATHING
FIFTH FORM:
ARCS OF JUSTICE!

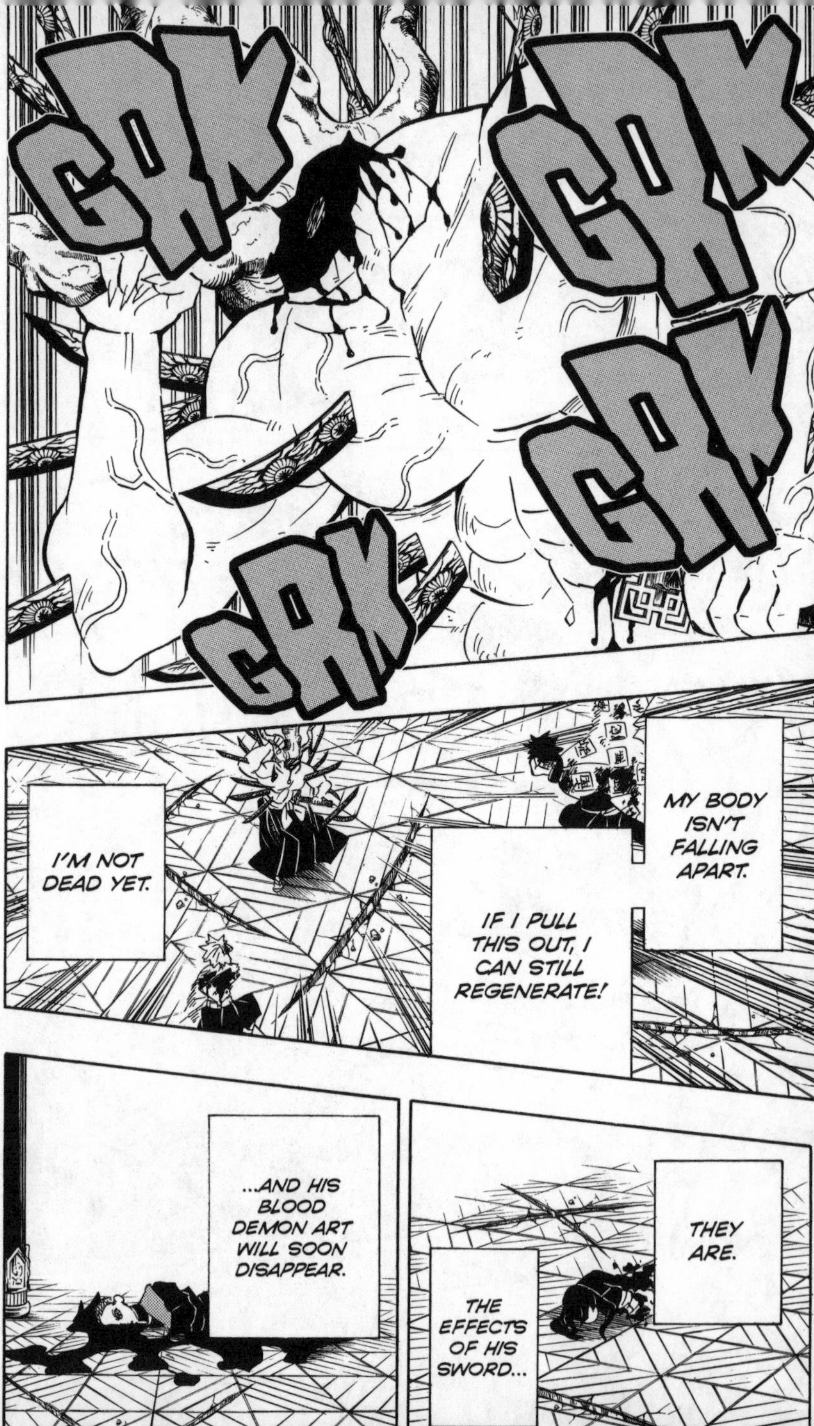
GAK
GAK
GAK
GAK
MY BODY ISN'T FALLING APART.
IF I PULL THIS OUT, I CAN STILL REGENERATE!
I'M NOT DEAD YET.
THEY ARE.
THE EFFECTS OF HIS SWORD...
...AND HIS BLOOD DEMON ART WILL SOON DISAPPEAR.

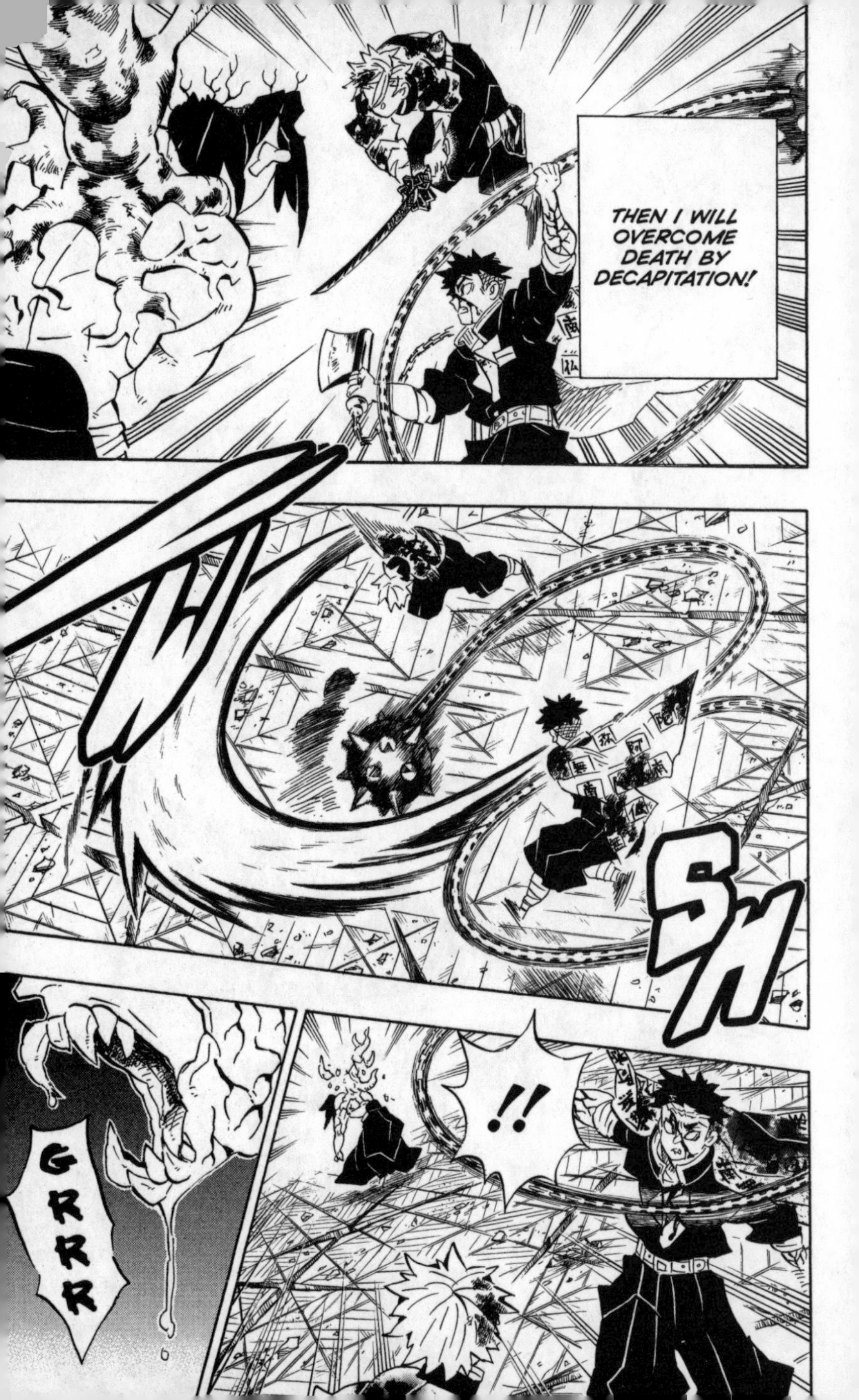
THEN I WILL OVERCOME DEATH BY DECAPITATION!
SH
!!
GRRR

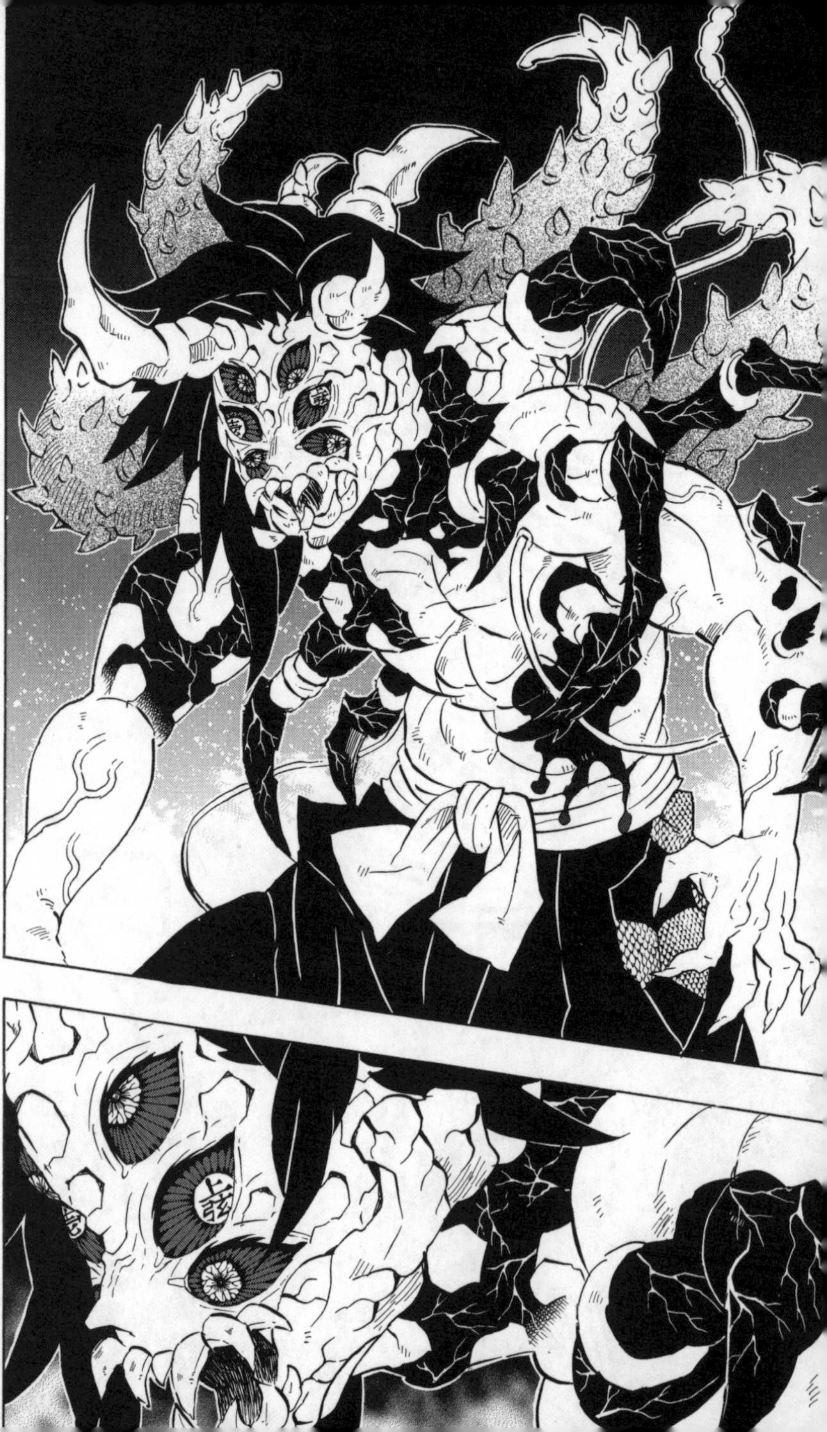
上弦

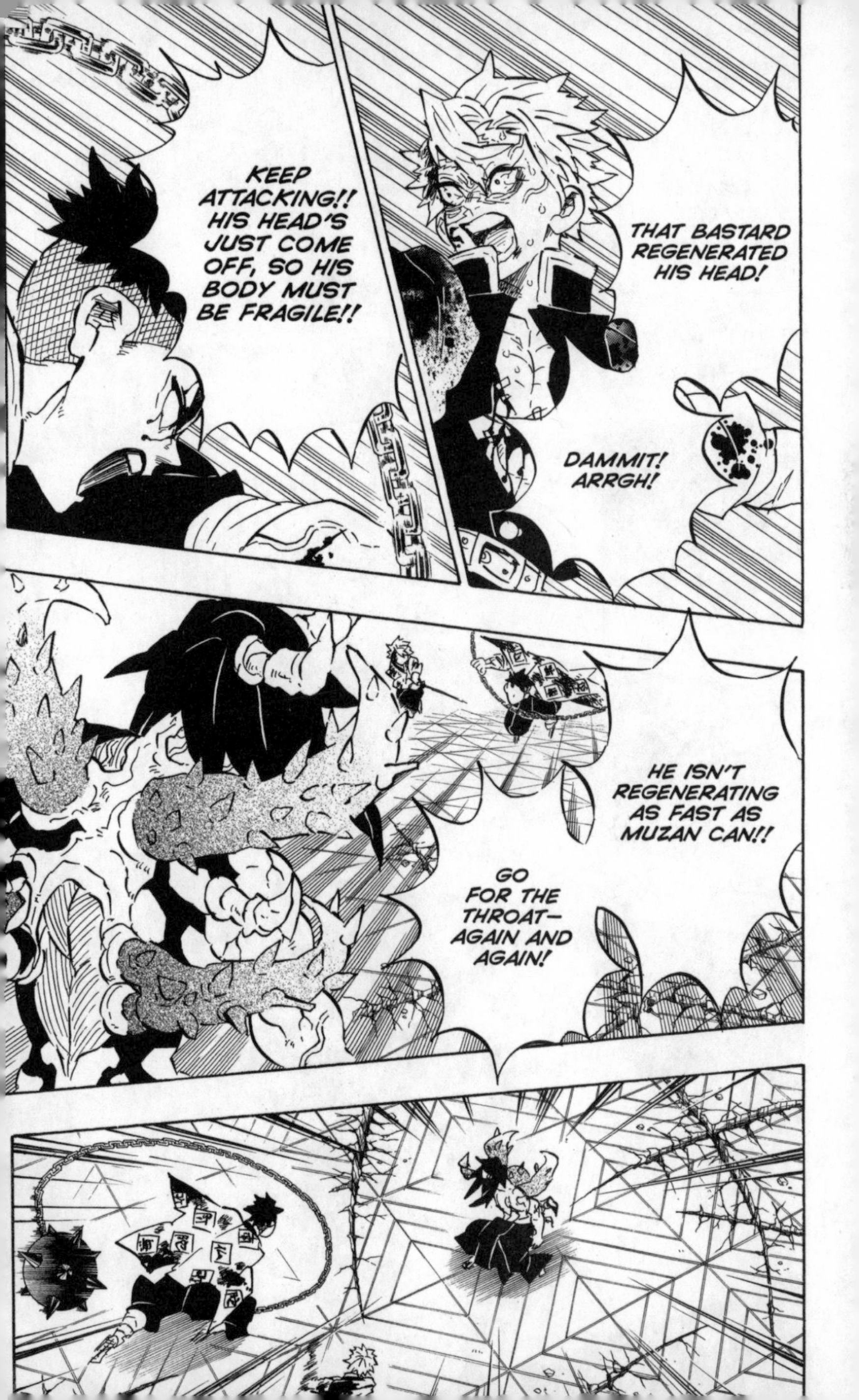
THAT BASTARD REGENERATED HIS HEAD!
DAMMIT! ARRGH!
KEEP ATTACKING!! HIS HEAD'S JUST COME OFF, SO HIS BODY MUST BE FRAGILE!!
HE ISN'T REGENERATING AS FAST AS MUZAN CAN!!
GO FOR THE THROAT— AGAIN AND AGAIN!

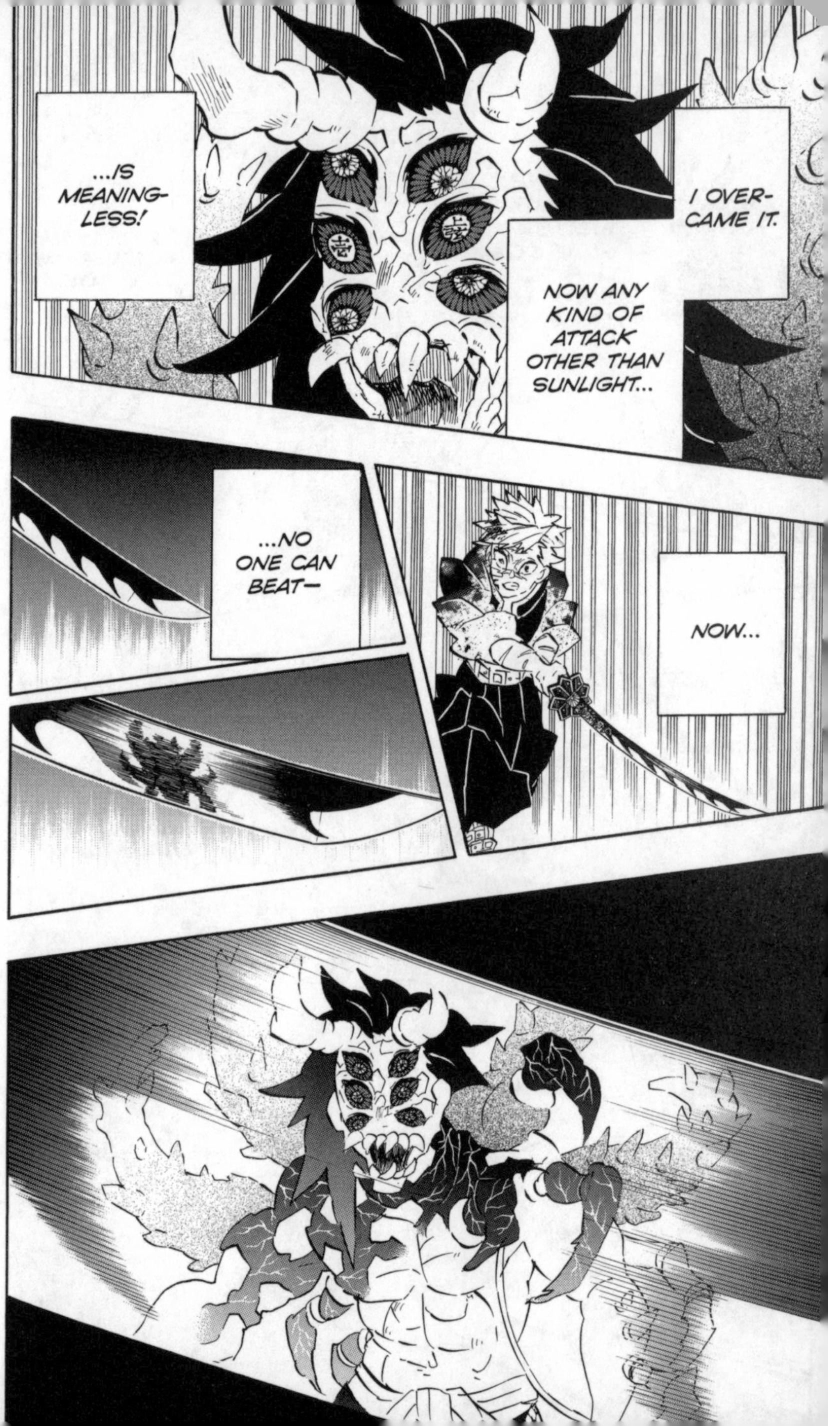
I OVERCAME IT.
NOW ANY KIND OF ATTACK OTHER THAN SUNLIGHT...
...IS MEANINGLESS!
NOW...
...NO ONE CAN BEAT—

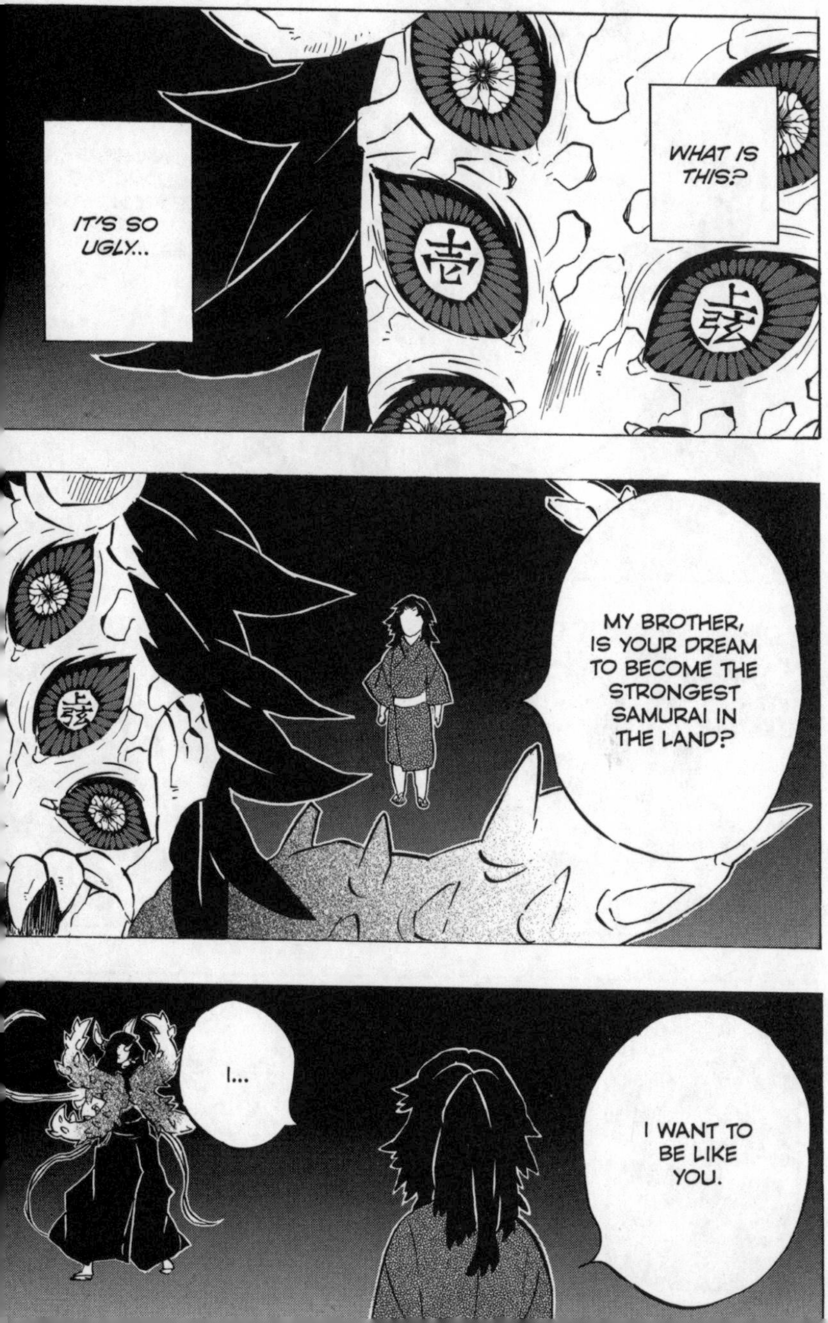
WHAT IS THIS?
IT'S SO UGLY...
MY BROTHER, IS YOUR DREAM TO BECOME THE STRONGEST SAMURAI IN THE LAND?
I...
I WANT TO BE LIKE YOU.

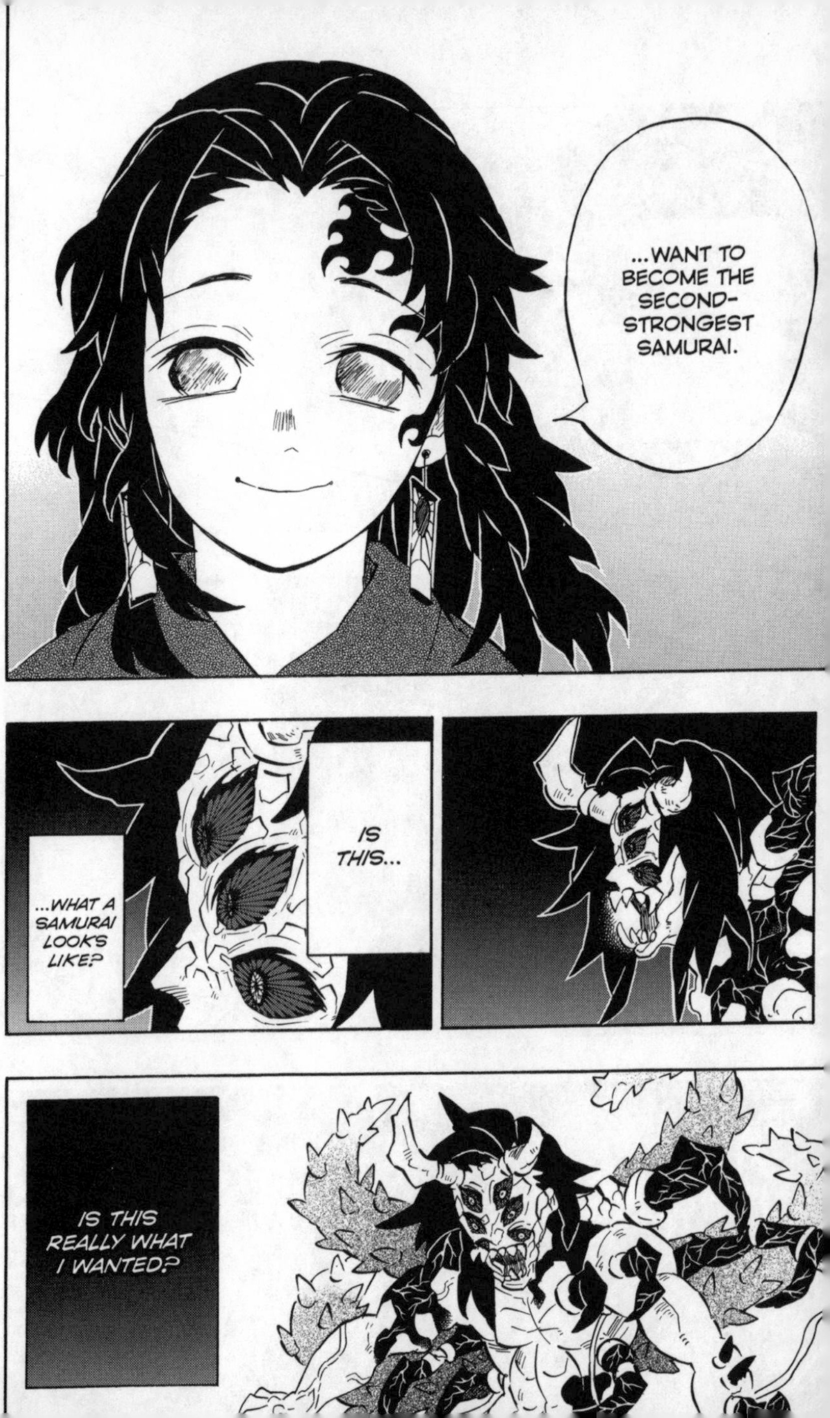
...WANT TO BECOME THE SECOND-STRONGEST SAMURAI.
IS THIS...
...WHAT A SAMURAI LOOKS LIKE?
IS THIS REALLY WHAT I WANTED?

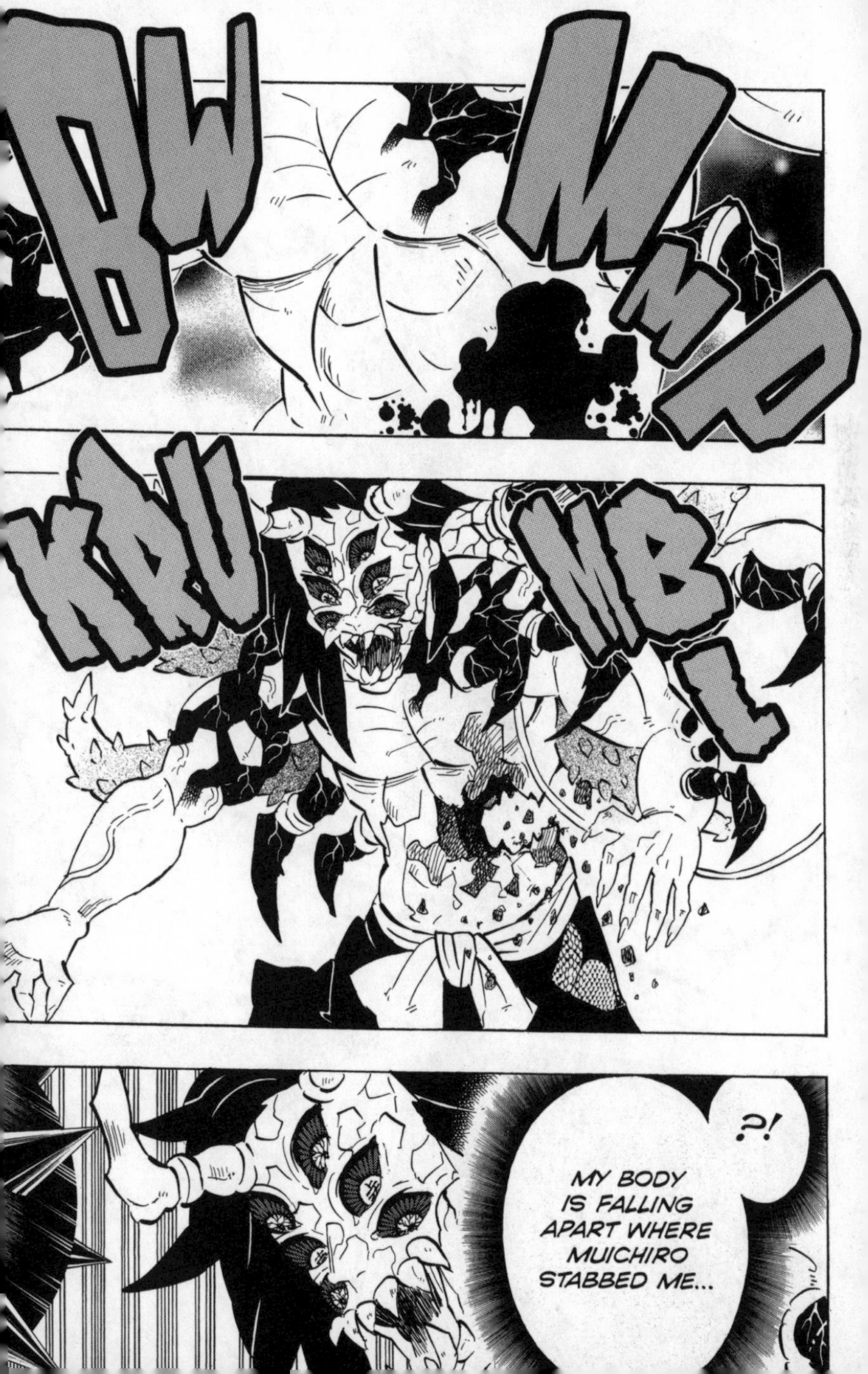
BWMMP
KRUMBL
?!
MY BODY IS FALLING APART WHERE MUICHIRO STABBED ME...

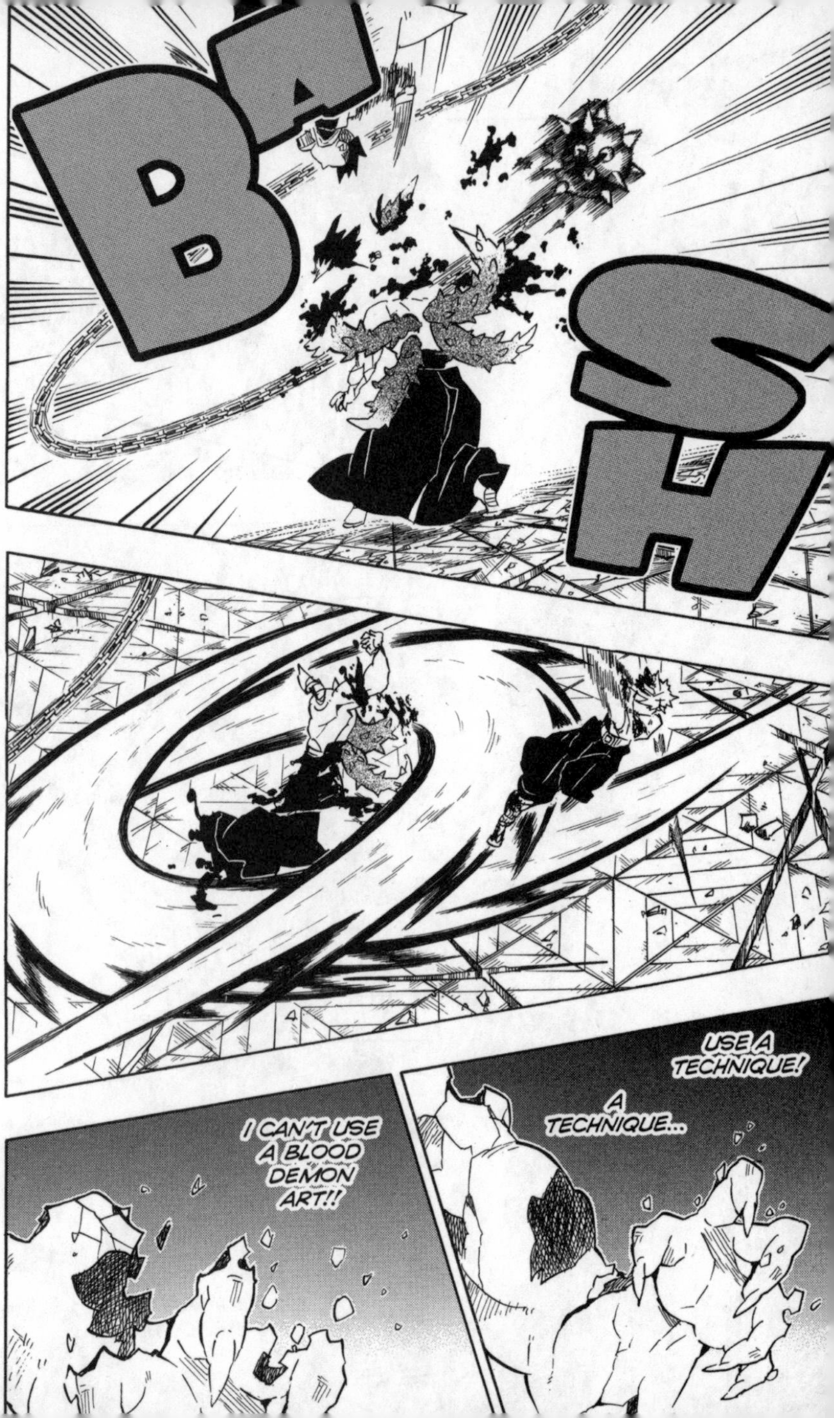
BASH
USE A TECHNIQUE!
A TECHNIQUE...
I CAN'T USE A BLOOD DEMON ART!!

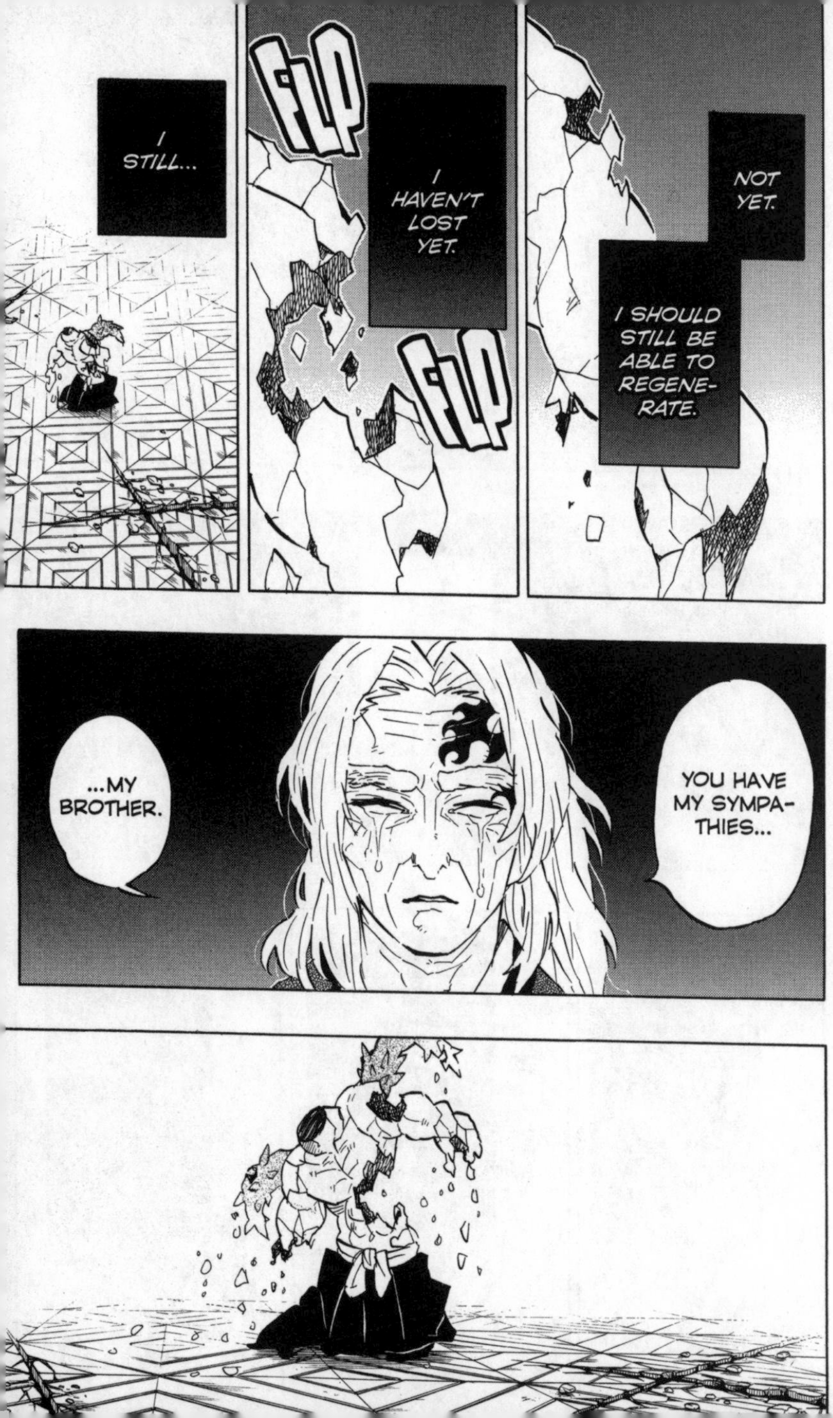
NOT YET.
I SHOULD STILL BE ABLE TO REGENERATE.
FLIP
I HAVEN'T LOST YET.
FLIP
I STILL...
YOU HAVE MY SYMPATHIES...
...MY BROTHER.

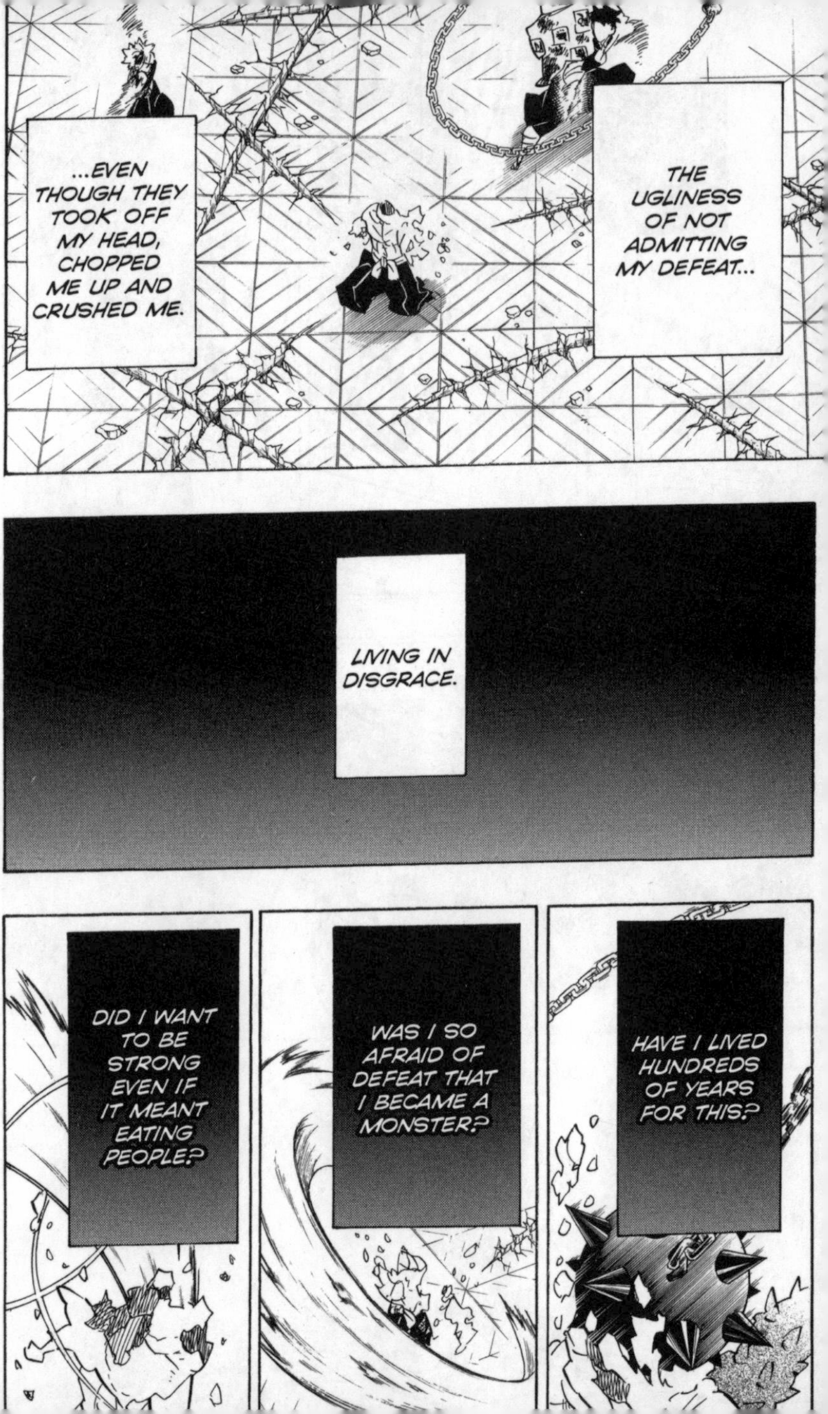
THE UGLINESS OF NOT ADMITTING MY DEFEAT...
...EVEN THOUGH THEY TOOK OFF MY HEAD, CHOPPED ME UP AND CRUSHED ME.
LIVING IN DISGRACE.
HAVE I LIVED HUNDREDS OF YEARS FOR THIS?
WAS I SO AFRAID OF DEFEAT THAT I BECAME A MONSTER?
DID I WANT TO BE STRONG EVEN IF IT MEANT EATING PEOPLE?

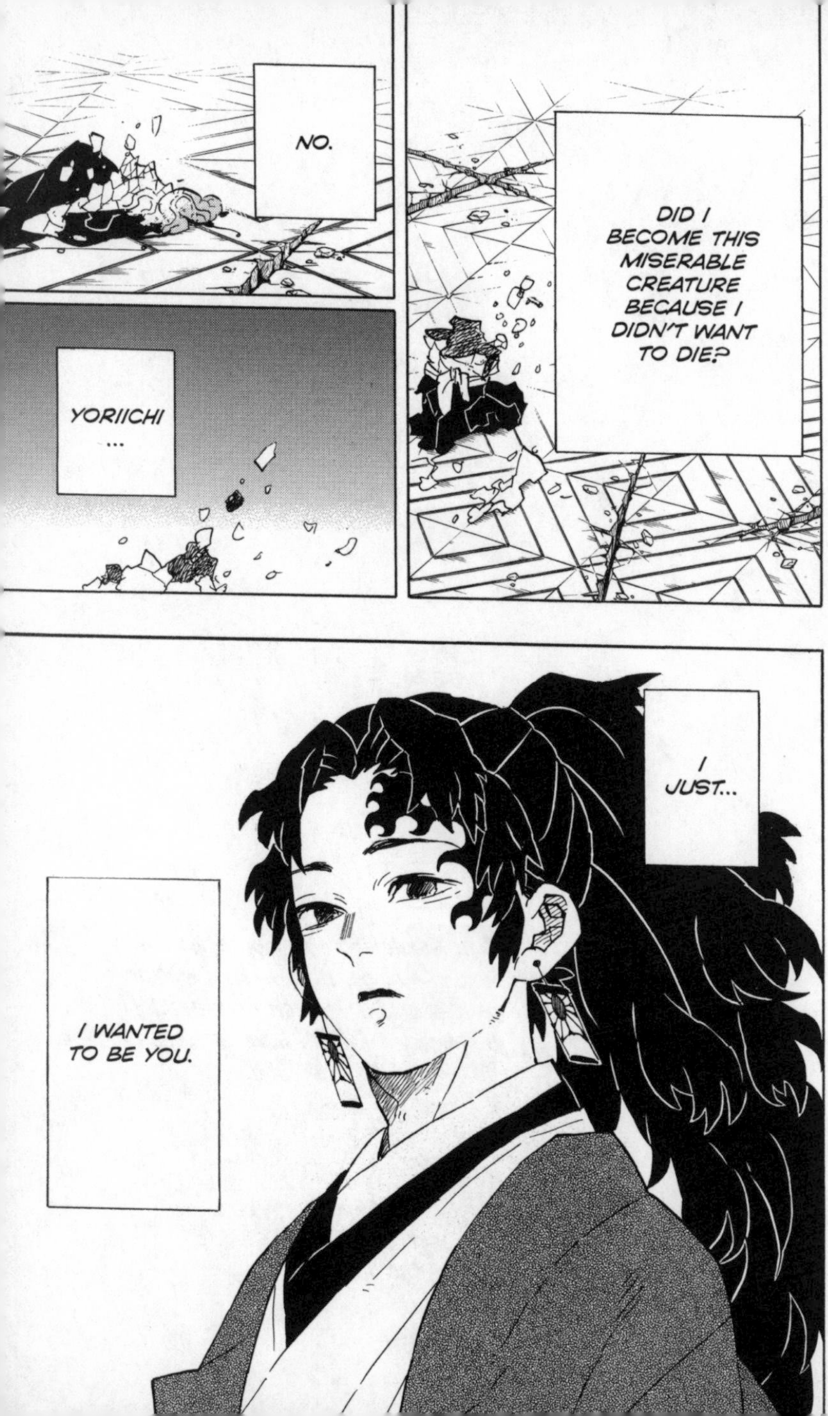
DID I BECOME THIS MISERABLE CREATURE BECAUSE I DIDN'T WANT TO DIE?
NO.
YORIICHI ...
I JUST...
I WANTED TO BE YOU.

When Kokushibo saw his reflection in Sanemi's blade, it was like a mirror, so it should have been reversed left to right, but I didn't have the time or skill to fix it.

Please, reverse it in your head.

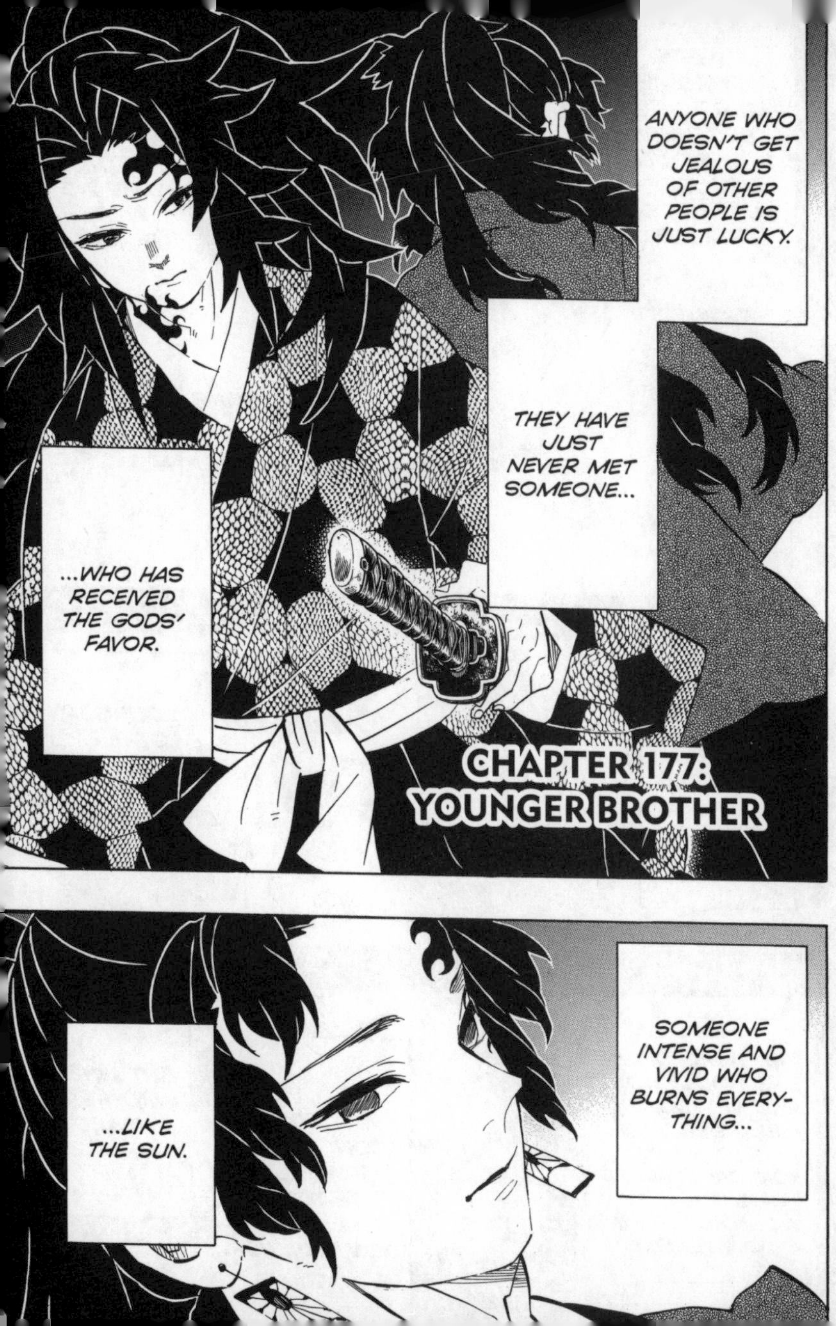
ANYONE WHO DOESN'T GET JEALOUS OF OTHER PEOPLE IS JUST LUCKY.
THEY HAVE JUST NEVER MET SOMEONE...
...WHO HAS RECEIVED THE GODS' FAVOR.
CHAPTER 177: YOUNGER BROTHER
SOMEONE INTENSE AND VIVID WHO BURNS EVERY-THING...
...LIKE THE SUN.

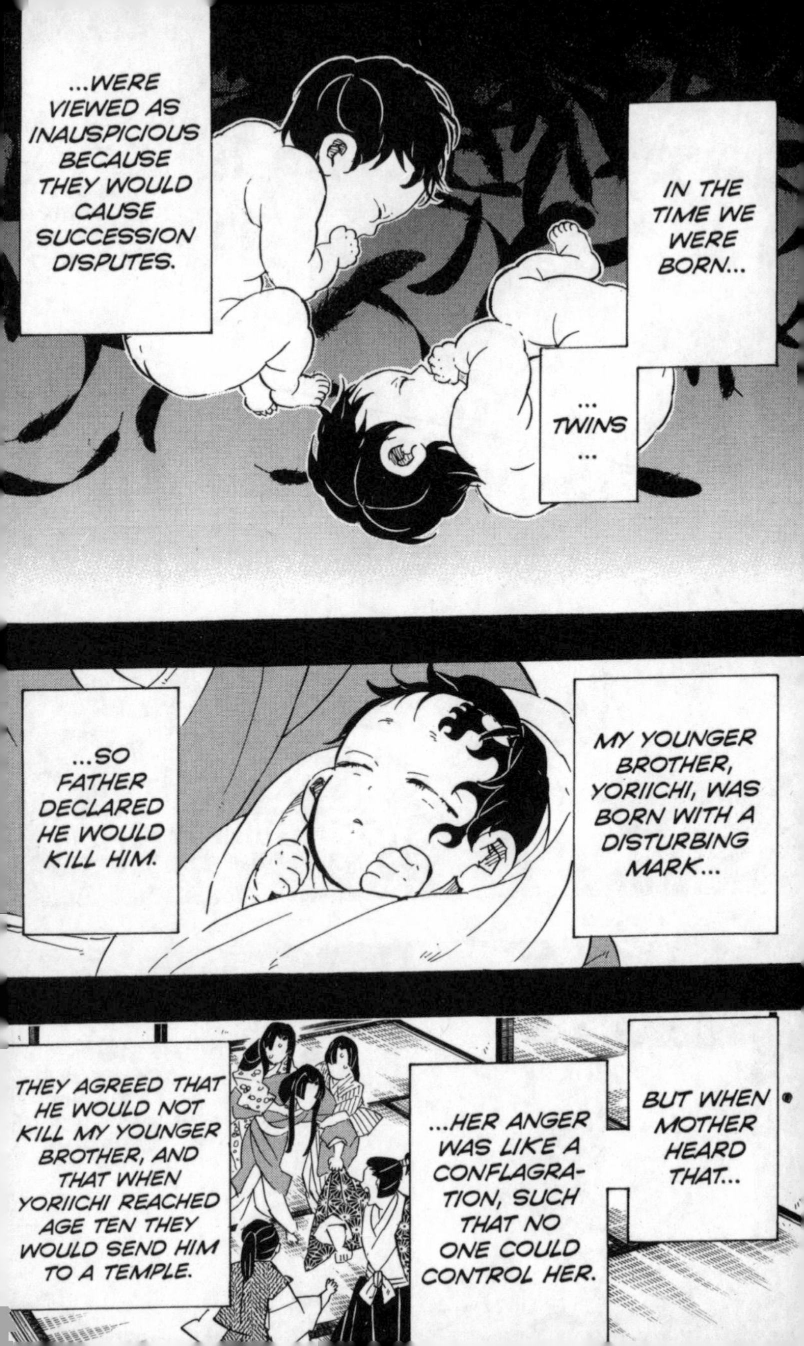
IN THE TIME WE WERE BORN...
... TWINS ...
...WERE VIEWED AS INAUSPICIOUS BECAUSE THEY WOULD CAUSE SUCCESSION DISPUTES.
MY YOUNGER BROTHER, YORIICHI, WAS BORN WITH A DISTURBING MARK...
...SO FATHER DECLARED HE WOULD KILL HIM.
BUT WHEN MOTHER HEARD THAT...
...HER ANGER WAS LIKE A CONFLAGRA-TION, SUCH THAT NO ONE COULD CONTROL HER.
THEY AGREED THAT HE WOULD NOT KILL MY YOUNGER BROTHER, AND THAT WHEN YORIICHI REACHED AGE TEN THEY WOULD SEND HIM TO A TEMPLE.

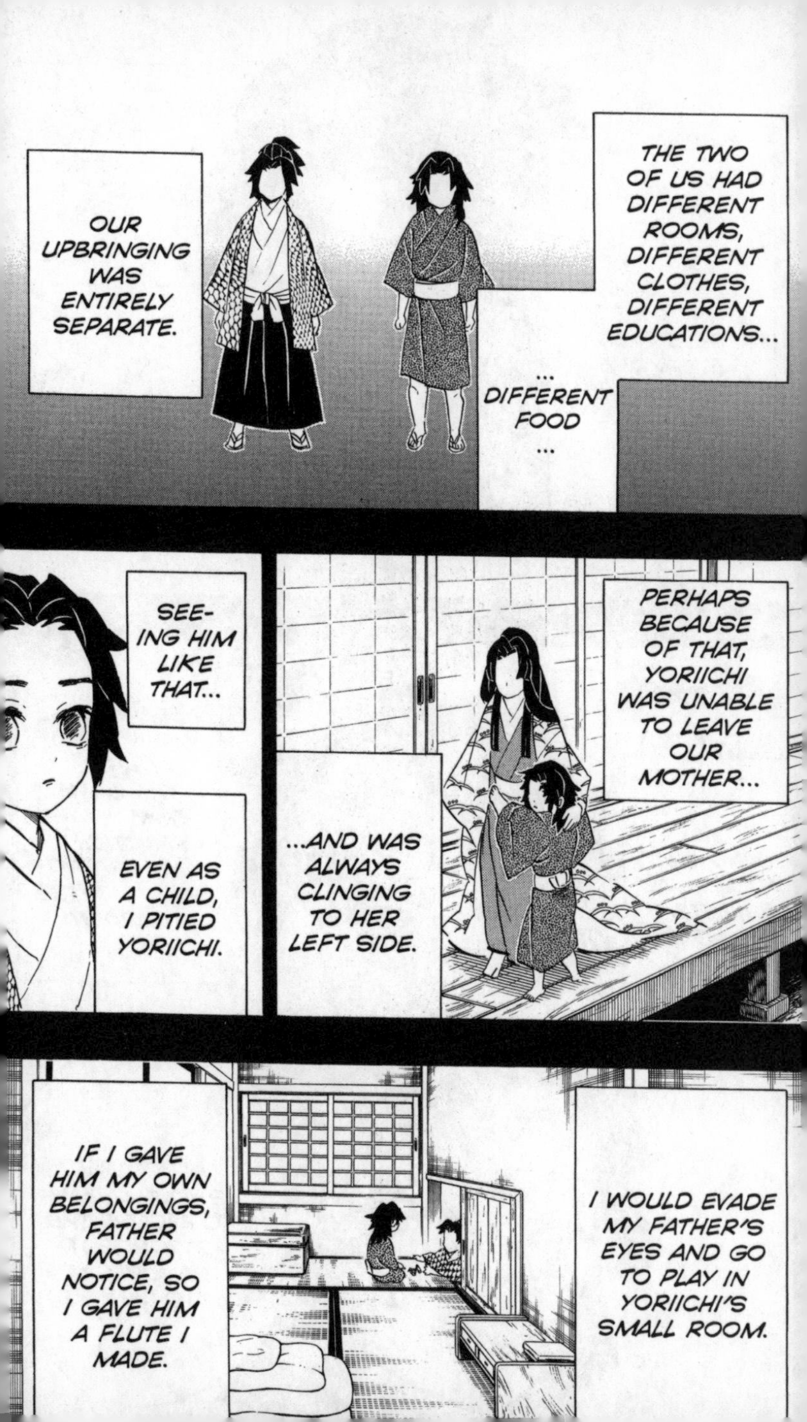
THE TWO OF US HAD DIFFERENT ROOMS, DIFFERENT CLOTHES, DIFFERENT EDUCATIONS...
... DIFFERENT FOOD ...
OUR UPBRINGING WAS ENTIRELY SEPARATE.
PERHAPS BECAUSE OF THAT, YORIICHI WAS UNABLE TO LEAVE OUR MOTHER...
...AND WAS ALWAYS CLINGING TO HER LEFT SIDE.
SEE-ING HIM LIKE THAT...
EVEN AS A CHILD, I PITIED YORIICHI.
I WOULD EVADE MY FATHER'S EYES AND GO TO PLAY IN YORIICHI'S SMALL ROOM.
IF I GAVE HIM MY OWN BELONGINGS, FATHER WOULD NOTICE, SO I GAVE HIM A FLUTE I MADE.

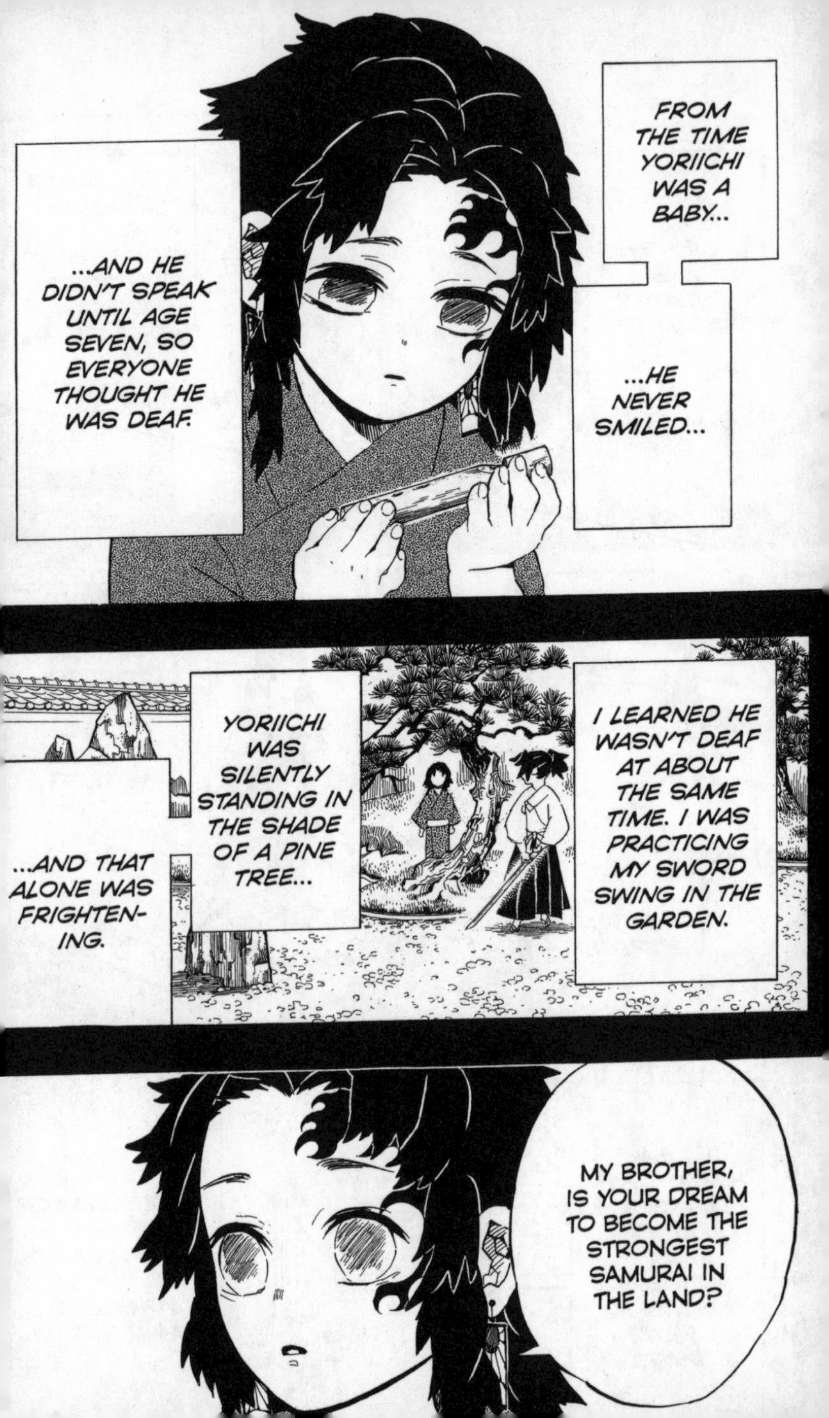
FROM THE TIME YORIICHI WAS A BABY...
...HE NEVER SMILED...
...AND HE DIDN'T SPEAK UNTIL AGE SEVEN, SO EVERYONE THOUGHT HE WAS DEAF.
I LEARNED HE WASN'T DEAF AT ABOUT THE SAME TIME. I WAS PRACTICING MY SWORD SWING IN THE GARDEN.
YORIICHI WAS SILENTLY STANDING IN THE SHADE OF A PINE TREE...
...AND THAT ALONE WAS FRIGHTEN-ING.
MY BROTHER, IS YOUR DREAM TO BECOME THE STRONGEST SAMURAI IN THE LAND?

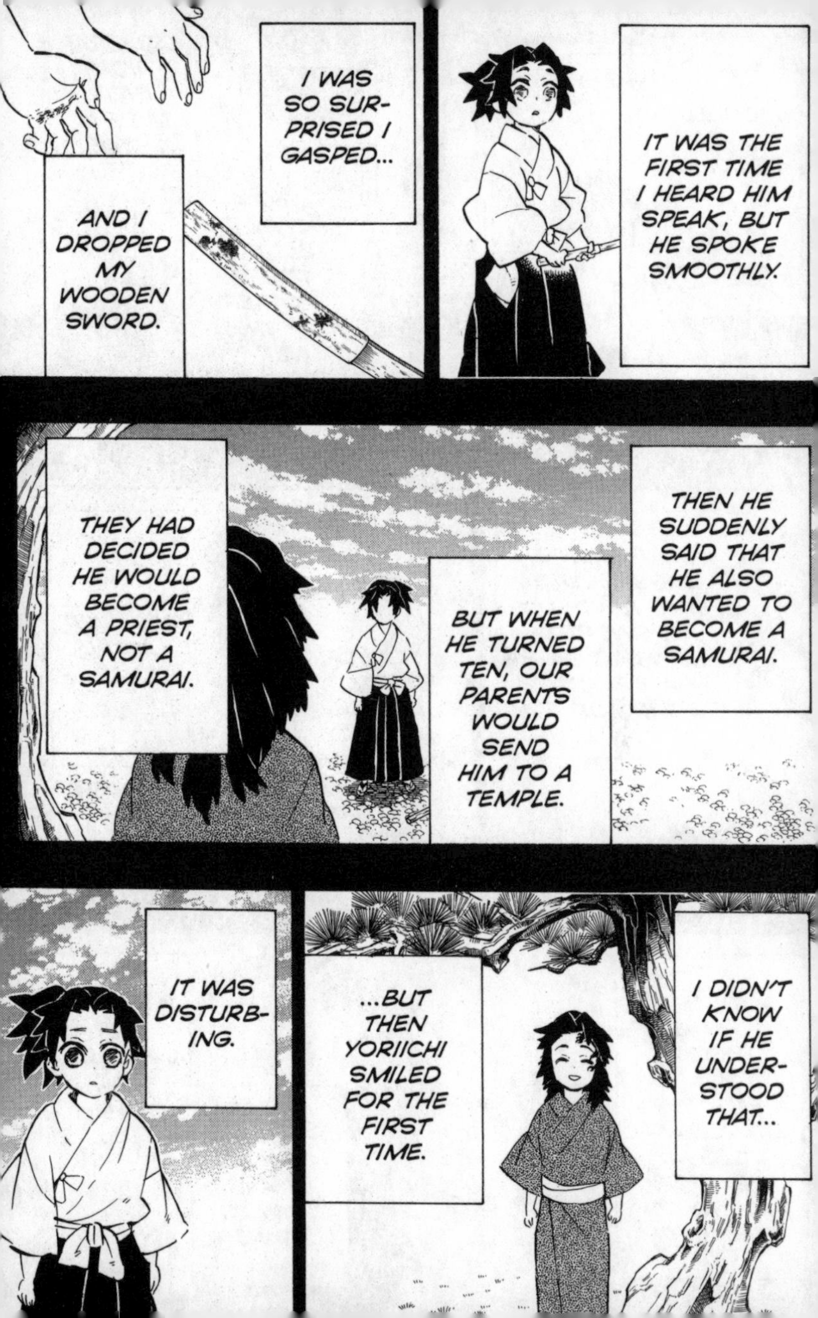
IT WAS THE FIRST TIME I HEARD HIM SPEAK, BUT HE SPOKE SMOOTHLY.
I WAS SO SUR-PRISED I GASPED...
AND I DROPPED MY WOODEN SWORD.
THEN HE SUDDENLY SAID THAT HE ALSO WANTED TO BECOME A SAMURAI.
BUT WHEN HE TURNED TEN, OUR PARENTS WOULD SEND HIM TO A TEMPLE.
THEY HAD DECIDED HE WOULD BECOME A PRIEST, NOT A SAMURAI.
I DIDN'T KNOW IF HE UNDER-STOOD THAT...
...BUT THEN YORIICHI SMILED FOR THE FIRST TIME.
IT WAS DISTURB-ING.

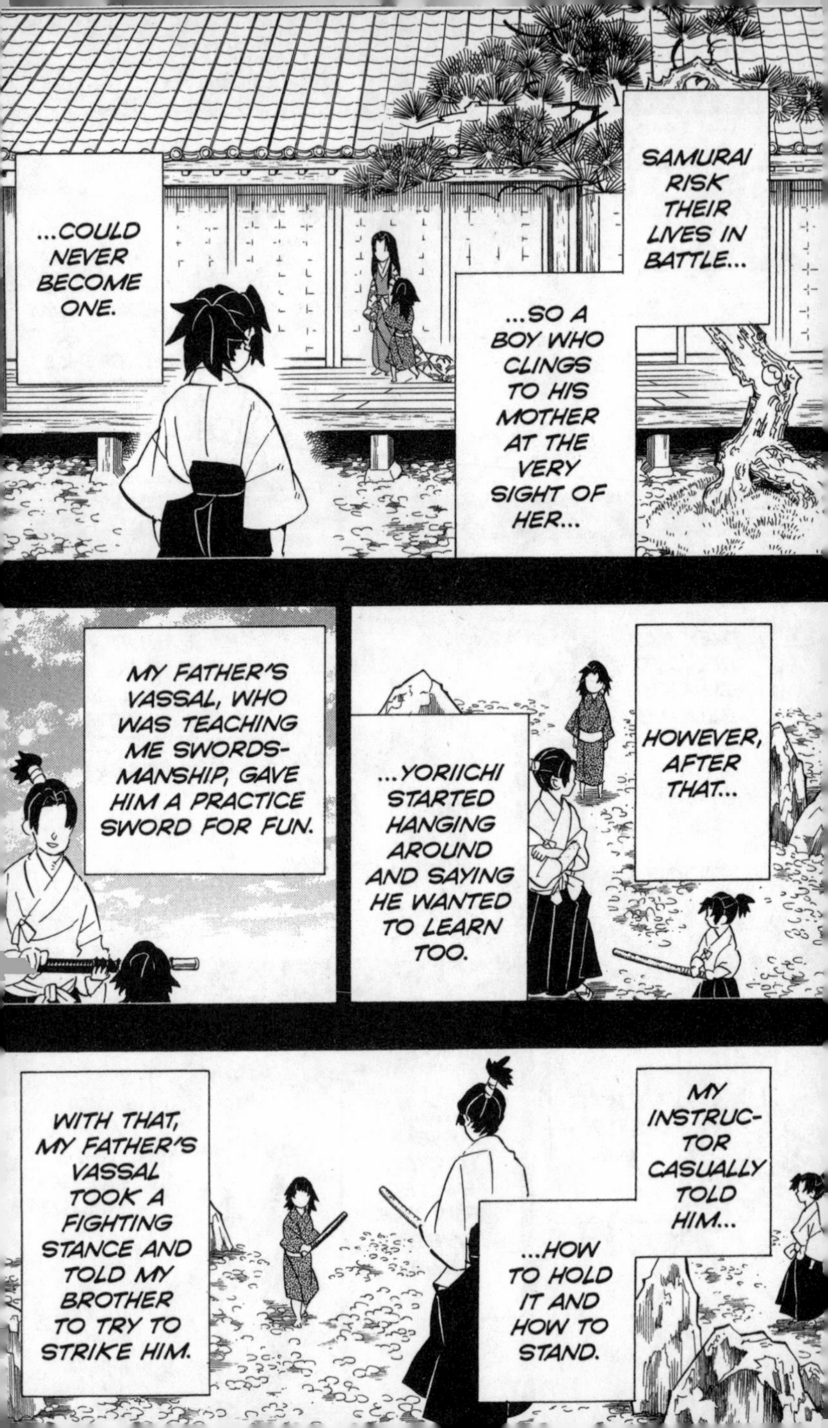
SAMURAI RISK THEIR LIVES IN BATTLE...
...SO A BOY WHO CLINGS TO HIS MOTHER AT THE VERY SIGHT OF HER...
...COULD NEVER BECOME ONE.
HOWEVER, AFTER THAT...
...YORIICHI STARTED HANGING AROUND AND SAYING HE WANTED TO LEARN TOO.
MY FATHER'S VASSAL, WHO WAS TEACHING ME SWORDS-MANSHIP, GAVE HIM A PRACTICE SWORD FOR FUN.
MY INSTRUC-TOR CASUALLY TOLD HIM...
...HOW TO HOLD IT AND HOW TO STAND.
WITH THAT, MY FATHER'S VASSAL TOOK A FIGHTING STANCE AND TOLD MY BROTHER TO TRY TO STRIKE HIM.

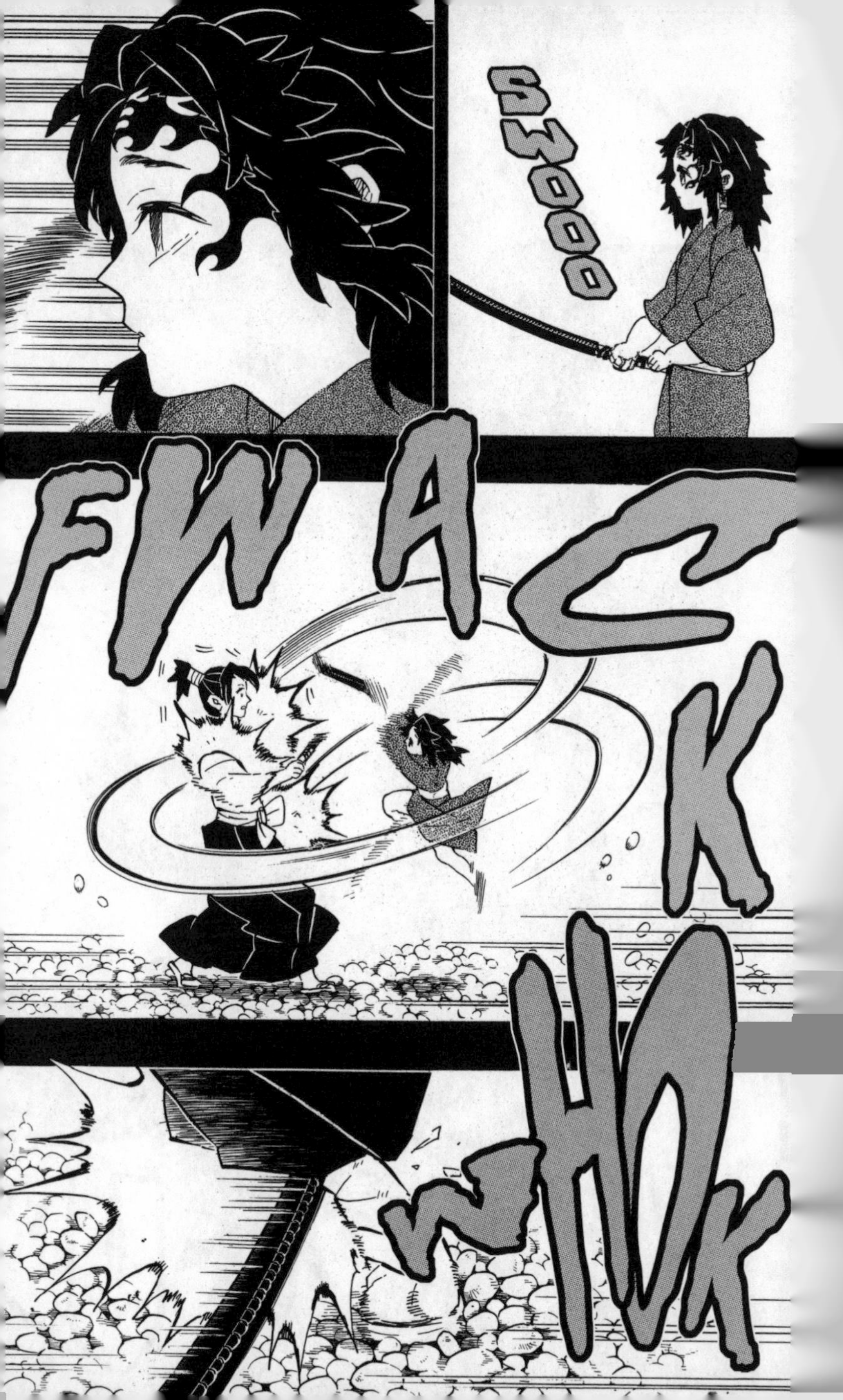
SWOOO
FWACK
WHOK

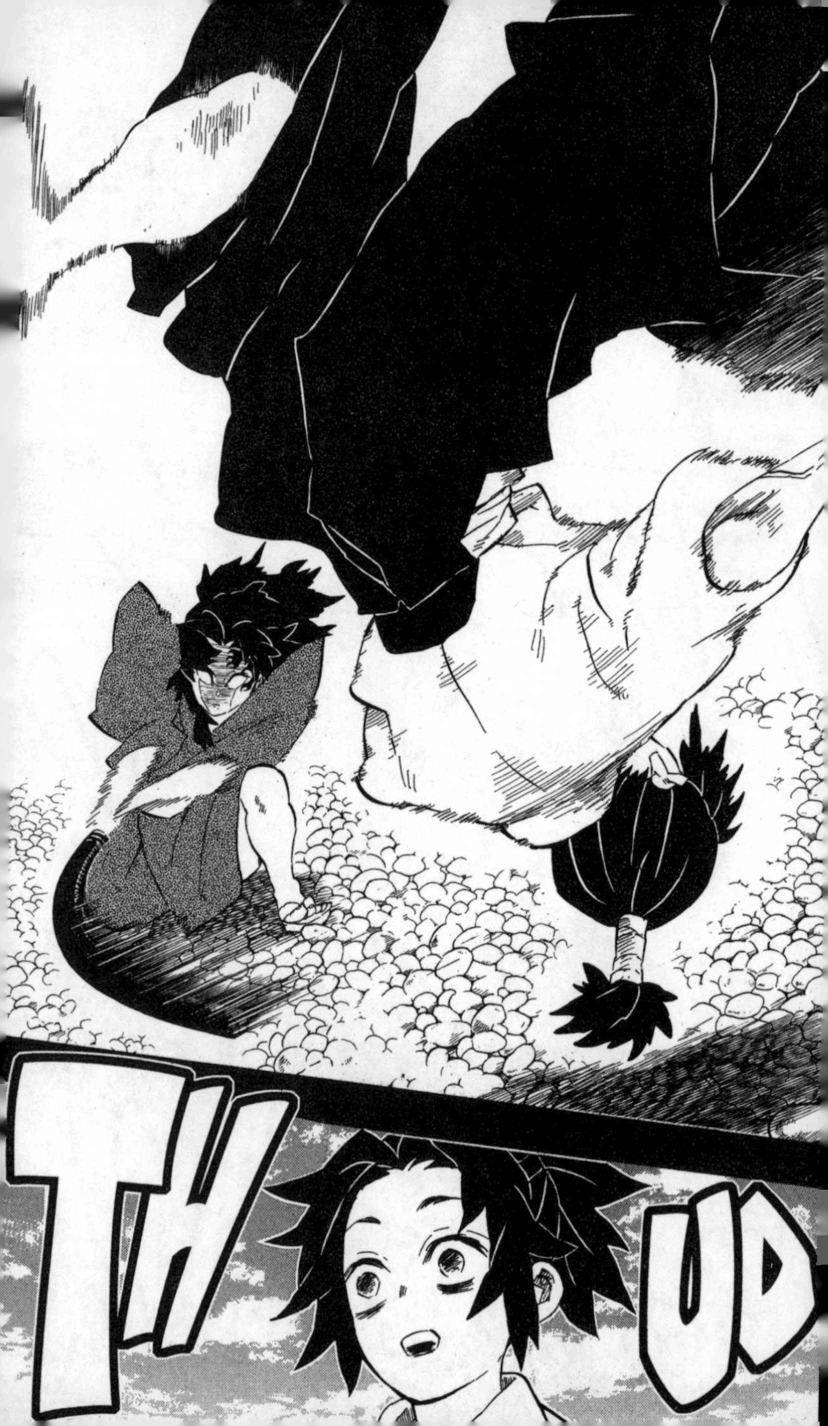
THUD

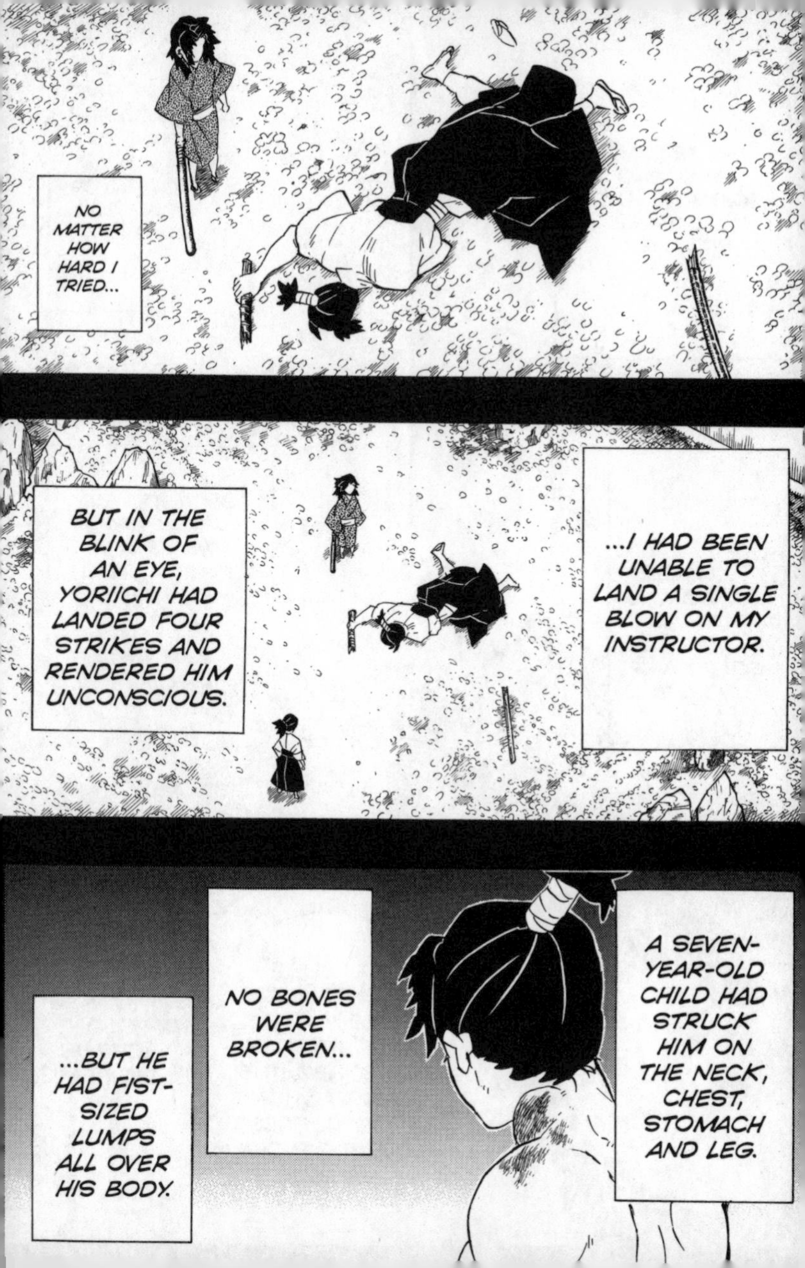
NO MATTER HOW HARD I TRIED...
...I HAD BEEN UNABLE TO LAND A SINGLE BLOW ON MY INSTRUCTOR.
BUT IN THE BLINK OF AN EYE, YORIICHI HAD LANDED FOUR STRIKES AND RENDERED HIM UNCONSCIOUS.
A SEVEN-YEAR-OLD CHILD HAD STRUCK HIM ON THE NECK, CHEST, STOMACH AND LEG.
NO BONES WERE BROKEN...
...BUT HE HAD FIST-SIZED LUMPS ALL OVER HIS BODY.

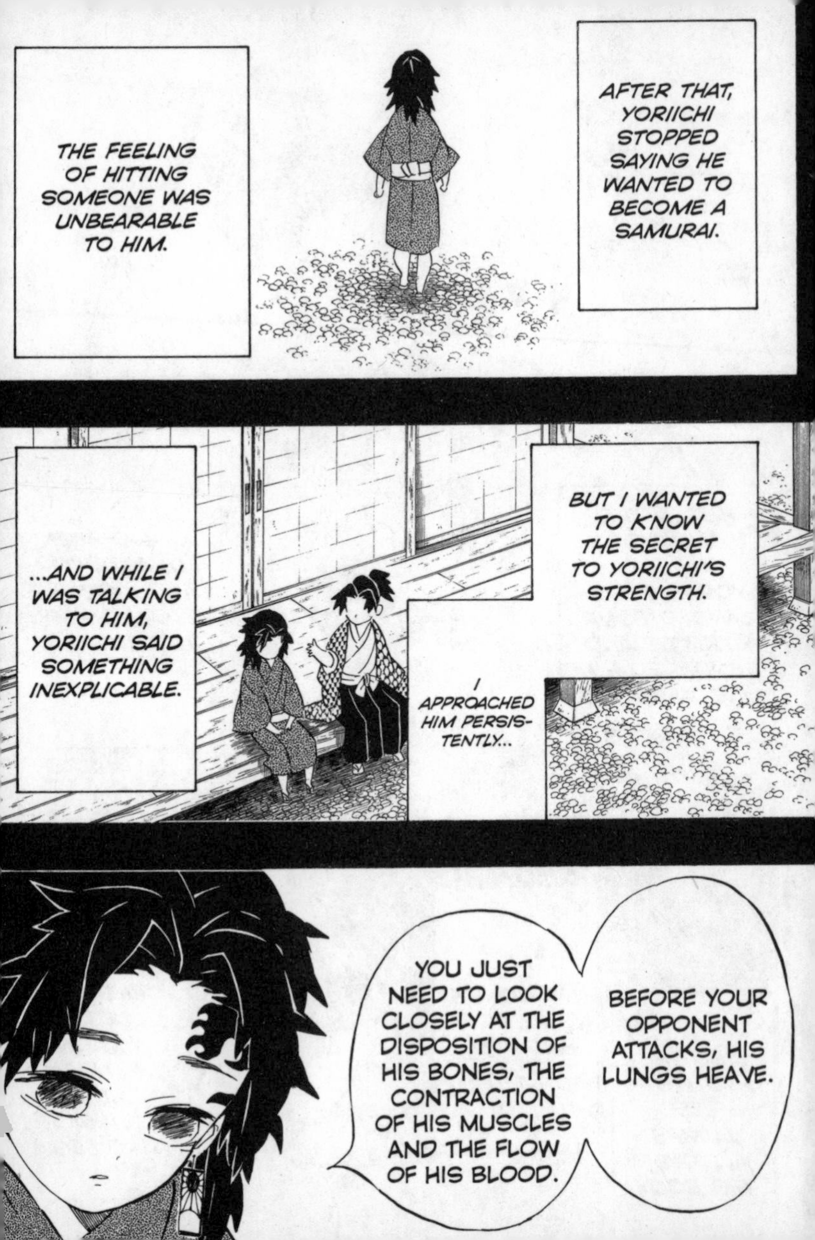
AFTER THAT, YORIICHI STOPPED SAYING HE WANTED TO BECOME A SAMURAI.
THE FEELING OF HITTING SOMEONE WAS UNBEARABLE TO HIM.
BUT I WANTED TO KNOW THE SECRET TO YORIICHI'S STRENGTH.
I APPROACHED HIM PERSIS-TENTLY...
...AND WHILE I WAS TALKING TO HIM, YORIICHI SAID SOMETHING INEXPLICABLE.
BEFORE YOUR OPPONENT ATTACKS, HIS LUNGS HEAVE.
YOU JUST NEED TO LOOK CLOSELY AT THE DISPOSITION OF HIS BONES, THE CONTRACTION OF HIS MUSCLES AND THE FLOW OF HIS BLOOD.

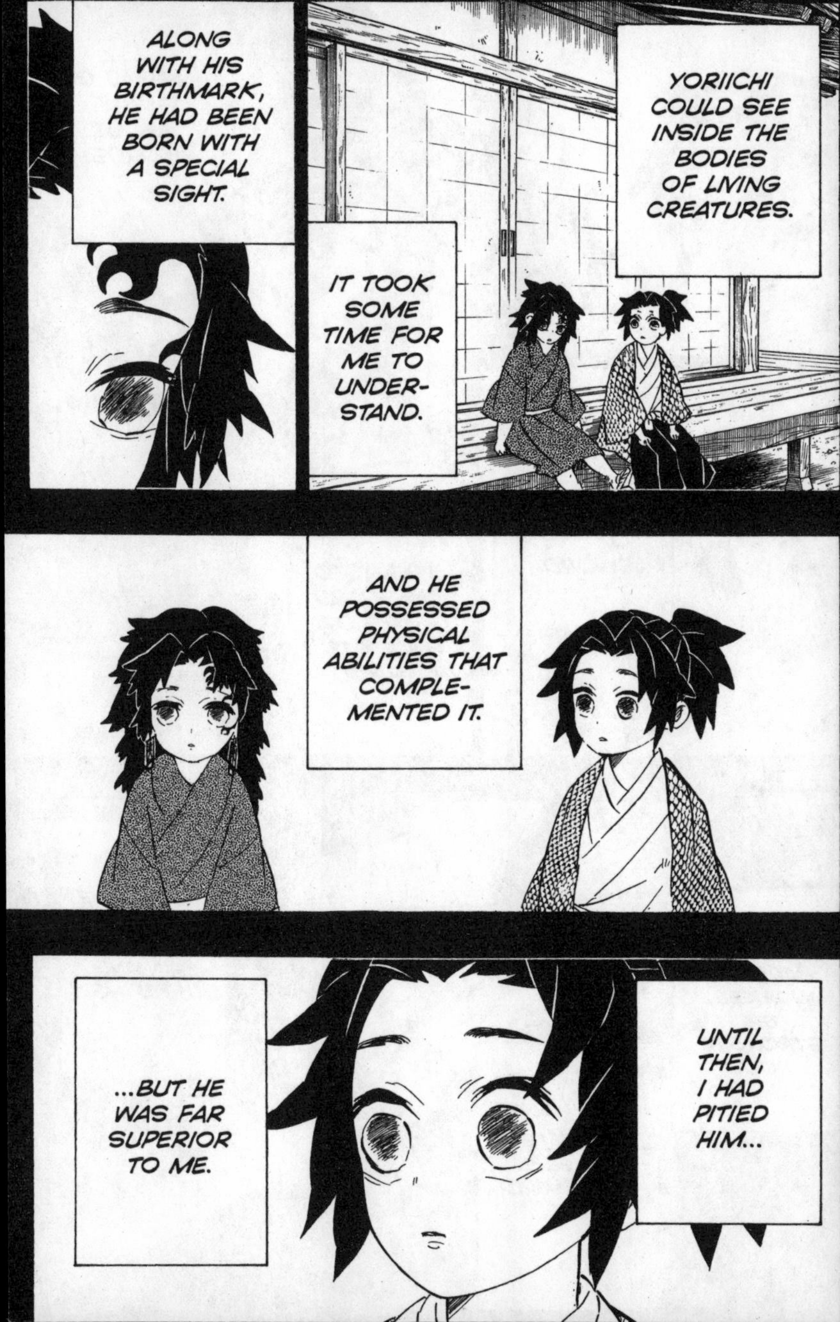
YORIICHI COULD SEE INSIDE THE BODIES OF LIVING CREATURES.
IT TOOK SOME TIME FOR ME TO UNDERSTAND.
ALONG WITH HIS BIRTHMARK, HE HAD BEEN BORN WITH A SPECIAL SIGHT.
AND HE POSSESSED PHYSICAL ABILITIES THAT COMPLEMENTED IT.
UNTIL THEN, I HAD PITIED HIM...
...BUT HE WAS FAR SUPERIOR TO ME.

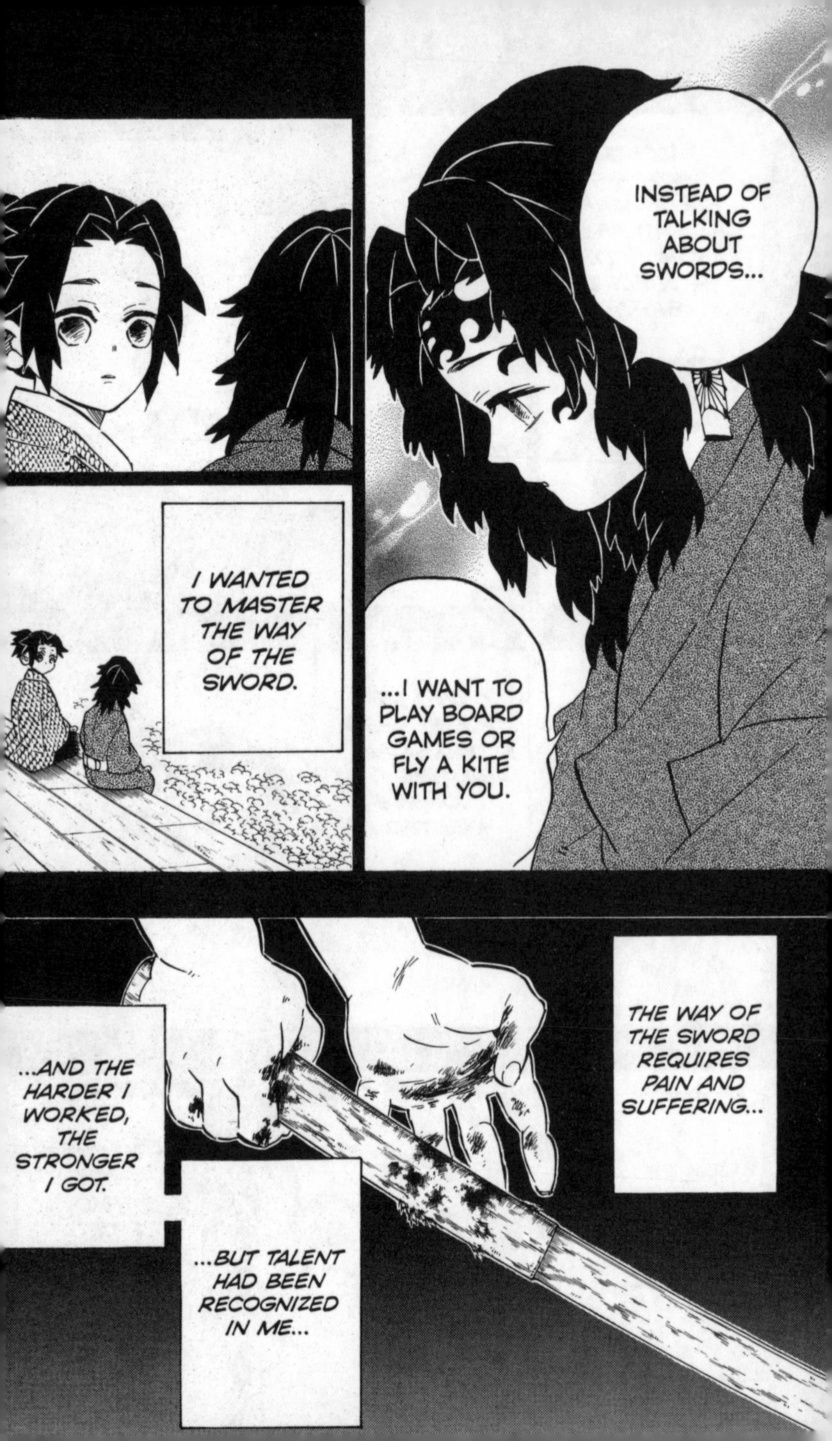
INSTEAD OF TALKING ABOUT SWORDS...
...I WANT TO PLAY BOARD GAMES OR FLY A KITE WITH YOU.
I WANTED TO MASTER THE WAY OF THE SWORD.
THE WAY OF THE SWORD REQUIRES PAIN AND SUFFERING...
...AND THE HARDER I WORKED, THE STRONGER I GOT.
...BUT TALENT HAD BEEN RECOGNIZED IN ME...

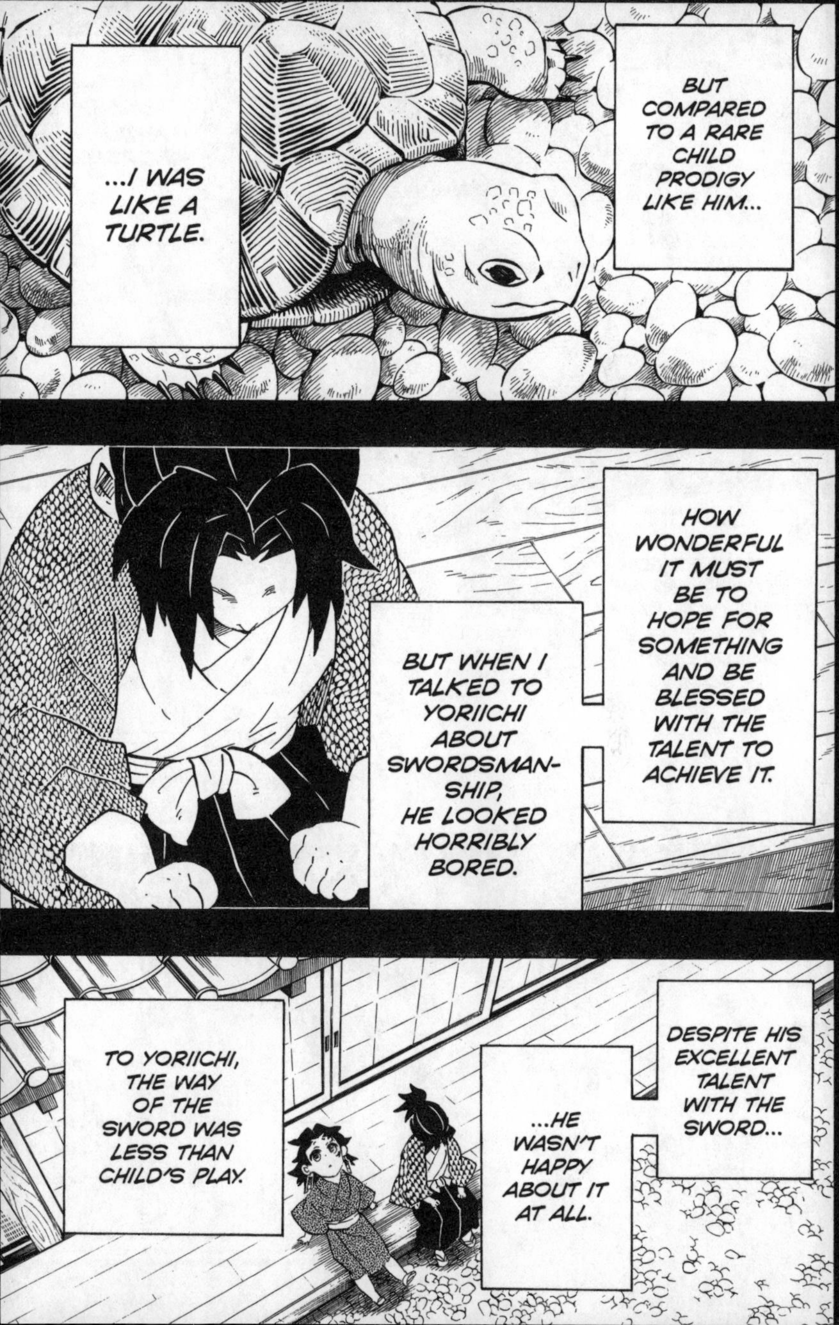
BUT COMPARED TO A RARE CHILD PRODIGY LIKE HIM...
...I WAS LIKE A TURTLE.
HOW WONDERFUL IT MUST BE TO HOPE FOR SOMETHING AND BE BLESSED WITH THE TALENT TO ACHIEVE IT.
BUT WHEN I TALKED TO YORIICHI ABOUT SWORDSMANSHIP, HE LOOKED HORRIBLY BORED.
DESPITE HIS EXCELLENT TALENT WITH THE SWORD...
...HE WASN'T HAPPY ABOUT IT AT ALL.
TO YORIICHI, THE WAY OF THE SWORD WAS LESS THAN CHILD'S PLAY.

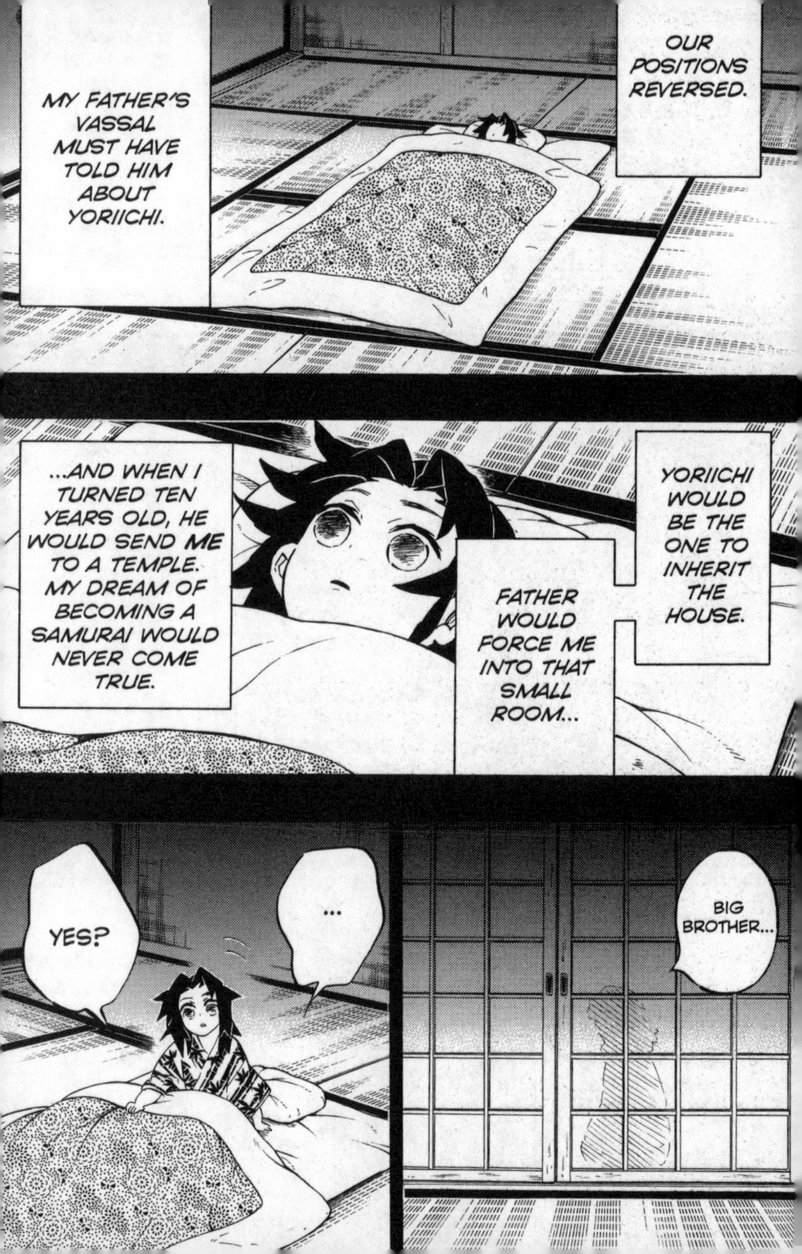
OUR POSITIONS REVERSED.
MY FATHER'S VASSAL MUST HAVE TOLD HIM ABOUT YORIICHI.
YORIICHI WOULD BE THE ONE TO INHERIT THE HOUSE.
FATHER WOULD FORCE ME INTO THAT SMALL ROOM...
...AND WHEN I TURNED TEN YEARS OLD, HE WOULD SEND ME TO A TEMPLE. MY DREAM OF BECOMING A SAMURAI WOULD NEVER COME TRUE.
BIG BROTHER...
...
YES?

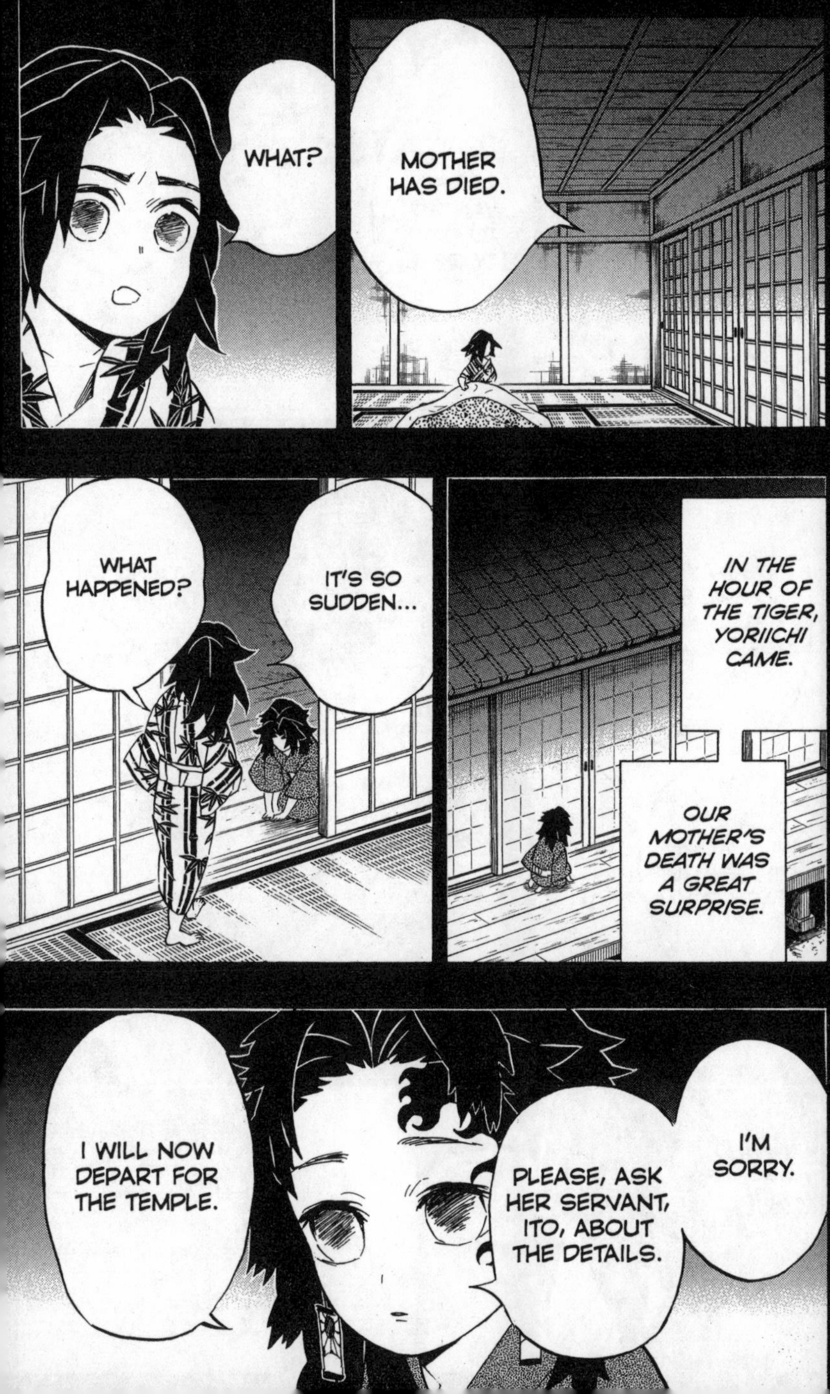
MOTHER HAS DIED.
WHAT?
IN THE HOUR OF THE TIGER, YORIICHI CAME.
OUR MOTHER'S DEATH WAS A GREAT SURPRISE.
IT'S SO SUDDEN...
WHAT HAPPENED?
I'M SORRY.
PLEASE, ASK HER SERVANT, ITO, ABOUT THE DETAILS.
I WILL NOW DEPART FOR THE TEMPLE.

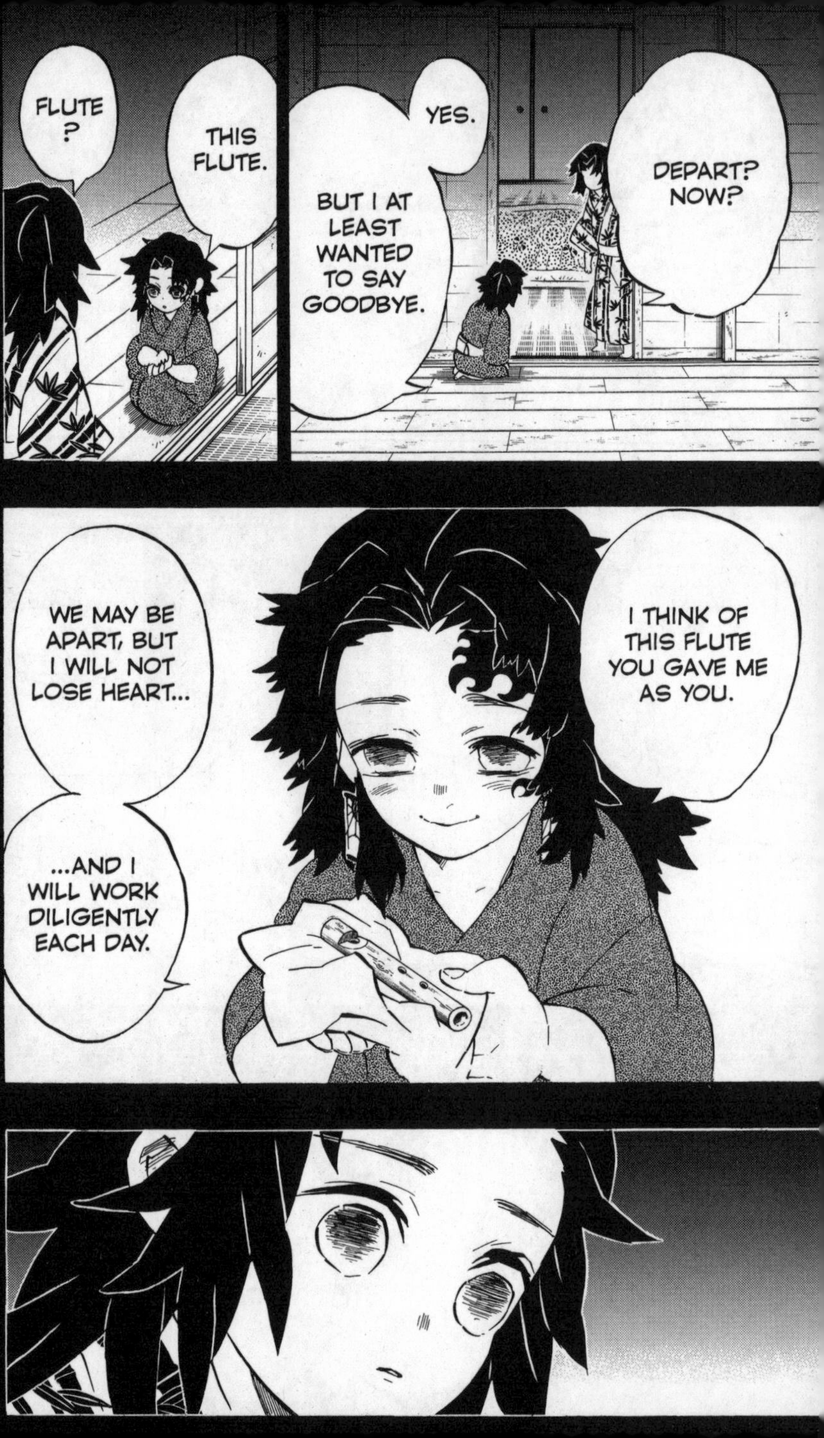
DEPART? NOW?
YES.
BUT I AT LEAST WANTED TO SAY GOODBYE.
THIS FLUTE.
FLUTE?
I THINK OF THIS FLUTE YOU GAVE ME AS YOU.
WE MAY BE APART, BUT I WILL NOT LOSE HEART...
...AND I WILL WORK DILIGENTLY EACH DAY.

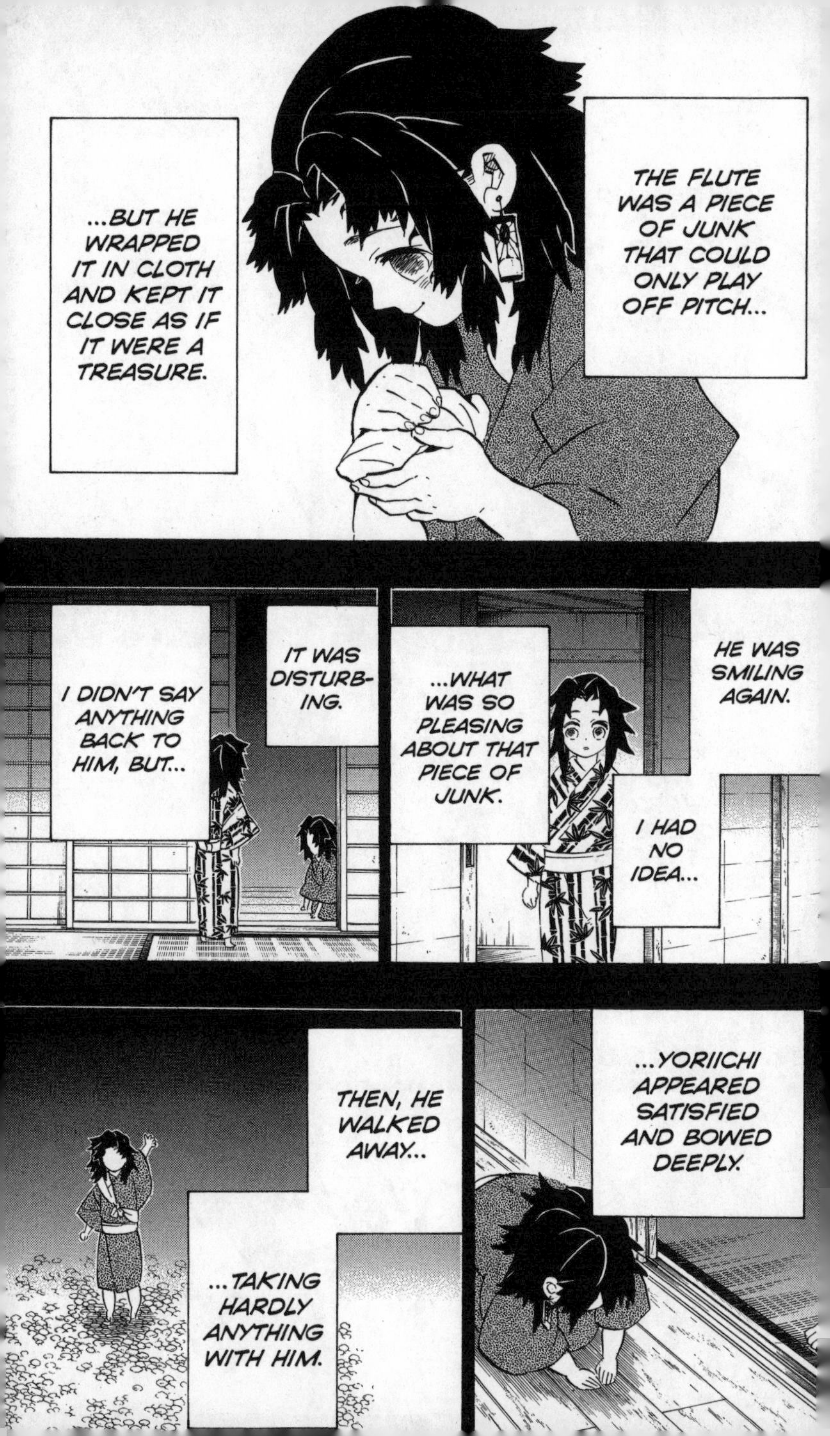
THE FLUTE WAS A PIECE OF JUNK THAT COULD ONLY PLAY OFF PITCH...
...BUT HE WRAPPED IT IN CLOTH AND KEPT IT CLOSE AS IF IT WERE A TREASURE.
HE WAS SMILING AGAIN.
I HAD NO IDEA...
...WHAT WAS SO PLEASING ABOUT THAT PIECE OF JUNK.
I DIDN'T SAY ANYTHING BACK TO HIM, BUT...
IT WAS DISTURB-ING.
...YORIICHI APPEARED SATISFIED AND BOWED DEEPLY.
THEN, HE WALKED AWAY...
...TAKING HARDLY ANYTHING WITH HIM.

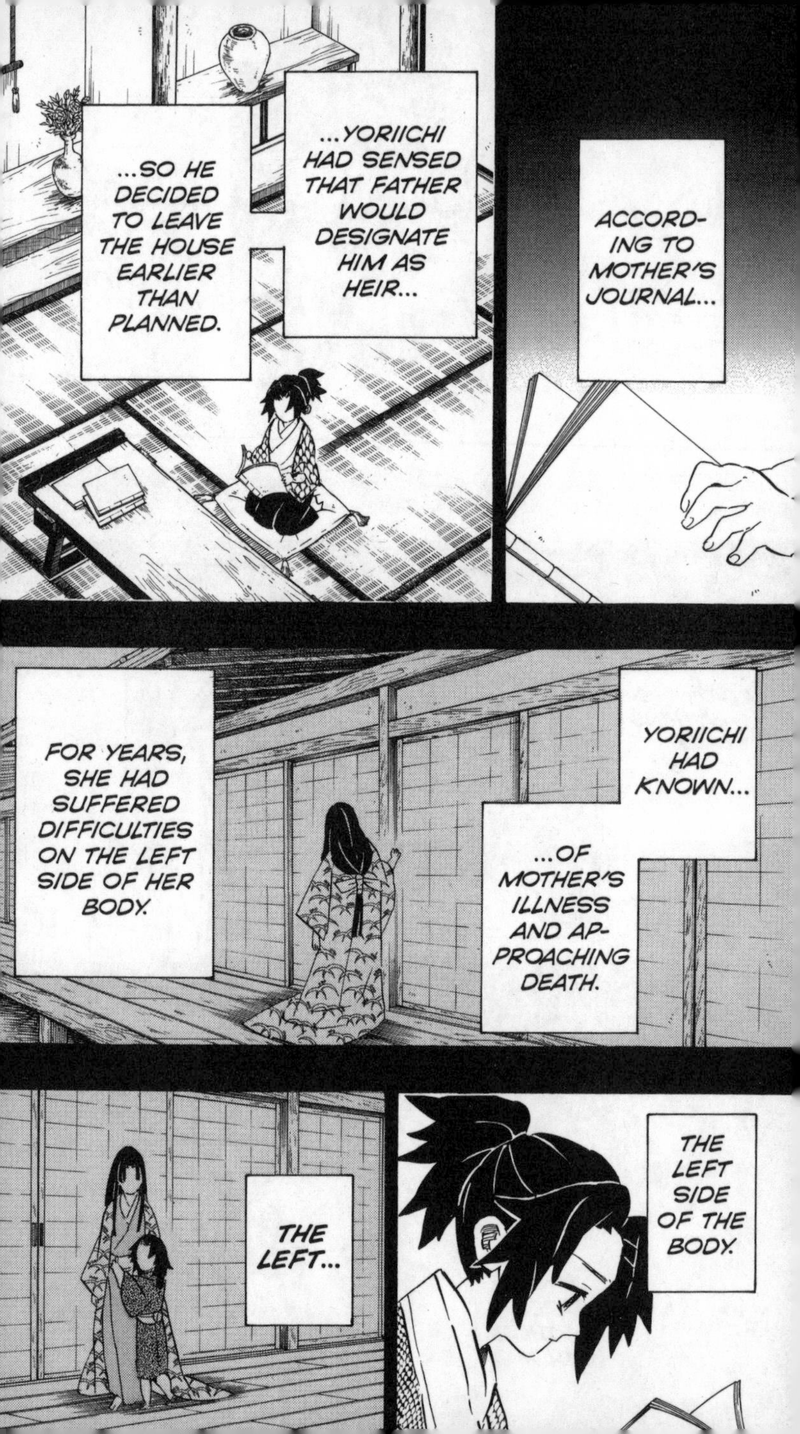
ACCORDING TO MOTHER'S JOURNAL...
...YORIICHI HAD SENSED THAT FATHER WOULD DESIGNATE HIM AS HEIR...
...SO HE DECIDED TO LEAVE THE HOUSE EARLIER THAN PLANNED.
YORIICHI HAD KNOWN...
...OF MOTHER'S ILLNESS AND APPROACHING DEATH.
FOR YEARS, SHE HAD SUFFERED DIFFICULTIES ON THE LEFT SIDE OF HER BODY.
THE LEFT SIDE OF THE BODY.
THE LEFT...

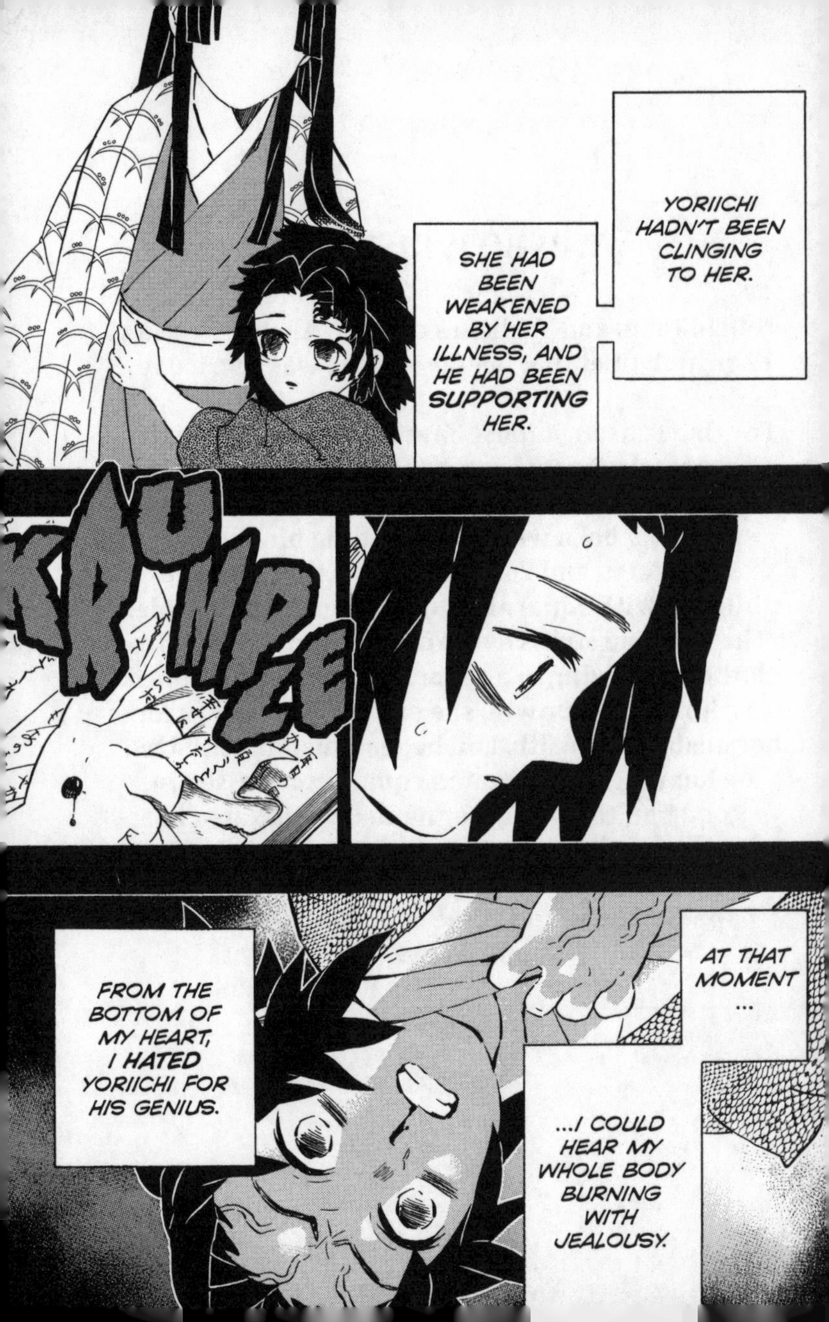
YORIICHI HADN'T BEEN CLINGING TO HER.
SHE HAD BEEN WEAKENED BY HER ILLNESS, AND HE HAD BEEN SUPPORTING HER.
KRUMPLE
AT THAT MOMENT ...
...I COULD HEAR MY WHOLE BODY BURNING WITH JEALOUSY.
FROM THE BOTTOM OF MY HEART, I HATED YORIICHI FOR HIS GENIUS.

TAISHO WHISPERS

Michikatsu and Yoriichi's mother, Akeno, was so calm and quiet that people say she was like a doll.

For that reason, it must have been shocking to the people who knew her when she flew into a rage at her husband for saying he would kill Yoriichi for being born with an unsettling birthmark. Michikatsu and Yoriichi's mother treated the children with equal affection as much as possible. The horrible stress over Yoriichi wearing shabby clothes and living in a room like a closet worsened her illness. In her will, she expressed concern for her husband's health, and begged that her children be kept together, treated equally and raised in good health. The father named Michikatsu in the hope that he would be strong and always be successful, while the mother named Yoriichi in the hope that he would value connections between people above all.

CHAPTER 178: EVEN IF YOU REACH OUT YOUR HAND

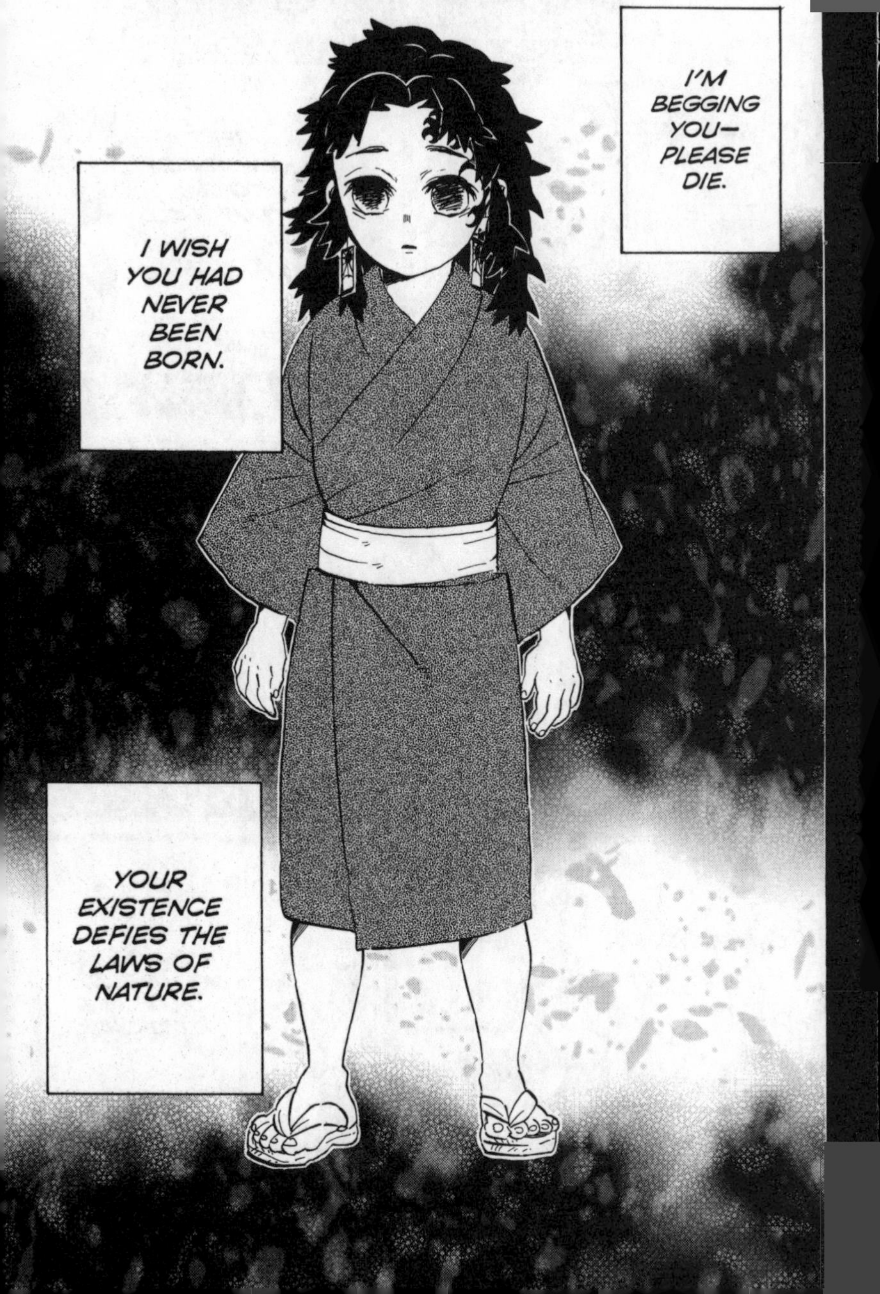
I'M BEGGING YOU—PLEASE DIE.
I WISH YOU HAD NEVER BEEN BORN.
YOUR EXISTENCE DEFIES THE LAWS OF NATURE.

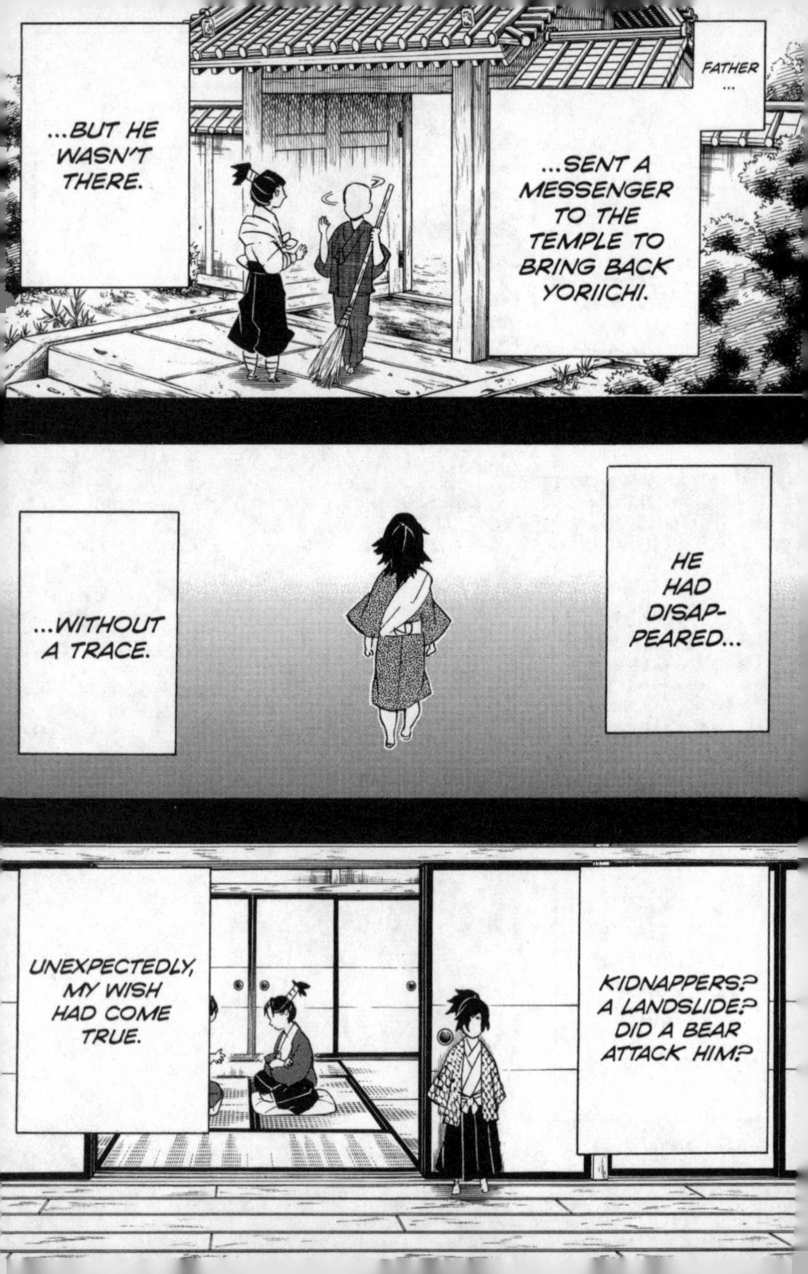
FATHER ...
...SENT A MESSENGER TO THE TEMPLE TO BRING BACK YORIICHI.
...BUT HE WASN'T THERE.
HE HAD DISAPPEARED...
...WITHOUT A TRACE.
KIDNAPPERS? A LANDSLIDE? DID A BEAR ATTACK HIM?
UNEXPECTEDLY, MY WISH HAD COME TRUE.

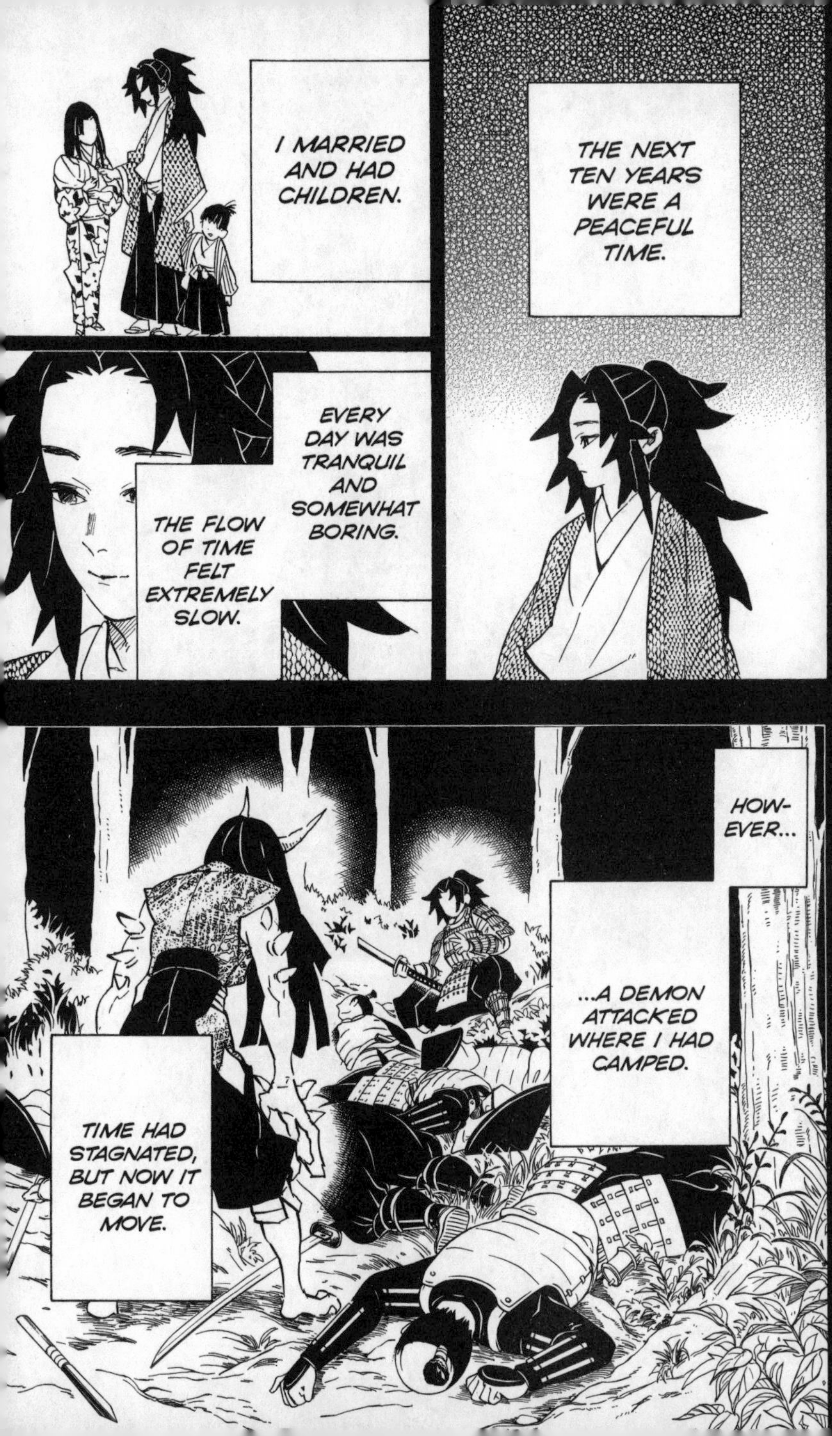
THE NEXT TEN YEARS WERE A PEACEFUL TIME.
I MARRIED AND HAD CHILDREN.
EVERY DAY WAS TRANQUIL AND SOMEWHAT BORING.
THE FLOW OF TIME FELT EXTREMELY SLOW.
HOW-EVER...
...A DEMON ATTACKED WHERE I HAD CAMPED.
TIME HAD STAGNATED, BUT NOW IT BEGAN TO MOVE.

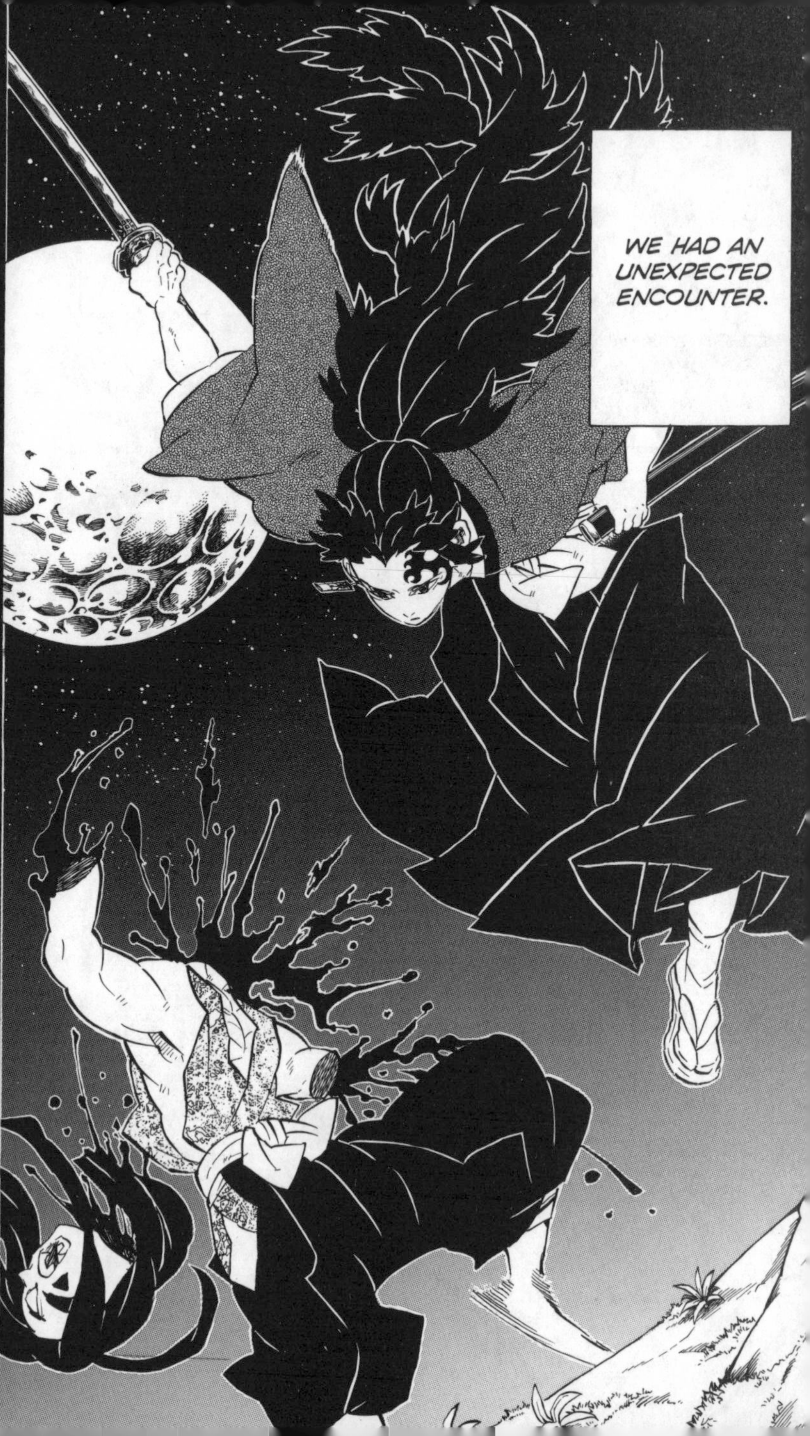
WE HAD AN UNEXPECTED ENCOUNTER.

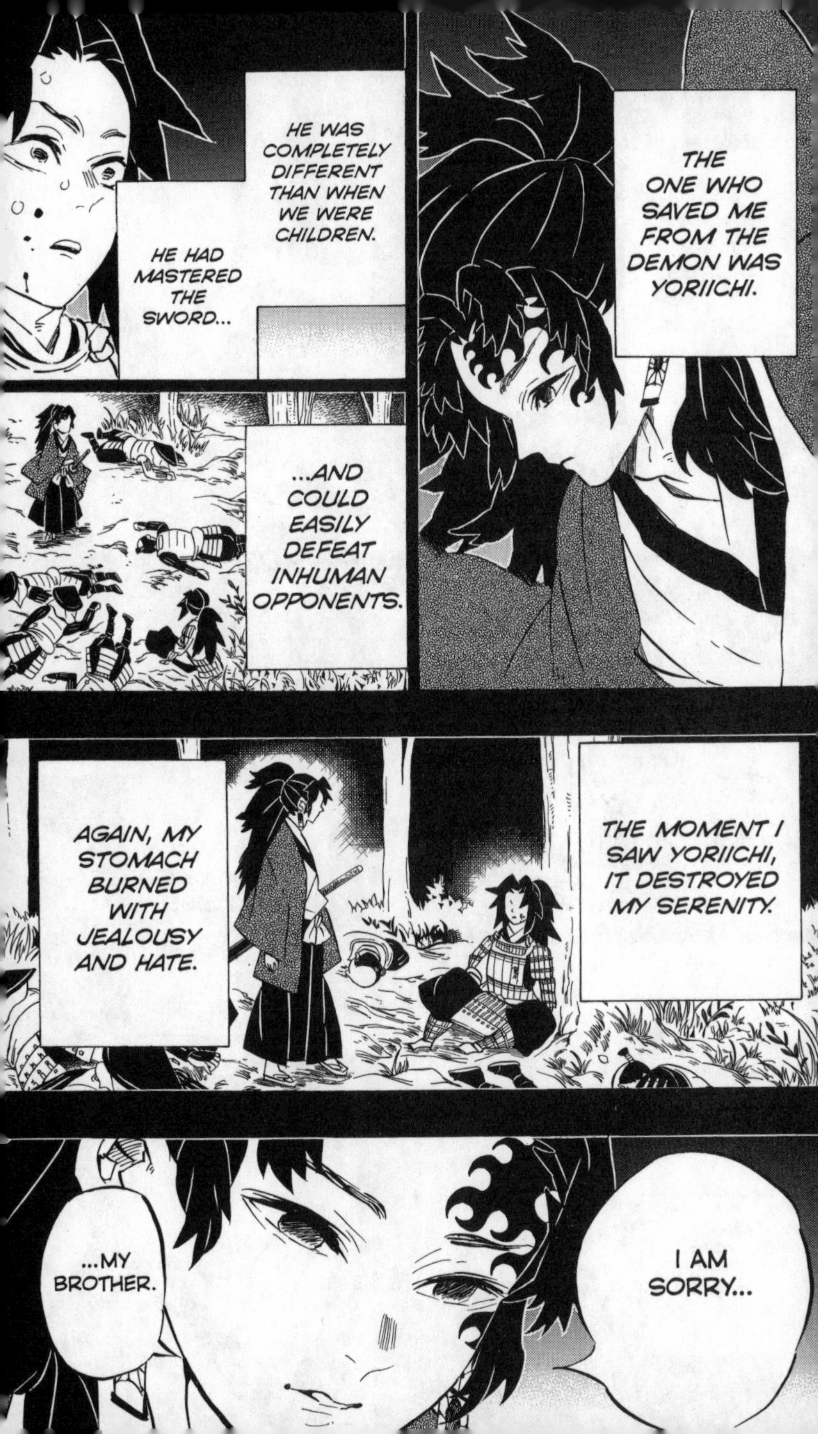
THE ONE WHO SAVED ME FROM THE DEMON WAS YORIICHI.
HE WAS COMPLETELY DIFFERENT THAN WHEN WE WERE CHILDREN.
HE HAD MASTERED THE SWORD...
...AND COULD EASILY DEFEAT INHUMAN OPPONENTS.
THE MOMENT I SAW YORIICHI, IT DESTROYED MY SERENITY.
AGAIN, MY STOMACH BURNED WITH JEALOUSY AND HATE.
I AM SORRY...
...MY BROTHER.

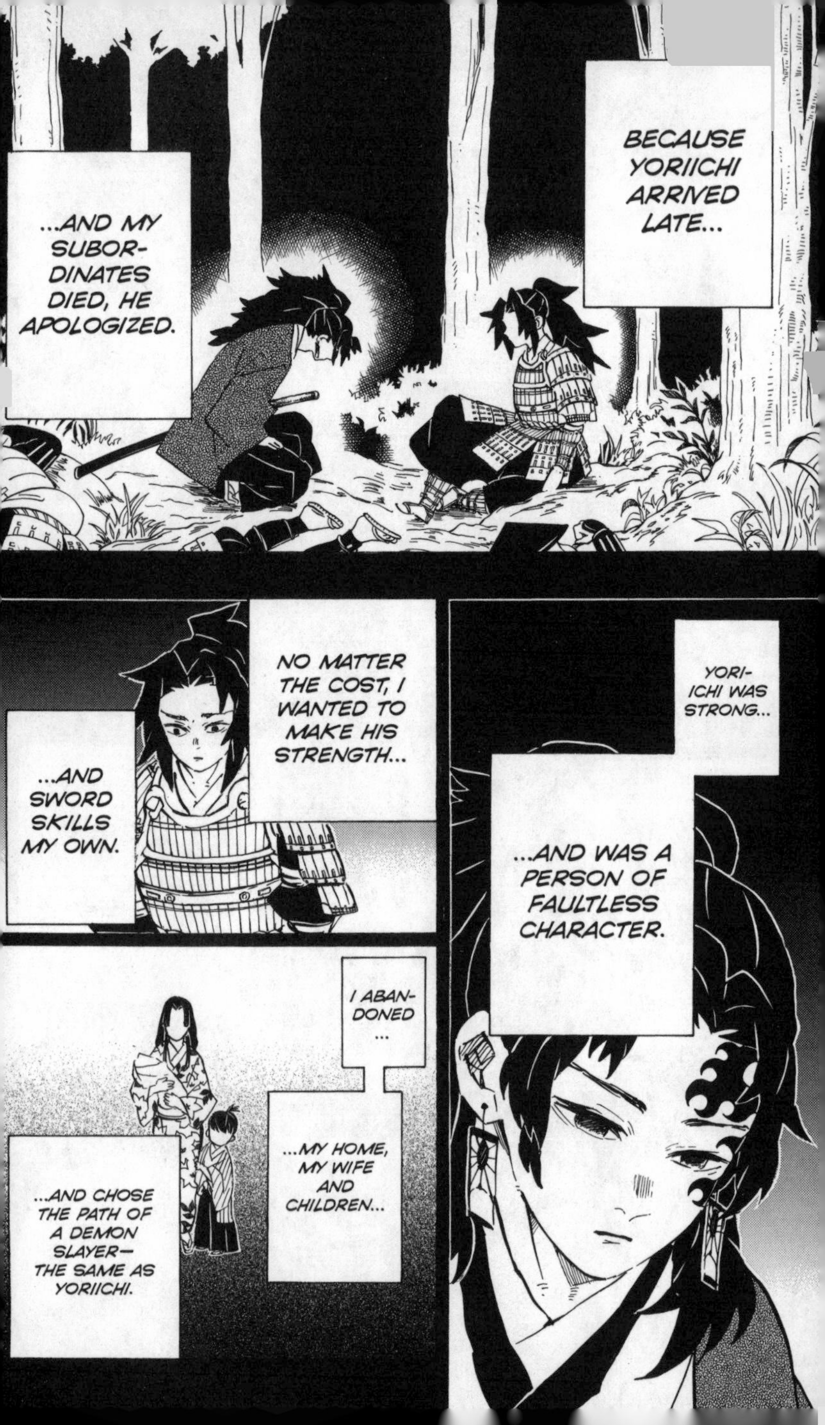
BECAUSE YORIICHI ARRIVED LATE...
...AND MY SUBOR-DINATES DIED, HE APOLOGIZED.
YORI-ICHI WAS STRONG...
...AND WAS A PERSON OF FAULTLESS CHARACTER.
NO MATTER THE COST, I WANTED TO MAKE HIS STRENGTH...
...AND SWORD SKILLS MY OWN.
I ABAN-DONED ...
...MY HOME, MY WIFE AND CHILDREN...
...AND CHOSE THE PATH OF A DEMON SLAYER—THE SAME AS YORIICHI.

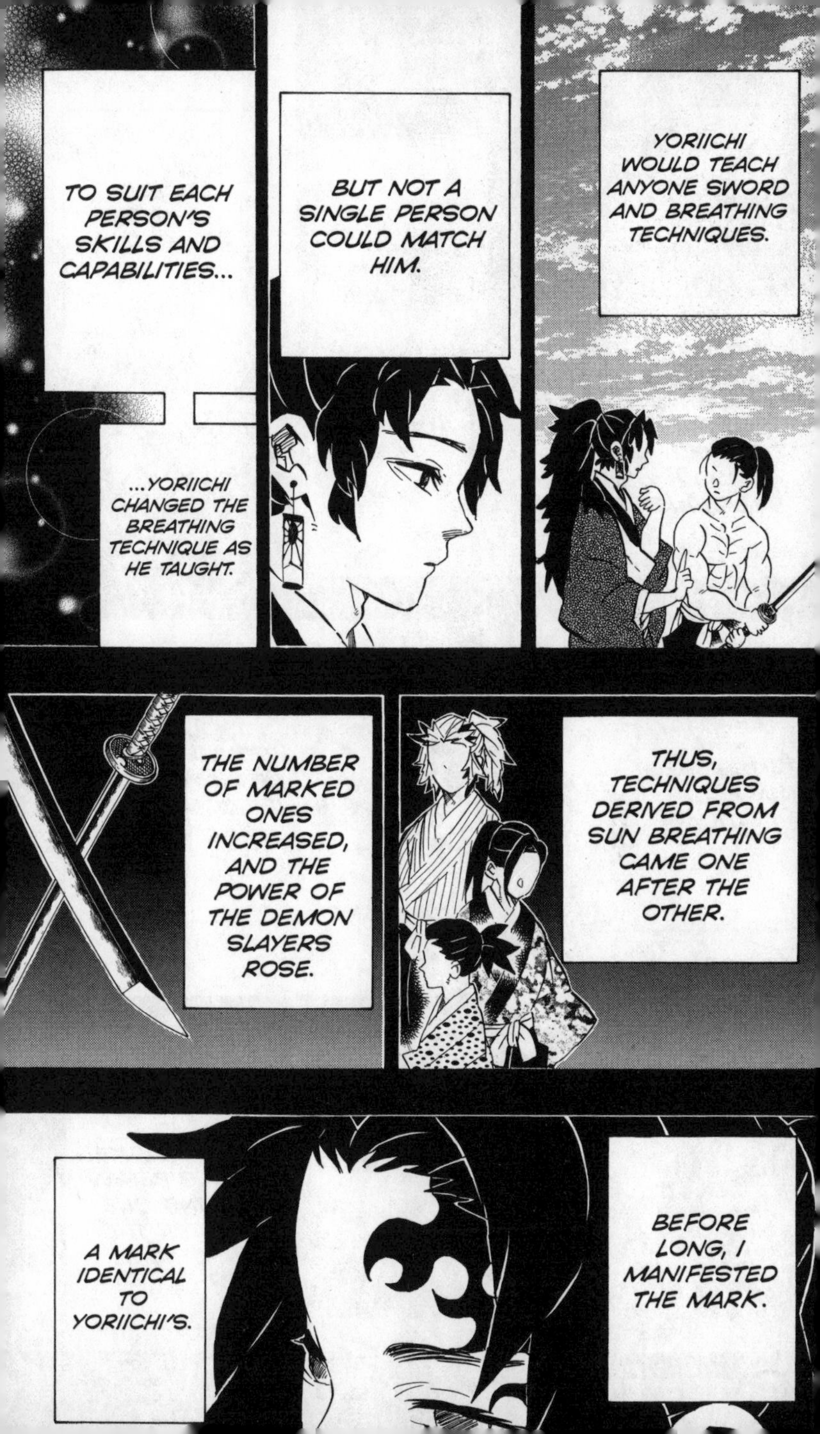
YORIICHI WOULD TEACH ANYONE SWORD AND BREATHING TECHNIQUES.
BUT NOT A SINGLE PERSON COULD MATCH HIM.
TO SUIT EACH PERSON'S SKILLS AND CAPABILITIES...
...YORIICHI CHANGED THE BREATHING TECHNIQUE AS HE TAUGHT.
THUS, TECHNIQUES DERIVED FROM SUN BREATHING CAME ONE AFTER THE OTHER.
THE NUMBER OF MARKED ONES INCREASED, AND THE POWER OF THE DEMON SLAYERS ROSE.
BEFORE LONG, I MANIFESTED THE MARK.
A MARK IDENTICAL TO YORIICHI'S.

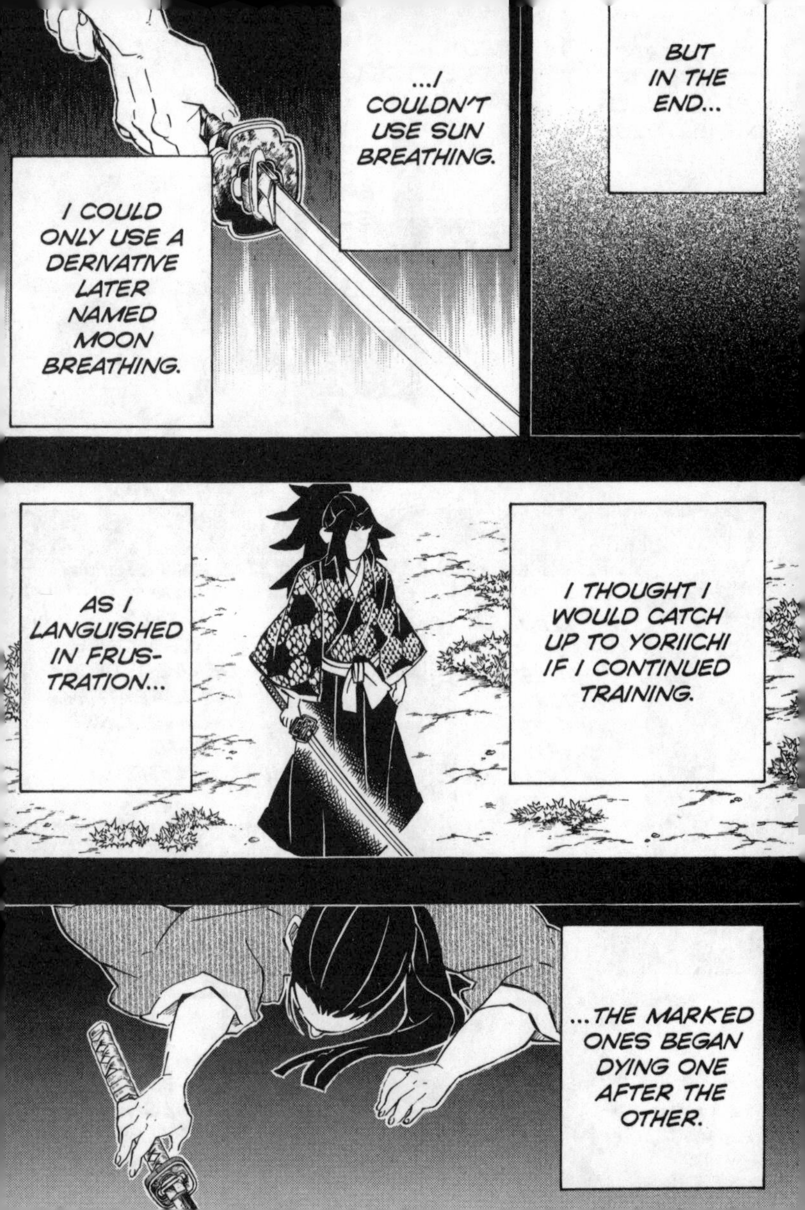
BUT IN THE END...
...I COULDN'T USE SUN BREATHING.
I COULD ONLY USE A DERIVATIVE LATER NAMED MOON BREATHING.
I THOUGHT I WOULD CATCH UP TO YORIICHI IF I CONTINUED TRAINING.
AS I LANGUISHED IN FRUSTRATION...
...THE MARKED ONES BEGAN DYING ONE AFTER THE OTHER.

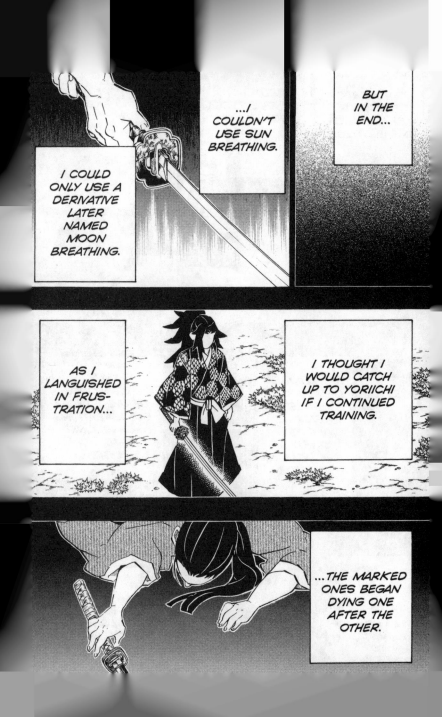

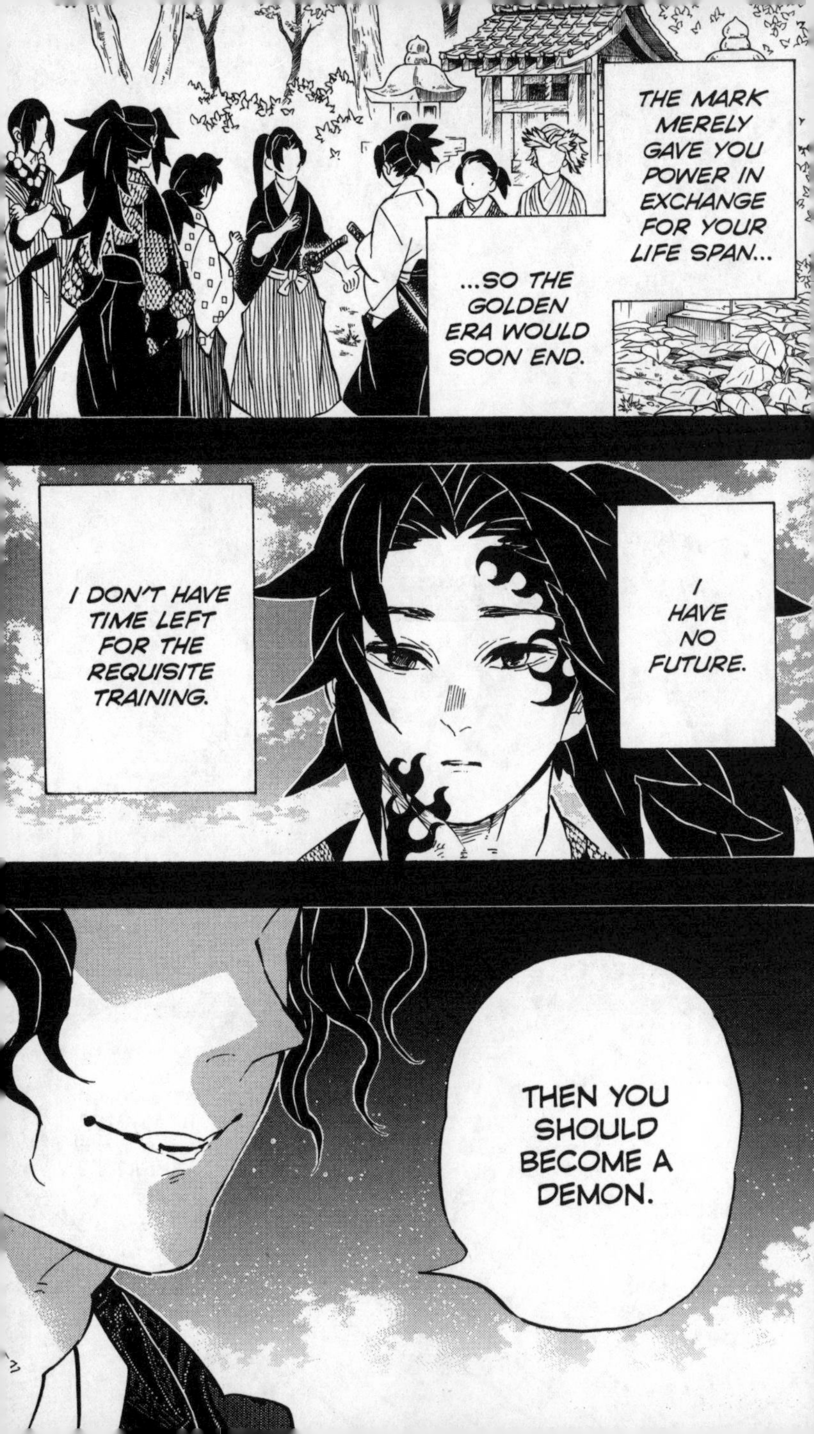
THE MARK MERELY GAVE YOU POWER IN EXCHANGE FOR YOUR LIFE SPAN...
...SO THE GOLDEN ERA WOULD SOON END.
I HAVE NO FUTURE.
I DON'T HAVE TIME LEFT FOR THE REQUISITE TRAINING.
THEN YOU SHOULD BECOME A DEMON.

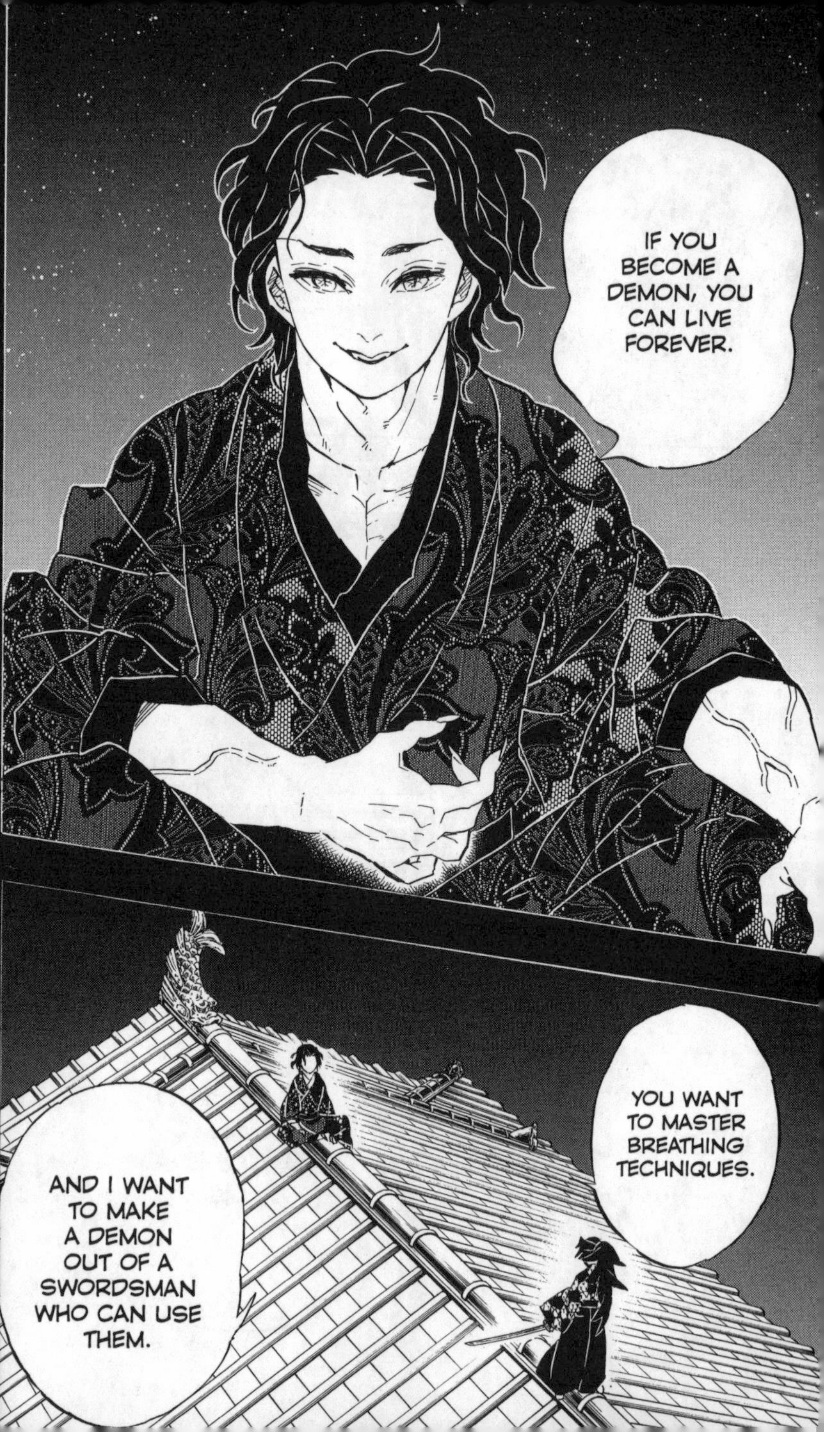
IF YOU BECOME A DEMON, YOU CAN LIVE FOREVER.
YOU WANT TO MASTER BREATHING TECHNIQUES.
AND I WANT TO MAKE A DEMON OUT OF A SWORDSMAN WHO CAN USE THEM.

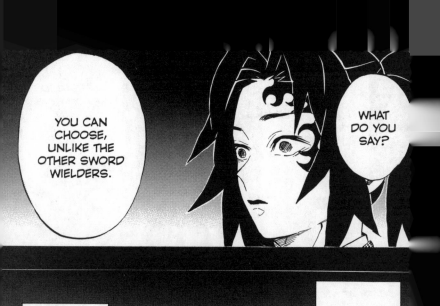

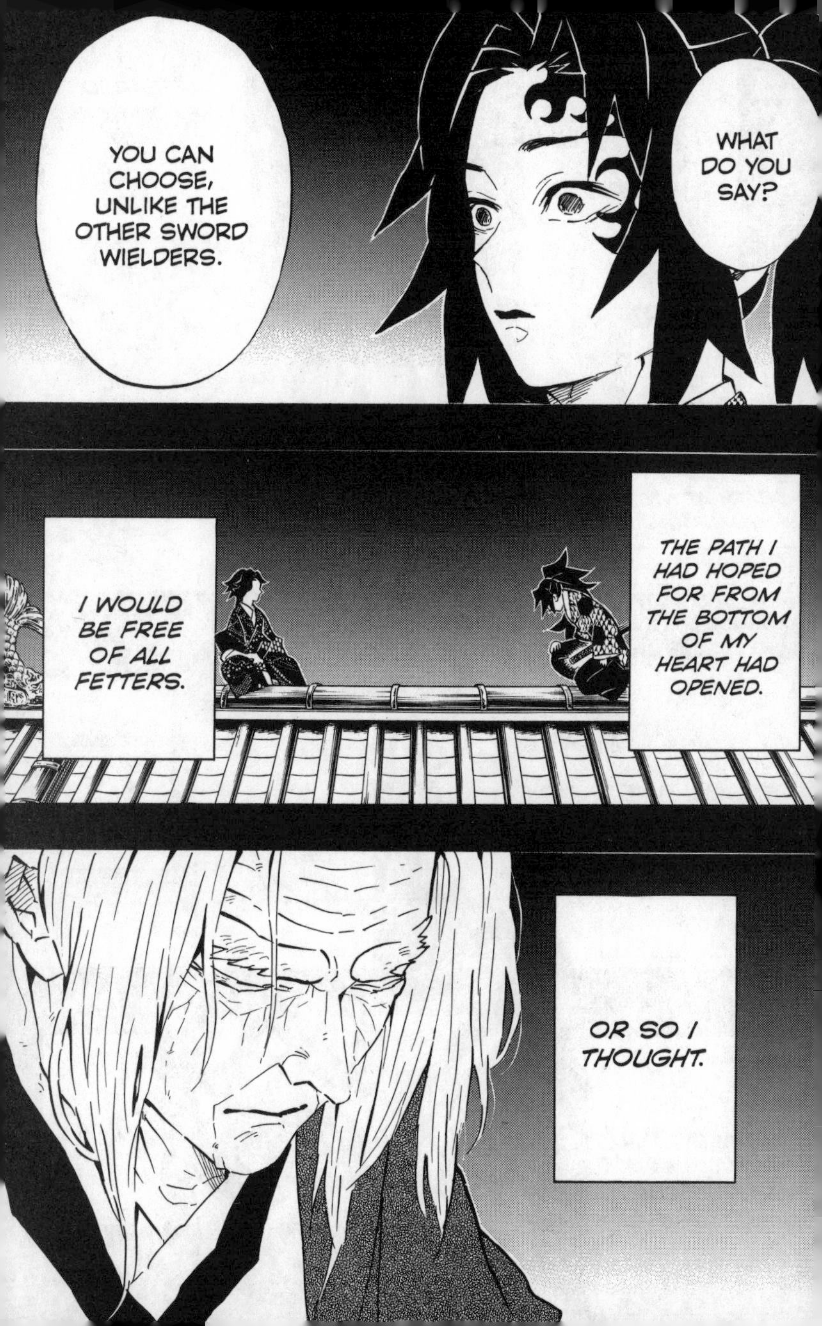
WHAT DO YOU SAY?
YOU CAN CHOOSE, UNLIKE THE OTHER SWORD WIELDERS.
THE PATH I HAD HOPED FOR FROM THE BOTTOM OF MY HEART HAD OPENED.
I WOULD BE FREE OF ALL FETTERS.
OR SO I THOUGHT.

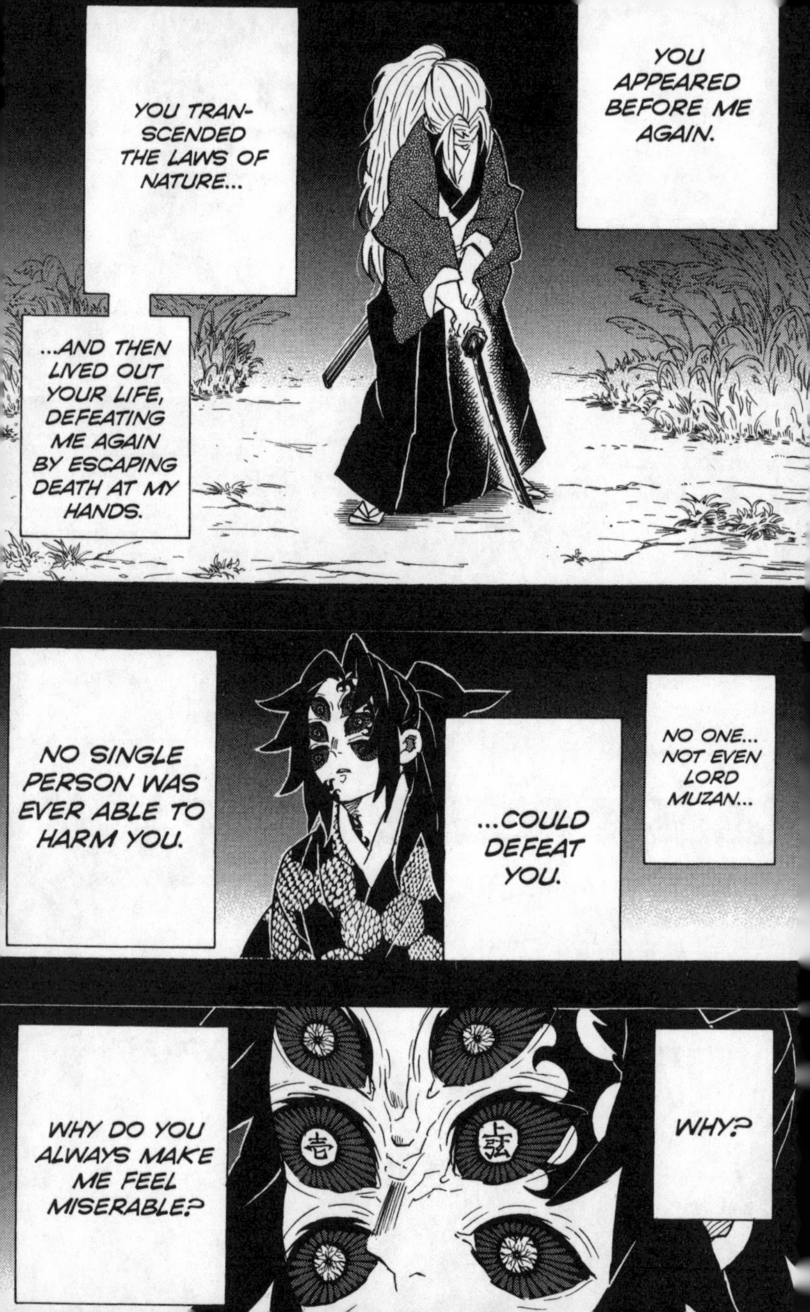
YOU APPEARED BEFORE ME AGAIN.
YOU TRAN-SCENDED THE LAWS OF NATURE...
...AND THEN LIVED OUT YOUR LIFE, DEFEATING ME AGAIN BY ESCAPING DEATH AT MY HANDS.
NO ONE... NOT EVEN LORD MUZAN...
...COULD DEFEAT YOU.
NO SINGLE PERSON WAS EVER ABLE TO HARM YOU.
WHY?
WHY DO YOU ALWAYS MAKE ME FEEL MISERABLE?

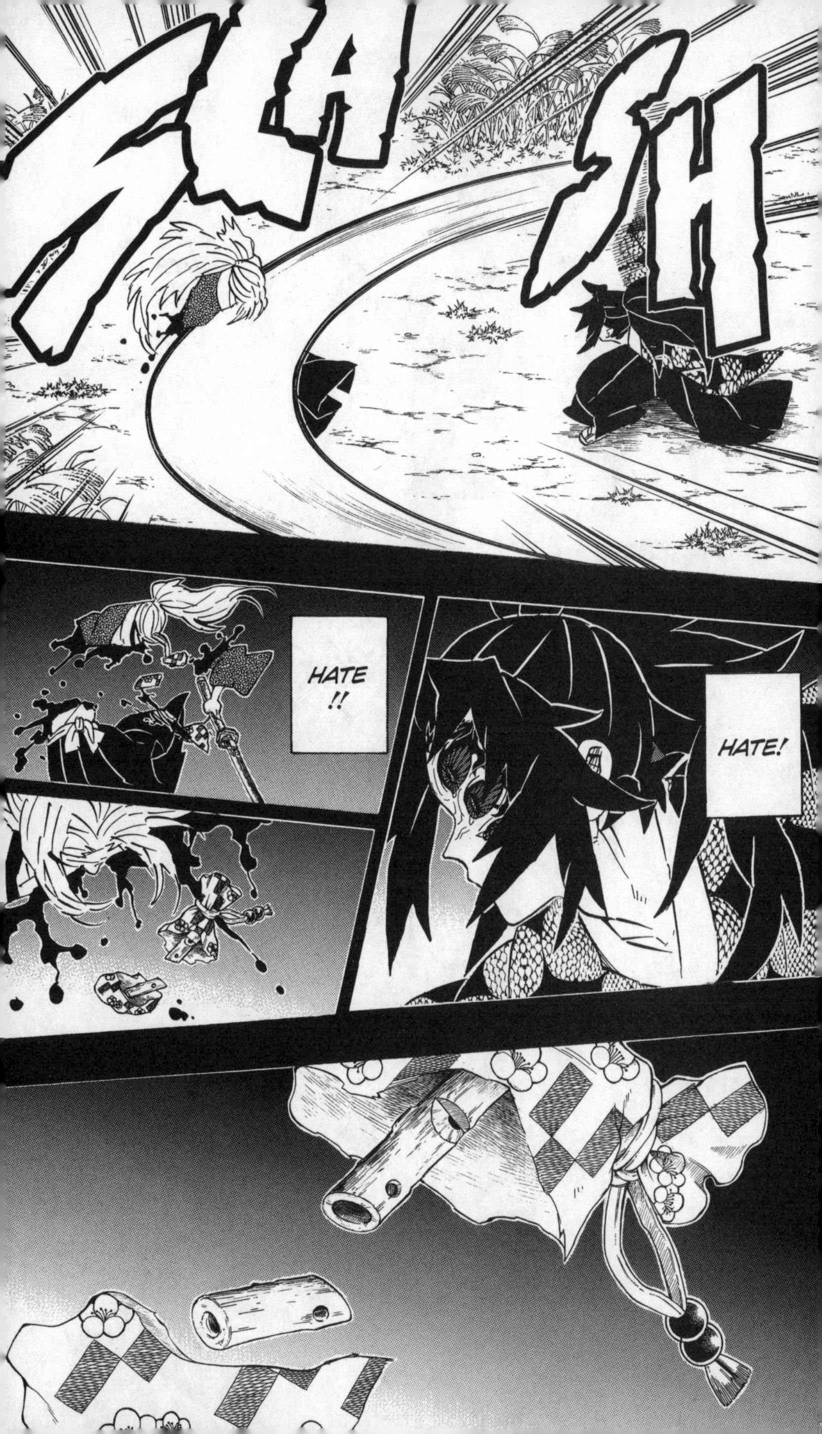
FLASH
HATE!
HATE !!

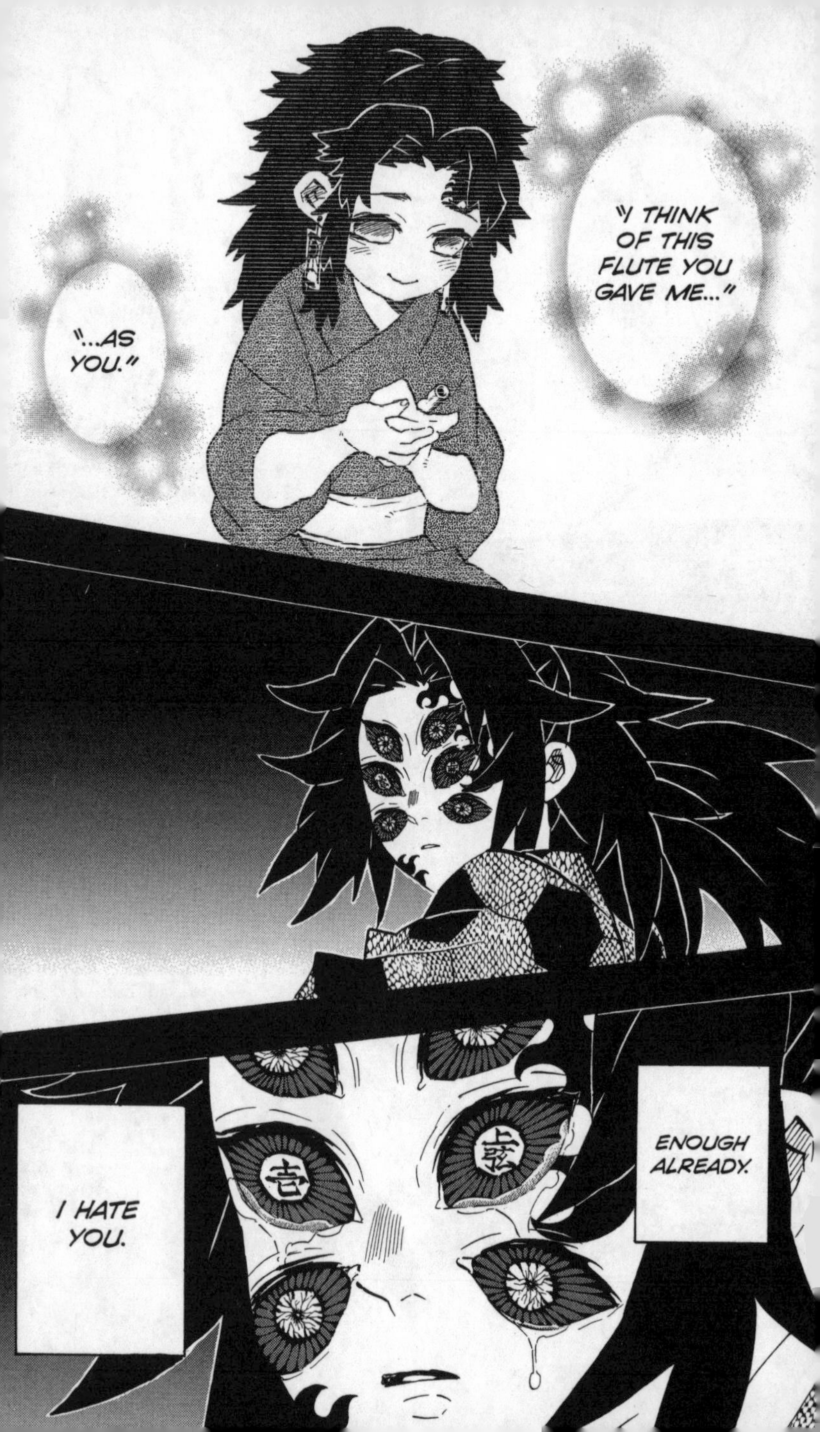
"I THINK OF THIS FLUTE YOU GAVE ME..."
"...AS YOU."
ENOUGH ALREADY.
I HATE YOU.

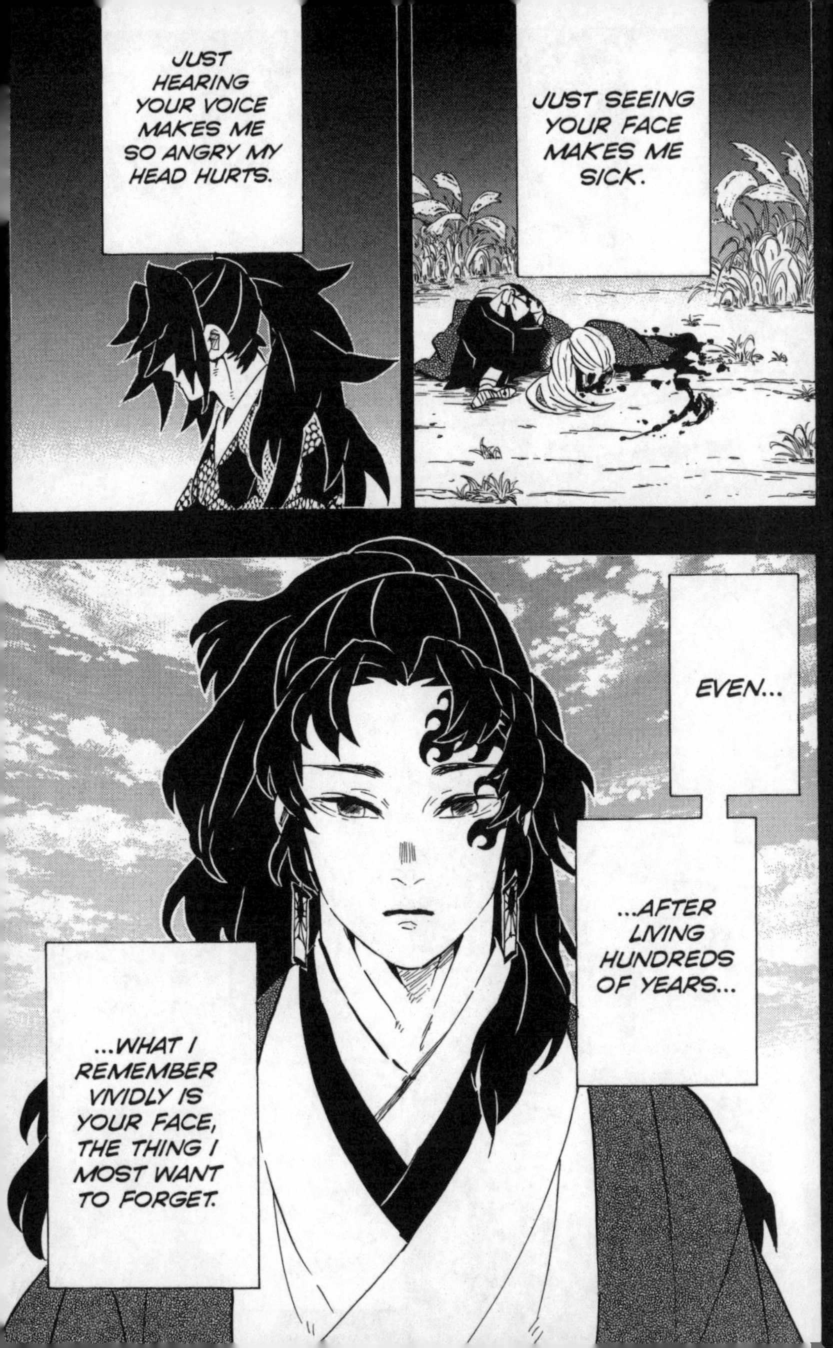
JUST SEEING YOUR FACE MAKES ME SICK.
JUST HEARING YOUR VOICE MAKES ME SO ANGRY MY HEAD HURTS.
EVEN...
...AFTER LIVING HUNDREDS OF YEARS...
...WHAT I REMEMBER VIVIDLY IS YOUR FACE, THE THING I MOST WANT TO FORGET.

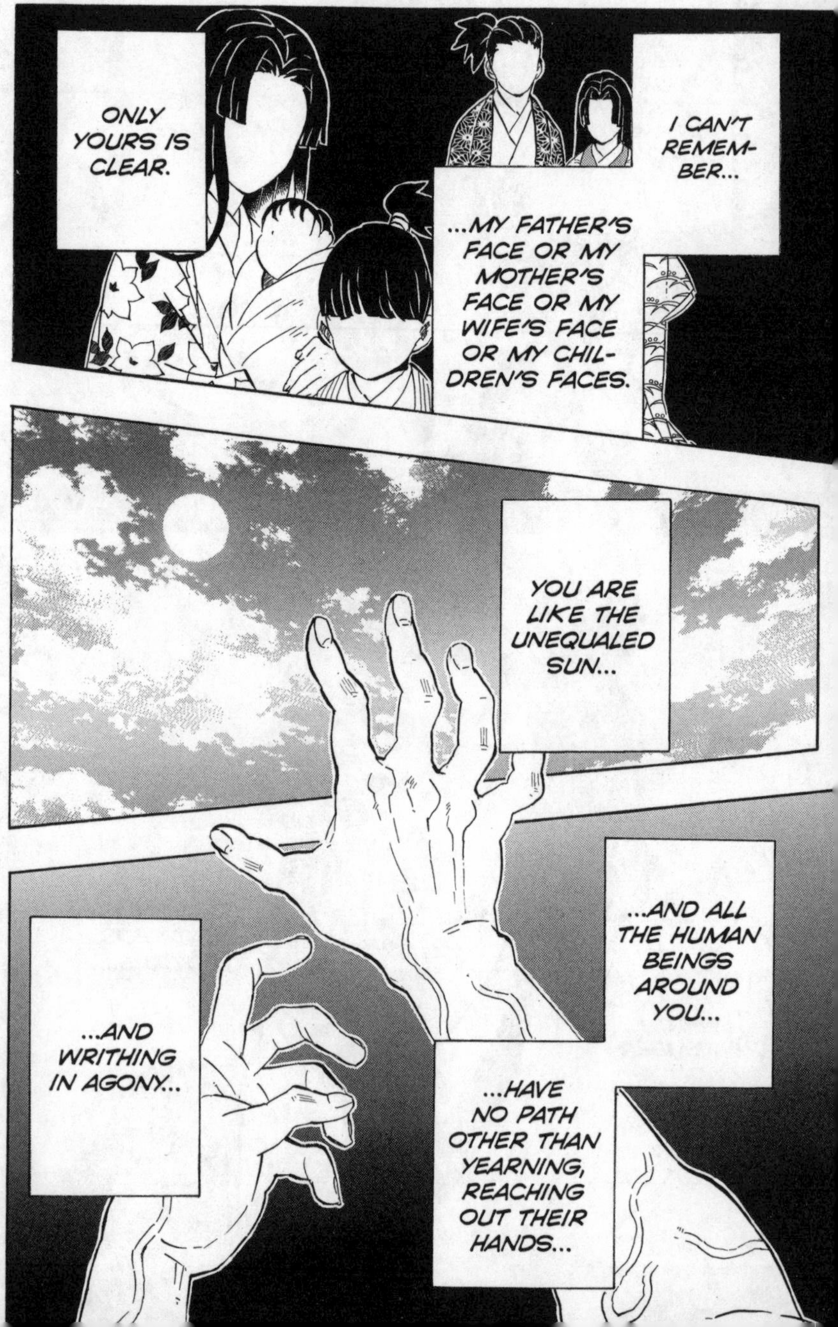
I CAN'T REMEMBER...
...MY FATHER'S FACE OR MY MOTHER'S FACE OR MY WIFE'S FACE OR MY CHILDREN'S FACES.
ONLY YOURS IS CLEAR.
YOU ARE LIKE THE UNEQUALED SUN...
...AND ALL THE HUMAN BEINGS AROUND YOU...
...HAVE NO PATH OTHER THAN YEARNING, REACHING OUT THEIR HANDS...
...AND WRITHING IN AGONY...

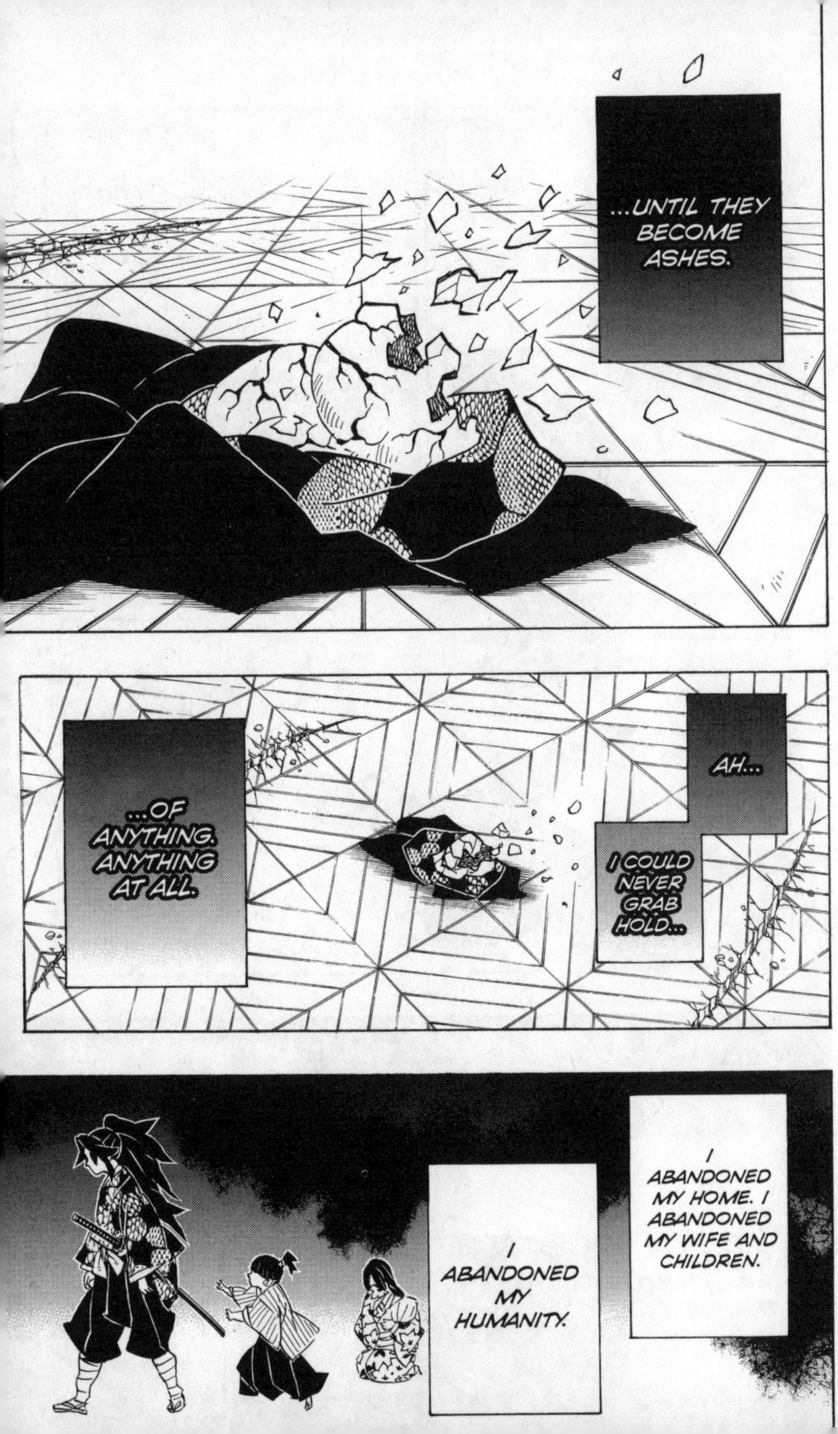
...UNTIL THEY BECOME ASHES.
AH...
I COULD NEVER GRAB HOLD...
...OF ANYTHING. ANYTHING AT ALL.
I ABANDONED MY HOME. I ABANDONED MY WIFE AND CHILDREN.
I ABANDONED MY HUMANITY.

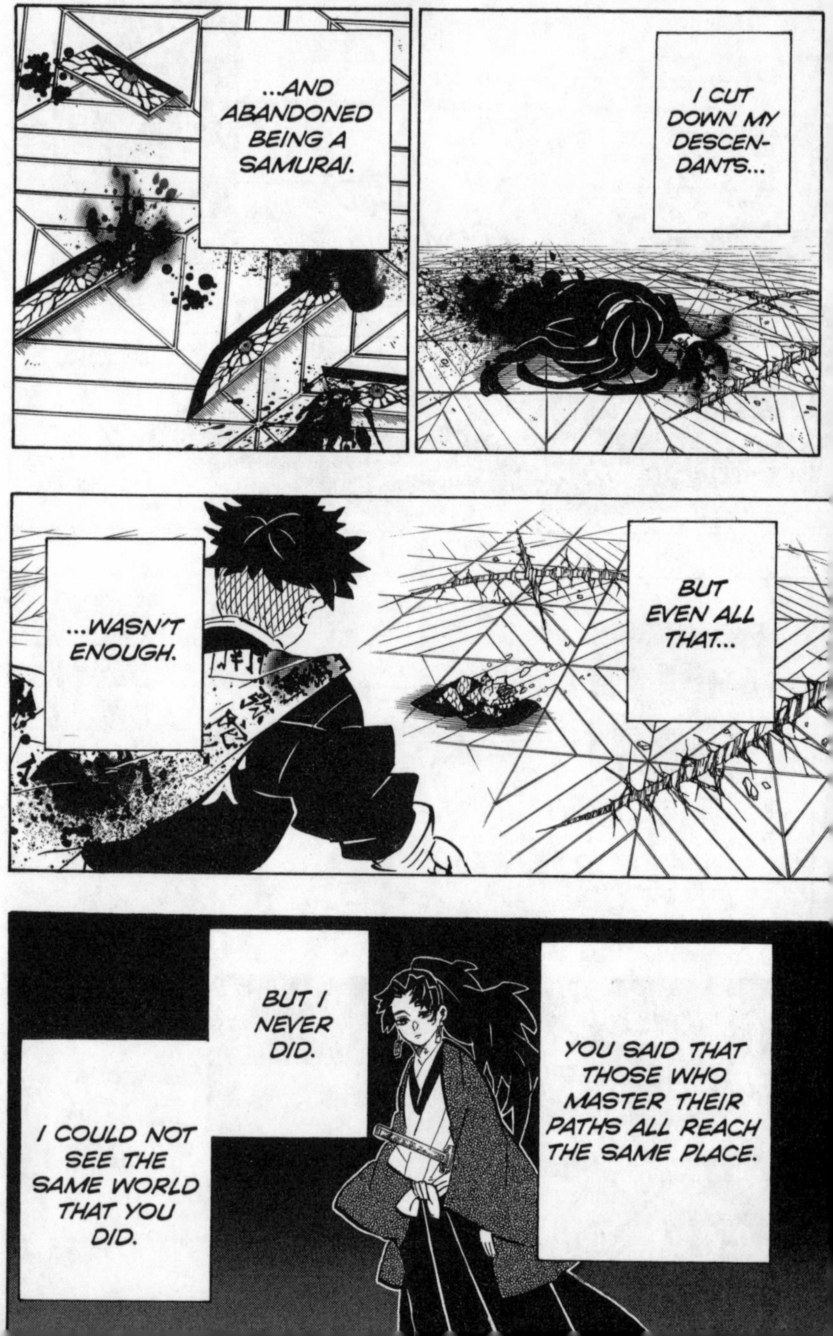
I CUT DOWN MY DESCEN-DANTS...
...AND ABANDONED BEING A SAMURAI.
BUT EVEN ALL THAT...
...WASN'T ENOUGH.
YOU SAID THAT THOSE WHO MASTER THEIR PATHS ALL REACH THE SAME PLACE.
BUT I NEVER DID.
I COULD NOT SEE THE SAME WORLD THAT YOU DID.

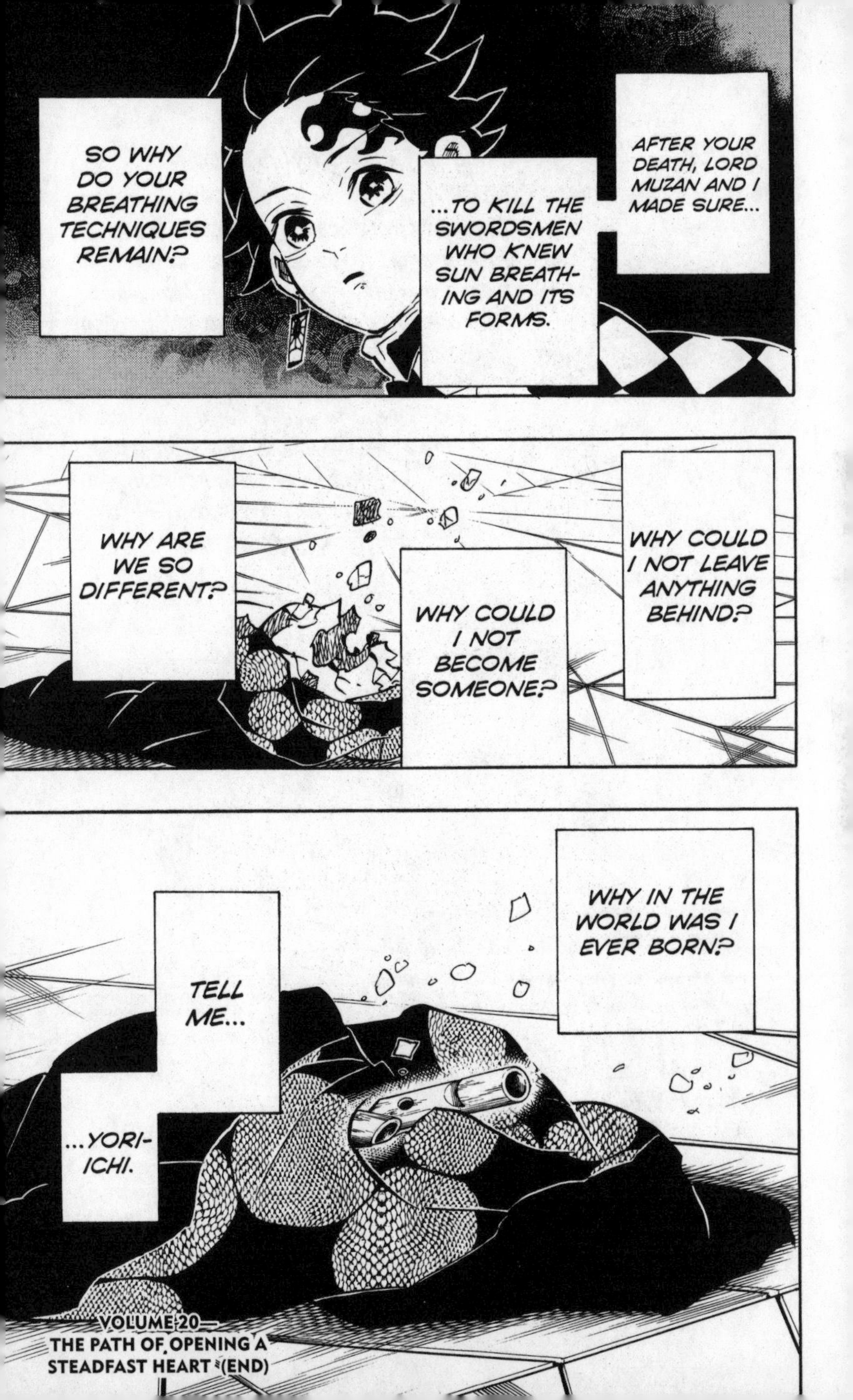
AFTER YOUR DEATH, LORD MUZAN AND I MADE SURE...
...TO KILL THE SWORDSMEN WHO KNEW SUN BREATHING AND ITS FORMS.
SO WHY DO YOUR BREATHING TECHNIQUES REMAIN?
WHY COULD I NOT LEAVE ANYTHING BEHIND?
WHY COULD I NOT BECOME SOMEONE?
WHY ARE WE SO DIFFERENT?
WHY IN THE WORLD WAS I EVER BORN?
TELL ME...
...YORI-ICHI.
VOLUME 20
THE PATH OF OPENING A STEADFAST HEART (END)

JUNIOR HIGH AND HIGH SCHOOL ☆ KIMETSU ACADEMY

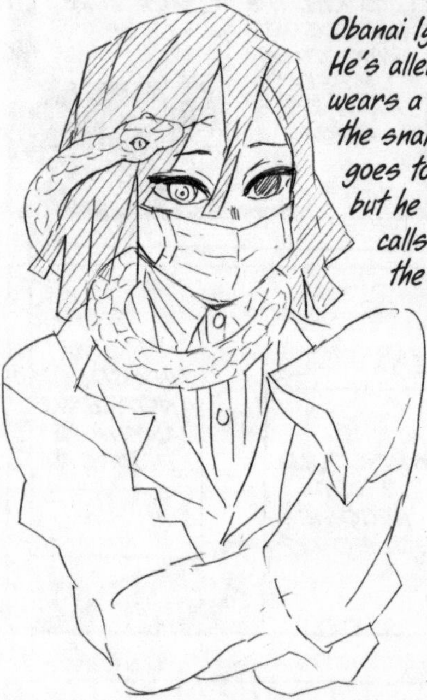

Obanai Iguro. Chemistry Teacher
He's allergic to women, so he always wears a mask. People say he also wears the snake to keep women away. He often goes to the diner run by Aoi's family, but he only drinks tea. He frequently calls ahead to see if the girl with the braids is there. When students get failing grades, he strings them up and fires plastic water bottle rockets at them.

Gyomei Himejima. Civics teacher • Bamboo Shoot Class, Year 1. He's so muscular that people were scared of him at first, but he often had items with cats on them, which was incredibly cute. Everyone soon thought, "Huh? Is he a gentle guy who likes cats?" Students often call him "father" by accident.

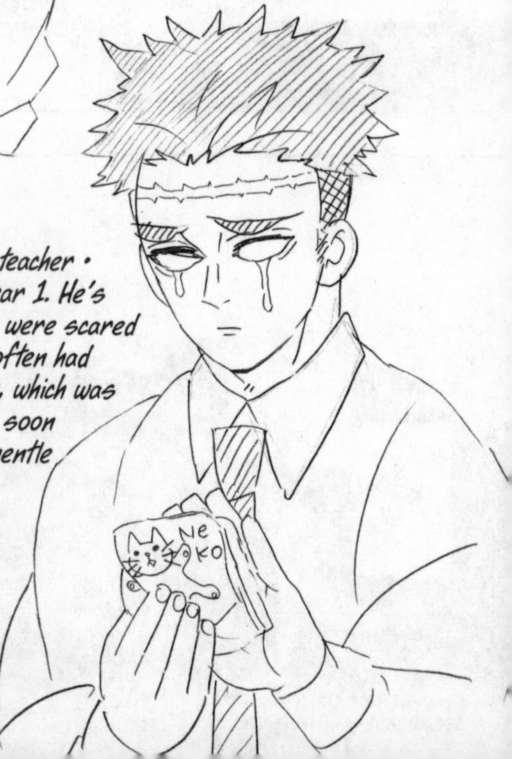
NE
KO

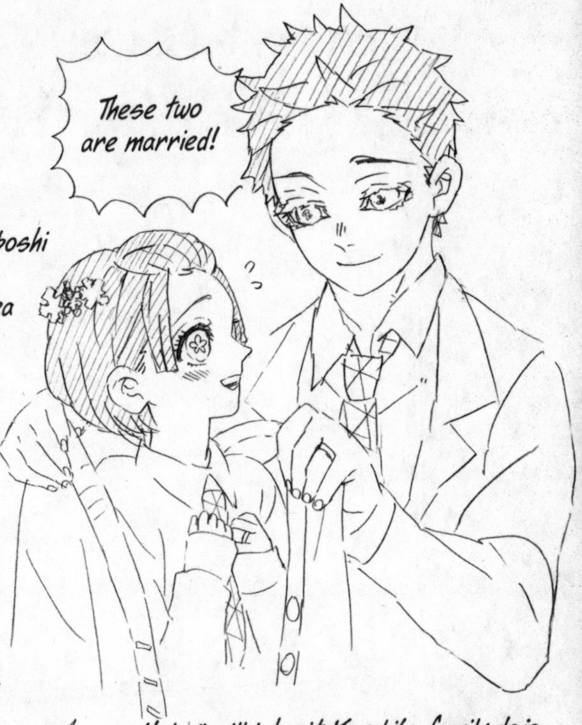
These two are married!

Hakuji Soyama (18), Eboshi Class, Year 3. Koyuki Soyama (16), Hydrangea Class, Year 1. As children, they lived in neighboring houses and promised to marry each other. Their parents approved, so they got married. Their pet names for each other are Princess and Lord Hakuji. They're both in the Handicraft Club.

Hakuji will inherit Koyuki's family dojo.

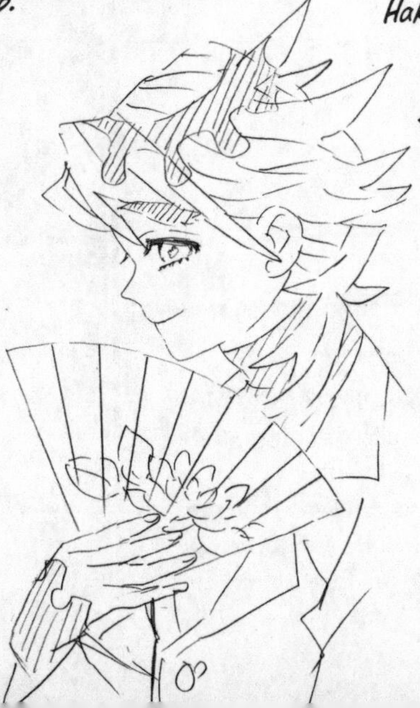

← He's a con man who performs marriages, among other things. He's notorious enough that there have been special programs about him on television. He has been involved in many scams, but there is never enough evidence to prosecute him. He spoke to a girl whose hair color gradually changed from green to pink and who later disappeared. An altercation between a man and woman that was overheard at the scene of the incident went like this: "I think you're lying!" "Guh!"

YOU'RE READING THE
WRONG WAY!

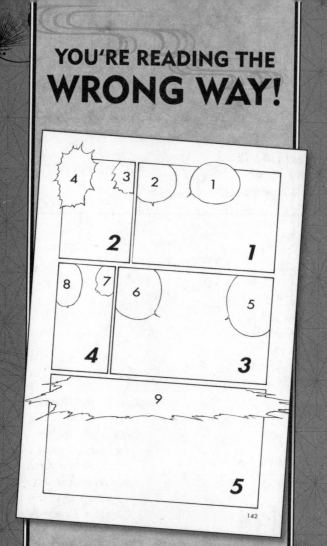

142

DEMON SLAYER: KIMETSU NO YAIBA reads from right to left, starting in the upper-right corner. Japanese is read from right to left, meaning that action, sound effects and word-balloon order are completely reversed from English order.